NATIONAL SAFETY COUNCIL
INJURY FACTS®
2017 EDITION

ALL INJURIES

OCCUPATIONAL

MOTOR VEHICLE

HOME AND COMMUNITY
STATE DATA

INTERNATIONAL

The National Safety Council, chartered by an act of Congress, is a nongovernmental, not-for-profit, public service organization. The mission of the National Safety Council is to eliminate preventable deaths at work, in homes and communities, and on the road through leadership, research, education and advocacy.

Injury Facts®, the Council's annual statistical report on unintentional injuries and their characteristics and costs, was prepared by:

Research and Safety Management Solutions Group:
Kenneth P. Kolosh, Manager, Statistics Department
Kevin T. Fearn, Sr. Statistical Associate
Kathleen T. Porretta, Technical Editor

Questions or comments about the content of *Injury Facts* should be directed to the Research and Safety Management Solutions Group, National Safety Council, 1121 Spring Lake Drive, Itasca, IL, 60143, by phone at (630) 775-2322, fax at (630) 285-0242, or email *rssdept@nsc.org*.

For price and ordering information, visit *www.nsc.org* or write:

Customer Service
National Safety Council, 1121 Spring Lake Drive, Itasca, IL, 60143, call (800) 621-7619, or fax (630) 285-0797.

Acknowledgments

The information presented in *Injury Facts* was made possible by the cooperation of many organizations and individuals, including state vital and health statistics authorities, state traffic authorities, state workers' compensation authorities, trade associations, Bureau of the Census, Bureau of Labor Statistics, Consumer Product Safety Commission, Federal Highway Administration, Federal Railroad Administration, International Labour Organization, National Center for Health Statistics, National Fire Protection Association, National Highway Traffic Safety Administration, National Transportation Safety Board, National Weather Service, Mine Safety and Health Administration, and the World Health Organization. Specific contributions are acknowledged in footnotes and source notes throughout the book.

Visit the National Safety Council website:
nsc.org
nsc.org/injuryfacts

Copyright ©2017 National Safety Council
All rights reserved.
The copyrighting of *Injury Facts®* is not intended to prevent use of the material for injury prevention purposes.
The information may be used (except where copyright is held by another organization), with credit to the
National Safety Council – the only restriction being that the original meaning shall be preserved.
Suggested citation: National Safety Council. (2017). *Injury Facts®, 2017 Edition*. Itasca, IL: Author.
Library of Congress Catalog Card Number: 99-74142
Printed in U.S.A. ISBN 978-0-87912-357-4   NSC Press Product No. 02333-0000

Table of Contents

Foreword .... iv-v

All Injuries 1
   All Unintentional Injuries 2-4
   While You Speak! 5
   Leading Cause by Age Graphic 6-7
   Costs 8-11
   Deaths by Type and Age Group 12-13
   EXPANDED Leading Causes by Age, Race, and Sex 14-21
   Sex and Age 22-23
   All Deaths Due to Injury 24-25
   Deaths by Event, Age, Sex, and Month 26-27
   National Health Interview Survey 28-31
   Top 10 Causes 32-33
   Disasters 34
   Intentional Injuries 35-37
   Children, Youths, and Adults 38-39
   Odds of Dying From 40-43
   Trends in Age-Adjusted Rates 44-45
   Historical Data 46-55

Occupational 57
   Work 58-61
   Costs and Time Lost 62
   On and Off the Job 63
   Workers' Compensation Claims by State 64
   NEW Transportation-Related injuries 65
   Workers' Compensation Claims Costs 66-67
   Forklift 68
   Falls 69-71
   NEW Fatigue 72
   Occupational Health 73
   Nature of Injury 74
   Part of Body 75
   Benchmarking Incidence Rates 76-77
   Injury and Illness Incidence Rates 78-83
   Event or Exposure 84
   Benchmarking Case and Demographic Data 85-101

Motor Vehicle 103
   Motor-Vehicle 104-105
   Deaths by Age and Type 106-107
   Major Safety Issues 108
   Costs 109
   State Laws 110
   Occupant Protection 111-113
   Alcohol 114-115
   Deaths, Injuries, Crashes by Type 116
   Speeding 117
   Distracted Driving 118
   NEW Assistive Safety Technology 119
   Improper Driving; Large Trucks 120
   Motorcycles 121
   School Bus Transportation 122
   Pedestrians 123
   Young Drivers 124
   NEW ATV 125
   Age of Driver 126
   NEW Impact of Recessions 127
   Crashes by Time of Day and Day of Week 128
   Deaths by Month; Holidays 129
   Work Zones; Emergency Vehicles 130
   NSC and NHTSA Differences 131
   Historical Data 132-139

Home and Community 141
   Home and Community Summary 142-143
   Home 144-145
   Home Deaths by Event and Age Group 146-147
   Public 148-149
   Public Deaths by Event and Age Group 150-151
   Weather 152
   NEW Playground injuries 153
   Sports and Recreation Injuries 154
   Product-Related Injuries 155
   Transportation 156-159
   Poisonings 160-162
   Falls 163
   NEW Fire-Related Fatalities and Injuries 164
   Pedalcycles 165
   Leading Risks by Age Groups 166-167
   Firearms 168
   Historical Data 169

State Data 171
   Summary 172-174
   Leading Causes by State 175-177
   Deaths by State and Event 178-179
   State and Year 180
   Fatal Occupational Injuries 181
   Occupational Incidence Rates 182-183
   Motor-Vehicle Deaths and Rates 184-185

International Data 187
   Summary 188
   Unintentional-Injuries 189
   Motor-Vehicle Injuries 190
   Poisoning 191
   Falls 192
   Drowning 193
   Occupational Deaths and Injuries 194-197

Technical Appendix 199-204

Other Sources 205

Glossary 206

Index 207-210

Foreword

All unintentional-injury deaths are preventable, yet we currently see little progress in reducing this preventable cause of death in the United States. After overtaking stroke in 2013, unintentional injuries are at an all-time high, and are now ranked as the fourth leading cause of death behind heart disease, cancer, and chronic lower respiratory disease. For a clearer picture of the increase, researchers refer to age-adjusted population death rates. Age-adjusted rates control for population size changes and demographic age shifts that occur over time and are the most appropriate way to track long term fatality trends. The current age-adjusted population death rate of 43.0 is 27% higher than the record low rate of 33.96 set in 1992.

The lack of success in reducing unintentional-injury deaths is even more shocking when contrasted with the success achieved in reducing the overall fatality rate in the United States. From a historical perspective, the overall death rate in the United States has decreased more consistently and to a greater extent than has the unintentional death rate. Using 1900 as the baseline year, the overall age-adjusted fatality rate has decreased by 71% while the unintentional fatality rate has decreased 50%. The chart on the facing page shows the percent change in age-adjusted death rates for both all deaths and unintentional deaths compared to the rate in 1900. As the chart indicates, progress in reducing the unintentional fatality rate has always lagged behind the progress in reducing the overall fatality rate. More recent trends are even more discouraging. Progress regarding the two death rates reached near parity in 1992. However since 1992, the overall fatality rate has decreased by over 19% while the unintentional fatality rate has *increased* 27%. If the unintentional fatality rate had kept pace with the improving overall fatality rate, over 58,000 fewer people would have died in 2015!

The historic slow progress in reducing unintentional-injury death and the recent increase in deaths since 1992 is unacceptable! For too long unintentional-injury deaths have been considered "accidents," unavoidable acts of God or fate that we are powerless to stop. To combat this complacency, the National Safety Council (NSC) has recently announced the goal to eliminate preventable deaths in our lifetime. Many may be skeptical of such an ambitious goal, but clearly the traditional incremental approach is not enough. To join the National Safety Council on this journey, please go to http://www.nsc.org/act/Pages/volunteer.aspx to learn how to get involved.

The latest data show a continuation of the recent negative trend with an increase of over 7% in unintentional-injury deaths in 2015 compared to 2014. Unintentional-injury deaths totaled 146,571 in 2015 compared to 136,053 in 2014.

The resident population of the United States was 321,418,000 in 2015, an increase of less than 1% from 2014. The unintentional death rate in 2015 was 45.6 per 100,000 population – an increase of nearly 7% from 2014.

A more complete summary of the situation in 2015 and recent trends is given on page 2.

Changes in the 2017 edition
Look for new data on…
- Expanded leading causes of death by age, race, and sex
- Workplace transportation related injuries
- Workplace fatigue related injuries
- Automobile assistive safety technologies
- ATV injuries
- Impact of recessions on motor-vehicle fatalities

And updated or expanded data on…
- General mortality
- Occupational injury and illness incidence rates by industry
- Occupational injury and illness profile data by industry sector
- Forklift injury trends
- Workers' compensation claims and costs
- Disasters
- Distracted driving
- Young drivers
- Comparing safety of transportation mode
- Traffic safety issues – alcohol, occupant protection, speeding, and others
- Consumer product-related injuries
- Unintentional deaths by states

We also continue to receive questions regarding a change made in the 2011 edition. Editions of *Injury Facts*® prior to 2011 included estimates of disabling injuries. Starting with the 2011 edition, NSC transitioned to the concept of "medically consulted injury" in place of "disabling injury." This new definition was adopted from the National Health Interview Survey, a household survey conducted by the National Center for Health Statistics (NCHS). A refinement of the medically consulted injury estimate was also made this year to better account for intentional injuries. This refinement makes comparison of medically consulted injuries to previous years inappropriate. A medically consulted injury is defined by NCHS as an injury serious enough that a medical professional was consulted. Moving *Injury Facts*® estimates from disabling injuries to medically consulted injuries provides several advantages. First and foremost, a medically consulted injury is a more inclusive definition that allows for more comprehensive estimates of the true burden of unintentional injuries. Second, medically consulted injury estimates are updated each year by NCHS allowing NSC to provide the most timely and accurate data possible. Finally, the previous definition of disabling injury was often misinterpreted as a workers' compensation injury. Using the term medically consulted injuries should help eliminate this confusion. For more information on medically consulted injuries, please see the technical appendix.

For more information on *Injury Facts*® and other products, visit NSC's web site (nsc.org), call Customer Service at 800-621-7619, or contact your local council.

Your comments and suggestions on how to improve *Injury Facts*® are welcome. Contact information is given on page ii.

Foreword (cont.)

Percent change of age adjusted death rates from 1900 to 2015 (indexed to 1900), United States

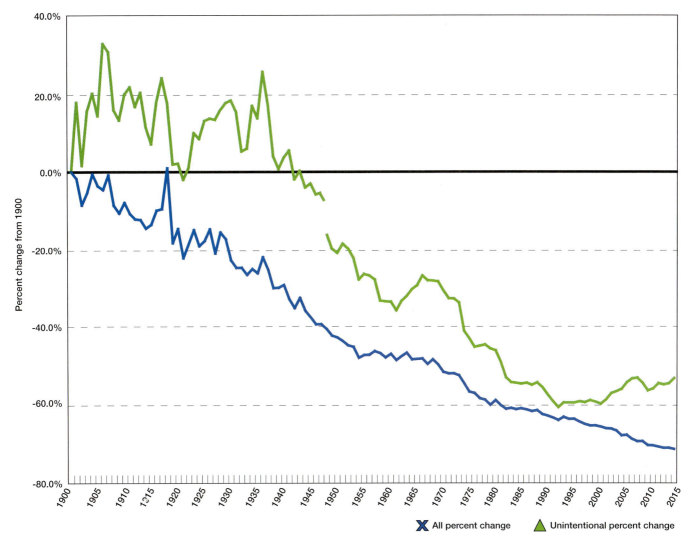

The break at 1948 shows the estimated effect of classification changes.
Adjusted to the year 2000 standard population to remove the influence of changes in age distribution between 1900 and 2015.

All Injuries

All Injuries Highlights

While you speak! — pg. 5

Cause of death graphic — pgs. 6-7

Costs — pgs. 8-11

NEW! Age, race, and ethnic origin fatality trends — pgs. 18-19

Disasters — pg. 34

Odds of dying — pg. 40

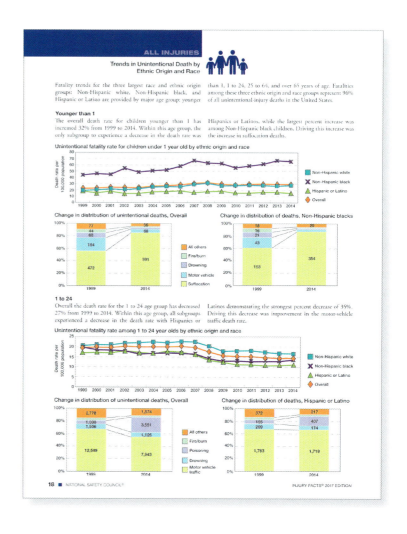

INJURY FACTS® 2017

The collection, analysis, and dissemination of unintentional injury and fatality statistics have been a focus for the National Safety Council since its inception. The first comprehensive statistical compendium ever produced relating to unintentional injuries and deaths was published in the early 1920s, shortly after the Council was formed. Since the 1920s, as a testament to its reliance on data as a measure of progress and guidance, statistical information has been published by the Council on an annual basis without interruption – first as *Accident Facts®* and more recently as *Injury Facts®*.

ALL INJURIES

All Unintentional Injuries, 2015

Unintentional-injury-related deaths were up 7.7% in 2015, compared to the 2014 estimate. Unintentional-injury-related deaths totaled 146,571 in 2015 and 136,053 in 2014. The 2015 estimate is 69% greater than the 1992 total of 86,777 (the lowest annual total since 1924).

The death rate in 2015 was 45.6 per 100,000 population – 34% greater than the lowest rate on record, which was 34.0 in 1992. The 2015 death rate increased 6.8% from the 2014 revised rate.

Comparing 2015 to 2014, work, motor-vehicle, home, and public deaths all increased. Similarly the population death rates also increased for all four classes.

The motor-vehicle death total increased 6.7% in 2015. The 2015 mileage death rate of 1.21 per 100,000,000 vehicle miles was up 3.4% from the revised 2014 rate of 1.17. The 2015 rate was up 2.5% from the revised 2013 rate of 1.18.

Unintentional injuries continued to be the fourth leading cause of death, exceeded only by heart disease, cancer, and chronic lower respiratory diseases. In 2013 unintentional injuries overtook strokes to become the fourth leading cause of death.

Nonfatal injuries also affect millions of Americans. In 2015, 40.6 million people – about 1 out of 8 – sought medical attention.

The economic impact of these fatal and nonfatal unintentional injuries amounted to $886.4 billion in 2015. This is equivalent to about $2,800 per capita, or about $7,100 per household. These are costs that every individual and household pays whether directly out of pocket, through higher prices for goods and services, or through higher taxes. Please note that the cost estimate model was extensively updated starting with the 2016 edition so current estimates are not comparable to earlier estimates.

Between 1912 and 2015, unintentional-injury-related deaths per 100,000 population were reduced about 45% (after adjusting for the classification change in 1948) from 82.5 to 45.6. The reduction in the overall rate during a period when the nation's population tripled has resulted in 6,400,000 fewer people being killed due to unintentional injuries than there would have been if the rate had not been reduced.

All unintentional injuries, 2015

Class	Deaths	Change from 2014	Deaths per 100,000 people	Medically consulted injuries[a]
All classes[b]	146,571	7.7%	45.6	40,600,000
Motor vehicle	37,757	6.7%	11.7	4,300,000
Public nonwork	35,751			4,100,000
Work	1,806			200,000
Home	200			([c])
Work	4,190	1.5%	1.3	4,400,000
Non-motor vehicle	2,384			4,200,000
Motor vehicle	1,806			200,000
Home	74,600	7.2%	23.2	20,700,000
Non-motor vehicle	74,400			20,700,000
Motor vehicle	200			([c])
Public	32,100	11.1%	10.0	11,400,000

Source: National Safety Council estimates (rounded) based on data from the National Center for Health Statistics (NCHS), state departments of health, and state traffic authorities, except for the work figures, which are from the Bureau of Labor Statistics, Census of Fatal Occupational Injuries (CFOI). The National Safety Council adopted the CFOI count for work-related unintentional injuries beginning with 1992 data. See the Glossary for definitions and the Technical Appendix for estimating procedures. Beginning with 1999 data, deaths are classified according to the 10th revision of the International Classification of Diseases. Caution should be used in comparing data classified under the two systems.

[a] The totals shown are approximations based on the National Safety Council's analysis of National Health Interview Survey results that is conducted by NCHS. The totals are the best estimates for the current year. They should not, however, be compared with totals shown in previous editions of this book to indicate year-to-year changes or trends. See the Glossary for definitions and the Technical Appendix for estimating procedures.

[b] Deaths and injuries above for the four separate classes add to more than the "All classes" figures due to rounding and because some deaths and injuries are included in more than one class. For example, 1,806 work deaths involved motor vehicles and are in both the work and motor-vehicle totals, and 200 motor-vehicle deaths occurred on home premises and are in both home and motor vehicle. The total of such duplication amounted to about 2,006 deaths and 200,000 injuries in 2014.

[c] Less than 10,000.

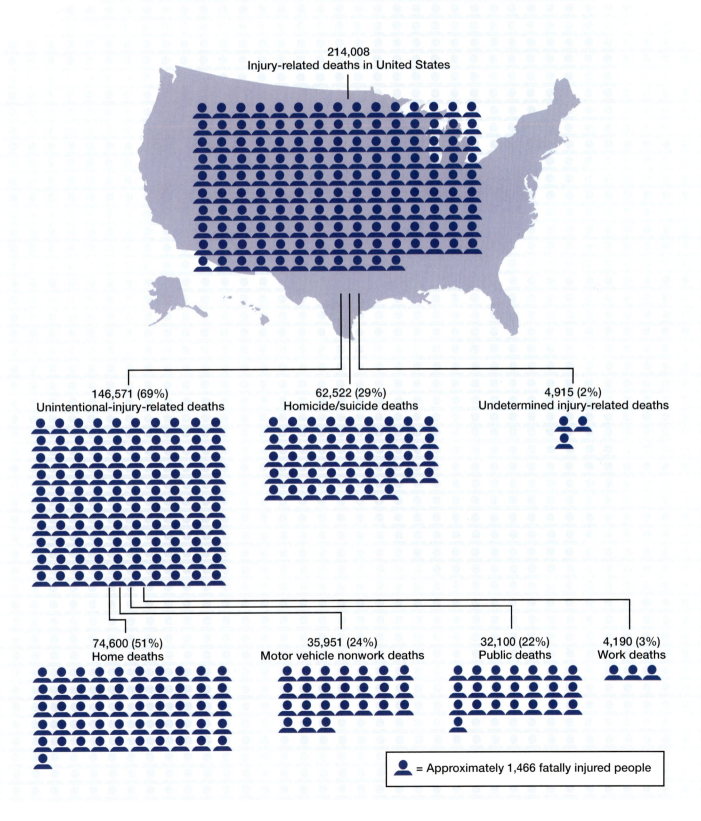

ALL INJURIES

All Injury-Related Deaths, 2015 (cont.)

Unintentional-injury-related deaths by class, United States, 2015

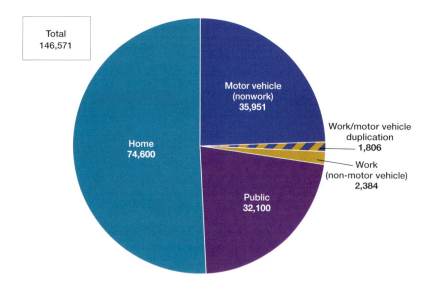

Unintentional medically consulted injuries[a] by class, United States, 2015

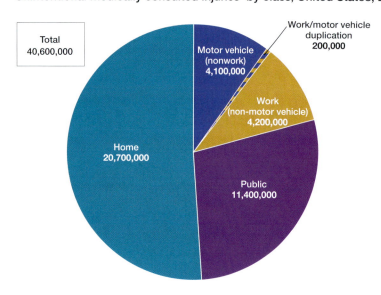

[a] Medically consulted injury estimate method was updated for the 2016 edition and is not comparable to estimates provided in earlier editions.

ALL INJURIES
While You Speak!

While you make a 10-minute safety speech, three people in the United States will be killed and about 772 will suffer an injury severe enough to require a consultation with a medical professional.[a] Costs will amount to $16,860,000. On average, 17 unintentional-injury-related deaths and about 4,630 medically consulted injuries occur every hour during the year. Deaths and medically consulted injuries by class occurred in the nation at the following rates in 2015:

Deaths and medically consulted injuries by class, 2015

Class	Severity	One every ...	Hour	Day	Week	2015 total
All	Deaths	4 minutes	17	402	2,820	146,571
	Injuries[a]	1 second	4,630	111,200	780,800	40,600,000
Motor vehicle	Deaths	14 minutes	4	103	730	37,757
	Injuries	7 seconds	490	11,800	82,700	4,300,000
Work	Deaths	125 minutes	<1	11	80	4,190
	Injuries	7 seconds	500	12,100	84,600	4,400,000
Workers off the job	Deaths	8 minutes	7	175	1,230	63,800
	Injuries	2 seconds	1,760	42,200	296,200	15,400,000
Home	Deaths	7 minutes	9	204	1,430	74,600
	Injuries	2 seconds	2,360	56,700	398,100	20,700,000
Public non-motor vehicle	Deaths	16 minutes	4	88	620	32,100
	Injuries	3 seconds	1,300	31,200	219,200	11,400,000

Source: National Safety Council estimates.
[a]Starting with the 2011 edition of Injury Facts, the National Safety Council adopted the definition of "medically consulted injuries" to replace "disabling injuries." For a full description of medically consulted injuries, please see the Technical Appendix. Please note that for the 2016 edition, the estimates were refined to better exclude intentional injuries and are not comparable to previous editions.

Deaths every hour...

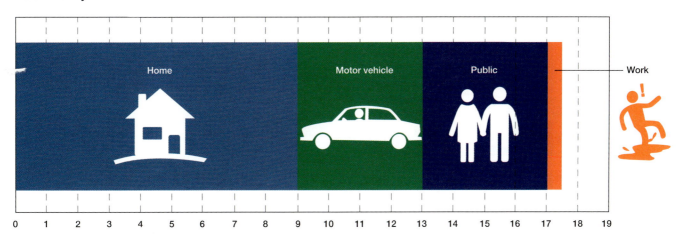

An unintentional-injury-related death occurs every four minutes.

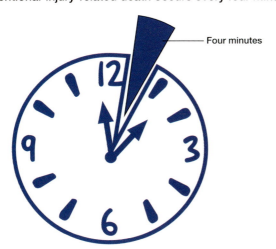

ALL INJURIES
Leading Causes of Total Unintentional Injuries

Percentage of Unintentional Deaths by Age Group, United States, 2014

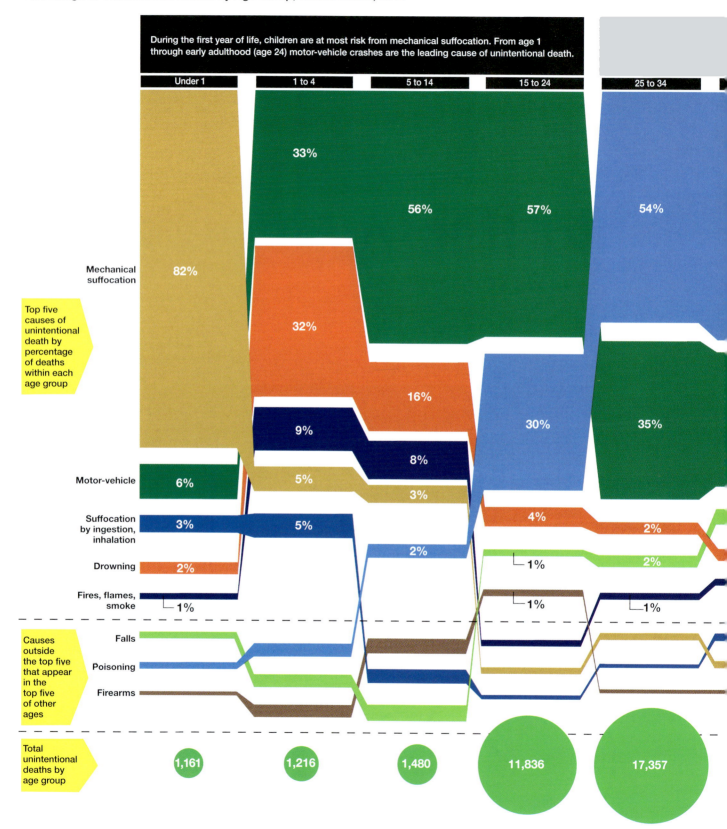

ALL INJURIES
Leading Causes of Total Unintentional Injuries (cont.)

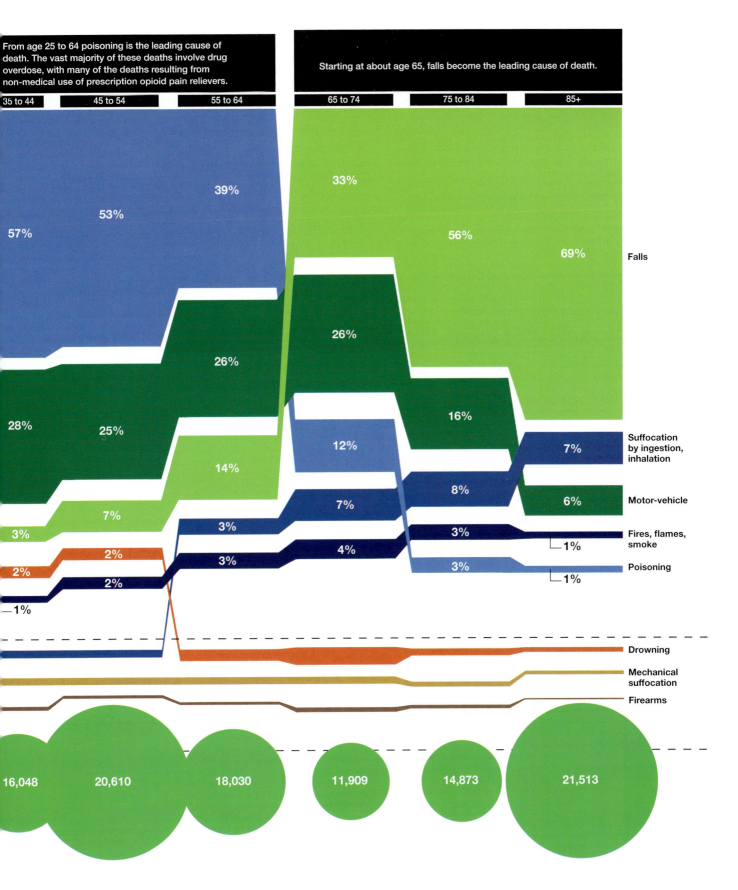

From age 25 to 64 poisoning is the leading cause of death. The vast majority of these deaths involve drug overdose, with many of the deaths resulting from non-medical use of prescription opioid pain relievers.

Starting at about age 65, falls become the leading cause of death.

INJURY FACTS® 2017 EDITION

ALL INJURIES

Costs of Unintentional Injuries by Class, 2015

Major revisions were made to the National Safety Council cost model for the 2016 edition that take advantage of data sources not previously available. Because of the changes made to the cost model, cost estimates provided in editions prior to 2016 are not comparable to currently published estimates.

The total cost of unintentional injuries in 2015, $886.4 billion, includes estimates of economic costs of fatal and nonfatal unintentional injuries together with employers' uninsured costs, vehicle damage costs, and fire losses. Wage and productivity losses, medical expenses, administrative expenses, and employers' uninsured costs are included in all four classes of injuries. Cost components unique to each class are identified below.

Motor-vehicle crash costs include property damage from motor-vehicle incidents. Work costs include the value of property damage in on-the-job motor-vehicle incidents and fires. Home and public costs include estimated fire losses, but do not include other property damage costs.

Besides the estimated $886.4 billion in economic losses from unintentional injuries in 2015, lost quality of life from those injuries is valued at an additional $3,538.1 billion, making the comprehensive cost $4,424.5 billion in 2015.

As mentioned, several cost benchmarks were updated starting with the 2016 edition of *Injury Facts*, making cost estimates not comparable to prior years. In addition, the method for estimating the number of medically attended injuries by class was also revised starting with the 2016 edition to use the latest National Health Interview Survey data. Estimated property damage costs in motor-vehicle crashes were re-benchmarked using data from the National Highway Traffic Safety Administration. Finally, the value of a statistical life was updated starting with the 2016 edition, affecting the comprehensive cost mentioned in the paragraph above.

Certain costs of unintentional injuries by class, 2015 ($ billions)

Cost	Total[a]	Motor vehicle	Work	Home	Public non-motor vehicle
Total	$886.4	$385.3	$142.5	$254.7	$132.6
Wage and productivity losses	458.0	178.6	45.8	161.4	79.1
Medical expenses	178.3	46.0	31.4	65.2	38.2
Administrative expenses[b]	139.2	84.5	46.1	14.1	9.5
Motor-vehicle damage	72.8	72.8	3.6	(c)	(c)
Employers' uninsured costs	23.8	3.4	11.3	6.3	3.5
Fire loss	14.3	(c)	4.3	7.7	2.3

Source: National Safety Council estimates. See the Technical Appendix. Cost-estimating procedures were revised extensively for the 1993, 2005-2006, and the 2016 editions of Injury Facts®. In general, cost estimates are not comparable from year to year. As additional data or new benchmarks become available, they are used from that point forward. Previously estimated figures are not revised.
[a] Duplication between work and motor vehicle, which amounted to $28.7 billion, was eliminated from the total.
[b] Home and public insurance administration costs may include costs of administering medical treatment claims for some motor-vehicle injuries filed through health insurance plans.
[c] Not included, see comments above.

Costs of unintentional injuries by class, 2015

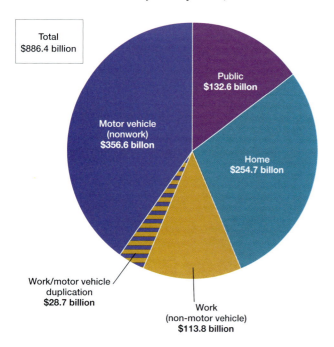

ALL INJURIES

Comprehensive Cost of Unintentional Injuries by Source of Payment

The two tables below provide estimates of the unintentional-injury-related costs that are paid by employers and government. These cost estimates reflect comprehensive costs including lost quality of life estimates. Employers and governments incur lost quality of life costs in part through higher wages paid to workers in high risk jobs. Because government agencies are also employers, the two tables are not mutually exclusive and should not be added together.

Comprehensive Cost of Unintentional Injuries Paid by Employers, 2015 ($ billions)

Cost category	Total	Motor vehicle (nonwork)	Work/motor vehicle duplication	Work (non-motor vehicle)	Home	Public
Total employer costs	**$622.75**	**$30.37**	**$68.65**	**$473.31**	**$32.01**	**$18.41**
Productivity and wage loss	$44.42	$8.92	$2.60	$15.27	$11.37	$6.26
Medical expenses (including employee health insurance)	$62.21	$9.11	$2.50	$28.93	$13.65	$8.00
Administrative expense (insurance administrative and legal)	$57.09	$9.65	$15.06	$31.07	$0.66	$0.64
Motor-vehicle damage	$4.37	$0.00	$4.37	$0.00	$0.00	$0.00
Employer uninsured costs	$23.83	$2.68	$0.71	$10.62	$6.32	$3.51
Fire loss	$4.28	$0.00	$0.00	$4.28	$0.00	$0.00
Wage risk premiums (higher wages paid for risky jobs)	$426.54	$0.00	$43.41	$383.13	$0.00	$0.00
Public services (police, etc)	$0.00	$0.00	$0.00	$0.00	$0.00	$0.00

Comprehensive Cost of Unintentional Injuries Paid by Government, 2015 ($ billions)

Cost category	Total	Motor vehicle (nonwork)	Work/motor vehicle duplication	Work (non-motor vehicle)	Home	Public
Total government costs	**$176.71**	**$25.39**	**$8.87**	**$45.16**	**$60.08**	**$37.20**
Productivity and wage loss	$31.79	$9.07	$0.81	$4.83	$10.75	$6.32
Medical expenses (including employee health insurance)	$88.68	$12.99	$0.19	$2.30	$46.15	$27.05
Administrative expense (insurance administrative and legal)	$9.66	$0.95	$1.83	$2.47	$2.24	$2.17
Motor-vehicle damage	$0.93	$0.37	$0.56	$0.00	$0.00	$0.00
Employer uninsured costs	$2.78	$0.40	$0.09	$0.84	$0.93	$0.52
Fire loss	$5.42	$0.00	$0.00	$4.28	$0.00	$1.14
Wage risk premiums (higher wages paid for risky jobs)	$35.72	$0.00	$5.29	$30.44	$0.00	$0.00
Public services (police, etc)	$1.72	$1.61	$0.10	$0.00	$0.00	$0.00

Source: National Safety Council estimates. See the Technical Appendix.

ALL INJURIES
Costs of Unintentional Injuries by Component

Major revisions were made to the National Safety Council cost model for this edition that take advantage of data sources not previously available. Because of the changes made to the cost model, cost estimates provided in this edition are not comparable to previously published estimates.

Wage and productivity losses
A person's contribution to the wealth of the nation usually is measured in terms of wages and household production. The total of wages and fringe benefits, together with an estimate of the replacement-cost value of household services, provides an estimate of this lost productivity. Also included is travel delay for motor-vehicle incidents.

Medical expenses
Doctor fees; hospital charges; the cost of medicines; future medical costs; and ambulance, helicopter, and other emergency medical services are included.

Administrative expenses
Includes the administrative cost of public and private insurance, as well as police and legal costs. Private insurance administrative costs are the difference between premiums paid to insurance companies and claims paid out by them. It is their cost of doing business and a part of the cost total. Claims paid by insurance companies are not identified separately, as every claim is compensation for losses such as wages, medical expenses, property damage, etc.

Motor-vehicle damage
Includes the value of damage to vehicles from motor-vehicle crashes. The cost of normal wear and tear to vehicles is not included.

Employers' uninsured costs
This is an estimate of the uninsured costs incurred by employers, representing the dollar value of time lost by uninjured workers. It includes time spent investigating and reporting injuries, administering first aid, hiring and training replacement workers, and the extra cost of overtime for uninjured workers.

Fire loss
Includes losses from both structure fires and nonstructure fires, such as vehicles, outside storage, crops, and timber.

Work – motor vehicle duplication
The cost of motor-vehicle crashes that involve people in the course of their work is included in both classes, but the duplication is eliminated from the total. The duplication in 2015 amounted to $28.7 billion and consists of $6.9 billion in wage and productivity losses, $2.5 billion in medical expenses, $15.0 billion in administrative expenses, $3.6 billion in vehicle damage, and $0.7 billion in employers' uninsured costs.

ALL INJURIES
Costs of Unintentional Injuries by Component (cont.)

Costs of unintentional injuries by component, 2015

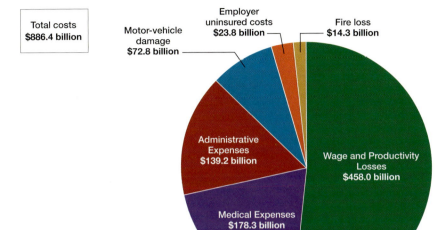

Total costs: $886.4 billion
- Motor-vehicle damage: $72.8 billion
- Employer uninsured costs: $23.8 billion
- Fire loss: $14.3 billion
- Administrative Expenses: $139.2 billion
- Wage and Productivity Losses: $458.0 billion
- Medical Expenses: $178.3 billion

ALL INJURIES
Cost Equivalents

The costs of unintentional injuries are immense – billions of dollars. Because figures this large can be difficult to comprehend, it is sometimes useful to reduce the numbers to a more understandable scale by relating them to quantities encountered in daily life. The table below shows how the costs of unintentional injuries compare to common quantities such as taxes, corporate profits, or stock dividends.

Cost equivalents, 2015

The cost of...	Is equivalent to...
...All injuries ($886.4 billion)	...58 cents of every dollar paid in federal personal income taxes, **or** ...52 cents of every dollar spent on food in the United States.
...Motor-vehicle crashes ($385.3 billion)	...purchasing 600 gallons of gasoline for each registered vehicle in the United States, **or** ...$1,800 per licensed driver.
...Work injuries ($142.5 billion)	...15 cents of every dollar of corporate dividends to stockholders, **or** ...7 cents of every dollar of pre-tax corporate profits, **or** ...exceeds the combined profits reported by the 9 largest Fortune 500 companies.
...Home injuries ($254.7 billion)	...a $365,900 rebate on each new single-family home built, **or** ...56 cents of every dollar of property taxes paid.
...Public injuries ($132.6 billion)	...a $14.6 million grant to each public library in the United States, **or** ...a $103,300 bonus for each police officer and firefighter.

Source: National Safety Council estimates.
[a]Major revisions were made to the National Safety Council cost model starting with the 2016 edition that take advantage of data sources not previously available. Because of the changes made to the cost model, cost estimates provided prior to the 2016 edition are not comparable to estimates published in later editions.

ALL INJURIES

Deaths Due to Unintentional Injuries, 2015

Type of event and age of victim

All unintentional injuries

The term "unintentional" covers most deaths from injury and poisoning. Excluded are homicides (including legal intervention), suicides, deaths for which none of these categories can be determined, and war deaths.

	Total	Change from 2014	Death rate[a]
Deaths	146,571	+7.7%	45.6

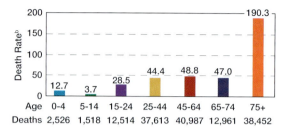

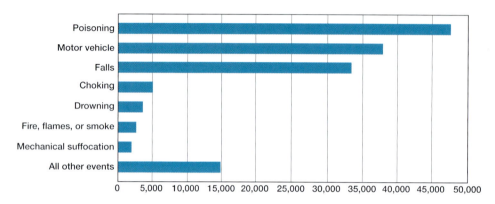

Poisoning

Includes deaths from drugs, medicines, other solid and liquid substances, and gases and vapors. Excludes poisonings from spoiled foods, *Salmonella*, etc., which are classified as disease deaths.

	Total	Change from 2014	Death rate[a]
Deaths	47,478	+13%	14.8

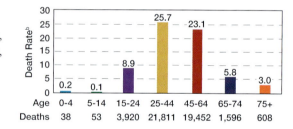

Motor-vehicle incidents

Includes deaths involving mechanically or electrically powered highway-transport vehicles in motion (except those on rails), both on and off the highway or street.

	Total	Change from 2014	Death rate[a]
Deaths	37,757	+7%	11.7

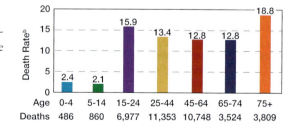

Falls

Includes deaths from falls from one level to another or on the same level. Excludes falls in or from transport vehicles, or while boarding or alighting from them.

	Total	Change from 2014	Death rate[a]
Deaths	33,381	+4%	10.4

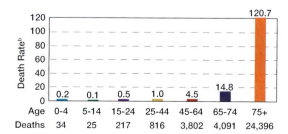

See footnotes on page 13.

ALL INJURIES
Deaths Due to Unintentional Injuries, 2015 (cont.)

Type of event and age of victim

Choking
Includes deaths from unintentional ingestion or inhalation of food or other objects resulting in the obstruction of respiratory passages.

	Total	Change from 2014	Death rate[a]
Deaths	5,051	+5%	1.6

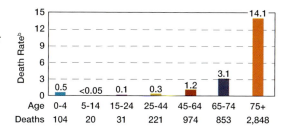

Drowning
Includes non-transport-related drownings such as those resulting from swimming, playing in the water, or falling in. Excludes drownings in floods and other cataclysms, which are classified to the cataclysm, and boating-related drownings.

	Total	Change from 2014	Death rate[a]
Deaths	3,602	+6%	1.1

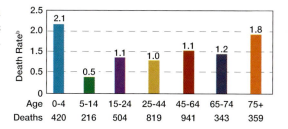

Fire, flames, or smoke
Includes deaths from exposure to fire, flames, or smoke, and from injuries in fires such as falls and struck by falling objects. Excludes burns from hot objects or liquids.

	Total	Change from 2014	Death rate[a]
Deaths	2,646	-2%	0.8

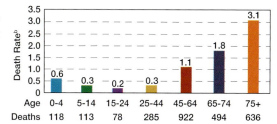

Mechanical suffocation
Includes deaths from hanging and strangulation, and suffocation in enclosed or confined spaces; cave-ins; or by bed clothes, plastic bags, or similar materials.

	Total	Change from 2014	Death rate[a]
Deaths	1,863	+6%	0.6

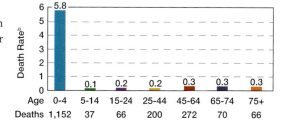

All other types
Most important types included are natural heat or cold; firearms; struck by or against object; machinery; electric current; and air, water, or rail transport.

	Total	Change from 2014	Death rate[a]
Deaths	14,793	+6%	4.6

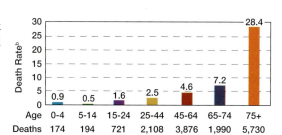

Note: Category descriptions have changed due to the adoption of ICD-10. See the Technical Appendix for comparability.
[a]Deaths per 100,000 population.
[b]Deaths per 100,000 population in each age group.

ALL INJURIES
Leading Causes of Death

Unintentional injuries are the fourth leading cause of death overall and first among people in age groups from 1 to 44. By single years of age, unintentional injuries are the leading cause of death from age 1 to 42.

Causes are ranked for both sexes combined. Some leading causes for males and females separately may not be shown. Beginning with 1999 data, deaths are classified according to the 10th revision of the *International Classification of Diseases*. See the Technical Appendix for comparability

Deaths and death rates by age and sex, 2014

Cause	Number of deaths Total	Male	Female	Death rates[a] Total	Male	Female
All ages[b]						
All causes	2,626,418	1,328,241	1,298,177	823.7	846.4	801.7
Heart disease	614,348	325,077	289,271	192.7	207.1	178.6
Cancer (malignant neoplasms)	591,699	311,296	280,403	185.6	198.4	173.2
Chronic lower respiratory diseases	147,101	69,456	77,645	46.1	44.3	48.0
Unintentional injuries	136,053	85,448	50,605	42.7	54.4	31.3
Poisoning	42,032	27,225	14,807	13.2	17.3	9.1
Motor-vehicle	35,398	25,158	10,240	11.1	16.0	6.3
Falls	31,959	16,029	15,930	10.0	10.2	9.8
Choking[c]	4,816	2,617	2,199	1.5	1.7	1.4
Drowning	3,406	2,640	766	1.1	1.7	0.5
All other unintentional injuries	18,442	11,779	6,663	5.8	7.5	4.1
Stroke (cerebrovascular disease)	133,103	55,471	77,632	41.7	35.3	47.9
Alzheimer's disease	93,541	28,362	65,179	29.3	18.1	40.3
Diabetes mellitus	76,488	41,111	35,377	24.0	26.2	21.8
Influenza and pneumonia	55,227	26,586	28,641	17.3	16.9	17.7
Nephritis and nephrosis	48,146	24,436	23,710	15.1	15.6	14.6
Suicide	42,773	33,113	9,660	13.4	21.1	6.0
Younger than 1						
All causes	23,215	12,886	10,329	588.0	638.6	535.0
Congenital anomalies	4,746	2,444	2,302	120.2	121.1	119.2
Short gestation, low birth weight, n.e.c.	4,173	2,370	1,803	105.7	117.5	93.4
Maternal complications of pregnancy	1,574	916	658	39.9	45.4	34.1
Sudden infant death syndrome	1,545	924	621	39.1	45.8	32.2
Unintentional injuries	1,161	663	498	29.4	32.9	25.8
Mechanical suffocation	951	545	406	24.1	27.0	21.0
Motor-vehicle	68	39	29	1.7	1.9	1.5
Choking[c]	40	27	13	1.0	1.3	0.7
Drowning	29	13	16	0.7	0.6	0.8
Fire, flames, or smoke	15	6	9	0.4	0.3	0.5
All other unintentional injuries	58	33	25	1.5	1.6	1.3
Complications of placenta, cord, membranes	965	499	466	24.4	24.7	24.1
Bacterial sepsis	544	298	246	13.8	14.8	12.7
Respiratory distress	460	269	191	11.7	13.3	9.9
Circulatory system disease	444	247	197	11.2	12.2	10.2
Neonatal hemorrhage	441	271	170	11.2	13.4	8.8
1-4 years						
All causes	3,830	2,172	1,658	24.0	26.7	21.3
Unintentional injuries	1,216	744	472	7.6	9.1	6.1
Motor-vehicle	405	226	179	2.5	2.8	2.3
Drowning	388	257	131	2.4	3.2	1.7
Fire, flames, or smoke	115	72	43	0.7	0.9	0.6
Mechanical suffocation	65	42	23	0.4	0.5	0.3
Choking[c]	55	39	16	0.3	0.5	0.2
All other unintentional injuries	188	108	80	1.2	1.3	1.0
Congenital anomalies	399	219	180	2.5	2.7	2.3
Homicide	364	196	168	2.3	2.4	2.2
Cancer (malignant neoplasms)	321	182	139	2.0	2.2	1.8
Heart disease	149	76	73	0.9	0.9	0.9
Influenza and pneumonia	109	57	52	0.7	0.7	0.7
Chronic lower respiratory diseases	53	30	23	0.3	0.4	0.3
Septicemia	53	23	30	0.3	0.3	0.4
Benign neoplasms	38	19	19	0.2	0.2	0.2
Perinatal period	38	24	14	0.2	0.3	0.2

See source and footnotes on page 16.

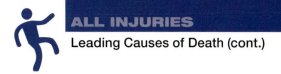

ALL INJURIES
Leading Causes of Death (cont.)

Deaths and death rates by age and sex, 2014 (cont.)

Cause	Number of deaths Total	Male	Female	Death rates[a] Total	Male	Female
5-14 years						
All causes	5,250	3,128	2,122	12.7	14.9	10.5
Unintentional injuries	1,480	968	512	3.6	4.6	2.5
Motor-vehicle	*829*	*499*	*330*	*2.0*	*2.4*	*1.6*
Drowning	*230*	*181*	*49*	*0.6*	*0.9*	*0.2*
Fire, flames, or smoke	*117*	*71*	*46*	*0.3*	*0.3*	*0.2*
Mechanical suffocation	*44*	*34*	*10*	*0.1*	*0.2*	*<0.1*
Poisoning	*31*	*17*	*14*	*0.1*	*0.1*	*0.1*
All other unintentional injuries	*229*	*166*	*63*	*0.6*	*0.8*	*0.3*
Cancer (malignant neoplasms)	852	488	364	2.1	2.3	1.8
Suicide	428	277	151	1.0	1.3	0.7
Congenital anomalies	348	185	163	0.8	0.9	0.8
Homicide	279	166	113	0.7	0.8	0.6
Heart disease	191	108	83	0.5	0.5	0.4
Chronic lower respiratory diseases	139	90	49	0.3	0.4	0.2
Influenza and pneumonia	98	50	48	0.2	0.2	0.2
Stroke (cerebrovascular disease)	88	47	41	0.2	0.2	0.2
Benign neoplasms	74	33	41	0.2	0.2	0.2
15-24 years						
All causes	28,791	21,117	7,674	65.5	93.8	35.8
Unintentional injuries	11,836	8,803	3,033	26.9	39.1	14.1
Motor-vehicle	*6,709*	*4,842*	*1,867*	*15.3*	*21.5*	*8.7*
Poisoning	*3,492*	*2,567*	*925*	*7.9*	*11.4*	*4.3*
Drowning	*507*	*465*	*42*	*1.2*	*2.1*	*0.2*
Falls	*174*	*143*	*31*	*0.4*	*0.6*	*0.1*
Firearms	*148*	*141*	*7*	*0.3*	*0.6*	*<0.1*
All other unintentional injuries	*806*	*645*	*161*	*1.8*	*2.9*	*0.8*
Suicide	5,079	4,089	990	11.5	18.2	4.6
Homicide	4,144	3,598	546	9.4	16.0	2.5
Cancer (malignant neoplasms)	1,569	952	617	3.6	4.2	2.9
Heart disease	953	616	337	2.2	2.7	1.6
Congenital anomalies	377	211	166	0.9	0.9	0.8
Influenza and pneumonia	199	116	83	0.5	0.5	0.4
Diabetes mellitus	181	115	66	0.4	0.5	0.3
Chronic lower respiratory diseases	178	116	62	0.4	0.5	0.3
Stroke (cerebrovascular disease)	177	102	75	0.4	0.5	0.3
25-34 years						
All causes	47,177	32,697	14,480	108.4	148.8	67.2
Unintentional injuries	17,357	12,841	4,516	39.9	58.4	21.0
Poisoning	*9,334*	*6,683*	*2,651*	*21.4*	*30.4*	*12.3*
Motor-vehicle	*6,030*	*4,568*	*1,462*	*13.9*	*20.8*	*6.8*
Drowning	*399*	*316*	*83*	*0.9*	*1.4*	*0.4*
Falls	*285*	*236*	*49*	*0.7*	*1.1*	*0.2*
Fire, flames, or smoke	*184*	*114*	*70*	*0.4*	*0.5*	*0.3*
All other unintentional injuries	*1,125*	*924*	*201*	*2.6*	*4.2*	*0.9*
Suicide	6,569	5,222	1,347	15.1	23.8	6.3
Homicide	4,159	3,477	682	9.6	15.8	3.2
Cancer (malignant neoplasms)	3,624	1,794	1,830	8.3	8.2	8.5
Heart disease	3,341	2,266	1,075	7.7	10.3	5.0
Chronic liver disease and cirrhosis	725	437	288	1.7	2.0	1.3
Diabetes mellitus	709	432	277	1.6	2.0	1.3
Human immunodeficiency virus infection	583	413	170	1.3	1.9	0.8
Stroke (cerebrovascular disease)	579	331	248	1.3	1.5	1.2
Influenza and pneumonia	549	288	261	1.3	1.3	1.2
35-44 years						
All causes	70,996	43,693	27,303	175.2	216.7	134.1
Unintentional injuries	16,048	11,066	4,982	39.6	54.9	24.5
Poisoning	*9,116*	*5,920*	*3,196*	*22.5*	*29.4*	*15.7*
Motor-vehicle	*4,488*	*3,310*	*1,178*	*11.1*	*16.4*	*5.8*
Falls	*504*	*383*	*121*	*1.2*	*1.9*	*0.6*
Drowning	*363*	*281*	*82*	*0.9*	*1.4*	*0.4*
Fire, flames, or smoke	*197*	*115*	*82*	*0.5*	*0.6*	*0.4*
All other unintentional injuries	*1,380*	*1,057*	*323*	*3.4*	*5.2*	*1.6*
Cancer (malignant neoplasms)	11,267	4,829	6,438	27.8	24.0	31.6
Heart disease	10,368	7,021	3,347	25.6	34.8	16.4
Suicide	6,706	5,035	1,671	16.6	25.0	8.2
Homicide	2,588	2,062	526	6.4	10.2	2.6
Chronic liver disease and cirrhosis	2,582	1,617	965	6.4	8.0	4.7
Diabetes mellitus	1,999	1,211	788	4.9	6.0	3.9
Stroke (cerebrovascular disease)	1,745	1,001	744	4.3	5.0	3.7
Human immunodeficiency virus infection	1,174	774	400	2.9	3.8	2.0
Influenza and pneumonia	1,125	616	509	2.8	3.1	2.5

See source and footnotes on page 16.

ALL INJURIES
Leading Causes of Death (cont.)

Deaths and death rates by age and sex, 2014 (cont.)

	Number of deaths			Death rates[a]		
Cause	Total	Male	Female	Total	Male	Female
45-54 years						
All causes	175,917	106,377	69,540	404.8	496.5	315.6
Cancer (malignant neoplasms)	44,834	22,053	22,781	103.2	102.9	103.4
Heart disease	34,791	24,316	10,475	80.1	113.5	47.5
Unintentional injuries	20,610	13,841	6,769	47.4	64.6	30.7
Poisoning	11,009	6,697	4,312	25.3	31.3	19.6
Motor-vehicle	5,251	3,889	1,362	12.1	18.2	6.2
Falls	1,340	986	354	3.1	4.6	1.6
Drowning	442	345	97	1.0	1.6	0.4
Fire, flames, or smoke	351	211	140	0.8	1.0	0.6
All other unintentional injuries	2,217	1,713	504	5.1	8.0	2.3
Suicide	8,767	6,420	2,347	20.2	30.0	10.7
Chronic liver disease and cirrhosis	8,627	5,727	2,900	19.9	26.7	13.2
Diabetes mellitus	6,062	3,795	2,267	13.9	17.7	10.3
Stroke (cerebrovascular disease)	5,349	2,995	2,354	12.3	14.0	10.7
Chronic lower respiratory diseases	4,402	2,002	2,400	10.1	9.3	10.9
Influenza and pneumonia	2,731	1,488	1,243	6.3	6.9	5.6
Septicemia	2,514	1,343	1,171	5.8	6.3	5.3
55-64 years						
All causes	348,808	212,198	136,610	870.3	1,098.2	658.2
Cancer (malignant neoplasms)	115,282	63,825	51,457	287.6	330.3	247.9
Heart disease	74,473	51,795	22,678	185.8	268.1	109.3
Unintentional injuries	18,030	12,174	5,856	45.0	63.0	28.2
Poisoning	7,013	4,242	2,771	17.5	22.0	13.4
Motor-vehicle	4,773	3,497	1,276	11.9	18.1	6.1
Falls	2,558	1,756	802	6.4	9.1	3.9
Choking[c]	581	342	239	1.4	1.8	1.2
Fire, flames, or smoke	508	337	171	1.3	1.7	0.8
All other unintentional injuries	2,597	2,000	597	6.5	10.4	2.9
Chronic lower respiratory diseases	16,492	8,549	7,943	41.2	44.2	38.3
Diabetes mellitus	13,342	8,196	5,146	33.3	42.4	24.8
Chronic liver disease and cirrhosis	12,792	8,871	3,921	31.9	45.9	18.9
Stroke (cerebrovascular disease)	11,727	6,796	4,931	29.3	35.2	23.8
Suicide	7,527	5,679	1,848	18.8	29.4	8.9
Septicemia	5,709	3,007	2,702	14.2	15.6	13.0
Influenza and pneumonia	5,390	3,076	2,314	13.4	15.9	11.1
65-74 years						
All causes	471,541	268,648	202,893	1,786.3	2,175.5	1,444.2
Cancer (malignant neoplasms)	159,208	87,914	71,294	603.1	711.9	507.5
Heart disease	101,683	64,917	36,766	385.2	525.7	261.7
Chronic lower respiratory diseases	35,617	18,096	17,521	134.9	146.5	124.7
Stroke (cerebrovascular disease)	19,663	10,504	9,159	74.5	85.1	65.2
Diabetes mellitus	18,204	10,599	7,605	69.0	85.8	54.1
Unintentional injuries	11,909	7,520	4,389	45.1	60.9	31.2
Falls	3,938	2,382	1,556	14.9	19.3	11.1
Motor-vehicle	3,153	2,103	1,050	11.9	17.0	7.5
Poisoning	1,410	810	600	5.3	6.6	4.3
Choking[c]	789	433	356	3.0	3.5	2.5
Fire, flames, or smoke	475	303	172	1.8	2.5	1.2
All other unintentional injuries	2,144	1,489	655	8.1	12.1	4.7
Nephritis and nephrosis	9,060	4,827	4,233	34.3	39.1	30.1
Septicemia	8,220	4,264	3,956	31.1	34.5	28.2
Influenza and pneumonia	7,861	4,368	3,493	29.8	35.4	24.9
Chronic liver disease and cirrhosis	7,809	4,999	2,810	29.6	40.5	20.0
75 years or older[b]						
All causes	1,450,893	625,325	825,568	7,311.2	7,814.4	6,971.1
Heart disease	388,082	173,788	214,294	1,955.6	2,171.7	1,809.5
Cancer (malignant neoplasms)	254,690	129,237	125,453	1,283.4	1,615.0	1,059.3
Stroke (cerebrovascular disease)	93,649	33,623	60,026	471.9	420.2	506.9
Chronic lower respiratory diseases	89,080	39,986	49,094	448.9	499.7	414.6
Alzheimer's disease	87,434	25,759	61,675	440.6	321.9	520.8
Influenza and pneumonia	36,979	16,438	20,541	186.3	205.4	173.4
Unintentional injuries	36,406	16,828	19,578	183.5	210.3	165.3
Falls	23,107	10,109	12,998	116.4	126.3	109.8
Motor-vehicle	3,692	2,185	1,507	18.6	27.3	12.7
Choking[c]	2,755	1,421	1,334	13.9	17.8	11.3
Fire, flames, or smoke	635	325	310	3.2	4.1	2.6
Poisoning	590	269	321	3.0	3.4	2.7
All other unintentional injuries	5,627	2,519	3,108	28.4	31.5	26.2
Diabetes mellitus	35,959	16,743	19,216	181.2	209.2	162.3
Nephritis and nephrosis	30,900	14,832	16,068	155.7	185.3	135.7
Parkinson's disease	22,051	12,969	9,082	111.1	162.1	76.7

Source: National Safety Council analysis of National Center for Health Statistics--Mortality Data for 2014 as compiled from data provided by the 57 vital statistics jurisdictions through the Vital Statistics Cooperative Program. Rates are National Safety Council estimates based on data from the National Center for Health Statistics and the U.S. Census Bureau.
[a]Deaths per 100,000 population in each age group. [b]Includes 163 deaths for which the age was unknown. [c]Inhalation or ingestion of food or other objects.

ALL INJURIES
Race and Hispanic Origin

The rank of unintentional injuries as a cause of death varies with race and Hispanic origin. While ranking fourth overall (following heart disease, cancer, and chronic lower respiratory diseases), unintentional injuries rank third for Hispanics after cancer and heart disease and fifth for non-Hispanics after heart disease, cancer, chronic lower respiratory disease, and stroke.

By race, unintentional injuries ranks fourth for whites, blacks, and for other non-black groups including Asians, Pacific Islanders, American Indians, and Alaskan Natives.

Unintentional-injury-related deaths and death rates by race, Hispanic origin, and sex, United States, 2014

Race and sex	Total Rank	Total Number	Total Rate	Non-Hispanic Rank	Non-Hispanic Number	Non-Hispanic Rate	Hispanic Rank	Hispanic Number	Hispanic Rate
All races	4	136,053	42.7	5	123,051	46.7	3	12,429	22.4
Males	3	85,448	54.4	3	76,076	59.0	3	8,982	32.1
Females	6	50,605	31.3	6	46,975	34.9	5	3,447	12.6
White	4	117,242	47.5	4	104,761	52.9	3	12,026	(b)
Males	3	72,884	59.6	3	63,873	65.5	3	8,702	(b)
Females	6	44,358	35.6	6	40,888	40.7	5	3,324	(b)
Black	4	14,168	33.6	4	13,849	35.0	3	221	(b)
Males	3	9,567	47.4	3	9,344	49.5	3	156	(b)
Females	7	4,601	20.9	8	4,505	21.8	4	65	(b)
Not white or black[a]	4	4,643	15.5	4	4,441	17.0	3	182	(b)
Males	3	2,997	20.6	3	2,859	22.8	3	124	(b)
Females	4	1,646	10.6	4	1,582	11.7	3	58	(b)

Source: National Safety Council analysis of National Center for Health Statistics (NCHS)–Mortality Data for 2014, as compiled from data provided by the 57 vital statistics jurisdictions through the Vital Statistics Cooperative Program. Rates are National Safety Council estimates based on data from NCHS and the U.S. Census Bureau.
Note: Rates are deaths per 100,000 population in each race/sex/Hispanic origin group. Total column includes 462 deaths for which Hispanic origin was not determined.
[a]Includes American Indian, Alaskan Native, Asian, Native Hawaiian, and Pacific Islander.
[b]Race is not well-reported for persons of Hispanic origin. Population death rates are unreliable.

Leading causes of unintentional-injury-related death by race, Hispanic origin, and sex, United States, 2014

Cause of death	All races Both	All races Male	All races Female	White Both	White Male	White Female	Black Both	Black Male	Black Female	Not White or Black[a] Both	Not White or Black[a] Male	Not White or Black[a] Female
Total	136,053	85,448	50,605	117,242	72,884	44,358	14,168	9,567	4,601	4,643	2,997	1,646
Poisoning	42,032	27,225	14,807	36,793	23,782	13,011	4,171	2,723	1,448	1,068	720	348
Motor vehicle	35,398	25,158	10,240	28,910	20,516	8,394	4,878	3,577	1,301	1,610	1,065	545
Fall	31,959	16,029	15,930	29,589	14,703	14,886	1,397	781	616	973	545	428
Choking[b]	4,816	2,617	2,199	4,179	2,279	1,900	515	273	242	122	65	57
Drowning	3,406	2,640	766	2,547	1,924	623	607	512	95	252	204	48
Fires, flames, or smoke	2,701	1,627	1,074	2,044	1,242	802	572	339	233	85	46	39
Population (thousands)	318,857	156,936	161,921	246,661	122,195	124,465	42,158	20,170	21,988	30,038	14,571	15,467

Cause of death	Non-Hispanic Both	Non-Hispanic Male	Non-Hispanic Female	Hispanic Both	Hispanic Male	Hispanic Female	Unknown Both	Unknown Male	Unknown Female
Total	123,051	76,076	46,975	12,429	8,982	3,447	573	390	183
Poisoning	38,226	24,405	13,821	3,544	2,642	902	262	178	84
Motor vehicle	30,197	21,286	8,911	5,082	3,782	1,300	119	90	29
Fall	30,102	14,926	15,176	1,760	1,048	712	97	55	42
Choking[b]	4,559	2,475	2,084	245	137	108	12	5	7
Drowning	2,996	2,302	694	397	329	68	13	9	4
Fires, flames, or smoke	2,531	1,515	1,016	152	99	53	18	13	5
Population (thousands)	263,470	128,919	134,551	55,388	28,018	27,370	—	—	—

Source: National Safety Council analysis of National Center for Health Statistics (NCHS)–Mortality Data for 2014, as compiled from data provided by the 57 vital statistics jurisdictions through the Vital Statistics Cooperative Program. Rates are National Safety Council estimates based on data from NCHS and the U.S. Census Bureau.
Note: Dashes (–) indicate not applicable.
[a]Includes American Indian, Alaskan Native, Asian, Native Hawaiian, and Pacific Islander.
[b]Suffocation by inhalation or ingestion.

ALL INJURIES

Trends in Unintentional Death by Ethnic Origin and Race

Fatality trends for the three largest race and ethnic origin groups: Non-Hispanic white, Non-Hispanic black, and Hispanic or Latino are provided by major age group: younger than 1, 1 to 24, 25 to 64, and over 65 years of age. Fatalities among these three ethnic origin and race groups represent 96% of all unintentional-injury deaths in the United States.

Younger than 1

The overall death rate for children younger than 1 has increased 32% from 1999 to 2014. Within this age group, the only subgroup to experience a decrease in the death rate was Hispanics or Latinos, while the largest percent increase was among Non-Hispanic black children. Driving this increase was the increase in suffocation deaths.

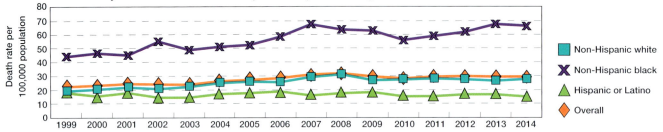

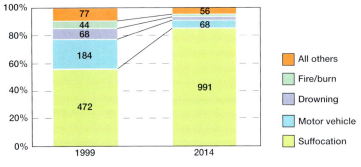

1 to 24

Overall the death rate for the 1 to 24 age group has decreased 27% from 1999 to 2014. Within this age group, all subgroups experienced a decrease in the death rate with Hispanics or Latinos demonstrating the strongest percent decrease of 35%. Driving this decrease was improvement in the motor-vehicle traffic death rate.

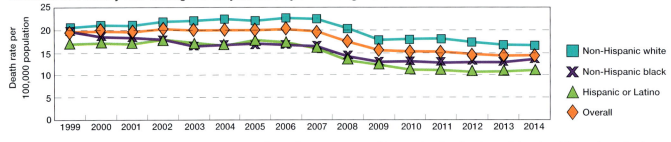

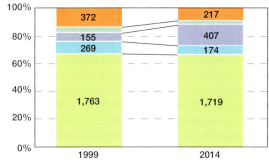

ALL INJURIES

Trends in Unintentional Death by Ethnic Origin and Race

25 to 64

The overall death rate for the 25 to 64 age group has increased 36% from 1999 to 2014. Within this age group, Hispanics or Latinos experienced nearly a 10% decrease in death rates while the death rate among Non-Hispanic whites increased 61%.

Among Non-Hispanic whites, the death rate for males increased 49% while females experienced a 91% increase. Driving this increase has been the increase in poisoning deaths primarily involving drugs, including opioid pain relievers.

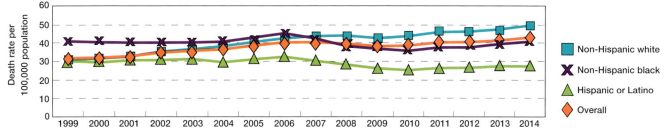

Unintentional fatality rate among 25 to 64 year olds by ethnic origin and race

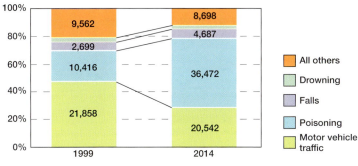

Change in distribution of unintentional deaths, Overall

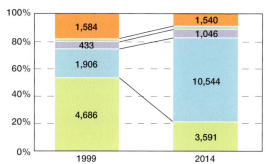

Change in distribution of deaths, Non-Hispanic white females

65 and older

Overall the death rate for the 65 and over age group has increased 13% from 1999 to 2014. Within this age group, the death rate among Non-Hispanic whites increased nearly 21% while decreasing 25% among Non-Hispanic blacks. Large increases in falls were experienced both overall and among Non-Hispanic blacks. The decrease in Non-Hispanic black death rates was driven by decreases in motor vehicle and suffocation deaths.

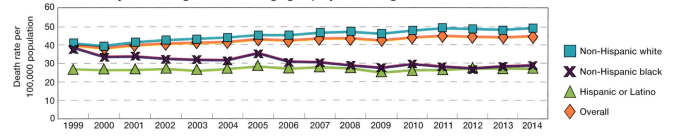

Unintentional fatality rate among 65 and older age group by ethnic origin and race

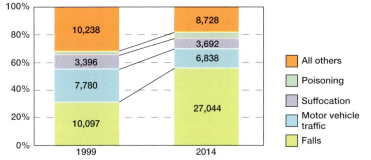

Change in distribution of unintentional deaths, Overall

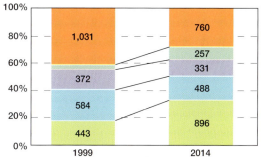

Change in distribution of deaths, Non-Hispanic blacks

ALL INJURIES

Leading Causes of Unintentional-Injury-Related Death by Age, 2014

Unintentional-injury-related deaths by age and event, United States, 2014

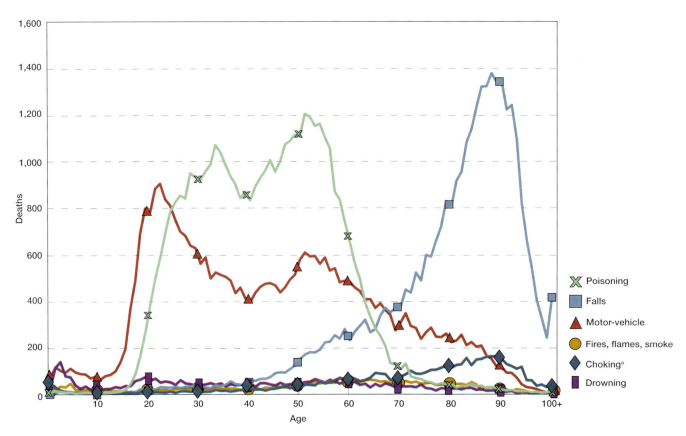

Poisonings; motor-vehicle crashes; falls; choking (suffocation by inhalation or ingestion of food or other object); drowning; and fire, flames, or smoke were the six leading causes of unintentional-injury-related death in the United States in 2014. The graph above depicts the number of deaths attributed to the top six causes by single years of age through age 99 and an aggregate age group of people 100 and older.

In 2014, poisonings were the leading cause of unintentional-injury-related death for all ages combined for the fourth consecutive year and were the leading cause of unintentional-injury-related death for each single year of age from 25 to 62. Among infants younger than 1, mechanical suffocation was the leading cause of death, followed by motor-vehicle deaths. Motor-vehicle deaths were the leading cause of death among 1-year-olds, followed by drowning. For 2-year-olds the reverse was true, with drowning the leading cause of death, followed by motor-vehicle fatalities.

The distribution of 2014 poisoning fatalities shows a sharp increase during early adulthood into middle age, rising from 163 for 18-year-olds to 1,200 for 51-year-olds. The greatest number of poisoning fatalities in 2014 occurred among people 51 years old.

The second leading cause of unintentional-injury-related death overall in 2014 was motor-vehicle crashes. Motor-vehicle fatalities reached a high of 900 for 22-year-olds, and were the leading cause of unintentional-injury-related death for people age 1, age 3 to 24, and age 63 to 66. Poisoning was the second leading cause of unintentional-injury-related death for people age 16 to 24, and from 63 to 65. Motor-vehicle fatalities were the second most common cause for every single year of age for those less than age 1, age 2, 25 to 62, and 67 to 87.

Falls were the third leading cause of unintentional-injury-related death in the United States in 2014. Falls were the leading cause of unintentional-injury-related death of people age 67 and older, and the second leading cause for those age 66. Deaths resulting from falls peaked at 1,374 for individuals age 88.

The fourth leading cause of unintentional-injury-related death in 2014 was choking.[a] Choking deaths peaked at age 88 with 158 deaths. Choking was the second leading cause of unintentional-injury-related death for people age 88 and older.

Drowning was the fifth leading cause of unintentional-injury-related death in 2014 and peaked at 135 fatalities for 2-year-olds, resulting in the leading cause of death for this age group. Drownings were the second leading cause of unintentional-injury-related death for children age 1 and age 3-15.

Fire, flames, or smoke was the sixth leading cause of unintentional-injury-related death in 2014. Fatalities due to fires, flames, or smoke peaked at 64 deaths among 58-year-olds.

Source: National Safety Council analysis of National Center for Health Statistics (NCHS)--Mortality Data for 2014, as compiled from data provided by the 57 vital statistics jurisdictions through the Vital Statistics Cooperative Program. Rates are National Safety Council estimates based on data from NCHS and the U.S. Census Bureau. See the Technical Appendix for ICD-10 codes for the leading causes and comparability with prior years.
[a]Inhalation or ingestion of food or other objects.

ALL INJURIES

Unintentional-Injury-Related Death Rates by Age, 2014

Unintentional-injury-related deaths per 100,000 population by age and event, United States, 2014

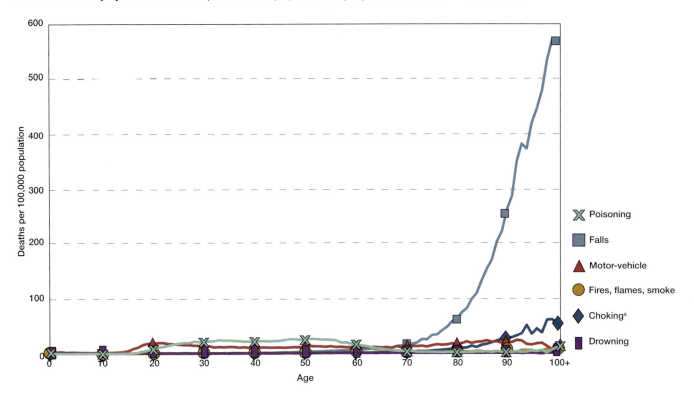

The graph above depicts U.S. death rates per 100,000 population for the six leading causes of unintentional-injury-related deaths in 2014 by age, through age 99 and an aggregate age group of people 100 and older.

Unintentional poisoning fatalities had the highest overall death rate, with an average of 13.2 deaths per 100,000 population. The poisoning death rate remained low until about age 15, when it started to increase steadily up to its peak rate of 26.7 at age 51 before falling again.

Motor-vehicle crashes had the second highest overall death rate from unintentional injury in the United States, with an average rate of 11.1 deaths per 100,000 population. Historically, motor-vehicle death rates peak for people in the 18-20 age group and, in 2014, there was such a peak among persons age 18-25 that reached a high of 19.6 for people age 21. However, in 2014 there was an even higher secondary peak among motor-vehicle death rates that began at age 76 and extended into the early 90s, with the highest rate among people age 92, at a rate of 24.3. This peak rate is followed by a rate of 23.7 occurring at age 86 and a rate of 23.1 for 93-year-olds.

Although motor-vehicle crashes were a significant problem for all ages, deaths resulting from falls for certain older ages had even higher death rates. Beginning at about age 67, the death rate from falls increased dramatically. The falls death rate surpassed that for motor vehicle for the first time at age 67 and remained higher throughout the remainder of the lifespan as it continued to rise steeply with increasing age, peaking for those age 99 with a rate of 571.4 per 100,000 population. The overall fatality rate for falls was 10.0.

Death rates due to choking on inhaled or ingested food or other objects were quite low for most ages. Rates rise rapidly beginning at about age 79. While relatively stable and low for all ages, the death rates for drownings showed peaks in the first few years of life and again at some very old ages. Death rates for fire, flames, or smoke were only slightly elevated at very young ages and began to climb at about age 75. The overall death rates per 100,000 U.S. population for choking; drowning; and fire, flames, or smoke did not exceed 1.5.

Source: National Safety Council analysis of National Center for Health Statistics (NCHS—Mortality Data for 2014, as compiled from data provided by the 57 vital statistics jurisdictions through the Vital Statistics Cooperative Program. Rates are National Safety Council estimates based on data from NCHS and the U.S. Census Bureau. See the Technical Appendix for ICD-10 codes for the leading causes and comparability with prior years.
[a]*Inhalation or ingestion of food or other objects.*

ALL INJURIES
Unintentional-Injury-Related Deaths by Sex and Age, 2014

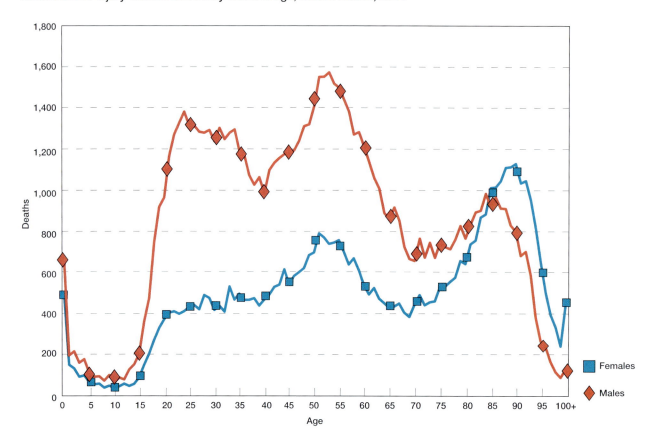

Unintentional-injury-related deaths by sex and age, United States, 2014

Males incurred more deaths due to unintentional injuries than females at all ages from birth to age 85 in 2014. The difference between the unintentional-injury-related death totals ranged from 20 more male deaths than female deaths at age 12 to 970 more deaths at age 24. The excess number of deaths for males compared to females was most evident from the late teen years to the mid-50s, when the gap begins to narrow. From age 85 on, deaths of females exceeded those of males by as little as 50 at age 86 to as much as 434 deaths nationwide at age 94.

Unintentional-injury-related deaths are at their lowest level for both sexes from about age 5 to about age 13. For males, the highest number of deaths (1,522) occurred at age 53, with high totals occurring from the late teens until the early 60s.

For females, however, the highest totals occurred among the elderly from the mid-80s through the early 90s. The greatest number of female deaths (1,129) occurred at age 90.

The graph above shows the number of unintentional-injury-related deaths in the United States during 2014 for each sex by single year of age from younger than 1 to age 99 and an aggregate age group of people 100 and older. It is based on death certificate data from the National Center for Health Statistics.

Source: National Safety Council analysis of National Center for Health Statistics (NCHS)—Mortality Data for 2014, as compiled from data provided by the 57 vital statistics jurisdictions through the Vital Statistics Cooperative Program. Rates are National Safety Council estimates based on data from NCHS and the U.S. Census Bureau. See the Technical Appendix for ICD-10 codes for the leading causes and comparability with prior years.

ALL INJURIES

Unintentional-Injury-Related Death Rates by Sex and Age, 2014

Unintentional-injury-related deaths per 100,000 population by sex and age, 2014

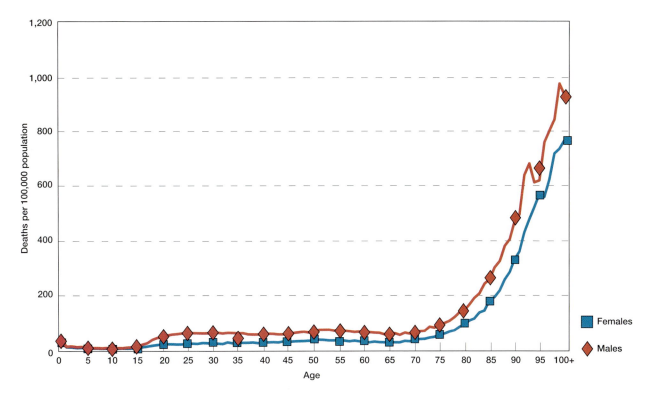

Males have greater unintentional-injury-related death rates for each year of age compared to females. The graph above shows the unintentional-injury-related death rates for males and females by single year of age from younger than 1 to age 99 and an aggregate age group of people 100 and older. It is based on National Center for Health Statistics mortality data and U.S. Census Bureau population data.

Death rates for both sexes are lowest from birth until the mid-teen years, where rates rise rapidly. Rates then remain fairly constant until the early 70's, where they again rise steadily with increasing age. Across all ages, males had an overall death rate of 54.4 unintentional-injury-related deaths per 100,000 males, while the rate among females in the United States was 31.3. The overall unintentional-injury-related death rate for all ages and both sexes was 42.7 deaths per 100,000 population.

Source: National Safety Council analysis of National Center for Health Statistics (NCHS)—Mortality Data for 2014, as compiled from data provided by the 57 vital statistics jurisdictions through the Vital Statistics Cooperative Program. Rates are National Safety Council estimates based on data from NCHS and the U.S. Census Bureau. See the Technical Appendix for ICD-10 codes for the leading causes and comparability with prior years.

ALL INJURIES
All Deaths Due to Injury

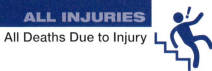

Mortality by selected external causes, United States, 2012-2014

Type of accident or manner of injury	2014[a]	2013	2012
All external causes of mortality, V01-Y89, *U01, *U03[b]	202,296	195,713	192,988
Deaths due to unintentional (accidental) injuries, V01-X59, Y85-Y86	136,053	130,557	127,792
Transport accidents, V01-V99, Y85	37,939	37,938	39,045
Motor-vehicle accidents, V02-V04, V09.0, V09.2, V12-V14, V19.0-V19.2, V19.4-V19.6, V20-V79, V80.3-V80.5, V81.0-V81.1, V82.0-V82.1, V83-V86, V87.0-V87.8, V88.0-V88.8, V89.0, V89.2	35,398	35,369	36,415
Pedestrian, V01-V09	6,258	5,974	6,020
Pedalcyclist, V10-V19	902	925	900
Motorcycle rider, V20-V29	4,106	4,230	4,643
Occupant of three-wheeled motor vehicle, V30-V39	3	7	7
Car occupant, V40-V49	6,274	6,625	7,632
Occupant of pick-up truck or van, V50-V59	1,277	1,474	1,729
Occupant of heavy transport vehicle, V60-V69	291	273	313
Bus occupant, V70-V79	26	29	38
Animal rider or occupant of animal-drawn vehicle, V80	97	91	106
Occupant of railway train or railway vehicle, V81	13	24	9
Occupant of streetcar, V82	1	1	2
Other and unspecified land transport accidents, V83-V89	17,141	16,716	15,997
Occupant of special industrial vehicle, V83	4	10	7
Occupant of special agricultural vehicle, V84	96	81	94
Occupant of special construction vehicle, V85	24	22	12
Occupant of all-terrain or other off-road motor vehicle, V86	940	934	908
Other and unspecified person, V87-V89	16,077	15,669	14,976
Water transport accidents, V90-V94	393	403	421
Drowning, V90, V92	300	310	314
Other and unspecified injuries, V91, V93-V94	93	93	107
Air and space transport accidents, V95-V97	412	412	432
Other and unspecified transport accidents and sequelae, V98-V99, Y85	745	754	796
Other specified transport accidents, V98	0	0	0
Unspecified transport accidents, V99	1	0	2
Nontransport unintentional (accidental) injuries, W00-X59, Y86	98,114	92,619	88,747
Falls, W00-W19	31,959	30,208	28,753
Fall on same level from slipping, tripping, and stumbling, W01	737	710	727
Other fall on same level, W00, W02-W03, W18	11,031	9,631	8,989
Fall involving bed, chair, other furniture, W06-W08	1,239	1,170	1,138
Fall on and from stairs and steps, W10	2,285	2,233	2,127
Fall on and from ladder or scaffolding, W11-W12	525	420	481
Fall from out of or through building or structure, W13	501	504	481
Other fall from one level to another, W09, W14-W17	668	605	650
Other and unspecified fall, W04-W05, W19	14,973	14,935	14,160
Exposure to inanimate mechanical forces, W20-W49	2,521	2,353	2,480
Struck by or striking against object, W20-W22	899	811	859
Caught between objects, W23	91	88	106
Contact with machinery, W24, W30-W31	605	588	627
Contact with sharp objects, W25-W29	106	130	122
Firearms discharge, W32-W34	586	505	548
Explosion and rupture of pressurized devices, W35-W38	21	11	23
Fireworks discharge, W39	6	6	8
Explosion of other materials, W40	116	128	110
Foreign body entering through skin or natural orifice, W44-W45	29	37	32
Other and unspecified inanimate mechanical forces, W41-W43, W49	62	49	45
Exposure to animate mechanical forces, W50-W64	143	133	144
Struck by or against another person, W50-W52	9	12	15
Bitten or struck by dog, W54	36	35	34
Bitten or struck by other mammals, W53, W55	83	59	80
Bitten or stung by nonvenomous insect and other arthropods, W57	6	13	5
Bitten or crushed by other reptiles, W59	0	0	0
Other and unspecified animate mechanical forces, W56, W58, W60, W64	9	14	10
Accidental drowning and submersion, W65-W74	3,406	3,391	3,551
Drowning and submersion while in or falling into bath-tub, W65-W66	438	464	416
Drowning and submersion while in or falling into swimming-pool, W67-W68	701	651	691
Drowning and submersion while in or falling into natural water, W69-W70	1,695	1,810	1,844
Other and unspecified drowning and submersion, W73-W74	572	466	600
Other accidental threats to breathing, W75-W84	6,580	6,601	6,238
Accidental suffocation and strangulation in bed, W75	913	903	798
Other accidental hanging and strangulation, W76	235	247	264
Threat to breathing due to cave-in, falling earth and other substances, W77	13	27	16
Inhalation of gastric contents, W78	295	319	313
Inhalation and ingestion of food causing obstruction of respiratory tract, W79	1,169	1,177	1,138
Inhalation and ingestion of other objects causing obstruction of respiratory tract, W80	3,352	3,368	3,183
Confined to or trapped in a low-oxygen environment, W81	9	3	9
Other and unspecified threats to breathing, W83-W84	594	557	517

See source and footnotes on page 25.

ALL INJURIES
All Deaths Due to Injury (cont.)

Mortality by selected external causes, United States, 2012-2014

Type of accident or manner of injury	2014[a]	2013	2012
Exposure to electric current, radiation, temperature, and pressure, W85-W99	266	273	287
Electric transmission lines, W85	58	66	61
Other and unspecified electric current, W86-W87	199	191	218
Radiation, W88-W91	0	0	0
Excessive heat or cold of man-made origin, W92-W93	8	5	3
High and low air pressure and changes in air pressure, W94	1	11	5
Other and unspecified man-made environmental factors, W99	0	0	0
Exposure to smoke, fire, and flames, X00-X09	2,701	2,760	2,464
Uncontrolled fire in building or structure, X00	2,198	2,266	1,941
Uncontrolled fire not in building or structure, X01	36	42	33
Controlled fire in building or structure, X02	15	14	22
Controlled fire not in building or structure, X03	42	22	36
Ignition of highly flammable material, X04	48	40	51
Ignition or melting of nightwear, X05	2	0	3
Ignition or melting of other clothing and apparel, X06	93	80	89
Other and unspecified smoke fire and flames, X08-X09	267	296	289
Contact with heat and hot substances, X10-X19	71	58	59
Contact with hot tap-water, X11	26	24	21
Other and unspecified heat and hot substances, X10, X12-X19	45	34	38
Contact with venomous animals and plants, X20-X29	91	91	83
Contact with venomous snakes and lizards, X20	5	4	6
Contact with venomous spiders, X21	7	7	7
Contact with hornets, wasps and bees, X23	64	62	59
Contact with other and unspecified venomous animal or plant, X22, X24-X29	15	18	11
Exposure to forces of nature, X30-X39	1,377	1,285	1,207
Exposure to excessive natural heat, X30	244	372	474
Exposure to excessive natural cold, X31	930	725	494
Lightning, X33	25	23	29
Earthquake and other earth movements, X34-X36	86	34	36
Cataclysmic storm, X37	61	63	138
Flood, X38	8	42	5
Exposure to other and unspecified forces of nature, X32, X39	23	26	31
Accidental poisoning by and exposure to noxious substances, X40-X49	42,032	38,851	36,332
Nonopioid analgesics, antipyretics, and antirheumatics, X40	224	233	210
Antiepileptic, sedative-hypnotic, antiparkinsonism, and psychotropic drugs n.e.c., X41	3,069	2,909	2,292
Narcotics and psychodysleptics [hallucinogens] n.e.c., X42	16,822	15,241	13,932
Other and unspecified drugs, medicaments, and biologicals, X43-X44	18,603	17,280	16,741
Alcohol, X45	2,283	2,244	2,176
Gases and vapors, X46-X47	847	753	792
Other and unspecified chemicals and noxious substances, X48-X49	184	191	189
Overexertion, travel, and privation, X50-X57	23	34	39
Accidental exposure to other and unspecified factors and sequelae, X58-X59, Y86	6,944	6,581	7,110
Intentional self-harm, X60-X84, Y87.0, *U03	42,773	41,149	40,600
Intentional self-poisoning, X60-X69	6,808	6,637	6,729
Intentional self-harm by hanging, strangulation, and suffocation, X70	11,407	10,062	10,088
Intentional self-harm by firearm, X72-X74	21,334	21,175	20,666
Other and unspecified means and sequelae, X71, X75-X84, Y87.0	3,224	3,275	3,117
Terrorism, *U03	0	0	0
Assault, X85-Y09, Y87.1, *U01	15,809	16,121	16,688
Assault by firearm, X93-X95	10,945	11,207	11,622
Assault by sharp object, X99	1,740	1,639	1,776
Other and unspecified means and sequelae, X85-X92, X96-X98, Y00-Y09, Y87.1	3,124	3,272	3,290
Terrorism, *U01	0	3	0
Event of undetermined intent, Y10-Y34, Y87.2, Y89.9	4,592	4,587	4,737
Poisoning, Y10-Y19	3,026	2,960	2,986
Hanging, strangulation, and suffocation, Y20	139	120	127
Drowning and submersion, Y21	185	238	278
Firearm discharge, Y22-Y24	270	281	256
Exposure to smoke, fire, and flames, Y26	155	132	153
Falling, jumping, or pushed from a high place, Y30	61	45	67
Other and unspecified means and sequelae, Y25, Y27-Y29, Y31-Y34,Y87.2, Y89.9	756	811	870
Legal intervention, Y35, Y89.0	515	516	550
Legal intervention involving firearm discharge, Y35.0	464	467	471
Legal execution, Y35.5	34	36	43
Other and unspecified means and sequelae, Y35.1-Y35.4, Y35.6-Y35.7, Y89.0	17	13	36
Operations of war and sequelae, Y36, Y89.1	14	15	18
Complications of medical and surgical care and sequelae, Y40-Y84, Y88.0-Y88.3	2,540	2,768	2,603

Source: National Center for Health Statistics–Mortality Data for 2014 as compiled from data provided by the 57 vital statistics jurisdictions through the Vital Statistics Cooperative Program. Deaths are classified on the basis of the 10th Revision of "The International Classification of Diseases" (ICD-10), which became effective in 1999.
Note: "n.e.c." means not elsewhere classified.
[a] Latest official figures.
[b] Numbers following titles refer to external cause of injury and poisoning classifications in ICD-10.

ALL INJURIES
Death by Age, Sex, and Type

Unintentional-injury-related deaths by age, sex, and type, United States, 2014[a]

Age and sex	Total[b]	Poisoning	Motor vehicle	Falls	Choking[c]	Drowning[d]	Fire, flames, or smoke	Mechanical suffocation	Natural heat or cold	All types Males	All types Females
Total	136,053	42,032	35,398	31,959	4,816	3,406	2,701	1,764	1,174	85,448	50,605
0-4	2,377	37	473	32	95	417	130	1,016	26	1,407	970
5-14	1,480	31	829	21	23	230	117	44	9	968	512
15-24	11,836	3,492	6,709	174	39	507	104	68	31	8,803	3,033
25-44	33,405	18,450	10,518	789	228	762	381	225	157	23,907	9,498
45-64	38,640	18,022	10,024	3,898	887	884	859	263	419	26,015	12,625
65-74	11,909	1,410	3,153	3,938	789	318	475	77	172	7,520	4,389
75 and older	36,406	590	3,692	23,107	2,755	288	635	71	360	16,828	19,578
Males	85,448	27,225	25,158	16,029	2,617	2,640	1,627	1,140	770		
Females	50,605	14,807	10,240	15,930	2,199	766	1,074	624	404		

Source: National Safety Council analysis of National Center for Health Statistics (NCHS)–Mortality Data for 2014, as compiled from data provided by the 57 vital statistics jurisdictions through the Vital Statistics Cooperative Program.
[a]Latest official figures.
[b]Includes types not shown separately.
[c]Inhalation or ingestion of food or other object obstructing breathing.
[d]Excludes water transport drownings.

Of the 136,053 unintentional-injury-related deaths in 2014, males accounted for 63% of all deaths. Females had the greatest share of deaths only in the 75 and older age group (54% female). Other than for falls, which is roughly split evenly between women and men, males are disproportionably represented over females. The largest differences in the proportion of fatalities were drowning (78% male) and motor-vehicle deaths (71% male). The smallest difference between the proportion of male and female fatalities was choking (54% male).

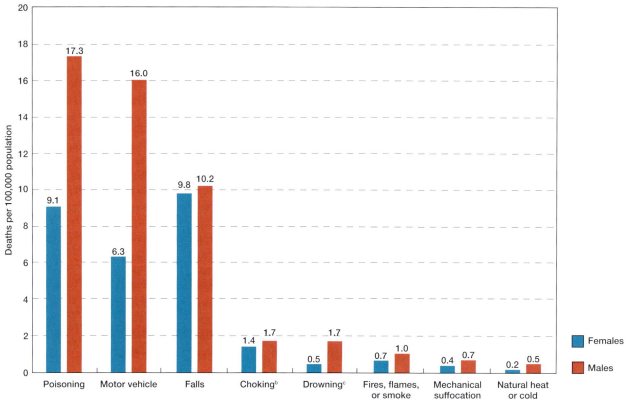

Unintentional-injury-related death rates by type and sex, United States, 2014[a]

[a]Latest official figures.
[b]Inhalation or ingestion of food or other objects.
[c]Excludes water transport drownings.

ALL INJURIES
Death by Age, Sex, and Type (cont.)

Unintentional-injury-related deaths by month and type, United States, 2014[a]

Month	All types	Poisoning	Motor vehicle	Falls	Choking[b]	Drowning[c]	Fire, flames, or smoke	Mechanical suffocation	Natural heat or cold	Struck by or against	All other types
Total	136,053	42,032	35,398	31,959	4,816	3,406	2,701	1,764	1,174	899	11,904
January	11,461	3,637	2,572	2,822	459	146	406	141	268	55	955
February	10,288	3,562	2,248	2,451	367	137	315	120	184	77	827
March	11,123	3,691	2,589	2,684	401	186	315	144	107	68	938
April	10,610	3,313	2,720	2,463	389	254	226	143	59	80	963
May	11,363	3,463	3,038	2,621	412	394	143	147	31	90	1,024
June	11,451	3,310	3,084	2,660	388	531	161	147	56	67	1,047
July	11,771	3,472	3,227	2,586	371	582	121	151	86	81	1,094
August	11,729	3,451	3,277	2,632	395	421	144	164	56	87	1,102
September	11,033	3,274	3,069	2,661	363	285	117	161	40	87	976
October	11,589	3,569	3,304	2,679	384	203	177	159	24	72	1,018
November	11,656	3,584	3,175	2,724	421	145	272	160	124	71	980
December	11,979	3,706	3,095	2,976	466	122	304	127	139	64	980
Average	11,338	3,503	2,950	2,663	401	284	225	147	98	75	992

Source: National Safety Council analysis of National Center for Health Statistics (NCHS)–Mortality Data for 2014, as compiled from data provided by the 57 vital statistics jurisdictions through the Vital Statistics Cooperative Program.
[a]Latest official figures.
[b]Inhalation or ingestion of food or other object obstructing breathing.
[c]Excludes water transport drownings.

Unintentional-injury-related deaths by month and type, United States, 2014[a]

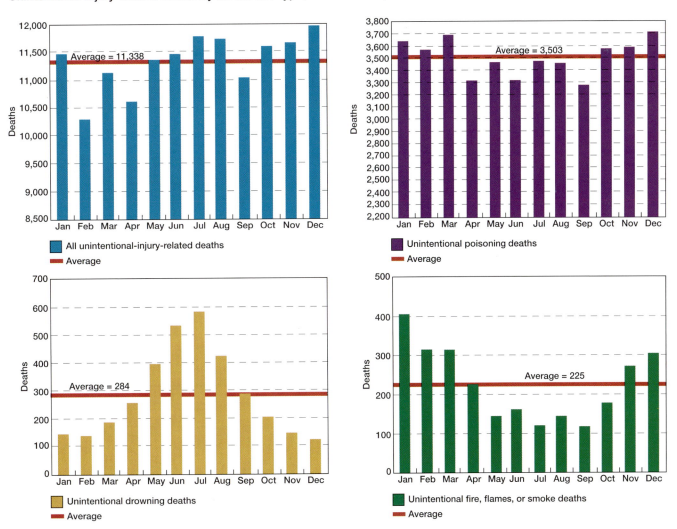

Cross-reference: See page 129 for motor-vehicle deaths by month and page 165 for pedalcycle deaths by month.

ALL INJURIES

The National Health Interview Survey, 2014

The National Health Interview Survey (NHIS), conducted by the National Center for Health Statistics, is a continuous, personal-interview sampling of households to obtain information about the health status of household members, including injuries experienced during the five weeks prior to the interview. Responsible family members residing in the household supplied the information used in the survey. In 2014, interviews were completed for 112,053 people living in 44,552 households throughout the United States. See page 29 for definitions.

Number of leading external causes of medically consulted injury and poisoning episodes by age, United States, 2014

	Population[a] (000)	External cause of injury and poisoning (number in thousands)						
		Falls	Struck by or against person or object	Transportation[b]	Overexertion	Cutting-piercing instructions	Other injury causes[b]	Poisoning[b]
All ages	313,090	14,963	4,228	3,293	3,699	3,191	9,546	629
Younger than 12	48,443	2,269	729	172[c]	(d)	168[c]	1,219	(d)
12-17 years	24,964	1,723	658	531	458[c]	172[c]	1,327	(d)
18-44 years	112,146	2,928	1,144	1,429	1,538	1,705	3,247	201[c]
45-64 years	82,604	3,728	994	809	1,104	746	2,586	(d)
65-74 years	26,210	1,865	263[c]	205[c]	202[c]	312[c]	630	(d)
75 and older	18,724	2,450	439[c]	(d)	252[c]	(d)	536	(e)

[a]Civilian noninstitutionalized population.
[b]"Transportation" includes motor vehicle, bicycle, motorcycle, pedestrian, train, boat, or airplane. "Poisoning" does not include food poisoning or allergic reaction. "Other injury causes" includes fire/burn/scald-related, animal or insect bites, machinery, other (not specified), and unknown causes.
[c]Estimate does not meet standard of reliability or precision and should be used with caution.
[d]Estimate is not shown because it does not meet standard of reliability or precision.
[e]Quantity zero.

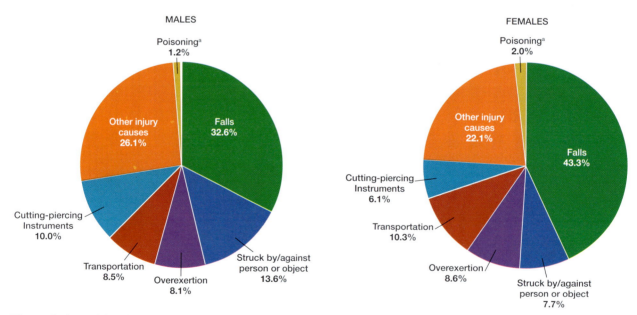

Leading external causes of injury and poisoning episodes by sex, United States, 2014

[a]The standard error of the poisoning estimate does not meet standard of reliability or precision.
Source: National Health Interview Survey tables of summary health statistics. Accessed June 30, 2016 at http://www.cdc.gov/nchs/nhis/SHS/tables.htm

ALL INJURIES
The National Health Interview Survey, 2014 (cont.)

In 2014, an estimated 39.5 million medically consulted injury and poisoning episodes were recorded, of which 50.8% were among males and 49.2% among females. The overall injury rate was 125.7 episodes per 1,000 population, with males experiencing higher rates (131.8 per 1,000 males) than females (119.6 per 1,000 females). Nearly half of all injuries occurred in or around the home (48.9%), followed by injuries at sport facilities, recreation areas, lakes, rivers, and pools (13.5%). Nationwide, injuries in public areas such as schools, hospitals, streets, recreational facilities, industrial and trade areas, and public buildings together accounted for 44.7% of the total injuries.

Among the 20.1 million injuries reported for males, the single most common place of injury occurrence was at home, with 23.7% occurring inside the home while injuries occurring outside contributed an additional 19.5%. About 54.9% of the injuries among females occurred in or around home. About 70% more injuries to females occurred inside the home than outside. Past findings have generally found twice as many injuries involving females occurring inside versus outside the home. Streets, parking lots, sidewalks, and highways, along with sport facility, recreation area, lake, river, or pools, were the next most common locations for injuries among females, accounting for 10.6% and 9.3% of injuries, respectively. For males, sport facilities and recreational areas were the most common nonhome places for injuries to occur (17.5%), followed by streets, parking lots, sidewalks, and highways (9.8%).

The 2014 NHIS injury definitions are listed below for comparability with prior years and other injury figures published in *Injury Facts*.

Number and percent of injury episodes by place of occurrence and sex, United States, 2014

Place of occurrence of injury episode	Both sexes No. of episodes (000)	Percent	Male No. of episodes (000)	Percent	Female No. of episodes (000)	Percent
Total episodes[a]	39,549	100.0	20,091	100.0	19,459	100.0
Home (inside)	11,496	29.1	4,771	23.7	6,725	34.6
Home (outside)	7,856	19.9	3,908	19.5	3,948	20.3
School, child care center, or preschool	3,563	9.0	1,826	9.1	1,737	8.9
Hospital or residential institution	591	1.5	273[b]	1.3[b]	317[b]	1.6[b]
Street, highway, sidewalk, or parking lot	4,032	10.2	1,969	9.8	2,064	10.6
Sport facility, recreation area, lake, river, or pool	5,330	13.5	3,517	17.5	1,814	9.3
Industrial, construction, or farm	1,444	3.7	1,310	6.5	135[b]	0.7[b]
Trade or service area	1,264	3.2	564	2.8	700	3.6
Other public building	1,441	3.6	722	3.6	719	3.7
Other (unspecified)	2,931	7.4	1,494	7.4	1,437	7.4

Source: National Health Interview Survey tables of summary health statistics. Accessed June 30, 2016 at http://www.cdc.gov/nchs/nhis/SHS/tables.htm
[a]Numbers and percentages may not sum to respective totals due to rounding and unknowns.
[b]Estimate does not meet standard of reliability or precision and should be used with caution.

INJURY DEFINITIONS

National Health Interview Survey definitions. The 2014 National Health Interview Survey (NHIS) figures include medically consulted injury and poisoning episodes (e.g., call to a poison control center; use of an emergency vehicle or emergency room; visit to a doctor's office or other health clinic; or phone call to a doctor, nurse, or other health care professional) that reportedly occurred during the three months prior to the date of the interview and resulted in one or more conditions. Beginning in 2004, injury and poisoning estimates were calculated using only those episodes that occurred five weeks or less before the interview date. This reflects a change from 1997 to 2003, when NHIS data contained injury and poisoning episodes that were reported to occur within four months of the interview, and estimates were calculated using a three-month recall period. Also, an imputation procedure was performed for injury and poisoning episodes to assign a date of occurrence if it was not reported. Therefore, figures for 2004 and subsequent years are not comparable to estimates from prior years.

In the 2014 NHIS Injury and Poisoning file, an injury episode refers to the traumatic event in which the person was injured one or more times from an external cause (e.g., a fall or a motor-vehicle traffic incident). An injury condition is the acute condition or the physical harm caused by the traumatic event. Likewise, a poisoning episode refers to the event resulting from ingestion of or contact with harmful substances, as well as overdoses or wrong use of any drug or medication, while a poisoning condition is the acute condition or the physical harm caused by the event. Each episode must have at least one injury condition or poisoning classified according to the nature-of-injury codes 800-909.2, 909.4, 909.9, 910-994.9, 995.5-995.59, and 995.80-995.85 in the Ninth Revision of the International Classification of Diseases (ICD-9-CM). Poisoning episodes exclude food poisoning, sun poisoning, or poison ivy rashes.

National Safety Council definition of injury. A medically consulted injury is defined as one that is serious enough that a medical professional was consulted or is a recordable work injury based on OSHA definitions (see Glossary). All injury totals labeled "medically consulted" in *Injury Facts* are based on this definition.

ALL INJURIES

The National Health Interview Survey, 2014 (cont.)

Of the 39.5 million medically consulted injuries in 2014, 34.2% were related to sports and leisure activities. Sports and leisure injuries accounted for 51.6% of all injury episodes among children younger than 12 and 60.2% of injury episodes among 12- to 17-year-olds.

The rate of injuries occurring during sports and leisure activities was substantially higher for males (50.9 cases per 1,000 males) than for females (38.1 cases per 1,000 females). The charts on this page illustrate these gender differences in terms of percentages and rates.

Number of injury episodes by age and activity at time of injury, United States, 2014

	Total episodes[a] (000)	Driving[c]	Working at paid job	Working around the house or yard	Attending school	Sports	Leisure activities	Other[d]
All ages	39,549	2,009	4,556	5,431	1,920	6,358	7,175	12,263
Younger than 12	4,782	(e)	0	(e)	589	834	1,632	1,718
12-17 years	4,972	(e)	(e)	(e)	1,000[f]	2,082	913	695
18-44 years	12,192	1,063	2,647	1,185	171[f]	2,461	1,719	2,906
45-64 years	10,140	506[f]	1,665	2,307	(e)	685	1,475	3,286
65-74 years	3,551	(e)	(e)	899	0	(e)	612	1,697
75 or older	3,913	(e)	(e)	802	0	225[f]	823	1,960

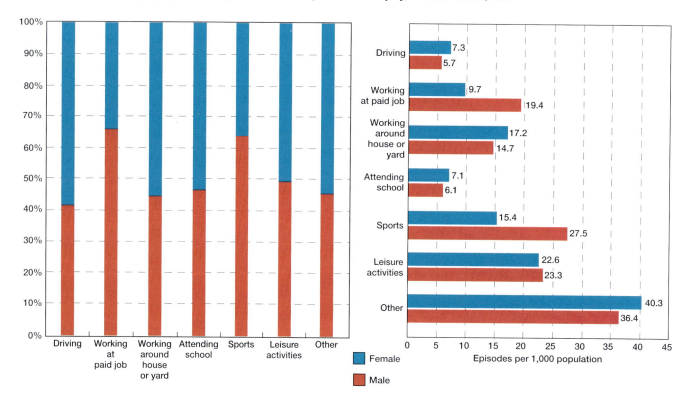

Percent and rates of injury episodes by sex and activity at time of injury, United States, 2014

Source: National Health Interview Survey tables of summary health statistics. Accessed June 30, 2016 at http://www.cdc.gov/nchs/nhis/SHS/tables.htm
[a]Numbers may not sum to respective totals due to rounding and unknowns.
[b]Activity at time of injury and poisoning episodes is based on the question, "What was [person] doing when the injury/poisoning happened?" Respondents could indicate up to two activities.
[c]Driving includes both drivers and passengers.
[d]"Other" includes unpaid work such as housework, shopping, volunteer work, sleeping, resting, eating, drinking, cooking, hands-on care from another person, and other unspecified activities.
[e]Estimate is not shown because it does not meet standard of reliability or precision.
[f]Estimate does not meet standard of reliability or precision and should be used with caution.

ALL INJURIES
The National Health Interview Survey, 2014 (cont.)

A body of evidence has accumulated pointing to socioeconomic factors such as income, wealth, and education as the fundamental causes of a wide range of health outcomes. In general, people with the highest levels of income and education are healthier than those with median income and education, who, in turn, tend to be in better health than the poor and least educated.[a]

Lower socioeconomic status is known to contribute to increased rates of fatal injuries. Although research provides some evidence of links between socioeconomic status and nonfatal injuries, studies based on morbidity data provide results somewhat less consistent than those of mortality studies. Nonetheless, numerous studies show considerable differences between socioeconomic groups even for nonfatal injuries.[b] The National Health Interview Survey provides an opportunity to look at the occurrence of unintentional injuries in the U.S. population as a function of socioeconomic position using two socioeconomic status measures – family income and education.[c]

Although NHIS data indicate that all people are affected by injuries, families whose poverty status was either poor (below the poverty threshold) or near poor (100% to less than 200% of the poverty threshold) had substantially higher injury rates than families who are not poor (200% of the poverty threshold and greater). In contrast, those with less than a high school diploma had the lowest medically consulted injury rate in 2014 (98.00 injuries per 1,000 population) while those with some college experienced the highest medically consulted injury rate (149.77). The finding that individuals with some college education have the highest rate of medically consulted injuries is consistent with past NHIS findings but does not seem to support the typical socioeconomic status pattern.

[a]Braveman, P. & Gottlieb, L. (2014). The social determinants of health: It's time to consider the causes of the causes. Public Health Reports, 2014 Supplement 2, Vol. 129, pp. 19-31.
[b]Laflamme, L., Burrows, S., & Hasselberg, M. (2009). Socioeconomic differences in injury risks–A review of findings and a discussion of potential countermeasures. Denmark: World Health Organization–Europe.
[c]Education data are shown for people 25 and older.

Percentages and rates of medically consulted injuries by poverty status, United States, 2014

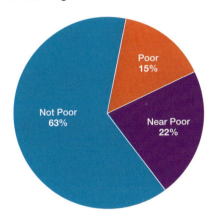
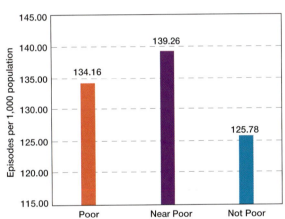

Percentages and rates of medically consulted injuries by level of education, United States, 2014

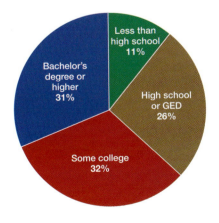
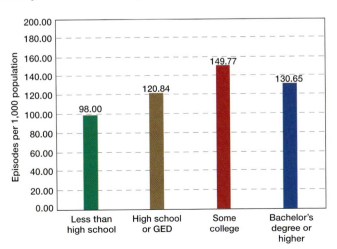

Source: National Health Interview Survey tables of summary health statistics. Accessed June 30, 2016 at http://www.cdc.gov/nchs/nhis/SHS/tables.htm

ALL INJURIES

Leading Causes of Fatal Unintentional Injuries

Poisoning is the leading cause of fatal unintentional injuries in the United States, according to the latest data from the National Center for Health Statistics. A total of 42,032 poisoning fatalities occurred in 2014, accounting for about 31% of all unintentional-injury-related deaths. Poisoning fatalities were the leading cause of unintentional-injury-related deaths in age groups from 25-34 through 55-64. Suffocation was the leading cause of unintentional-injury-related deaths for people younger than 1, while falls were the leading cause for those age 65 and older. Motor-vehicle fatalities were the leading cause of death in the 1-4 through 15-24 age groups. Overall motor-vehicle deaths include both traffic and non-traffic deaths as per all other motor-vehicle fatality totals in *Injury Facts* and thus are not comparable to motor-vehicle traffic fatalities previously reported in this table. Taken together, poisoning, motor vehicle, and falls accounted for more than four-fifths of all unintentional-injury-related deaths. In addition to these three causes, drowning was a leading cause of unintentional-injury-related deaths for most age groups.

Leading causes of fatal unintentional injuries by age group, United States, 2014

Rank	All ages	Younger than 1	1-4	5-9	10-14	15-24	25-34	35-44	45-54	55-64	65 or older
1	Poisoning 42,032	Suffocation 991	Motor vehicle overall 405	Motor vehicle overall 390	Motor vehicle overall 439	Motor vehicle overall 6,709	Poisoning 9,334	Poisoning 9,116	Poisoning 11,009	Poisoning 7,013	Falls 27,044
2	Motor vehicle overall 35,398	Motor vehicle overall 68	Drowning 388	Drowning 125	Drowning 105	Poisoning 3,492	Motor vehicle overall 6,030	Motor vehicle overall 4,488	Motor vehicle overall 5,251	Motor vehicle overall 4,773	Motor vehicle traffic 6,838
3	Falls 31,959	Drowning 29	Suffocation 120	Fire/burn 68	Fire/burn 49	Drowning 507	Drowning 399	Falls 504	Falls 1,340	Falls 2,558	Unspecified 4,590
4	Suffocation 6,580	Natural/environment 17	Fire/burn 117	Suffocation 34	Suffocation 33	Falls 174	Falls 285	Drowning 363	Suffocation 452	Suffocation 698	Suffocation 3,692
5	Unspecified 5,848	Fire/burn 15	Struck by/against 38	Natural/environment 22	Poisoning 22	Firearms 148	Suffocation 194	Suffocation 259	Drowning 442	Unspecified 530	Poisoning 1,993
6	Drowning 3,406	Unspecified 12	Natural/environment 35	Struck by/against 16	Other transport 16	Suffocation 107	Fire/burn 187	Other specified, classifiable 210	Fire/burn 363	Fire/burn 517	Fire/burn 1,151
7	Fire/burn 2,772	Poisoning 9	Poisoning 28	Firearms 14	Falls 13	Fire/burn 105	Other specified, classifiable 183	Fire/burn 198	Unspecified 316	Drowning 442	Natural/environment 654
8	Natural/environment 1,625	Falls 8	Falls 24	Other transport 12	Struck by/against 13	Other specified, classifiable 101	Other transport 123	Unspecified 180	Other specified, classifiable 292	Natural/environment 347	Drowning 604
9	Other specified, classifiable 1,323	Other specified, classifiable 5	Firearms 22	Poisoning 9	Firearms 12	Pedestrian, other 88	Unspecified 115	Natural/environment 148	Natural/environment 238	Other specified, classifiable 265	Other specified, n.e.c.[a] 569
10	Other specified, n.e.c.[a] 1,096	Struck by/against 4	Unspecified 13	Falls 8	Natural/environment 11	Other transport 86	Natural/environment 95	Other transport 110	Other specified, n.e.c.[a] 172	Other specified, n.e.c.[a] 194	Struck by/against 259
All causes of fatal unintentional injury											
Number	136,053	1,161	1,216	730	750	11,836	17,357	16,048	20,610	18,030	48,315[b]
Per 100,000 population	42.7	29.4	7.6	3.6	3.6	26.9	39.9	39.6	47.4	45.0	104.5[b]

Source: Centers for Disease Control and Prevention, National Center for Injury Prevention and Control. Web-based Injury Statistics Query and Reporting System (WISQARS), data accessed July 11, 2016, at www.cdc.gov/injury/wisqars/index.html.
[a]"n.e.c." means not elsewhere classified.
[b]Includes 20 cases with age unknown.

KEY
- Poisoning
- Falls
- Drowning
- Overexertion
- Motor-vehicle overall
- Suffocation
- Stuck by/against
- Cut/pierce

ALL INJURIES
Leading Causes of Nonfatal Unintentional Injuries

Falls are the leading cause of nonfatal unintentional injuries that are treated in hospital emergency departments, according to data from the All Injury Program, a cooperative program involving the National Center for Injury Prevention and Control, the Centers for Disease Control and Prevention, and the Consumer Product Safety Commission. Nearly 9.2 million people were treated in an emergency department for fall-related injuries in 2014. Falls were the leading cause of nonfatal injuries for all age groups except for the 10- to 14 and 15- to 24-year-old age groups, for which struck by or against an object or person was the leading cause. Struck by or against, overexertion, and motor vehicle crashes involving vehicle occupants also were leading causes for most age groups (please see color key at the bottom of the opposite page).

Leading causes of nonfatal unintentional injuries treated in hospital emergency departments by age group, United States, 2014[a]

Rank	All ages	Younger than 1	1-4	5-9	10-14	15-24	25-34	35-44	45-54	55-64	65 or older
1	Falls 9,163,980	Falls 129,404	Falls 818,850	Falls 622,225	Struck by/against 535,500	Struck by/against 865,847	Falls 764,225	Falls 726,920	Falls 943,379	Falls 1,001,304	Falls 2,791,459
2	Struck by/against 4,083,298	Struck by/against 28,577	Struck by/against 317,648	Struck by/against 386,752	Falls 533,032	Falls 832,979	Overexertion 596,781	Overexertion 506,447	Overexertion 444,754	Overexertion 276,676	Stuck by/against 281,308
3	Overexertion 3,132,271	Other bite/sting[b] 12,042	Other bite/sting[b] 165,536	Other bite/sting[b] 117,961	Overexertion 282,976	Overexertion 636,085	Struck by/against 589,679	Struck by/against 418,522	Struck by/against 395,394	Struck by/against 264,024	Overexertion 222,387
4	Motor vehicle occupant 2,412,109	Foreign body 10,891	Foreign body 122,229	Cut/pierce 100,315	Cut/pierce 111,781	Motor vehicle occupant 594,353	Motor vehicle occupant 513,641	Motor vehicle occupant 370,982	Other specified[c] 394,517	Motor vehicle occupant 243,750	Motor vehicle occupant 191,849
5	Cut/pierce 1,959,505	Inhalation/suffocation 10,441	Overexertion 78,491	Overexertion 83,021	Pedalcyclist 84,383	Cut/pierce 408,048	Cut/pierce 390,725	Other specified[c] 306,042	Motor vehicle occupant 342,581	Other specified[c] 213,974	Cut/pierce 147,739
6	Other specified[c] 1,751,918	Other specified[c] 9,266	Cut/pierce 78,428	Pedalcyclist 70,964	Unknown/unspecified 72,270	Other specified[c] 291,986	Other specified[c] 338,244	Cut/pierce 296,099	Poisoning 273,232	Cut/pierce 185,389	Poisoning 119,150
7	Poisoning 1,231,033	Fire/burn 8,087	Other specified[c] 63,396	Foreign body 61,112	Motor vehicle occupant 69,008	Other bite/sting[b] 185,547	Poisoning 220,487	Poisoning 209,879	Cut/pierce 265,317	Poisoning 181,339	Other bite/sting[b] 103,084
8	Other bite/sting[b] 1,216,927	Cut/pierce 5,507	Fire/burn 48,389	Motor vehicle occupant 56,511	Other bite/sting[b] 68,770	Poisoning 175,948	Other bite/sting[b] 181,712	Other bite/sting[b] 138,422	Other bite/sting[b] 141,378	Other bite/sting[b] 102,454	Other specified[c] 92,209
9	Unknown/unspecified 722,811	Unknown/unspecified 5,445	Unknown/unspecified 38,409	Dog bite 43,369	Other transport[d] 37,456	Unknown/unspecified 132,016	Unknown/unspecified 112,258	Unknown/unspecified 91,609	Unknown/unspecified 97,250	Unknown/unspecified 68,220	Other transport[d] 80,011
10	Foreign body 531,277	Overexertion 4,623	Dog bite 33,771	Other transport[d] 33,210	Dog bite 31,790	Other transport[d] 91,805	Other transport[d] 76,068	Other transport[d] 65,952	Other transport[d] 67,338	Other transport[d] 49,252	Unknown/unspecified 75,150
All causes of nonfatal unintentional injury											
Number	28,728,927	234,572	1,880,144	1,668,218	1,925,790	4,646,758	4,158,992	3,425,716	3,667,832	2,806,269	4,314,635[e]
Per 100,000 population	9,010.0	5,941.0	11,803.6	8,129.9	9,316.2	10,565.7	9,557.3	8,455.8	8,439.8	7,002.1	9,330.3[e]

Source: NEISS All Injury Program, Office of Statistics and Programming, National Center for Injury Prevention and Control, the Centers for Disease Control and Prevention, and Consumer Product Safety Commission.
[a]See color key on opposite page.
[b]Other than dog bite.
[c]Injury associated with any other specified cause that does not fit another category. Includes electric current, explosions, fireworks, radiation, animal scratch, etc. Excludes all causes listed in the table and bb/pellet gunshot, drowning and near drowning, firearm gunshot, suffocation, machinery, natural and environmental conditions, pedestrians, and motorcyclists.
[d]Includes occupant of any transport vehicle other than a motor vehicle or motorcycle (e.g., airplane, space vehicle, railcar, boat, all-terrain vehicle, animal and animal-drawn conveyances, battery-powered carts, ski lifts, and other cable cars not on rails).
[e]Includes 4,475 cases with age unknown.

ALL INJURIES
Disaster Deaths, 2015

Disasters are front-page news, even though the lives lost in the United States are relatively few when compared to the day-to-day life losses from unintentional injuries (see "While You Speak!" on page 5). Listed below are the U.S. disasters, of which the National Safety Council is aware, that occurred in 2015 and took five or more lives.

Disaster — events resulting in five or more deaths, United States, 2015

Type and location	No. of deaths	Date of disaster
Flash flood, Utah	20	September 14
Flash flood and debris flow, Missouri	15	December 26-28
Flash flood, Texas	14	May 23-24
Tornado, Texas	13	December 26
Heat wave, Nevada	13	July 1-4
Tornado, Mississippi	11	December 23
Motor-vehicle traffic crash, Texas	10	January 14
Motor-vehicle traffic crash, Florida	8	March 30
Flash flood, Texas	8	May 25
Single-family home fire, New York	7	March 21
Dense fog related car crash, California	6	January 13
Motor-vehicle traffic crash, Texas	6	January 15
Single-family home fire, Maryland	6	January 15
Motor-vehicle traffic crash, New York	6	Feburary 3
Winter storm, Kentucky	6	February 15-20
Winter storm, Tennessee	6	February 17
Motor-vehicle traffic crash, South Carolina	6	March 19
Marine Thunderstorm with high winds, off the Alabama cost	6	April 25
Motor-vehicle traffic crash, Kentucky	6	May 1
Motor-vehicle traffic crash, Tennessee	6	May 7
Motor-vehicle traffic crash, Texas	6	June 24
Motor-vehicle traffic crash, Tennessee	6	June 25
Flash flood and debris flow, Alaska	6	August 18
Wildfire, California	6	September 9-12
Motor-vehicle traffic crash, Texas	6	September 24
Motor-vehicle traffic crash, Arkansas	6	November 6
Flash flood, Illinois	6	December 26
Single-family home fire, Ohio	5	January 6
Motor-vehicle traffic crash, Maryland	5	January 10
Motor-vehicle traffic crash, California	5	January 13
Motor-vehicle traffic crash, Alaska	5	January 24
Motor-vehicle traffic crash, Texas	5	February 26
Motor-vehicle traffic crash, South Carolina	5	March 21
Motor-vehicle traffic crash, Iowa	5	April 9
Motor-vehicle traffic crash, Texas	5	April 12
Motor-vehicle traffic crash, Georgia	5	April 22
Motor-vehicle traffic crash, Georgia	5	May 19
Heavy rain, Texas	5	May 23
Flash flood, Texas	5	May 29
Motor-vehicle traffic crash, Florida	5	June 16
Motor-vehicle traffic crash, New Mexico	5	July 4
Motor-vehicle traffic crash, Indiana	5	July 23
Motor-vehicle traffic crash, Florida	5	July 27
Motor-vehicle traffic crash, Florida	5	August 9
Motor-vehicle traffic crash, Arizona	5	August 13
Motor-vehicle traffic crash, Washington	5	September 24
Motor-vehicle traffic crash, Florida	5	October 4
Single-family home fire, Kentucky	5	October 20
Motor-vehicle traffic crash, California	5	October 24
Flash flood, Texas	5	October 30
Motor-vehicle traffic crash, Arizona	5	November 29
Vacant single-family dwelling, California	5	December 13
Motor-vehicle traffic crash, Texas	5	December 14
Motor-vehicle traffic crash, Louisiana	5	December 22
Flash flood and tornado, Tennessee	5	December 23
Motor-vehicle traffic crash, Illinois	5	December 26
Motor-vehicle traffic crash, Florida	5	December 30
Motor-vehicle traffic crash, California	5	December 31

Source: The National Climatic Data Center, National Fire Protection Association, and National Highway Traffic Safety Administration.
Note: Some death totals are estimates and may differ among sources.

ALL INJURIES
Intentional Injuries

Injuries may be divided into three broad groups – unintentional, intentional, and undetermined intent. Most of *Injury Facts* presents data on unintentional injuries. This page and the next two present data on intentional injuries.

Under the World Health Organization's Safe Communities initiative, for which the National Safety Council is the affiliate support center in the United States, injury prevention is not limited to unintentional injuries. Data on intentional injuries are presented here to support Safe Communities and to provide context to the unintentional-injury data provided in *Injury Facts*.

Intentional injuries may be divided into four subgroups – intentional self-harm (suicide), assault (homicide), legal intervention, and operations of war. The diagram below illustrates the injury groupings and shows the death totals for 2014.

Injury deaths by intent, United States, 2014

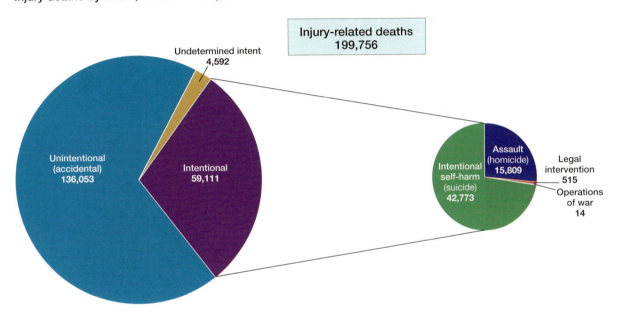

Intentional self-harm includes suicide and attempted suicide by purposely self-inflicted poisoning or injury. The most common methods of intentional self-harm that result in death are firearms; hanging, strangulation, and suffocation; and poisoning.

Assault includes homicide and injuries inflicted by another person with intent to injure or kill (excluding legal intervention and operations of war). The most common means of homicide are firearms; sharp objects; and hanging, strangulation, and suffocation.

Legal intervention includes legal execution. Operations of war include injuries to military personnel and civilians caused by war and civil insurrection. The death must have occurred in the United States. In the vital statistics system, war deaths (and other deaths) occurring outside the United States are counted by the country in which they occurred.

ALL INJURIES
Intentional Injuries by Age and Sex

The three most frequent causes of injury death are also among the top 20 causes of all deaths in the United States in 2014. Unintentional (accidental) injuries ranked 4th, intentional self-harm (suicide) ranked 10th, and assault (homicide) ranked 17th.

Intentional self-harm ranked as high as second (after unintentional injuries) for people ages 13-18, and 20-34, and ranked third for those 11, 12, 19, and 35 to 37. Suicide deaths were highest at age 49 (964) and ranked fourth at this age after cancer, heart disease, and unintentional injuries. Assault ranked as high as second (after unintentional injuries) for people 2, 3, and 19 years old. It ranked third among people 1, 6, 15 to 18, and 20 to 30 years old. Homicide deaths were highest at age 22 (562). For people 15-30 years old, unintentional, homicide, and suicide are the three leading causes of death. The graph below shows the number of deaths due to injuries by single year of age from 0 to 100.

Injury deaths by age, United States, 2014

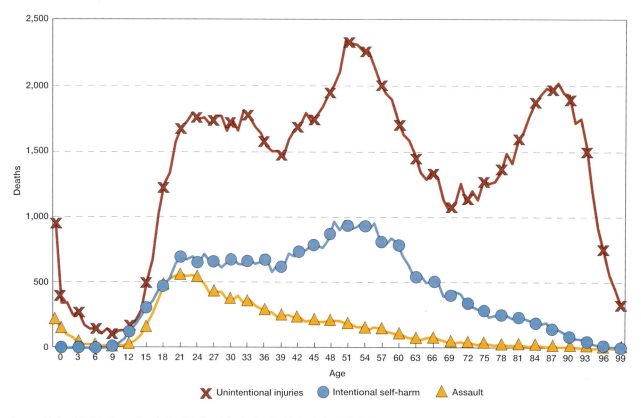

Source: National Safety Council analysis of National Center for Health Statistics (NCHS)–Mortality Data for 2014, as compiled from data provided by the 57 vital statistics jurisdictions through the Vital Statistics Cooperative Program.

Males have higher death rates than females for injuries of all intents. Males also have higher nonfatal injury rates than females for unintentional injuries and assault. Females, however, have a higher injury rate than males for intentional self-harm.

Death and nonfatal injury rates by intent and sex, United States, 2014

Sex	Deaths per 100,000 population			Nonfatal injuries per 100,000 population		
	Unintentional	Homicide	Suicide	Unintentional	Assault	Self-harm
Both sexes	42.7	5.0	13.4	9,010	489	147
Males	54.4	8.0	21.1	9,720	594	119
Females	31.3	2.0	6.0	8,322	386	174
Ratio of male to female	1.7	3.9	3.5	1.2	1.5	0.7

Source: National Safety Council analysis of National Center for Health Statistics (NCHS)–Mortality Data for 2014, as compiled from data provided by the 57 vital statistics jurisdictions through the Vital Statistics Cooperative Program. Rates are National Safety Council estimates based on data from NCHS and the U.S. Census Bureau.

ALL INJURIES
Unintentional and Intentional Injury Trends

The graph below shows the trends from 1992 to 2014 in injury deaths and death rates. Unintentional-injury-related deaths and death rates increased by 62.1% and 30.4%, respectively. Suicide deaths increased 40.3%, while the death rate increased 12.9%. Homicide deaths and death rates decreased 37.1% and 49.4%, respectively, over the 1992-2014 period. Age-adjusted death rates, which remove the effects of the changing age distribution of the population, increased 21.6% for unintentional injuries, increased 8.2% for suicide, and decreased 46.5% for homicide.

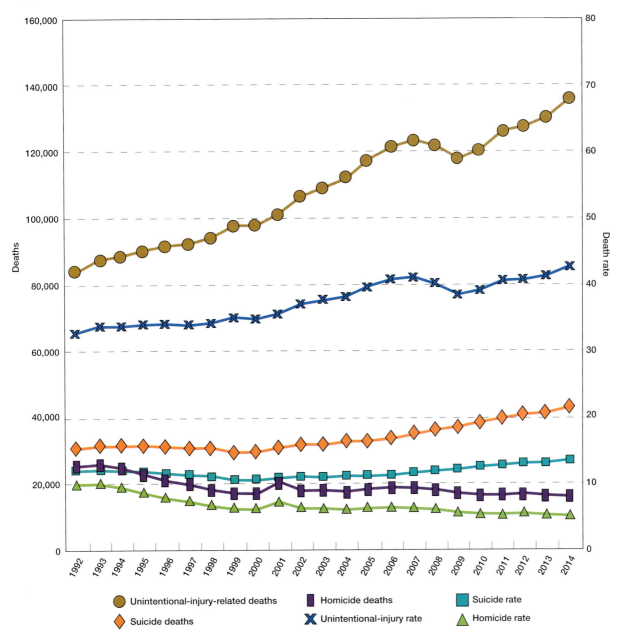

Injury deaths and death rates, United States, 1992-2014

*Deaths per 100,000 population.
Source: National Safety Council analysis of National Center for Health Statistics (NCHS)–Mortality Data for 2014, as compiled from data provided by the 57 vital statistics jurisdictions through the Vital Statistics Cooperative Program. Rates are National Safety Council estimates based on data from NCHS and the U.S. Census Bureau.

Cross-reference: See page 168 for additional information on firearm related deaths.

ALL INJURIES
Children and Adolescents

■ *Motor-vehicle crashes are the leading cause of injury-related deaths among children.*

Unintentional injuries are a major public health concern affecting children and adolescents in the United States. They are the underlying cause of death in over one-third of childhood mortality cases for people 1-19 years old, and about 39% of the deaths among 15- to 19-year-olds.

Fatal injuries in the first year of life numbered 1,162 in 2014, or approximately 29 deaths per 100,000 population. Mechanical suffocation constituted the majority (82%) of all unintentional injury-related mortality cases for infants. Motor-vehicle crashes were the second leading cause of injury mortality. In addition, 249 infant deaths that year were attributed to homicide (for more information on intentional injuries, see pages 35-37).

In the second and third year of life, the risk of fatal injury is reduced by more than two-thirds. In 2014, 345 fatal injury cases were recorded among 1-year-old children and 346 cases among 2-year-old children, with an identical mortality rate of about 9 deaths per 100,000 population for each age. Motor-vehicle crashes led drowning as the leading cause of injury death for 1-year-olds, while the reverse was true for 2-year-olds.

In the following two-year period (ages 3-4) the injury mortality rate dropped even lower, averaging over 6 deaths per 100,000 population in 2014. Motor-vehicle crashes were the leading cause of death at each age, followed by drowning and fire, flames, or smoke.

From the age of 5 to early adolescence (ages 12-14), the injury mortality rate shows a general U-shaped pattern, reaching its lowest level at around age 10. Motor-vehicle crashes, unintentional drowning, and incidents related to fire, flames, or smoke were the leading causes of injury mortality for children 5-14 years old in 2014.

Teens (15-19 years) made up 27% of the U.S. population between the ages of 1 and 19 and 58% of all injury mortality cases in that age group. Most importantly, about 67% of teen injury deaths are attributed to motor-vehicle crashes. Of the 3,736 injury deaths among teens in 2014, 2,515 occurred in crashes. The overall injury rate for this age group was 17.7 per 100,000 population and it varied from a low of 6.9 for 15-year-olds to a high of 28.8 for 19-year-olds.

For all children and adolescents age 19 and younger, the injury mortality rate by age can be described as a J-shaped relationship, peaking during infancy and again in the late teen years.

Unintentional injury deaths by event, ages 0-19, United States, 2014

Age	Population (000)	Total	Rates[a]	Motor vehicle	Drowning	Poisoning	Fire, flames, or smoke	Mechanical suffocation	Choking[b]	Firearms	Falls	All Other
<1 year	3,948	1,162	29.4	69	29	9	15	951	40	2	8	39
1-19 years	78,187	6,432	8.2	3,749	863	626	272	137	92	104	102	487
1 year	3,962	345	8.7	113	110	10	17	32	26	3	4	30
2 years	3,958	346	8.7	97	135	8	30	13	14	5	9	35
3 years	4,005	251	6.3	89	74	5	26	7	8	9	9	24
4 years	4,003	274	6.8	106	69	5	42	13	7	5	2	25
5 years	4,005	175	4.4	90	34	0	15	6	3	2	1	24
6 years	4,134	146	3.5	83	20	2	13	3	4	2	1	18
7 years	4,154	151	3.6	81	30	2	14	4	1	2	3	14
8 years	4,120	111	2.7	64	16	2	10	2	1	3	3	10
9 years	4,107	147	3.6	72	25	3	16	8	2	5	0	16
10 years	4,115	101	2.5	59	17	2	10	2	1	1	1	8
11 years	4,086	132	3.2	74	19	4	13	5	4	2	1	10
12 years	4,069	136	3.3	79	19	3	7	3	3	3	3	16
13 years	4,169	173	4.1	94	27	5	10	4	1	4	3	25
14 years	4,232	208	4.9	133	23	8	9	7	3	2	5	18
15 years	4,164	288	6.9	190	32	16	9	5	1	8	4	23
16 years	4,167	509	12.2	362	31	40	2	5	3	8	8	50
17 years	4,185	676	16.2	482	53	85	6	4	0	8	7	31
18 years	4,226	1,017	24.1	688	59	163	10	8	5	15	19	50
19 years	4,326	1,246	28.8	793	70	263	13	6	5	17	19	60
0-4 years	19,876	2,378	12.0	474	417	37	130	1,016	95	24	32	153
5-9 years	20,520	730	3.6	390	125	9	68	23	11	14	8	82
10-14 years	20,671	750	3.6	439	105	22	49	21	12	12	13	77
15-19 years	21,068	3,736	17.7	2,515	245	567	40	28	14	56	57	214

Source: National Safety Council analysis of National Center for Health Statistics (NCHS)—Mortality Data for 2014 as compiled from data provided by the 57 vital statistics jurisdictions through the Vital Statistics Cooperative Program. Rates are National Safety Council estimates based on data from NCHS and the U.S. Census Bureau.
Note: Data do not include "age unknown" cases, which totaled 20 in 2014.
[a]Deaths per 100,000 population in each age group.
[b]Suffocation by inhalation or ingestion of food or other object.

ALL INJURIES
Adults

■ *Injury mortality and fall-related mortality rates increase with age.*

Unintentional injuries cause significant mortality among adults in the United States. In 2014 alone, injuries were responsible for over 128,400 deaths among Americans 20 and older.

The leading causes of injury mortality include poisoning, motor-vehicle crashes, falls, choking, drowning, and fire, flames and smoke. Poisoning (32%), falls (25%), and motor-vehicle crashes (25%), the three leading causes of injury mortality, combined to account for over four-fifths of all fatal unintentional injuries sustained by adults older than 20 in 2014.

Age plays an important role in the occurrence of injuries. Motor-vehicle crashes are the leading cause of injury mortality through the early to mid-20s. Starting with the mid-20s, incidences of poisoning become the leading cause of death, with prevalence peaking in the early 50s. Beginning in the late 60s, motor-vehicle crashes once again take over as the leading cause of injury mortality until superseded by falls beginning in the early 70s.

The increase in the incidence of fatal falls appears to be the driving force behind a surge in the overall injury mortality rate in later life. The highest fall mortality rates occur among adults beginning at age 70 and older. As the table below illustrates, the number of injury-related deaths per 100,000 population in 2013 increased from 52 for 70- to 74-year-olds to 451 for 90- to 94-year-olds – a nearly nine-fold increase.

A 2015 report from the Consumer Product Safety Commission (CPSC) examined non-fall related fatalities among victims age 65 years old and older from 2009 to 2011[a]. Of the total 12,540 consumer product-related senior fatalities during this time period, 9,140 (73%) were fall fatalities and 3,400 (27%) were non-fall fatalities. The majority of reported senior non-fall fatalities were due to mechanical hazards (55%), followed by fire-related fatalities (32%), and carbon monoxide poisoning fatalities (5%). The top five product group hazards associated with non-fall senior fatalities included submersions involving 'Swimming activity, pools, equipment,' fire-related fatalities involving 'Clothing, All,' submersions involving 'Bathtub and shower structures,' fire-related fatalities involving 'Cigarettes, etc., lighters, fuel,' and fire-related fatalities involving 'Home fires/CO/gas vapors with unknown product.' In contrast to fall fatality reports that peak for those between 84 and 89 years old, there were more non-fall fatality reports for seniors between 65 and 69 years old than for older seniors. Males experienced 64% of the reported non-fall fatalities among seniors and females 36% at a time when the population of seniors age 65 and older in the United States was 43% male and 57% female.

[a]Suchy, A. (October 2015). Consumer product-related non-fall fatalities involving victims 65 years of age and older. Bethesda, MD: U.S. Consumer Product Safety Commission. Downloaded August 3, 2016 from http://www.cpsc.gov/Global/Safety%20Education/Sports%20and%20Recreation/SeniorNonFallFatalityReport2015.pdf.

Unintentional-injury-related deaths by event, age 20 or older, United States, 2014

Age	Population (000)	Total	Rates[a]	Poisoning	Motor vehicle	Falls	Choking[b]	Drowning	Fire, flames, or smoke	Natural heat or cold	Stuck by or against	Mechanical suffocation	All other
20-24	22,912	8,100	35.4	2,925	4,194	117	25	262	64	18	33	40	422
25-29	21,988	8,737	39.7	4,381	3,373	142	42	206	101	30	32	53	377
30-34	21,529	8,620	40.0	4,953	2,657	143	47	193	83	25	55	52	412
35-39	19,922	7,860	39.5	4,518	2,271	203	58	172	94	39	47	52	406
40-44	20,591	8,188	39.8	4,598	2,217	301	81	191	103	63	58	68	508
45-49	20,888	9,271	44.4	5,211	2,343	489	127	191	138	58	74	72	568
50-54	22,571	11,339	50.2	5,798	2,908	851	179	251	213	112	87	74	866
55-59	21,511	10,250	47.7	4,591	2,600	1,198	272	243	252	131	76	65	822
60-64	18,566	7,780	41.9	2,422	2,173	1,360	309	199	256	118	96	52	795
65-69	15,325	6,113	39.9	981	1,710	1,690	374	169	248	73	73	49	746
70-74	11,073	5,796	52.3	429	1,443	2,248	415	149	227	99	55	28	703
75-79	7,922	6,613	83.5	217	1,279	3,379	517	91	198	88	53	19	772
80-84	5,760	8,260	143.4	157	1,116	4,878	625	99	203	95	30	17	1,040
85-89	3,827	9,826	256.8	131	822	6,576	762	64	120	91	31	17	1,212
90-94	1,799	8,122	451.5	55	386	5,705	606	25	85	62	9	13	1,176
95-99	464	2,989	644.2	22	74	2,159	206	6	23	23	5	3	468
100 and older	72	576	800.0	1	8	409	39	1	4	1	0	2	111
20 and older	236,720	128,440	54.3	41,390	31,574	31,848	4,684	2,512	2,412	1,126	814	676	11,404
25 and older	213,808	120,340	56.3	38,465	27,380	31,731	4,659	2,250	2,348	1,108	781	636	10,982
35 and older	170,291	102,983	60.5	29,131	21,350	31,446	4,570	1,851	2,164	1,053	694	531	10,193
45 and older	129,778	86,935	67.0	20,015	16,862	30,942	4,431	1,488	1,967	951	589	411	9,279
55 and older	86,319	66,325	76.8	9,006	11,611	29,602	4,125	1,046	1,616	781	428	265	7,845
65 and older	46,242	48,295	104.4	1,993	6,838	27,044	3,544	604	1,108	532	256	148	6,228
75 and older	19,844	36,386	183.4	583	3,685	23,106	2,755	286	633	360	128	71	4,779

Source: National Safety Council analysis of National Center for Health Statistics—Mortality Data for 2014, as compiled from data provided by the 57 vital statistics jurisdictions through the Vital Statistics Cooperative Program. Rates are National Safety Council estimates based on data from NCHS and the U.S. Census Bureau.
Note: Data do not include "age unknown" cases, which totaled 20 in 2014.
[a]Deaths per 100,000 population in each age group.
[b]Suffocation by inhalation or ingestion of food or other object.

ALL INJURIES
The Odds of Dying From…

Fear is a natural and healthy response that helps us avoid and respond quicker to potential dangers. However, fear can also be counterproductive when people misjudge the actual level of risk. Over-estimating the level of risk can result in anxiety that interferes with normal daily activities. Underestimating risk, on the flip side, can lead to unsafe activities or environments resulting in injury or even death. It can be very difficult to accurately estimate actual risk levels. To help more accurately judge and compare the risk of death from various events, the table on the following pages was prepared. With this information one can better judge and compare the odds of dying from a diverse set of events including lightning, plane crashes, and dog bites.

The odds given in the table are statistical averages over the whole U.S. population and do not necessarily reflect the chances of death for a particular person from a particular external cause. Any individual's odds of dying from various external causes are affected by the activities in which they participate, where they live and drive, what kind of work they do, among other factors.

The table has four columns. The first column gives the manner of injury such as motor-vehicle crash, fall, fire, etc. The second column gives the total number of deaths nationwide due to the manner of injury in 2014 (the latest year for which data are available). The third column gives the odds of dying in one year due to the manner of injury. The fourth column gives the lifetime odds of dying from the manner of injury. Statements about the odds or chances of dying from a given cause of death may be made as follows:

- The odds of dying from (manner of injury) in 2014 were 1 in (value given in the one-year odds column).

- The lifetime odds of dying from (manner of injury) for a person born in 2014 were 1 in (value given in the lifetime odds column).

For example, referring to the first line of the table:
- The odds of dying from an injury in 2014 were 1 in 1,576.
- The lifetime odds of dying from an injury for a person born in 2014 were 1 in 20.

The one year odds are approximated by dividing the 2014 population (318,857,056) by the number of deaths. The lifetime odds are approximated by dividing the one-year odds by the life expectancy of a person born in 2014 (78.8 years). Please note that odds based on less than 20 deaths are likely to be unstable from year to year and are therefore not included in the table and figure on the following pages.

The figure on page 43 visually represents the lifetime odds of death for selected causes from the odds table. The total lifetime odds of death from any cause are 1 in 1, or 100%, and thus the largest shaded area representing the total odds actually extends off the page in all directions to infinity. The circles for selected causes are sized according to their relative lifetime probabilities, with the least probable event – death from a lightning strike – depicted using the smallest circle.

Source: National Safety Council estimates based on data from National Center for Health Statistics—Mortality Data for 2014, as compiled from data provided by the 57 vital statistics jurisdictions through the Vital Statistics Cooperative Program. Population and life expectancy data are from the U.S. Census Bureau. Deaths are classified on the basis of the 10th Revision of the World Health Organization's "The International Classification of Diseases" (ICD). Numbers following titles refer to External Cause of Morbidity and Mortality classifications in ICD-10.

ALL INJURIES
The Odds of Dying From... (cont.)

Odds of death due to injury, United States, 2014[a]

Type of accident or manner of injury	Deaths	One-year odds	Lifetime odds
All external causes of mortality, V01-Y89, *U01, *U03[b]	202,296	1,576	20
Deaths due to unintentional (accidental) injuries, V01-X59, Y85-Y86	136,053	2,344	30
Transport accidents, V01-V99, Y85	37,939	8,404	107
Motor vehicle accidents, V02-V04, V09.0, V09.2, V12-V14, V19.0-V19.2, V19.4-V19.6, V20-V79, V80.3-V80.5, V81.0-V81.1, V82.0-V82.1, V83-V86, V87.0-V87.8, V88.0-V88.8, V09.0, V89.2	35,398	9,008	114
Pedestrian, V01-V09	6,258	50,952	647
Pedalcyclist, V10-V19	902	353,500	4,486
Motorcycle rider, V20-V29	4,106	77,656	985
Occupant of three-wheeled motor vehicle, V30-V39	3	(c)	(c)
Car occupant, V40-V49	6,274	50,822	645
Occupant of pick-up truck or van, V50-V59	1,277	249,692	3,169
Occupant of heavy transport vehicle, V60-V69	291	1,095,729	13,905
Bus occupant, V70-V79	26	12,263,733	155,631
Animal rider or occupant of animal-drawn vehicle, V80	97	3,287,186	41,716
Occupant of railway train or railway vehicle, V81	13	24,527,466	311,262
Occupant of streetcar, V82	1	(c)	(c)
Other and unspecified land transport accidents, V83-V89	17,141	18,602	236
Occupant of special industrial vehicle, V83	4	(c)	(c)
Occupant of special agricultural vehicle, V84	96	3,321,428	42,150
Occupant of special construction vehicle, V85	24	13,285,711	168,600
Occupant of all-terrain or other off-road motor vehicle, V86	940	339,210	4,305
Other and unspecified person, V87-V89	16,077	19,833	252
Water transport accidents, V90-V94	393	811,341	10,296
Drowning, V90, V92	300	1,062,857	13,488
Other and unspecified injuries, V91, V93-V94	93	3,428,570	43,510
Air and space transport accidents, V95-V97	412	773,925	9,821
Other and unspecified transport accidents and sequelae, V98-V99, Y85	745	427,996	5,431
Other specified transport accidents, V98	0	(c)	(c)
Unspecified transport accidents, V99	1	(c)	(c)
Nontransport unintentional (accidental) injuries, W00-X59, Y86	98,114	3,250	41
Falls, W00-W19	31,959	9,977	127
Fall on same level from slipping, tripping, and stumbling, W01	737	432,642	5,490
Other fall on same level, W00, W02-W03, W18	11,031	28,906	367
Fall involving bed, chair, or other furniture, W06-W08	1,239	257,350	3,266
Fall on and from stairs and steps, W10	2,285	139,544	1,771
Fall on and from ladder or scaffolding, W11-W12	525	607,347	7,707
Fall from out of or through building or structure, W13	501	636,441	8,077
Other fall from one level to another, W09, W14-W17	668	477,331	6,057
Other and unspecified fall, W04-W05, W19	14,973	21,295	270
Exposure to inanimate mechanical forces, W20-W49	2,521	126,480	1,605
Struck by or striking against object, W20-W22	899	354,680	4,501
Caught between objects, W23	91	3,503,924	44,466
Contact with machinery, W24, W30-W31	605	527,036	6,688
Contact with sharp objects, W25-W29	106	3,008,085	38,174
Firearms discharge, W32-W34	586	544,125	6,905
Explosion and rupture of pressurized devices, W35-W38	21	(c)	(c)
Fireworks discharge, W39	6	(c)	(c)
Explosion of other materials, W40	116	2,748,768	34,883
Foreign body entering through skin or natural orifice, W44-W45	29	10,995,071	139,531
Other and unspecified inanimate mechanical forces, W41-W43, W49	62	5,142,856	65,265
Exposure to animate mechanical forces, W50-W64	143	2,229,770	28,297
Struck by or against another person, W50-W52	9	(c)	(c)
Bitten or struck by dog, W54	36	8,857,140	112,400
Bitten or struck by other mammals, W53, W55	83	3,841,651	48,752
Bitten or stung by nonvenomous insect and other arthropods, W57	6	(c)	(c)
Bitten or crushed by other reptiles, W59	0	(c)	(c)
Other and unspecified animate mechanical forces, W56, W58, W60, W64	9	(c)	(c)
Accidental drowning and submersion, W65-W74	3,406	93,616	1,188
Drowning and submersion while in or falling into bath-tub, W65-W66	438	727,984	9,238
Drowning and submersion while in or falling into swimming-pool, W67-W68	701	454,860	5,772
Drowning and submersion while in or falling into natural water, W69-W70	1,695	188,116	2,387
Other and unspecified drowning and submersion, W73-W74	572	557,442	7,074
Other accidental threats to breathing, W75-W84	6,580	48,459	615
Accidental suffocation and strangulation in bed, W75	913	349,241	4,432
Other accidental hanging and strangulation, W76	235	1,356,839	17,219
Threat to breathing due to cave-in, falling earth and other substances, W77	13	24,527,466	311,262
Inhalation of gastric contents, W78	295	1,080,871	13,717
Inhalation and ingestion of food causing obstruction of respiratory tract, W79	1,169	272,761	3,461
Inhalation and ingestion of other objects causing obstruction of respiratory tract, W80	3,352	95,124	1,207
Confined to or trapped in a low-oxygen environment, W81	9	(c)	(c)
Other and unspecified threats to breathing, W83-W84	594	536,796	6,812

See source and footnotes on page 42.

ALL INJURIES

The Odds of Dying From... (cont.)

Odds of death due to injury, United States, 2014[a] (cont.)

Type of accident or manner of injury	Deaths	One-year odds	Lifetime odds
Exposure to electric current, radiation, temperature, and pressure, W85-W99	266	1,198,711	15,212
Electric transmission lines, W85	58	5,497,535	69,766
Other and unspecified electric current, W86-W87	199	1,602,297	20,334
Radiation, W88-W91	0	([c])	([c])
Excessive heat or cold of man-made origin, W92-W93	8	([c])	([c])
High and low air pressure and changes in air pressure, W94	1	([c])	([c])
Other and unspecified man-made environmental factors, W99	0	([c])	([c])
Exposure to smoke, fire, and flames, X00-X09	2,701	118,051	1,498
Uncontrolled fire in building or structure, X00	2,198	145,067	1,841
Uncontrolled fire not in building or structure, X01	36	8,857,140	112,400
Controlled fire in building or structure, X02	15	([c])	([c])
Controlled fire not in building or structure, X03	42	7,591,835	96,343
Ignition of highly flammable material, X04	48	6,642,855	84,300
Ignition or melting of nightwear, X05	2	([c])	([c])
Ignition or melting of other clothing and apparel, X06	93	3,428,570	43,510
Other and unspecified smoke fire and flames, X08-X09	267	1,194,221	15,155
Contact with heat and hot substances, X10-X19	71	4,490,944	56,992
Contact with hot tap-water, X11	26	12,263,733	155,631
Other and unspecified heat and hot substances, X10, X12-X19	45	7,085,712	89,920
Contact with venomous animals and plants, X20-X29	91	3,503,924	44,466
Contact with venomous snakes and lizards, X20	5	([c])	([c])
Contact with venomous spiders, X21	7	([c])	([c])
Contact with hornets, wasps and bees, X23	64	4,982,142	63,225
Contact with other and unspecified venomous animal or plant, X22, X24-X29	15	([c])	([c])
Exposure to forces of nature, X30-X39	1,377	231,559	2,939
Exposure to excessive natural heat, X30	244	1,306,791	16,584
Exposure to excessive natural cold, X31	930	342,857	4,351
Lightning, X33	25	12,754,282	161,856
Earthquake and other earth movements, X34-X36	86	3,707,640	47,051
Cataclysmic storm, X37	61	5,227,165	66,335
Flood, X38	8	39,857,132	505,801
Exposure to other and unspecified forces of nature, X32, X39	23	13,863,350	175,931
Accidental poisoning by and exposure to noxious substances, X40-X49	42,032	7,586	96
Nonopioid analgesics, antipyretics, and antirheumatics, X40	224	1,423,469	18,064
Antiepileptic, sedative-hypnotic, antiparkinsonism, and psychotropic drugs n.e.c., X41	3,069	103,896	1,318
Narcotics and psychodysleptics [hallucinogens] n.e.c., X42	16,822	18,955	241
Other and unspecified drugs, medicaments, and biologicals, X43-X44	18,603	17,140	218
Alcohol, X45	2,283	139,666	1,772
Gases and vapors, X46-X47	847	376,455	4,777
Other and unspecified chemicals and noxious substances, X48-X49	184	1,732,919	21,991
Overexertion, travel, and privation, X50-X57	23	13,863,350	175,931
Accidental exposure to other and unspecified factors and sequelae, X58-X59, Y86	6,944	45,918	583
Intentional self-harm, X60-X84, Y87.0, *U03	**42,773**	**7,455**	**95**
Intentional self-poisoning, X60-X69	6,808	46,836	594
Intentional self-harm by hanging, strangulation, and suffocation, X70	11,407	27,953	355
Intentional self-harm by firearm, X72-X74	21,334	14,946	190
Other and unspecified means and sequelae, X71, X75-X84, Y87.0	3,224	98,901	1,255
Terrorism, *U03	0	([c])	([c])
Assault, X85-Y09, Y87.1, *U01	**15,809**	**20,169**	**256**
Assault by firearm, X93-X95	10,945	29,133	370
Assault by sharp object, X99	1,740	183,251	2,326
Other and unspecified means and sequelae, X85-X92, X96-X98, Y00-Y09, Y87.1	3,124	102,067	1,295
Terrorism, *U01	0	([c])	([c])
Event of undetermined intent, Y10-Y34, Y87.2, Y89.9	**4,592**	**69,438**	**881**
Poisoning, Y10-Y19	3,026	105,372	1,337
Hanging, strangulation, and suffocation, Y20	139	2,293,936	29,111
Drowning and submersion, Y21	185	1,723,552	21,872
Firearm discharge, Y22-Y24	270	1,180,952	14,987
Exposure to smoke, fire, and flames, Y26	155	2,057,142	26,106
Falling, jumping, or pushed from a high place, Y30	61	5,227,165	66,335
Other and unspecified means and sequelae, Y25, Y27-Y29, Y31-Y34, Y87.2, Y89.9	756	421,769	5,352
Legal intervention, Y35, Y89.0	**515**	**619,140**	**7,857**
Legal intervention involving firearm discharge, Y35.0	464	687,192	8,721
Legal execution, Y35.5	34	9,378,149	119,012
Other and unspecified means and sequelae, Y35.1-Y35.4, Y35.6-Y35.7, Y89.0	17	([c])	([c])
Operations of war and sequelae, Y36, Y89.1	**14**	**([c])**	**([c])**
Complications of medical and surgical care and sequelae, Y40-Y84, Y88.0-Y88.3	**2,540**	**125,534**	**1,593**

Source: National Center for Health Statistics–Mortality Data for 2014, as compiled from data provided by the 57 vital statistics jurisdictions through the Vital Statistics Cooperative Program. Deaths are classified on the basis of the 10th Revision of "The International Classification of Diseases" (ICD-10), which became effective in 1999.
Note: "n.e.c." means not elsewhere classified.
[a]Latest official figures.
[b]Numbers following titles refer to external cause of injury and poisoning classifications in ICD-10.
[c]Rates based on less than 20 deaths are likely to be unstable from year to year and therefore are not included.

ALL INJURIES

The Odds of Dying From… (cont.)

Lifetime odds of death for selected causes, United States, 2014[a]

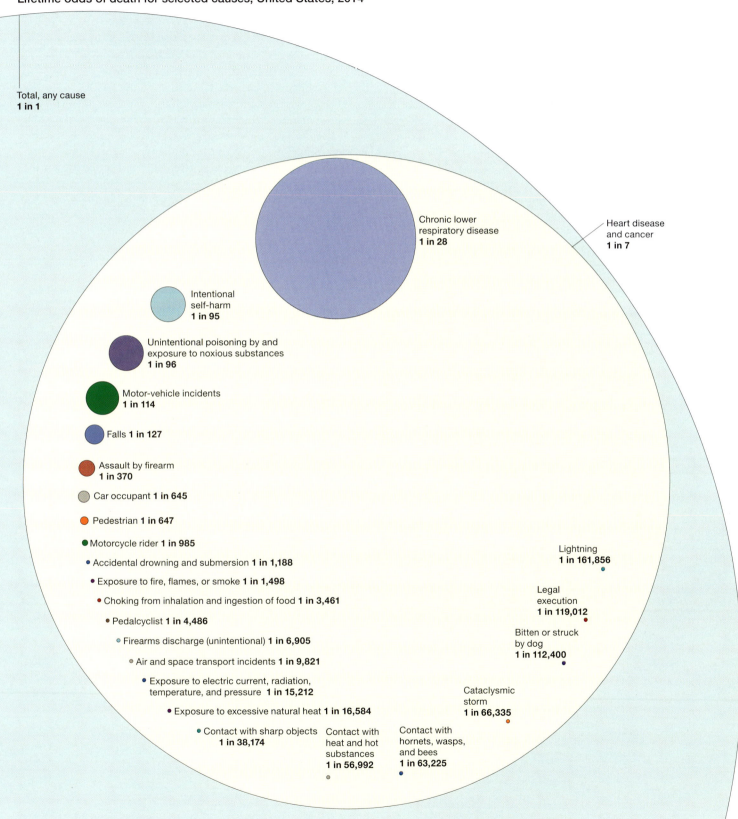

- Total, any cause **1 in 1**
- Heart disease and cancer **1 in 7**
- Chronic lower respiratory disease **1 in 28**
- Intentional self-harm **1 in 95**
- Unintentional poisoning by and exposure to noxious substances **1 in 96**
- Motor-vehicle incidents **1 in 114**
- Falls **1 in 127**
- Assault by firearm **1 in 370**
- Car occupant **1 in 645**
- Pedestrian **1 in 647**
- Motorcycle rider **1 in 985**
- Accidental drowning and submersion **1 in 1,188**
- Exposure to fire, flames, or smoke **1 in 1,498**
- Choking from inhalation and ingestion of food **1 in 3,461**
- Pedalcyclist **1 in 4,486**
- Firearms discharge (unintentional) **1 in 6,905**
- Air and space transport incidents **1 in 9,821**
- Exposure to electric current, radiation, temperature, and pressure **1 in 15,212**
- Exposure to excessive natural heat **1 in 16,584**
- Contact with sharp objects **1 in 38,174**
- Contact with heat and hot substances **1 in 56,992**
- Contact with hornets, wasps, and bees **1 in 63,225**
- Cataclysmic storm **1 in 66,335**
- Bitten or struck by dog **1 in 112,400**
- Legal execution **1 in 119,012**
- Lightning **1 in 161,856**

Source: National Safety Council estimates based on data from National Center for Health Statistics—Mortality Data for 2014 as compiled from data provided by the 57 vital statistics jurisdictions through the Vital Statistics Cooperative Program. Population and life expectancy data are from the U.S. Census Bureau. For mortality figures, estimated one-year and lifetime odds, and external cause classification codes based on the 10th Revision of "The International Classification of Diseases" (ICD) for the causes illustrated, see table on pages 41–42.
[a]Latest official figures.

ALL INJURIES

Trends in Unintentional-Injury-Related Death Rates

Age-adjusted rates, which eliminate the effect of shifts in the age distribution of the population, decreased 57% from 1912 to 2015 – from 100.4 to 43.0 deaths per 100,000 population. The adjusted rates, which are shown in the graphs on the opposite page, are standardized to the year 2000 standard U.S. population. The break in the lines at 1948 shows the estimated effect of changes in the International Classification of Diseases (ICD). The break in the lines at 1992 resulted from the adoption of the Bureau of Labor Statistics Census of Fatal Occupational Injuries for work-related deaths. Another change in the ICD in 1999 also affects the trends. See the Technical Appendix for comparability.

The table below shows the change in the age distribution of the population since 1910. The age-adjusted death rate for all unintentional injuries increased and decreased significantly several times during the period from 1910 to 1940 (top of facing page). Since 1940, there were some setbacks, such as in the early 1960s, but the overall trend through the early 1990s was positive. However, since 1992 the overall age-adjusted death rate has demonstrated an increasing trend. The age-adjusted death rates for unintentional-injury-related deaths in the work and home classes declined fairly steadily since they became available in the late 1920s, and the home class rates have increased since the early 1990s. The rates in the public class declined for three decades, rose in the 1960s, and then continued declining until leveling out in the 1990s to present. The age-adjusted motor-vehicle death rate rose steadily from 1910 to the late 1930s as the automobile became more widely used. A sharp drop in use occurred during World War II and a sharp rise in rates occurred in the 1960s, with death rates reflecting economic cycles and a long-term downward trend since then.

United States population, selected years

Year	All ages	Younger than 15	15-24	25-44	45-64	65 or older
Number (in thousands)						
1910	91,973[a]	29,499	18,121	26,810	13,424	3,950
2000[b]	274,634	58,964	38,077	81,892	60,991	34,710
2015	321,419	61,017	43,848	84,727	84,066	47,761
Percent						
1910	100.0%	32.1%	19.7%	29.2%	14.6%	4.3%
2000[b]	100.0%	21.5%	13.9%	29.8%	22.2%	12.6%
2015	100.0%	19.0%	13.6%	26.4%	26.2%	14.9%

Looking at individual leading causes (bottom chart on next page), at the turn of the last century falls were the leading cause of unintentional-injury-related death, while motor vehicle and poisoning deaths were only minor concerns. Today, although falls continue to be a major concern, poisonings and motor-vehicle incidents have become the two leading causes of unintentional-injury-related deaths.

For 1910: U.S. Census Bureau. (1960). Historical Statistics of the United States, Colonial Times to 1957. Series A 71-85. Washington, DC: U.S. Government Printing Office. For 2000: Anderson, R.N., & Rosenberg, H.M. (1998). Age standardization of death rates: Implementation of the year 2000 standard. National Vital Statistics Reports, Issue 47, No. 3 p. 13. For 2013: U.S. Census Bureau.
[a]*Includes 169,000 people with age unknown.*
[b]*This is the population used for standardization (age adjustment) and differs slightly from the actual 2000 population, which totaled 275,306,000.*

ALL INJURIES
Trends in Unintentional-Injury-Related Death Rates (cont.)

Age-adjusted death rates by class of injury, United States, 1910-2015

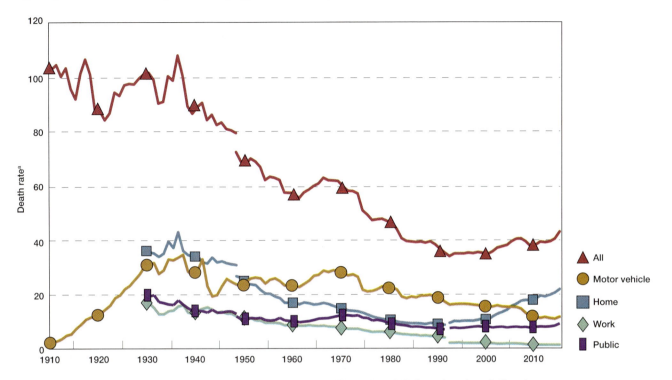

[a] Deaths per 100,000 population adjusted to the year 2000 standard population. The break at 1948 shows the estimated effect of classification changes. The break at 1992 is due to the adoption of the Bureau of Labor Statistics' Census of Fatal Occupational Injuries for work-related deaths.

Age-adjusted death rates by leading cause of unintentional injury, United States, 1910-2015

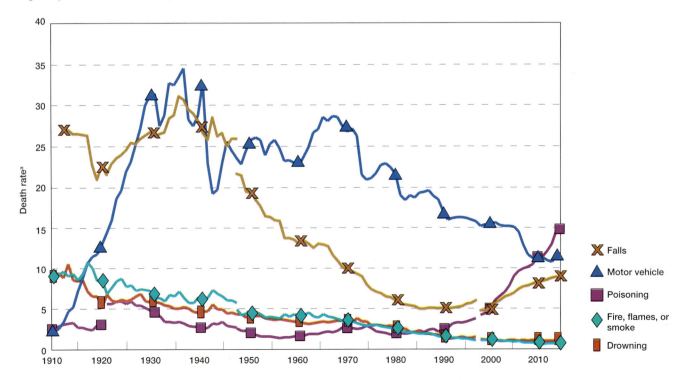

[a] Deaths per 100,000 population adjusted to the year 2000 standard population. Breaks in graph lines signify changes in fatal injury coding.

INJURY FACTS® 2017 EDITION — NATIONAL SAFETY COUNCIL® ■ 45

ALL INJURIES
Principal Classes of Unintentional-Injury-Related Deaths

Principal classes of unintentional-injury-related deaths, United States, 1903-2015

Year	Total[a] Deaths	Rate[b]	Motor vehicle Deaths	Rate[b]	Work Deaths	Rate[b]	Home Deaths	Rate[b]	Public non-motor vehicle Deaths	Rate[b]
1903	70,600	87.2	(c)	–	(c)	–	(c)	–	(c)	–
1904	71,500	86.6	(c)	–	(c)	–	(c)	–	(c)	–
1905	70,900	84.2	(c)	–	(c)	–	(c)	–	(c)	–
1906	80,000	93.2	400	0.5	(c)	–	(c)	–	(c)	–
1907	81,900	93.6	700	0.8	(c)	–	(c)	–	(c)	–
1908	72,300	81.2	800	0.9	(c)	–	(c)	–	(c)	–
1909	72,700	80.1	1,300	1.4	(c)	–	(c)	–	(c)	–
1910	77,900	84.4	1,900	2.0	(c)	–	(c)	–	(c)	–
1911	79,300	84.7	2,300	2.5	(c)	–	(c)	–	(c)	–
1912	78,400	82.5	3,100	3.3	(c)	–	(c)	–	(c)	–
1913	82,500	85.5	4,200	4.4	(c)	–	(c)	–	(c)	–
1914	77,000	78.6	4,700	4.8	(c)	–	(c)	–	(c)	–
1915	76,200	76.7	6,600	6.6	(c)	–	(c)	–	(c)	–
1916	84,800	84.1	8,200	8.1	(c)	–	(c)	–	(c)	–
1917	90,100	88.2	10,200	10.0	(c)	–	(c)	–	(c)	–
1918	85,100	82.1	10,700	10.3	(c)	–	(c)	–	(c)	–
1919	75,500	71.9	11,200	10.7	(c)	–	(c)	–	(c)	–
1920	75,900	71.2	12,500	11.7	(c)	–	(c)	–	(c)	–
1921	74,000	68.4	13,900	12.9	(c)	–	(c)	–	(c)	–
1922	76,300	69.4	15,300	13.9	(c)	–	(c)	–	(c)	–
1923	84,400	75.7	18,400	16.5	(c)	–	(c)	–	(c)	–
1924	85,600	75.6	19,400	17.1	(c)	–	(c)	–	(c)	–
1925	90,000	78.4	21,900	19.1	(c)	–	(c)	–	(c)	–
1926	91,700	78.7	23,400	20.1	(c)	–	(c)	–	(c)	–
1927	92,700	78.4	25,800	21.8	(c)	–	(c)	–	(c)	–
1928	95,000	79.3	28,000	23.4	19,000	15.8	30,000	24.9	21,000	17.4
1929	98,200	80.8	31,200	25.7	20,000	16.4	30,000	24.6	20,000	16.4
1930	99,100	80.5	32,900	26.7	19,000	15.4	30,000	24.4	20,000	16.3
1931	97,300	78.5	33,700	27.2	17,500	14.1	29,000	23.4	20,000	16.1
1932	89,000	71.3	29,500	23.6	15,000	12.0	29,000	23.2	18,000	14.4
1933	90,932	72.4	31,363	25.0	14,500	11.6	29,500	23.6	18,500	14.7
1934	100,977	79.9	36,101	28.6	16,000	12.7	34,000	26.9	18,000	14.2
1935	99,773	78.4	36,369	28.6	16,500	13.0	32,000	25.2	18,000	14.2
1936	110,052	85.9	38,089	29.7	18,500	14.5	37,000	28.9	19,500	15.2
1937	105,205	81.7	39,643	30.8	19,000	14.8	32,000	24.8	18,000	14.0
1938	93,805	72.3	32,582	25.1	16,000	12.3	31,000	23.9	17,000	13.1
1939	92,623	70.8	32,386	24.7	15,500	11.8	31,000	23.7	16,000	12.2
1940	96,885	73.4	34,501	26.1	17,000	12.9	31,500	23.9	16,500	12.5
1941	101,513	76.3	39,969	30.0	18,000	13.5	30,000	22.5	16,500	12.4
1942	95,889	71.6	28,309	21.1	18,000	13.4	30,500	22.8	16,000	12.0
1943	99,038	73.8	23,823	17.8	17,500	13.0	33,500	25.0	17,000	12.7
1944	95,237	71.7	24,282	18.3	16,000	12.0	32,500	24.5	16,000	12.0
1945	95,918	72.4	28,076	21.2	16,500	12.5	33,500	25.3	16,000	12.1
1946	98,033	70.0	33,411	23.9	16,500	11.8	33,000	23.6	17,500	12.5
1947	99,579	69.4	32,697	22.8	17,000	11.9	34,500	24.1	18,000	12.6
1948 (5th Rev.)[d]	98,001	67.1	32,259	22.1	16,000	11.0	35,000	24.0	17,000	11.6
1948 (6th Rev.)[d]	93,000	63.7	32,259	22.1	16,000	11.0	31,000	21.2	16,000	11.0
1949	90,106	60.6	31,701	21.3	15,000	10.1	31,000	20.9	15,000	10.1
1950	91,249	60.3	34,763	23.0	15,500	10.2	29,000	19.2	15,000	9.9
1951	95,871	62.5	36,996	24.1	16,000	10.4	30,000	19.6	16,000	10.4
1952	96,172	61.8	37,794	24.3	15,000	9.6	30,500	19.6	16,000	10.3
1953	95,032	60.1	37,955	24.0	15,000	9.5	29,000	18.3	16,500	10.4
1954	90,032	55.9	35,586	22.1	14,000	8.7	28,000	17.4	15,500	9.6
1955	93,443	56.9	38,426	23.4	14,200	8.6	28,500	17.3	15,500	9.4
1956	94,780	56.6	39,628	23.7	14,300	8.5	28,000	16.7	16,000	9.6
1957	95,307	55.9	38,702	22.7	14,200	8.3	28,000	16.4	17,500	10.3
1958	90,604	52.3	36,981	21.3	13,300	7.7	26,500	15.3	16,500	9.5
1959	92,080	52.2	37,910	21.5	13,800	7.8	27,000	15.3	16,500	9.3
1960	93,806	52.1	38,137	21.2	13,800	7.7	28,000	15.6	17,000	9.4
1961	92,249	50.4	38,091	20.8	13,500	7.4	27,000	14.8	16,500	9.0
1962	97,139	52.3	40,804	22.0	13,700	7.4	28,500	15.3	17,000	9.2
1963	100,669	53.4	43,564	23.1	14,200	7.5	28,500	15.1	17,500	9.3
1964	105,000	54.9	47,700	25.0	14,200	7.4	28,000	14.6	18,500	9.7
1965	108,004	55.8	49,163	25.4	14,100	7.3	28,500	14.7	19,500	10.1
1966	113,563	58.1	53,041	27.1	14,500	7.4	29,500	15.1	20,000	10.2
1967	113,169	57.3	52,924	26.8	14,200	7.2	29,000	14.7	20,500	10.4
1968	114,864	57.6	54,862	27.5	14,300	7.2	28,000	14.0	21,500	10.8
1969	116,385	57.8	55,791	27.7	14,300	7.1	27,500	13.7	22,500	11.2
1970	114,638	56.2	54,633	26.8	13,800	6.8	27,000	13.2	23,500	11.5
1971	113,439	54.8	54,381	26.3	13,700	6.6	26,500	12.8	23,500	11.4
1972	115,448	55.2	56,278	26.9	14,000	6.7	26,500	12.7	23,500	11.2
1973	115,821	54.8	55,511	26.3	14,300	6.8	26,500	12.5	24,500	11.6

See source and footnotes on page 47.

ALL INJURIES

Principal Classes of Unintentional-Injury-Related Deaths (cont.)

Principal classes of unintentional-injury-related deaths, United States, 1903-2015 (cont.)

Year	Total[a] Deaths	Rate[b]	Motor vehicle Deaths	Rate[b]	Work Deaths	Rate[b]	Home Deaths	Rate[b]	Public non-motor vehicle Deaths	Rate[b]
1974	104,622	49.0	46,402	21.8	13,500	6.3	26,000	12.2	23,000	10.8
1975	103,030	47.8	45,853	21.3	13,000	6.0	25,000	11.6	23,000	10.6
1976	100,761	46.3	47,038	21.6	12,500	5.7	24,000	11.0	21,500	10.0
1977	103,202	47.0	49,510	22.5	12,900	5.9	23,200	10.6	22,200	10.1
1978	105,561	47.5	52,411	23.6	13,100	5.9	22,800	10.3	22,000	9.9
1979	105,312	46.9	53,524	23.8	13,000	5.8	22,500	10.0	21,000	9.4
1980	105,718	46.5	53,172	23.4	13,200	5.8	22,800	10.0	21,300	9.4
1981	100,704	43.9	51,385	22.4	12,500	5.4	21,700	9.5	19,800	8.6
1982	94,082	40.6	45,779	19.8	11,900	5.1	21,200	9.2	19,500	8.4
1983	92,488	39.6	44,452	19.0	11,700	5.0	21,200	9.1	19,400	8.3
1984	92,911	39.4	46,263	19.6	11,500	4.9	21,200	9.0	18,300	7.8
1985	93,457	39.3	45,901	19.3	11,500	4.8	21,600	9.1	18,800	7.9
1986	95,277	39.7	47,865	19.9	11,100	4.6	21,700	9.0	18,700	7.8
1987	95,020	39.2	48,290	19.9	11,300	4.7	21,400	8.8	18,400	7.6
1988	97,100	39.7	49,078	20.1	11,000	4.5	22,700	9.3	18,400	7.5
1989	95,028	38.5	47,575	19.3	10,900	4.4	22,500	9.1	18,200	7.4
1990	91,983	36.9	46,814	18.8	10,100	4.0	21,500	8.6	17,400	7.0
1991	89,347	35.4	43,536	17.3	9,800	3.9	22,100	8.8	17,600	7.0
1992	86,777	34.0	40,982	16.1	4,968[e]	1.9[e]	24,000[e]	9.4[e]	19,000[e]	7.4[e]
1993	90,523	35.1	41,893	16.3	5,035	2.0	26,100	10.1	19,700	7.6
1994	91,437	35.1	42,524	16.3	5,338	2.1	26,300	10.1	19,600	7.5
1995	93,320	35.5	43,363	16.5	5,018	1.9	27,200	10.3	20,100	7.6
1996	94,948	35.8	43,649	16.5	5,058	1.9	27,500	10.4	21,000	7.9
1997	95,644	35.7	43,458	16.2	5,162	1.9	27,700	10.3	21,700	8.1
1998	97,835	36.2	43,501	16.1	5,120	1.9	29,000	10.7	22,600	8.4
1999[f]	97,860	35.9	42,401	15.5	5,185	1.9	30,500	11.2	22,200	8.1
2000	97,900	35.6	43,354	15.7	5,022	1.8	29,200	10.6	22,700	8.2
2001	101,537	35.6	43,788	15.4	5,042	1.8	33,200	11.6	21,800	7.6
2002	106,742	37.1	45,380	15.8	4,726	1.6	36,400	12.6	22,500	7.8
2003	109,277	37.6	44,757	15.4	4,725	1.6	38,800	13.3	23,200	8.0
2004	112,012	38.1	44,933	15.3	5,000	1.7	41,700	14.2	22,700	7.7
2005	117,809	39.7	45,343	15.3	4,987	1.7	46,400	15.6	23,400	7.9
2006	121,599	40.8	45,316	15.2	5,092	1.7	49,600	16.6	23,900	8.0
2007	123,706	41.1	43,945	14.6	4,833	1.6	53,500	17.8	23,700	7.9
2008	121,902	40.0	39,790	13.1	4,425	1.5	55,200	18.1	24,500	8.0
2009	118,046	38.5	36,216	11.8	3,744	1.2	55,800	18.2	24,000	7.8
2010	120,859	39.0	35,332	11.4	3,902	1.3	58,100	18.7	25,300	8.2
2011	126,438	40.6	35,303	11.3	3,975	1.3	62,400	20.0	26,400	8.5
2012	127,792	40.7	36,415	11.6	3,904	1.2	62,800	20.0	26,600	8.5
2013	130,557	41.3	35,369	11.2	3,899	1.2	65,700	20.8	27,300	8.6
2014[g]	136,053	42.7	35,398	11.1	4,127	1.3	69,600	21.8	28,900	9.1
2015	146,571	45.6	37,757	11.7	4,190	1.3	74,600	23.2	32,100	10.0
Changes										
2006 to 2015	20.5%	12%	-17%	-23%	-18%	-24%	50%	40%	34%	25%
2014 to 2015	7.7%	7%	7%	5%	2%	0%	7%	6%	11%	10%
Total deaths and average death rates										
Since 2006	1,273,523	41.0	380,841	12.3	42,091	1.4	607,300	19.5	262,700	8.5
Since 1996	2,210,139	38.9	777,756	14.0	87,060	1.6	920,200	15.8	465,500	8.2
Since 1986	3,230,899	38.2	1,273,325	15.4	171,709	2.2	1,159,200	13.8	654,600	8.0
Since 1976	4,225,095	39.6	1,762,760	16.9	295,509	3.0	1,381,400	12.8	858,400	8.2

Source: Total and motor-vehicle deaths, 1903-1932 based on National Center for Health Statistics (NCHS) death registration states; 1933-1948 (5th Rev.), 1949-1963, 1965-2015 are NCHS totals for the United States. Work deaths for 1992-2015 are from the Bureau of Labor Statistics Census of Fatal Occupational Injuries. All other figures are National Safety Council estimates.

[a] Duplications between motor vehicle, work, and home are eliminated in the total column.
[b] Rates are deaths per 100,000 population.
[c] Data insufficient to estimate yearly totals.
[d] In 1948, a revision was made in the International Classification of Diseases. The first figures for 1948 are comparable with those for earlier years, the second with those for later years.
[e] Adoption of the Census of Fatal Occupational Injuries figure for the work class necessitated adjustments to the home and public classes. See the Technical Appendix for details.
[f] In 1999, a revision was made in the International Classification of Diseases. See the Technical Appendix for comparability with earlier years.
[g] Revised.

ALL INJURIES
Unintentional-Injury-Related Deaths by Age

Unintentional-injury-related deaths by age, United States, 1903-2015

Year	All ages	Younger than 5 years	5-14 years	15-24 years	25-44 years	45-64 years	65-74 years	75 years and older[a]
1903	70,600	9,400	8,200	10,300	20,100	12,600	10,000	
1904	71,500	9,700	9,000	10,500	19,900	12,500	9,900	
1905	70,900	9,800	8,400	10,600	19,600	12,600	9,900	
1906	80,000	10,000	8,400	13,000	24,000	13,600	11,000	
1907	81,900	10,500	8,300	13,400	24,900	14,700	10,100	
1908	72,300	10,100	7,600	11,300	20,500	13,100	9,700	
1909	72,700	9,900	7,400	10,700	21,000	13,300	10,400	
1910	77,900	9,900	7,400	11,900	23,600	14,100	11,000	
1911	79,300	11,000	7,500	11,400	22,400	15,100	11,900	
1912	78,400	10,600	7,900	11,500	22,200	14,700	11,500	
1913	82,500	9,800	7,400	12,200	24,500	16,500	12,100	
1914	77,000	10,600	7,900	11,000	21,400	14,300	11,800	
1915	76,200	10,300	8,200	10,800	20,500	14,300	12,100	
1916	84,800	11,600	9,100	7,700	24,900	17,800	13,700	
1917	90,100	11,600	9,700	11,700	24,400	18,500	14,200	
1918	85,100	10,600	10,100	10,600	21,900	17,700	14,200	
1919	75,500	10,100	10,000	10,200	18,600	13,800	12,800	
1920	75,900	10,200	9,900	10,400	18,100	13,900	13,400	
1921	74,000	9,600	9,500	9,800	18,000	13,900	13,200	
1922	76,300	9,700	9,500	10,000	18,700	14,500	13,900	
1923	84,400	9,900	9,800	11,000	21,500	16,900	15,300	
1924	85,600	10,200	9,900	11,900	20,900	16,800	15,900	
1925	90,000	9,700	10,000	12,400	22,200	18,700	17,000	
1926	91,700	9,500	9,900	12,600	22,700	19,200	17,800	
1927	92,700	9,200	9,900	12,900	22,900	19,700	18,100	
1928	95,000	8,900	9,800	13,100	23,300	20,600	19,300	
1929	98,200	8,600	9,800	14,000	24,300	21,500	20,000	
1930	99,100	8,200	9,100	14,000	24,300	22,200	21,300	
1931	97,300	7,800	8,700	13,500	23,100	22,500	21,700	
1932	89,000	7,100	8,100	12,000	20,500	20,100	21,200	
1933	90,932	6,948	8,195	12,225	21,005	20,819	21,740	
1934	100,977	7,034	8,272	13,274	23,288	24,197	24,912	
1935	99,773	6,971	7,808	13,168	23,411	23,457	24,958	
1936	110,052	7,471	7,866	13,701	24,990	26,535	29,489	
1937	105,205	6,969	7,704	14,302	23,955	24,743	27,532	
1938	93,805	6,646	6,593	12,129	20,464	21,689	26,284	
1939	92,628	6,668	6,378	12,066	20,164	20,842	26,505	
1940	96,885	6,851	6,466	12,763	21,166	21,840	27,799	
1941	101,513	7,052	6,702	14,346	22,983	22,509	27,921	
1942	95,889	7,220	6,340	13,732	21,141	20,764	26,692	
1943	99,038	8,039	6,636	15,278	20,212	20,109	28,764	
1944	95,237	7,912	6,704	14,750	19,115	19,097	27,659	
1945	95,918	7,741	6,836	12,446	19,393	20,097	29,405	
1946	98,033	7,949	6,545	13,366	20,705	20,249	29,219	
1947	99,579	8,219	6,069	13,166	21,155	20,513	30,457	
1948 (5th Rev.)[b]	98,001	8,387	5,859	12,595	20,274	19,809	31,077	
1948 (6th Rev.)[b]	93,000	8,350	5,850	12,600	20,300	19,300	9,800	16,800
1949	90,106	8,469	5,539	11,522	19,432	18,302	9,924	16,918
1950	91,249	8,389	5,519	12,119	20,663	18,665	9,750	16,144
1951	95,871	8,769	5,892	12,366	22,363	19,610	10,218	16,653
1952	96,172	8,871	5,980	12,787	21,950	19,892	10,026	16,667
1953	95,032	8,678	6,136	12,837	21,422	19,479	9,927	16,553
1954	90,032	8,380	5,939	11,801	20,023	18,299	9,652	15,938
1955	93,443	8,099	6,099	12,742	29,911	19,199	9,929	16,464
1956	94,780	8,173	6,319	13,545	20,986	19,207	10,160	16,393
1957	95,307	8,423	6,454	12,973	20,949	19,495	10,076	16,937
1958	90,604	8,789	6,514	12,744	19,658	18,095	9,431	15,373
1959	92,080	8,748	6,511	13,269	19,666	18,937	9,475	15,474
1960	93,806	8,950	6,836	13,457	19,600	19,385	9,689	15,829
1961	92,249	8,622	6,717	13,431	19,273	19,134	9,452	15,620
1962	97,139	8,705	6,751	14,557	19,955	20,335	10,149	16,687
1963	100,669	8,688	6,962	15,889	20,529	21,262	10,194	17,145
1964	100,500	8,670	7,400	17,420	22,080	22,100	10,400	16,930
1965	108,004	8,586	7,391	18,688	22,228	22,900	10,430	17,781
1966	113,563	8,507	7,958	21,030	23,134	24,022	10,706	18,206
1967	113,169	7,825	7,874	21,645	23,255	23,826	10,645	18,099
1968	114,864	7,263	8,369	23,012	23,684	23,896	10,961	17,679
1969	116,385	6,973	8,186	24,668	24,410	24,192	10,643	17,313
1970	114,638	6,594	8,203	24,336	23,979	24,164	10,644	16,718
1971	113,439	6,496	8,143	24,733	23,535	23,240	10,494	16,798
1972	115,448	6,142	8,242	25,762	23,852	23,658	10,446	17,346
1973	115,821	6,037	8,102	26,550	24,750	23,059	10,243	17,080

See source and footnotes on page 49.

ALL INJURIES
Unintentional-Injury-Related Deaths by Age (cont.)

Unintentional-injury-related deaths by age, United States, 1903-2015 (cont.)

Year	All ages	Younger than 5 years	5-14 years	15-24 years	25-44 years	45-64 years	65-74 years	75 years and older[a]
1974	104,622	5,335	7,037	24,200	22,547	20,334	9,323	15,846
1975	103,030	4,948	6,818	24,121	22,877	19,643	9,220	15,403
1976	100,761	4,692	6,308	24,316	22,399	19,000	8,823	15,223
1977	103,202	4,470	6,305	25,619	23,460	19,167	9,006	15,175
1978	105,561	4,766	6,118	26,622	25,024	18,774	9,072	15,185
1979	105,312	4,429	5,689	26,574	26,097	18,346	9,013	15,164
1980	105,718	4,479	5,224	26,206	26,722	18,140	8,997	15,950
1981	100,704	4,130	4,866	23,582	26,928	17,339	8,639	15,220
1982	94,082	4,108	4,504	21,306	25,135	15,907	8,224	14,898
1983	92,488	3,999	4,321	19,756	24,996	15,444	8,336	15,636
1984	92,911	3,652	4,198	19,801	25,498	15,273	8,424	16,065
1985	93,457	3,746	4,252	19,161	25,940	15,251	8,583	16,524
1986	95,277	3,843	4,226	19,975	27,201	14,733	8,499	16,800
1987	95,020	3,871	4,198	18,695	27,484	14,807	8,686	17,279
1988	97,100	3,794	4,215	18,507	28,279	15,177	8,971	18,157
1989	95,028	3,770	4,090	16,738	28,429	15,046	8,812	18,143
1990	91,983	3,496	3,650	16,241	27,663	14,607	8,405	17,921
1991	89,347	3,626	3,660	15,278	26,526	13,693	8,137	18,427
1992	86,777	3,286	3,388	13,662	25,808	13,882	8,165	18,586
1993	90,523	3,488	3,466	13,966	27,277	14,434	8,125	19,767
1994	91,437	3,406	3,508	13,898	27,012	15,200	8,279	20,134
1995	93,320	3,067	3,544	13,842	27,660	16,004	8,400	20,803
1996	94,948	2,951	3,433	13,809	27,092	16,717	8,780	22,166
1997	95,644	2,770	3,371	13,367	27,129	17,521	8,578	22,908
1998	97,835	2,689	3,254	13,349	27,172	18,286	8,892	24,193
1999c	97,860	2,743	3,091	13,656	27,121	18,924	8,208	24,117
2000	97,900	2,707	2,979	14,113	27,182	19,783	7,698	23,438
2001	101,537	2,690	2,836	14,411	27,784	21,002	7,835	24,979
2002	106,742	2,587	2,718	15,412	29,279	23,020	8,086	25,640
2003	109,277	2,662	2,618	15,272	29,307	25,007	8,081	26,330
2004	112,012	2,693	2,666	15,449	29,503	26,593	8,116	26,992
2005	117,809	2,747	2,415	15,753	30,916	29,192	8,632	28,154
2006	121,599	2,757	2,258	16,229	32,488	31,121	8,420	28,326
2007	123,706	2,873	2,194	15,897	31,908	32,508	8,753	29,573
2008	121,902	2,784	1,859	14,089	30,653	33,136	8,994	30,387
2009	118,046	2,674	1,680	12,454	29,159	32,945	8,976	30,158
2010	120,859	2,504	1,643	12,341	29,365	33,690	9,407	31,909
2011	126,438	2,540	1,635	12,330	30,748	35,907	10,014	33,264
2012	127,792	2,522	1,550	11,908	30,885	36,216	10,558	34,153
2013	130,557	2,472	1,521	11,619	31,563	37,414	10,967	35,001
2014	136,053	2,377	1,480	11,836	33,405	38,640	11,909	36,406
2015	146,571	2,526	1,518	12,514	37,613	40,987	12,961	38,452
Changes								
2006 to 2015	21%	-8%	-33%	-23%	16%	32%	54%	36%
2014 to 2015	8%	6%	3%	6%	13%	6%	9%	6%

Source: 1903-1932 based on National Center for Health Statistics (NCHS) data for registration states; 1933-1948 (5th Rev.), 1949-1963, 1965-2015 are NCHS totals. All other figures are National Safety Council estimates. See Technical Appendix for comparability.
[a]Includes age unknown. In 2015, they numbered 18.
[b]In 1948, a revision was made in the International Classification of Diseases. The first figures for 1948 are comparable with those for earlier years, the second with those for later years.
[c]In 1999, a revision was made in the International Classification of Diseases. See the Technical Appendix for comparability with earlier years.

ALL INJURIES
Unintentional-Injury-Related Death Rates by Age

Unintentional-injury-related death rates[a] by age, United States, 1903-2015

Year	Standardized rate[b]	All ages	Younger than 5 years	5-14 years	15-24 years	25-44 years	45-64 years	65-74 years	75 years and older[c]
1903	99.4	87.2	98.7	46.8	65.0	87.4	111.7	299.8	
1904	103.4	86.6	99.1	50.9	64.9	84.6	108.1	290.0	
1905	98.4	84.2	98.6	47.0	64.1	81.4	106.2	282.5	
1906	114.2	93.2	99.1	46.5	77.1	97.3	111.7	306.0	
1907	112.4	93.6	102.7	45.5	78.0	98.8	117.8	274.2	
1908	99.7	81.2	97.5	41.2	64.4	79.5	102.2	256.7	
1909	97.4	80.1	94.2	39.6	59.9	79.6	101.0	268.2	
1910	103.0	84.4	92.8	39.1	65.3	87.3	104.0	276.0	
1911	104.7	84.7	101.9	39.3	62.1	81.4	108.7	292.1	
1912	100.4	82.5	97.1	40.5	62.3	79.2	103.2	275.8	
1913	103.5	85.5	88.4	37.4	65.2	85.6	112.5	281.7	
1914	95.9	78.6	94.3	38.9	58.5	73.2	94.6	268.1	
1915	92.1	76.7	90.8	39.7	57.3	69.0	92.1	268.8	
1916	101.4	84.1	101.4	43.3	40.8	82.5	112.1	297.6	
1917	106.7	88.2	108.4	45.3	62.1	79.8	113.8	301.2	
1918	101.2	82.1	91.0	46.5	58.7	72.2	106.3	294.2	
1919	87.7	71.9	87.2	45.9	55.3	60.1	81.8	262.0	
1920	87.8	71.2	87.4	44.9	55.5	56.9	85.6	289.5	
1921	84.3	68.4	80.8	42.4	51.4	55.5	79.4	259.8	
1922	86.9	69.4	80.6	41.5	51.4	57.1	81.4	265.1	
1923	94.5	75.7	82.0	42.4	55.6	64.5	92.6	282.8	
1924	93.3	75.6	82.9	42.4	58.6	61.7	90.2	283.5	
1925	97.2	78.4	78.6	42.3	59.7	64.7	97.8	293.9	
1926	97.7	78.7	77.9	41.4	59.9	65.4	98.2	298.7	
1927	97.5	78.4	75.9	41.0	60.2	65.2	98.0	295.4	
1928	99.6	79.3	74.4	40.4	59.9	65.6	99.9	306.2	
1929	101.2	80.8	73.3	40.0	63.1	67.7	102.1	308.9	
1930	101.8	80.5	71.8	36.9	62.3	67.0	102.9	317.9	
1931	99.2	78.5	69.9	35.2	59.7	63.0	102.1	313.3	
1932	90.5	71.3	65.1	32.8	52.7	55.6	89.3	296.9	
1933	91.1	72.4	65.5	33.4	53.6	56.3	90.8	295.3	
1934	100.5	79.9	68.1	33.9	57.8	61.8	103.3	328.5	
1935	97.9	78.4	68.5	32.2	56.9	61.6	98.0	319.8	
1936	108.1	85.9	74.4	32.9	58.8	65.3	108.6	367.4	
1937	100.7	81.7	69.6	32.7	60.9	62.1	99.3	333.4	
1938	89.4	72.3	65.3	28.5	51.3	52.5	85.4	308.9	
1939	86.7	70.8	62.9	28.2	50.7	51.2	81.0	300.0	
1940	89.1	73.4	64.8	28.8	53.5	53.2	83.4	305.7	
1941	90.7	76.3	65.0	29.7	60.9	57.2	84.8	297.4	
1942	84.3	71.6	63.9	27.9	59.8	52.4	77.1	275.5	
1943	86.3	73.8	66.9	29.0	69.7	50.3	73.6	287.8	
1944	82.5	71.7	63.2	29.1	72.9	48.9	68.9	268.6	
1945	83.4	72.4	59.8	29.5	64.5	50.5	71.6	277.6	
1946	81.0	70.0	60.2	28.1	61.7	48.8	70.9	267.9	
1947	80.5	69.4	57.4	25.8	59.6	49.0	70.6	270.7	
1948 (5th Rev.)[d]	79.5	67.1	56.3	24.6	56.8	46.2	66.8	267.4	
1948 (6th Rev.)[d]	72.5	63.7	56.0	24.5	56.8	46.2	65.1	122.4	464.3
1949	69.0	60.6	54.4	23.0	52.2	43.5	60.6	120.4	450.7
1950	68.1	60.3	51.4	22.6	55.0	45.6	60.5	115.8	414.7
1951	70.1	62.5	50.8	23.6	57.7	49.0	62.7	117.1	413.6
1952	69.0	61.8	51.5	22.5	60.9	47.7	62.7	111.1	399.8
1953	67.0	60.1	49.5	22.1	61.4	46.4	60.5	106.7	383.6
1954	62.2	55.9	46.7	20.5	56.4	43.0	55.9	100.7	354.4
1955	63.4	56.9	43.9	20.7	60.1	44.7	57.7	100.8	350.2
1956	63.0	56.6	43.3	20.2	63.3	44.7	56.7	100.6	335.6
1957	62.2	55.9	43.5	19.9	59.5	44.6	56.6	97.5	333.3
1958	57.5	52.3	44.5	19.6	56.2	42.0	51.7	89.3	292.6
1959	57.4	52.2	43.6	18.9	56.5	42.1	53.2	87.7	284.7
1960	57.3	52.1	44.0	19.1	55.6	42.0	53.6	87.6	281.4
1961	55.4	50.4	42.0	18.1	54.0	41.2	52.1	83.8	267.9
1962	57.5	52.3	42.6	18.0	55.0	42.7	54.6	88.5	277.7
1963	58.6	53.4	42.8	18.2	57.2	44.0	56.3	87.9	277.0
1964	60.0	54.9	43.1	19.1	59.9	47.3	57.6	88.9	263.9
1965	61.9	55.8	43.4	18.7	61.6	47.7	58.8	88.5	268.7
1966	63.0	58.1	44.4	19.9	66.9	49.6	60.7	89.8	267.4
1967	62.1	57.3	42.2	19.4	66.9	49.7	59.2	88.5	257.4
1968	62.0	57.6	40.6	20.5	69.2	50.1	58.5	90.2	244.0
1969	61.8	57.8	40.2	20.0	71.8	51.2	58.4	86.6	232.0
1970	59.8	56.2	38.4	20.1	68.0	49.8	57.6	85.2	219.6
1971	58.1	54.8	37.7	20.1	66.1	48.4	54.7	82.7	213.2
1972	58.0	55.2	35.9	20.6	67.6	47.5	55.2	80.8	214.2
1973	57.1	54.8	35.8	20.6	68.2	48.0	53.3	77.3	206.3

See source and footnotes on page 51.

ALL INJURIES
Unintentional-Injury-Related Death Rates by Age (cont.)

Unintentional-injury-related death rates[a] by age, United States, 1903-2015 (cont.)

Year	Standardized rate[b]	All ages	Younger than 5 years	5-14 years	15-24 years	25-44 years	45-64 years	65-74 years	75 years and older[c]
1974	50.9	49.0	32.4	18.2	60.9	42.7	46.7	68.7	186.7
1975	49.3	47.8	30.7	17.8	59.5	42.3	44.9	66.2	175.5
1976	47.3	46.3	30.0	16.7	58.9	40.3	43.2	62.0	168.4
1977	47.6	47.0	28.7	17.0	61.3	40.9	43.4	61.5	164.0
1978	47.8	47.5	30.3	16.9	63.1	42.3	42.4	60.5	159.7
1979	47.0	46.9	27.6	16.1	62.6	42.7	41.3	58.8	154.8
1980	46.5	46.5	27.2	15.0	61.7	42.3	40.8	57.5	158.6
1981	44.0	43.9	24.4	14.2	55.9	41.2	39.0	54.4	147.4
1982	40.6	40.6	23.8	13.2	51.2	37.3	35.8	50.9	140.0
1983	39.6	39.6	22.8	12.7	48.2	36.0	34.7	50.8	142.8
1984	39.4	39.4	20.6	12.4	48.9	35.7	34.3	50.7	142.8
1985	39.2	39.3	21.0	12.6	47.9	35.3	34.2	50.9	143.0
1986	39.4	39.7	21.4	12.6	50.5	36.1	33.0	49.6	141.5
1987	39.0	39.2	21.4	12.4	48.1	35.7	33.0	49.8	141.6
1988	39.5	39.7	20.9	12.3	48.5	36.1	33.4	50.9	145.3
1989	38.4	38.5	20.4	11.8	44.8	35.7	32.8	49.3	141.5
1990	36.8	36.9	18.5	10.4	44.0	34.2	31.6	46.4	136.5
1991	35.3	35.4	18.9	10.2	42.0	32.3	29.3	44.5	136.7
1992	34.0	34.0	16.8	9.3	37.8	31.3	28.7	44.2	134.5
1993	35.0	35.1	17.7	9.4	38.8	33.0	29.1	43.6	139.9
1994	35.0	35.1	17.3	9.4	38.4	32.5	29.9	44.3	139.2
1995	35.0	35.5	15.7	9.3	38.2	33.2	30.6	44.8	140.6
1996	35.3	35.8	15.3	8.9	38.1	32.3	31.1	47.0	145.9
1997	35.1	35.7	14.5	8.7	36.5	32.5	31.6	46.3	146.2
1998	35.5	36.2	14.2	8.3	35.9	32.6	31.9	48.3	151.1
1999[e]	35.2	35.9	14.5	7.8	36.1	32.7	32.0	45.0	147.7
2000	34.8	35.6	14.3	7.5	36.7	33.0	32.3	42.3	140.8
2001	35.7	35.6	13.9	6.9	36.1	32.7	32.6	42.8	146.8
2002	37.1	37.1	13.2	6.6	37.9	34.7	34.6	44.2	148.2
2003	37.6	37.6	13.5	6.4	37.0	34.8	36.4	44.0	149.6
2004	38.1	38.1	13.4	6.5	37.1	35.1	37.6	43.9	151.4
2005	39.5	39.7	13.5	6.0	37.4	36.8	40.1	46.3	155.2
2006	40.4	40.8	13.5	5.6	38.5	38.9	41.6	44.5	154.4
2007	40.5	41.1	13.9	5.5	37.5	38.2	42.4	45.2	159.2
2008	39.4	40.0	13.2	4.6	32.8	36.8	42.6	44.7	162.8
2009	37.7	38.5	12.6	4.1	28.9	35.1	41.5	43.2	160.6
2010	38.1	39.0	11.7	4.0	28.6	35.3	41.7	44.1	168.2
2011	39.3	40.6	12.6	4.0	28.2	37.3	43.4	44.5	175.9
2012	39.1	40.7	12.6	3.8	27.1	37.3	43.7	47.0	178.3
2013	39.4	41.3	12.4	3.7	26.4	37.9	45.0	43.5	179.6
2014	40.4	42.7	12.0	3.6	26.9	39.8	46.3	45.1	183.5
2015	43.0	45.6	12.7	3.7	28.5	44.4	48.8	47.0	190.3
Changes									
2006 to 2015	12%	-6%	-34%	-26%	14%	17%	6%	23%	
2014 to 2015	7%	6%	3%	6%	12%	5%	4%	4%	
2015 population (thousands)									
Total[f]		321,419	19,907	41,110	43,848	84,727	84,066	27,550	20,210
Male		158,229	10,178	20,980	22,466	42,503	41,014	12,892	8,198
Female		163,190	9,730	20,130	21,382	42,224	43,052	14,658	12,012

Source: All figures are National Safety Council estimates. See Technical Appendix for comparability.
[a] Rates are deaths per 100,000 resident population in each age group.
[b] Adjusted to the year 2000 standard population to remove the influence of changes in age distribution between 1903 and 2015.
[c] Includes age unknown.
[d] In 1948, a revision was made in the International Classification of Diseases. The first figures for 1948 are comparable with those for earlier years, the second with those for later years.
[e] In 1999, a revision was made in the International Classification of Diseases. See the Technical Appendix for comparability.
[f] Sum of parts may not equal total due to rounding.

ALL INJURIES
Principal Types of Unintentional-Injury-Related Deaths

Principal types of unintentional-injury-related deaths, United States, 1903-1998

Year	Total	Motor vehicle	Falls	Drowning[a]	Fire, flames, or smoke[b]	Choking[b]	Firearms	Poison (solid or liquid)	Poison (gas or vapor)	All other
1903	70,600	[c]	[c]	9,200	[c]	[c]	2,500	[c]	[c]	58,900
1904	71,500	[c]	[c]	9,300	[c]	[c]	2,800	[c]	[c]	59,400
1905	70,900	[c]	[c]	9,300	[c]	[c]	2,000	[c]	[c]	59,600
1906	80,000	400	[c]	9,400	[c]	[c]	2,100	[c]	[c]	68,100
1907	81,900	700	[c]	9,000	[c]	[c]	1,700	[c]	[c]	70,500
1908	72,300	800	[c]	9,300	[c]	[c]	1,900	[c]	[c]	60,300
1909	72,700	1,300	[c]	8,500	[c]	[c]	1,600	[c]	[c]	61,300
1910	77,900	1,900	[c]	8,700	[c]	[c]	1,900	[c]	[c]	65,400
1911	79,300	2,300	[c]	9,000	[c]	[c]	2,100	[c]	[c]	65,900
1912	78,400	3,100	[c]	8,600	[c]	[c]	2,100	[c]	[c]	64,600
1913	82,500	4,200	15,100	10,300	8,900	[c]	2,400	3,200	[c]	38,400
1914	77,000	4,700	15,000	8,700	9,100	[c]	2,300	3,300	[c]	33,900
1915	76,200	6,600	15,000	8,600	8,400	[c]	2,100	2,800	[c]	32,700
1916	84,800	8,200	15,200	8,900	9,500	[c]	2,200	2,900	[c]	37,900
1917	90,100	10,200	15,200	7,600	10,800	[c]	2,300	2,800	[c]	41,200
1918	85,100	10,700	13,200	7,000	10,200	[c]	2,500	2,700	[c]	38,800
1919	75,500	11,200	11,900	9,100	9,100	[c]	2,800	3,100	[c]	28,300
1920	75,900	12,500	12,600	6,100	9,300	[c]	2,700	3,300	[c]	29,400
1921	74,000	13,900	12,300	7,800	7,500	[c]	2,800	2,900	[c]	26,800
1922	76,300	15,300	13,200	7,000	8,300	[c]	2,900	2,800	[c]	26,800
1923	84,400	18,400	14,100	6,800	9,100	[c]	2,900	2,800	2,700	27,600
1924	85,600	19,400	14,700	7,400	7,400	[c]	2,900	2,700	2,900	28,200
1925	90,000	21,900	15,500	7,300	8,600	[c]	2,800	2,700	2,800	28,400
1926	91,700	23,400	16,300	7,500	8,800	[c]	2,800	2,600	3,200	27,100
1927	92,700	25,800	16,500	8,100	8,200	[c]	3,000	2,600	2,700	25,800
1928	95,000	28,000	17,000	8,600	8,400	[c]	2,900	2,800	2,800	24,500
1929	98,200	31,200	17,700	7,600	8,200	[c]	3,200	2,600	2,800	24,900
1930	99,100	32,900	18,100	7,500	8,100	[c]	3,200	2,600	2,500	24,200
1931	97,300	33,700	18,100	7,600	7,100	[c]	3,100	2,600	2,100	23,000
1932	89,000	29,500	18,600	7,500	7,100	[c]	3,000	2,200	2,100	19,000
1933	90,932	31,363	18,962	7,158	6,781	[c]	3,014	2,135	1,633	19,886
1934	100,977	36,101	20,725	7,077	7,456	[c]	3,033	2,148	1,643	22,794
1935	99,773	36,369	21,378	6,744	7,253	[c]	2,799	2,163	1,654	21,413
1936	110,052	38,089	23,562	6,659	7,939	[c]	2,817	2,177	1,665	27,144
1937	105,205	39,643	22,544	7,085	7,214	[c]	2,576	2,190	1,675	22,278
1938	93,805	32,582	23,239	6,881	6,491	[c]	2,726	2,077	1,428	18,381
1939	92,623	32,386	23,427	6,413	6,675	[c]	2,618	1,963	1,440	17,701
1940	96,885	34,501	23,356	6,202	7,521	[c]	2,375	1,847	1,583	19,500
1941	101,513	39,969	22,764	6,389	6,922	[c]	2,396	1,731	1,464	19,878
1942	95,889	28,309	22,632	6,696	7,901	[c]	2,678	1,607	1,741	24,325
1943	99,038	23,823	24,701	7,115	8,726	921	2,282	1,745	2,014	27,711
1944	95,237	24,282	22,989	6,511	8,372	896	2,392	1,993	1,860	25,942
1945	95,918	28,076	23,847	6,624	7,949	897	2,385	1,987	2,120	22,033
1946	98,033	33,411	23,109	6,442	7,843	1,076	2,801	1,961	1,821	19,569
1947	99,579	32,697	24,529	6,885	8,033	1,206	2,439	1,865	1,865	14,060
1948 (5th Rev.)[d]	98,001	32,259	24,836	6,428	7,743	1,315	2,191	1,753	2,045	19,611
1948 (6th Rev.)[d]	93,000	32,259	22,000	6,500	6,800	1,299	2,330	1,600	2,020	17,192
1949	90,106	31,701	22,308	6,684	5,982	1,341	2,326	1,634	1,617	16,513
1950	91,249	34,763	20,783	6,131	6,405	1,350	2,174	1,584	1,769	16,290
1951	95,871	36,996	21,376	6,489	6,788	1,456	2,247	1,497	1,627	17,395
1952	96,172	37,794	20,945	6,601	6,922	1,434	2,210	1,440	1,397	17,429
1953	95,032	37,955	20,631	6,770	6,579	1,603	2,277	1,391	1,223	16,603
1954	90,032	35,586	19,771	6,334	6,083	1,627	2,271	1,339	1,223	15,798
1955	93,443	38,426	20,192	6,344	6,352	1,608	2,120	1,431	1,163	15,807
1956	94,780	39,628	20,282	6,263	6,405	1,760	2,202	1,422	1,213	15,605
1957	95,307	38,702	20,545	6,613	6,269	2,043	2,369	1,390	1,143	16,233
1958	90,604	36,981	18,248	6,582[e]	7,291[e]	2,191[e]	2,172	1,429	1,187	14,523
1959	92,080	37,910	18,774	6,434	6,898	2,189	2,258	1,661	1,141	14,815
1960	93,806	38,137	19,023	6,529	7,645	2,397	2,334	1,679	1,253	14,809
1961	92,249	38,091	18,691	6,525	7,102	2,499	2,204	1,804	1,192	14,141
1962	97,139	40,804	19,589	6,439	7,534	1,813	2,092	1,833	1,376	15,659
1963	100,669	43,564	19,335	6,347	8,172	1,949	2,263	2,061	1,489	15,489
1964	105,000	47,700	18,941	6,709	7,379	1,865	2,275	2,100	1,360	16,571
1965	108,004	49,163	19,984	6,799	7,347	1,836	2,344	2,110	1,526	16,895
1966	113,563	53,041	20,066	7,084	8,084	1,831	2,558	2,283	1,648	16,968
1967	113,169	52,924	20,120	7,076	7,423	1,980	2,896	2,506	1,574	16,670
1968	114,864	54,862	18,651	7,372[e]	7,335	3,100[e]	2,394[e]	2,583	1,526	17,041
1969	116,385	55,791	17,827	7,699	7,163	3,712	2,309	2,967	1,549	16,368
1970	114,638	54,633	16,926	7,860	6,718	2,753	2,406	3,679	1,620	18,043
1971	113,439	54,381	16,755	7,396	6,776	2,877	2,360	3,710	1,646	17,538
1972	115,448	56,278	16,744	7,586	6,714	2,830	2,442	3,728	1,690	17,436
1973	115,821	55,511	16,506	8,725	6,503	3,013	2,618	3,683	1,652	17,610

See source and footnotes on page 53.

ALL INJURIES
Principal Types of Unintentional-Injury-Related Deaths (cont.)

Principal types of unintentional-injury-related deaths, United States, 1903-1998 (cont.)

Year	Total	Motor vehicle	Falls	Drowning[a]	Fire, flames, or smoke[b]	Choking[b]	Firearms	Poison (solid or liquid)	Poison (gas or vapor)	All other
1974	104,622	46,402	16,339	7,876	6,236	2,991	2,513	4,016	1,518	16,731
1975	103,030	45,853	14,896	8,000	6,071	3,106	2,380	4,694	1,577	16,453
1976	100,761	47,038	14,136	6,827	6,338	3,033	2,059	4,161	1,569	15,600
1977	103,202	49,510	13,773	7,126	6,357	3,037	1,982	3,374	1,596	16,447
1978	105,561	52,411	13,690	7,026	6,163	3,063	1,806	3,035	1,737	16,630
1979	105,312	53,524	13,216	6,872	5,991	3,243	2,004	3,165	1,472	15,825
1980	105,718	53,172	13,294	7,257	5,822	3,249	1,955	3,089	1,242	16,638
1981	100,704	51,385	12,628	6,277	5,697	3,331	1,871	3,243	1,280	14,992
1982	94,082	45,779	12,077	6,351	5,210	3,254	1,756	3,474	1,259	14,922
1983	92,488	44,452	12,024	6,353	5,028	3,387	1,695	3,382	1,251	14,916
1984	92,911	46,263	11,937	5,388	5,010	3,541	1,668	3,808	1,103	14,193
1985	93,457	45,901	12,001	5,316	4,938	3,551	1,649	4,091	1,079	14,931
1986	95,277	47,865	11,444	5,700	4,835	3,692	1,452	4,731	1,009	14,549
1987	95,020	48,290	11,733	5,100	4,710	3,688	1,440	4,415	900	14,744
1988	97,100	49,078	12,096	4,966	4,965	3,805	1,501	5,353	873	14,463
1989	95,028	47,575	12,151	4,015	4,716	3,578	1,489	5,603	921	14,980
1990	91,983	46,814	12,313	4,685	4,175	3,303	1,416	5,055	748	13,474
1991	89,347	43,536	12,662	4,818	4,120	3,240	1,441	5,698	736	13,096
1992	86,777	40,982	12,646	3,542	3,958	3,182	1,409	6,449	633	13,976
1993	90,523	41,893	13,141	3,807	3,900	3,160	1,521	7,877	660	14,564
1994	91,437	42,524	13,450	3,942	3,986	3,065	1,356	8,309	685	14,120
1995	93,320	43,363	13,986	4,350	3,761	3,185	1,225	8,461	611	14,378
1996	94,948	43,649	14,986	3,959	3,741	3,206	1,134	8,872	638	14,763
1997	95,644	43,458	15,447	4,051	3,490	3,275	981	9,587	576	14,779
1998	97,835	43,501	16,274	4,406	3,255	3,515	866	10,255	546	15,217

Principal types of unintentional-injury-related deaths, United States, 1999-2015

Year	Total	Motor vehicle	Falls	Poisoning	Choking[b]	Drowning[f]	Fire, flames, or smoke[b]	Mechanical suffocation	Firearms	All other
1999[g]	97,860	42,401	13,162	12,186	3,885	3,529	3,348	1,618	824	16,907
2000	97,900	43,354	13,322	12,757	4,313	3,482	3,377	1,335	776	15,184
2001	101,537	43,788	15,019	14,078	4,185	3,281	3,309	1,370	802	15,705
2002	106,742	45,380	16,257	17,550	4,128	3,447	3,159	1,389	762	13,670
2003	109,277	44,757	17,229	19,457	4,272	3,306	3,369	1,309	730	14,850
2004	112,012	44,933	18,807	20,950	4,470	3,308	3,229	1,421	649	14,245
2005	117,809	45,343	19,656	23,617	4,386	3,582	3,197	1,514	789	15,725
2006	121,599	45,316	20,823	27,531	4,332	3,579	3,109	1,580	642	14,687
2007	123,706	43,945	22,631	29,846	4,344	3,443	3,286	1,653	613	14,558
2008	121,902	39,790	24,013	31,116	4,366	3,548	2,912	1,759	592	14,398
2009	118,046	36,216	24,792	31,758	4,370	3,517	2,756	1,569	554	13,068
2010	120,859	35,332	26,009	33,041	4,570	3,782	2,782	1,595	606	13,748
2011	126,438	35,303	27,483	36,280	4,708	3,556	2,746	1,534	591	14,237
2012	127,792	36,415	28,756	36,332	4,634	3,551	2,464	1,604	548	13,488
2013	130,557	35,369	30,208	38,851	4,864	3,391	2,760	1,737	505	12,872
2014	136,053	35,398	31,959	42,032	4,816	3,406	2,701	1,764	586	13,391
2015	146,571	37,757	33,381	47,478	5,051	3,602	2,646	1,863	489	14,304
Changes										
2006 to 2015	21%	-17%	60%	72%	17%	1%	-15%	18%	-24%	-3%
2014 to 2015	8%	7%	4%	13%	5%	6%	-2%	6%	-17%	7%

Source: National Center for Health Statistics and National Safety Council. See Technical Appendix for comparability.
[a] Includes drowning in water transport incidents.
[b] Fires, flames, or smoke includes burns by fire and deaths resulting from conflagration regardless of nature of injury. Choking is the inhalation of food or other object obstructing breathing.
[c] Comparable data not available.
[d] In 1948, a revision was made in the International Classification of Diseases. The first figures for 1948 are comparable with those for earlier years, the second with those for later years.
[e] Data are not comparable to previous years shown due to classification changes in 1958 and 1968.
[f] Excludes water transport drownings.
[g] In 1999, a revision was made in the International Classification of Diseases. See the Technical Appendix for comparability.

ALL INJURIES

Unintentional-Injury-Related Death Rates for Principal Types

Unintentional-injury-related death rates[a] for principal types, United States, 1903-1998

Year	Total	Motor vehicle	Falls	Drowning[b]	Fire, flames, or smoke[c]	Choking[c]	Firearms	Poison (solid or liquid)	Poison (gas or vapor)	All other
1903	87.2	[d]	[d]	11.4	[d]	[d]	3.1	[d]	[d]	72.7
1904	86.6	[d]	[d]	11.3	[d]	[d]	3.4	[d]	[d]	71.9
1905	84.2	[d]	[d]	11.1	[d]	[d]	2.4	[d]	[d]	70.7
1906	93.2	0.5	[d]	11.0	[d]	[d]	2.4	[d]	[d]	79.3
1907	93.6	0.8	[d]	10.4	[d]	[d]	2.0	[d]	[d]	80.4
1908	81.2	0.9	[d]	10.5	[d]	[d]	2.1	[d]	[d]	67.7
1909	80.1	1.4	[d]	9.4	[d]	[d]	1.8	[d]	[d]	67.5
1910	84.4	2.0	[d]	9.4	[d]	[d]	2.1	[d]	[d]	70.9
1911	84.7	2.5	[d]	9.6	[d]	[d]	2.2	[d]	[d]	70.4
1912	82.5	3.3	[d]	9.0	[d]	[d]	2.2	[d]	[d]	68.0
1913	85.5	4.4	15.5	10.6	9.1	[d]	2.5	3.3	[d]	40.1
1914	78.6	4.8	15.1	8.8	9.1	[d]	2.3	3.3	[d]	35.2
1915	76.7	6.6	14.9	8.6	8.4	[d]	2.1	2.8	[d]	33.3
1916	84.1	8.1	14.9	8.7	9.3	[d]	2.2	2.8	[d]	38.1
1917	88.2	10.0	14.7	7.4	10.5	[d]	2.2	2.7	[d]	40.7
1918	82.1	10.3	12.8	6.8	9.9	[d]	2.4	2.6	[d]	37.3
1919	71.9	10.7	11.4	6.9	8.7	[d]	2.7	3.0	[d]	28.5
1920	71.2	11.7	11.8	5.7	8.7	[d]	2.5	3.1	[d]	27.7
1921	68.4	12.9	11.3	7.2	6.9	[d]	2.6	2.7	[d]	24.8
1922	69.4	13.9	12.0	6.4	7.5	[d]	2.6	2.5	[d]	24.5
1923	75.7	16.5	12.6	6.1	8.1	[d]	2.6	2.5	2.4	24.9
1924	75.6	17.1	12.9	6.5	8.4	[d]	2.5	2.4	2.5	23.3
1925	78.4	19.1	13.4	6.3	7.4	[d]	2.4	2.3	2.4	25.1
1926	78.7	20.1	13.9	6.4	7.5	[d]	2.4	2.2	2.7	23.5
1927	78.4	21.8	13.9	6.8	6.9	[d]	2.5	2.2	2.3	22.0
1928	79.3	23.4	14.1	7.1	7.0	[d]	2.4	2.3	2.3	20.7
1929	80.8	25.7	14.5	6.2	6.7	[d]	2.6	2.1	2.3	20.7
1930	80.5	26.7	14.7	6.1	6.6	[d]	2.6	2.1	2.0	19.7
1931	78.5	27.2	14.6	6.1	5.7	[d]	2.5	2.1	1.7	18.6
1932	71.3	23.6	14.9	6.0	5.7	[d]	2.4	1.8	1.7	15.2
1933	72.4	25.0	15.1	5.7	5.4	[d]	2.4	1.7	1.3	15.8
1934	79.9	28.6	16.4	5.6	5.9	[d]	2.4	1.7	1.3	18.0
1935	78.4	28.6	16.8	5.3	5.7	[d]	2.2	1.7	1.3	16.8
1936	85.9	29.7	18.4	5.2	6.2	[d]	2.2	1.7	1.3	21.2
1937	81.7	30.8	17.5	5.5	5.6	[d]	2.0	1.7	1.3	17.3
1938	72.3	25.1	17.9	5.3	5.0	[d]	2.1	1.6	1.1	14.2
1939	70.8	24.7	17.9	4.9	5.1	[d]	2.0	1.5	1.1	13.6
1940	73.4	26.1	17.7	4.7	5.7	[d]	1.8	1.4	1.2	14.8
1941	76.3	30.0	17.1	4.8	5.2	[d]	1.8	1.3	1.1	15.0
1942	71.6	21.1	16.9	5.0	5.9	[d]	2.0	1.2	1.3	18.2
1943	73.8	17.8	18.4	5.3	6.5	0.7	1.7	1.3	1.5	20.6
1944	71.7	18.3	17.3	4.9	6.3	0.7	1.8	1.5	1.4	19.5
1945	72.4	21.2	18.0	5.0	6.0	0.7	1.8	1.5	1.6	16.6
1946	70.0	23.9	16.5	4.6	5.6	0.8	2.0	1.4	1.3	13.9
1947	69.4	22.8	17.1	4.8	5.6	0.8	1.7	1.3	1.3	14.0
1948 (5th Rev.)[e]	67.1	22.1	17.0	4.4	5.3	0.9	1.5	1.2	1.4	13.3
1948 (6th Rev.)[e]	63.7	22.1	15.1	4.5	4.7	0.9	1.6	1.1	1.4	12.3
1949	60.6	21.3	15.0	4.5	4.0	0.9	1.6	1.1	1.1	11.1
1950	60.3	23.0	13.7	4.1	4.2	0.9	1.4	1.1	1.2	10.7
1951	62.5	24.1	13.9	4.2	4.4	1.0	1.5	1.0	1.1	11.3
1952	61.8	24.3	13.5	4.2	4.5	0.9	1.4	0.9	0.9	11.2
1953	60.1	24.0	13.0	4.3	4.2	1.0	1.4	0.9	0.8	10.2
1954	55.9	22.1	12.3	3.9	3.8	1.0	1.4	0.8	0.8	9.8
1955	56.9	23.4	12.3	3.9	3.9	1.0	1.3	0.9	0.7	9.5
1956	56.6	23.7	12.1	3.7	3.8	1.1	1.3	0.8	0.7	9.4
1957	55.9	22.7	12.1	3.9	3.7	1.2	1.4	0.8	0.7	9.4
1958	52.3	21.3	10.5	3.8[f]	4.2[f]	1.3[f]	1.3	0.8	0.7	8.4
1959	52.2	21.5	10.6	3.7	3.9	1.2	1.3	0.9	0.7	8.4
1960	52.1	21.2	10.6	3.6	4.3	1.3	1.3	0.9	0.7	8.2
1961	50.4	20.8	10.2	3.6	3.9	1.4	1.2	1.0	0.7	7.6
1962	52.3	22.0	10.5	3.5	4.1	1.0	1.1	1.0	0.7	8.4
1963	53.4	23.1	10.3	3.4	4.3	1.0	1.2	1.1	0.8	8.2
1964	54.9	25.0	9.9	3.5	3.9	1.0	1.2	1.1	0.7	8.4
1965	55.8	25.4	10.3	3.5	3.8	1.0	1.2	1.1	0.8	8.7
1966	58.1	27.1	10.3	3.6	4.8	0.9	1.3	1.2	0.8	8.1
1967	57.3	26.8	10.2	3.6	3.8	1.0	1.5	1.3	0.8	8.3
1968	57.6	27.5	9.4	3.7[f]	3.7[f]	1.6[f]	1.2[f]	1.3	0.8	8.4
1969	57.8	27.7	8.9	3.8	3.6	1.8	1.2	1.5	0.8	8.5
1970	56.2	26.8	8.3	3.9	3.3	1.4	1.2	1.8	0.8	8.7
1971	54.8	26.3	8.1	3.6	3.3	1.4	1.1	1.8	0.8	8.4
1972	55.2	26.9	8.0	3.6	3.2	1.4	1.2	1.8	0.8	8.3
1973	54.8	26.3	7.8	4.1	3.1	1.4	1.2	1.7	0.8	8.4

See source and footnotes on page 55.

ALL INJURIES

Unintentional-Injury-Related Death Rates for Principal Types (cont.)

Unintentional-injury-related death rates[a] for principal types, United States, 1903-1998 (cont.)

Year	Total	Motor vehicle	Falls	Drowning[b]	Fire, flames, or smoke[c]	Choking[c]	Firearms	Poison (solid or liquid)	Poison (gas or vapor)	All other
1974	49.0	21.8	7.7	3.7	2.9	1.4	1.2	1.8	0.7	7.8
1975	47.8	21.3	6.9	3.7	2.8	1.4	1.1	2.2	0.7	7.7
1976	46.3	21.6	6.5	3.1	2.9	1.4	0.9	1.9	0.7	7.3
1977	47.0	22.5	6.3	3.2	2.9	1.4	0.9	1.5	0.7	7.6
1978	47.5	23.6	6.2	3.2	2.8	1.4	0.8	1.4	0.8	7.3
1979	46.9	23.8	5.9	3.1	2.7	1.4	0.9	1.4	0.7	7.0
1980	46.5	23.4	5.9	3.2	2.6	1.4	0.9	1.4	0.5	7.2
1981	43.9	22.4	5.5	2.7	2.5	1.5	0.8	1.4	0.6	6.5
1982	40.6	19.8	5.2	2.7	2.2	1.4	0.8	1.5	0.5	6.5
1983	39.6	19.0	5.1	2.7	2.2	1.4	0.7	1.4	0.5	6.6
1984	39.4	19.6	5.1	2.3	2.1	1.5	0.7	1.6	0.5	6.0
1985	39.3	19.3	5.0	2.2	2.1	1.5	0.7	1.7	0.5	6.3
1986	39.7	19.9	4.8	2.4	2.0	1.5	0.6	2.0	0.4	6.1
1987	39.2	19.9	4.8	2.1	1.9	1.5	0.6	1.8	0.4	6.2
1988	39.7	20.1	4.9	2.0	2.0	1.6	0.6	2.2	0.4	5.9
1989	38.5	19.3	4.9	1.9	1.9	1.4	0.6	2.3	0.4	5.8
1990	36.9	18.8	4.9	1.9	1.7	1.3	0.6	2.0	0.3	5.4
1991	35.4	17.3	5.0	1.8	1.6	1.3	0.6	2.3	0.3	5.2
1992	34.0	16.1	5.0	1.4	1.6	1.2	0.6	2.5	0.2	5.4
1993	35.1	16.3	5.1	1.5	1.5	1.2	0.6	3.1	0.3	5.5
1994	35.1	16.3	5.2	1.5	1.5	1.2	0.5	3.2	0.3	5.4
1995	35.5	16.5	5.3	1.7	1.4	1.2	0.5	3.2	0.2	5.5
1996	35.8	16.5	5.6	1.5	1.4	1.2	0.4	3.3	0.2	5.7
1997	35.7	16.2	5.8	1.5	1.3	1.2	0.4	3.6	0.2	5.5
1998	36.2	16.1	6.0	1.6	1.2	1.3	0.3	3.8	0.2	5.7

Unintentional-injury-related death rates[a] for principal types, United States, 1999-2015

Year	Total	Motor vehicle	Falls	Poisoning	Choking[c]	Drowning[g]	Fire, flames, or smoke[c]	Mechanical suffocation	Firearms	All other
1999[h]	35.9	15.5	4.8	4.5	1.4	1.3	1.2	0.6	0.3	6.3
2000	35.6	15.7	4.8	4.6	1.6	1.3	1.2	0.5	0.3	5.5
2001	35.6	15.4	5.3	4.9	1.5	1.2	1.2	0.5	0.3	5.5
2002	37.1	15.8	5.6	6.4	1.4	1.2	1.1	0.5	0.3	4.7
2003	37.6	15.4	5.9	6.7	1.5	1.1	1.2	0.4	0.3	5.1
2004	38.1	15.3	6.4	7.1	1.5	1.1	1.1	0.5	0.2	4.9
2005	39.7	15.3	6.6	8.0	1.5	1.2	1.1	0.5	0.3	5.3
2006	40.8	15.2	7.0	9.2	1.5	1.2	1.0	0.5	0.2	4.9
2007	41.1	14.6	7.5	9.9	1.4	1.1	1.1	0.5	0.2	4.8
2008	40.0	13.1	7.9	10.2	1.4	1.2	1.0	0.6	0.2	4.7
2009	38.5	11.8	8.1	10.3	1.4	1.1	0.9	0.5	0.2	4.1
2010	39.0	11.4	8.4	10.7	1.5	1.2	0.9	0.5	0.2	4.4
2011	40.6	11.3	8.8	11.6	1.5	1.1	0.9	0.5	0.2	4.6
2012	40.7	11.6	9.2	11.6	1.5	1.1	0.8	0.5	0.2	4.3
2013	41.3	11.2	9.6	12.3	1.5	1.1	0.9	0.5	0.2	4.1
2014	42.7	11.1	10.0	13.2	1.5	1.1	0.8	0.6	0.2	4.2
2015	45.6	11.7	10.4	14.8	1.6	1.1	0.8	0.6	0.2	4.5
Changes										
2006 to 2015	12%	-23%	49%	61%	7%	-8%	-20%	20%	0%	-8%
2014 to 2015	7%	5%	4%	12%	7%	0%	0%	0%	0%	7%

Source: National Safety Council estimates. See Technical Appendix for comparability.
[a] Deaths per 100,000 population.
[b] Includes drowning in water transport incidents.
[c] Fires, flames, or smoke includes burns by fire and deaths resulting from conflagration regardless of nature of injury. Choking is the inhalation of food or other object obstructing breathing.
[d] Comparable data not available.
[e] In 1948, a revision was made in the International Classification of Diseases. The first figures for 1948 are comparable with those for earlier years, the second with those for later years.
[f] Data are not comparable to previous years shown due to classification changes in 1958 and 1968.
[g] Excludes water transport drownings.
[h] In 1999, a revision was made in the International Classification of Diseases. See the Technical Appendix for comparability.

INJURY FACTS® 2017 EDITION   NATIONAL SAFETY COUNCIL® ■ 55

Occupational

Occupational Highlights

Costs — pg. 62

NEW! Transportation-related injuries — pg. 65

Workers' compensation — pgs. 66-67

Falls — pgs. 69-71

NEW! Fatigue — pg. 72

Industry rate — pgs. 80-82

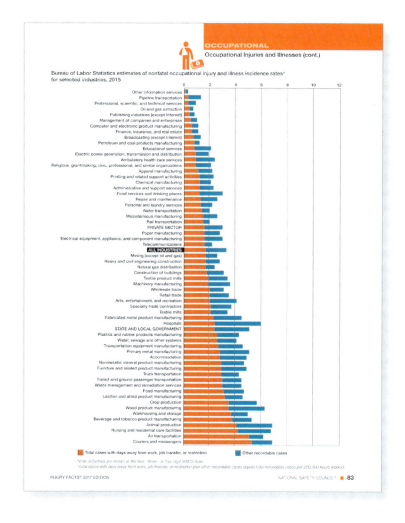

 # INJURY FACTS® 2017

Fatigue — pg. 72

Analysis of National Health Interview Survey data by Luckhaupt (2010) assessed the prevalence of short sleep duration by industry. This analysis found that, on average, 30% of civilian employed workers from 2004 to 2007 received six or less hours of sleep a day. Short sleep duration was most prevalent among management companies and enterprises (40%), followed by transportation and warehousing (37%). Concerningly, the prevalence of short sleep duration appears to be getting worse. In a combined sample from 1985 and 1990, only 24% of workers reported short sleep duration.

OCCUPATIONAL

Work, 2015

All Census of Fatal Occupational Injuries fatal injury rates published by the Bureau of Labor Statistics (BLS) for the years 1992-2007 were employment-based, and measured the risk of fatal injury for those employed during a given period of time, regardless of hours worked. Starting in 2008, BLS moved to hours-based rates to measure fatal injury risk per standardized length of exposure, which are generally considered more accurate than employment-based rates. Caution should be used when comparing fatality rates prior to 2008.

In addition to unintentional fatal work injuries, 646 homicides and suicides occurred in the workplace in 2015. These intentional injuries are not included in the unintentional-injury data shown here.

The State Data section, which begins on page 171, shows fatal occupational injuries and nonfatal injury and illness incidence rates by state.

Unintentional-injury-related deaths	4,190
Unintentional-injury-related deaths per 100,000 full-time equivalent workers[a]	3.0
Medically consulted injuries	4,400,000
Workers	150,031,000
Costs	$142.5 billion

Unintentional injuries at work by industry (preliminary), United States, 2015

Industry division	Hours worked[a] (millions)	Deaths[a] 2015	Deaths[a] Change from 2014	Deaths per 100,000 full-time equivalent workers[a] 2015	Deaths per 100,000 full-time equivalent workers[a] Change from 2014	Medically consulted injuries[c]
All industries	277,470	4,190	1%	3.0	0%	4,400,000
Agriculture[b]	4,859	548	-3%	22.6	-11%	130,000
Mining[b]	2,104	119	-34%	11.3	-20%	10,000
Construction	18,562	908	6%	9.8	3%	320,000
Manufacturing	31,180	316	1%	2.0	0%	530,000
Wholesale trade	7,413	156	-9%	4.2	-9%	110,000
Retail trade	29,203	142	10%	1.0	11%	500,000
Transportation and warehousing	11,027	707	1%	12.8	0%	240,000
Utilities	1,956	22	57%	2.2	57%	20,000
Information	5,509	35	6%	1.3	18%	30,000
Financial activities	19,220	60	-18%	0.6	-25%	100,000
Professional and business services	32,205	420	17%	2.6	13%	210,000
Educational and health services	41,469	108	-8%	0.5	-17%	790,000
Leisure and hospitality	22,148	139	-4%	1.3	-7%	370,000
Other services[b]	12,656	153	11%	2.4	9%	150,000
Government	37,789	357	7%	1.9	6%	910,000

Source: Deaths are final data from the Bureau of Labor Statistics (BLS) Census of Fatal Occupational Injuries. All other figures are National Safety Council estimates based on data from BLS.

[a] Deaths include persons of all ages. Workers and death rates include persons 16 years and older. The rate is calculated as: (number of fatal work injuries x 200,000,000/total hours worked). The base for 100,000 full-time equivalent workers is 200,000,000 hours. Prior to 2008, rates were based on estimated employment – not hours worked.
[b] Agriculture includes forestry, fishing, and hunting. Mining includes oil and gas extraction. "Other services" excludes public administration.
[c] See Technical Appendix for the definition of medically consulted injury.

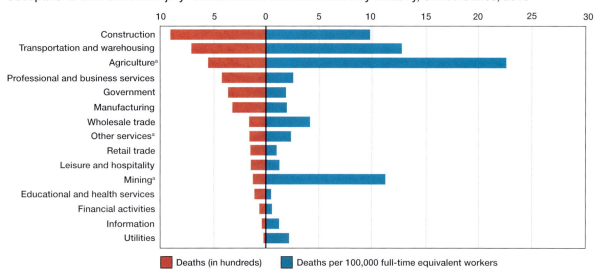

Occupational unintentional-injury-related deaths and death rates by industry, United States, 2015

[a] Agriculture includes forestry, fishing, and hunting. Mining includes oil and gas extraction. "Other services" excludes public administration.

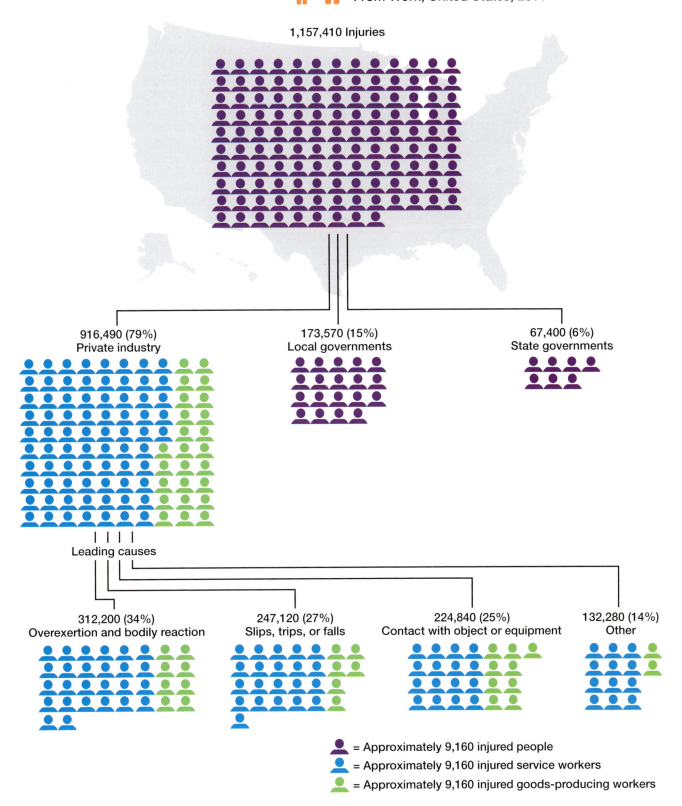

OCCUPATIONAL
Work, 2015 (cont.)

Unintentional-work-related-injury deaths and death rates, United States, 1992-2015

Year	Deaths	Workers (in thousands)	Hours worked[a] (in millions)	Deaths per 100,000 workers[a]
1992	4,965	119,168		4.2
1993	5,034	120,778		4.2
1994	5,338	124,470		4.3
1995	5,015	126,248		4.0
1996	5,069	127,997		4.0
1997	5,160	130,810		3.9
1998	5,117	132,772		3.9
1999	5,184	134,688		3.8
2000	5,022	136,402		3.7
2001	5,042	136,246		3.7
2002	4,726	137,731		3.4
2003	4,725	138,988		3.4
2004	4,995	140,504		3.6
2005	4,984	142,946		3.5
2006	5,088	145,607		3.5
2007	4,829	147,203		3.3
2008[a]	4,423	146,535	271,958	3.3[a]
2009	3,744	141,102	254,771	2.9
2010	3,896	140,298	255,948	3.0
2011	3,901	140,298	258,293	3.0
2012	3,903	143,709	264,374	3.0
2013	3,899	145,171	268,127	2.9
2014[b]	4,132	146,307	272,663	3.0
2015	4,190	150,031	277,470	3.0

Source: Deaths are from the Bureau of Labor Statistics (BLS) Census of Fatal Occupational Injuries (CFOI). Employment is from BLS and is based on the Current Population Survey. All other data are National Safety Council estimates.
Note: Deaths include persons of all ages. Workers and death rates include persons 16 and older. Workers are persons 16 years and older who are gainfully employed, including owners, managers, other paid employees, the self-employed, unpaid family workers, and active-duty resident military personnel. Because of adoption of CFOI, deaths and rates from 1992 to present are not comparable to prior years. See the Technical Appendix for additional information.
[a]Starting in 2008, BLS moved from employment-based rates to hours-based rates to measure fatal injury risk per standardized length of exposure, which are generally considered more accurate than employment-based rates. Caution should be used when comparing with rates prior to 2008.
[b]Revised.

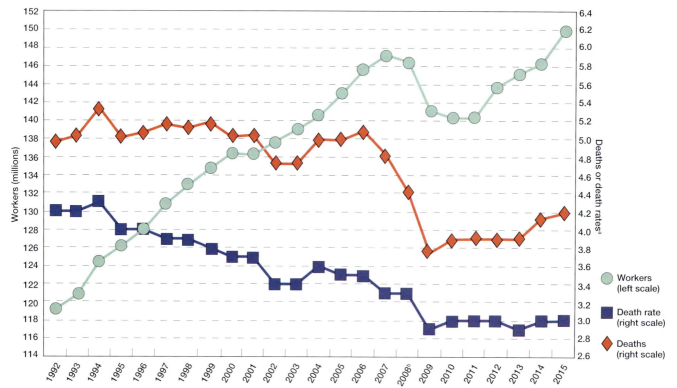

Workers, unintentional-work-related-injury deaths, and death rates, United States, 1992-2015

[a]Deaths in thousands; rate per 100,000 workers.
[b]Starting in 2008, the Bureau of Labor Statistics changed from an employment-based rate to an hours-based rate.

OCCUPATIONAL
Work, 2015 (cont.)

Occupational injury-related deaths and death rates, United States, 1994-2002

Year	Total	Homicide and suicide	Unintentional All industries[a]	Agriculture[b]	Mining, quarrying[c]	Construction	Manufacturing	Transportation and public utilities	Trade[d]	Services[e]	Government
Deaths											
1994	6,632	1,294	5,338	814	177	1,000	734	819	492	676	534
1995	6,275	1,260	5,015	769	155	1,021	640	784	461	608	528
1996	6,202	1,133	5,069	762	151	1,025	660	883	451	615	321
1997	6,238	1,078	5,160	799	156	1,075	678	882	451	593	504
1998	6,055	938	5,117	808	143	1,136	631	830	443	634	465
1999	6,054	870	5,184	776	122	1,168	671	918	425	623	451
2000	5,920	898	5,022	693	153	1,114	624	872	447	643	460
2001	5,915	873[f]	5,042	714	169	1,183	546	844	431	636	507
2002	5,534	808	4,726	758	120	1,092	523	843	381	569	437
Deaths per 100,000 workers											
1994	5.3	1.0	4.3	22.8	26.5	14.4	3.7	11.6	1.9	1.7	2.7
1995	4.9	1.0	4.0	21.4	24.8	14.3	3.1	11.0	1.8	1.5	2.7
1996	4.8	0.9	4.0	21.2	26.6	13.7	3.2	12.2	1.7	1.4	1.6
1997	4.8	0.8	3.9	22.5	24.7	13.7	3.3	11.6	1.7	1.3	2.6
1998	4.5	0.7	3.9	22.7	23.1	14.1	3.1	10.8	1.6	1.4	2.4
1999	4.5	0.6	3.8	22.6	21.7	13.8	3.4	11.5	1.5	1.3	2.2
2000	4.3	0.7	3.7	20.1	29.4	12.4	3.1	10.8	1.6	1.4	2.3
2001	4.3	0.6[f]	3.7	22.0	29.9	13.0	2.9	10.4	1.6	1.3	2.5
2002	4.0	0.6	3.4	21.8	23.3	11.9	2.9	10.5	1.4	1.1	2.1

Source: Deaths are from the Bureau of Labor Statistics (BLS) Census of Fatal Occupational Injuries. Rates are National Safety Council estimates based on BLS employment data. Deaths include persons of all ages. Death rates include persons 16 years and older. Industry divisions are based on the Standard Industrial Classification Manual.
[a] Includes deaths with industry unknown.
[b] Agriculture includes forestry, fishing, and agricultural services.
[c] Mining includes oil and gas extraction.
[d] Trade includes wholesale and retail trade.
[e] Services includes finance, insurance, and real estate.
[f] Excludes 2,886 homicides of workers on Sept. 11, 2001.

Occupational injury-related deaths and death rates, United States, 2003-2015

Year	Total	Homicide and suicide	Unintentional All industries[a]	Agriculture, forestry, fishing, and hunting	Mining	Construction	Manufacturing	Wholesale trade	Retail trade	Transportation and warehousing	Utilities	Information	Financial activities	Professional and business services	Educational and health services	Leisure and hospitality	Other services	Government
Deaths																		
2003	5,575	850	4,725	676	141	1,094	379	169	148	735	29	57	82	396	116	142	123	434
2004	5,764	769	4,995	651	151	1,203	421	187	189	779	49	49	68	401	123	144	144	432
2005	5,734	750	4,984	697	154	1,161	357	197	198	831	28	56	66	442	122	114	149	404
2006	5,840	752	5,088	635	190	1,199	423	210	190	803	52	61	82	407	142	136	142	409
2007	5,657	828	4,829	564	180	1,163	364	193	160	819	33	70	69	415	121	138	116	421
2008	5,214	791	4,423	640	173	937	364	157	158	724	37	36	65	351	110	118	130	414
2009	4,551	807	3,744	545	96	793	290	168	137	576	13	28	58	363	101	119	110	347
2010	4,690	794	3,896	603	170	744	284	157	148	595	26	32	65	316	133	142	131	350
2011	4,692	791	3,901	532	148	706	293	173	133	692	34	47	49	374	109	137	122	352
2012	4,628	725	3,903	500	177	775	284	185	149	670	22	31	56	360	106	136	122	327
2013	4,585	686	3,899	479	155	799	280	179	140	670	24	34	50	369	105	110	136	371
2014[b]	4,821	689	4,132	565	181	860	312	172	129	699	14	33	73	359	117	145	138	335
2015	4,836	646	4,190	548	119	908	316	156	142	707	22	35	60	420	108	139	153	357
Deaths per 100,000 workers[c]																		
2003	4.0	0.6	3.4	30.0	26.9	11.4	2.3	3.8	0.9	16.0	3.3	1.6	0.9	2.9	0.6	1.3	1.8	2.1
2004	4.1	0.5	3.6	29.7	28.1	11.7	2.6	4.1	1.2	16.7	5.9	1.5	0.7	2.9	0.7	1.3	2.1	2.0
2005	4.0	0.5	3.5	31.7	24.8	10.8	2.2	4.3	1.2	16.7	3.4	1.7	0.7	3.2	0.6	1.0	2.1	1.9
2006	4.0	0.5	3.5	29.1	27.8	10.6	2.6	4.6	1.1	15.7	6.2	1.8	0.8	2.8	0.7	1.2	2.0	1.9
2007	3.8	0.5	3.3	26.9	24.7	10.2	2.2	4.4	1.0	15.6	3.9	2.1	0.7	2.7	0.6	1.2	1.7	1.9
2008[c]	3.8	0.6	3.3	29.4	17.8	9.4	2.3	3.8	1.1	13.6	4.0	1.1	0.7	2.4	0.6	1.1	2.1	2.1
2009	3.6	0.6	2.9	26.3	12.2	9.5	2.1	4.4	1.0	12.1	1.4	1.0	0.6	2.7	0.5	1.2	1.8	1.8
2010	3.7	0.6	3.0	27.9	19.6	9.4	2.0	4.1	1.1	12.4	2.8	1.1	0.7	2.3	0.7	1.4	2.2	1.8
2011	3.6	0.6	3.0	24.1	15.2	8.8	2.0	4.5	1.0	14.2	3.7	1.6	0.6	2.6	0.5	1.4	2.1	1.9
2012	3.5	0.5	3.0	23.1	15.6	9.6	1.9	4.9	1.1	13.2	2.5	1.1	0.6	2.4	0.5	1.3	2.0	1.8
2013	3.4	0.5	2.9	22.6	12.4	9.4	1.9	4.8	1.0	12.8	2.7	1.2	0.5	2.4	0.5	1.0	2.2	2.0
2014[b]	3.5	0.5	3.0	25.3	14.1	9.5	2.0	4.6	0.9	12.8	1.4	1.1	0.8	2.3	0.6	1.4	2.2	1.8
2015	3.5	0.5	3.0	22.6	11.3	9.8	2.0	4.2	1.0	12.8	2.2	1.3	0.6	2.6	0.5	1.3	2.4	1.9

Source: Deaths are from the Bureau of Labor Statistics (BLS) Census of Fatal Occupational Injuries. Rates are National Safety Council estimates based on BLS employment data. Deaths include persons of all ages. Death rates include persons 16 years and older. Industry sectors are based on the North American Industry Classification System.
[a] Includes deaths with industry unknown.
[b] Revised.
[c] Starting in 2008, BLS moved from employment-based rates to hours-based rates to measure fatal injury risk per standardized length of exposure. Caution should be used when comparing with rates prior to 2008.

INJURY FACTS® 2017 EDITION — NATIONAL SAFETY COUNCIL® — 61

OCCUPATIONAL
Work Injury Costs

The true cost to the nation, employers, and individuals of work-related deaths and injuries is much greater than the cost of workers' compensation insurance alone. The figures presented below show National Safety Council estimates of the total economic costs of occupational deaths and injuries. Major revisions were made to the National Safety Council cost model starting with the 2016 edition that take advantage of data sources not previously available. Because of the changes made to the cost model, cost estimates provided prior to the 2016 edition are not comparable to current estimates. For this reason, **costs should not be compared to prior years.**

TOTAL COST IN 2015 .... **$142.5 Billion**
Includes wage and productivity losses of $45.8 billion, medical costs of $31.4 billion, and administrative expenses of $46.1 billion. Includes employers' uninsured costs of $11.3 billion, such as the money value of time lost by workers other than those with disabling injuries; who are directly or indirectly involved in injuries; and the cost of time required to investigate injuries, write up injury reports, etc. Also includes damage to motor vehicles in work-related injuries of $3.6 billion and fire losses of $4.3 billion.

COST PER WORKER **$900**
Includes the value of goods or services each worker must produce to offset the cost of work injuries. It is *not* the average cost of a work-related injury.

COST PER DEATH **$1,000,000**

COST PER MEDICALLY CONSULTED INJURY **$31,000**
Includes estimates of wage losses, medical expenses, administrative expenses, and employer costs; excludes property damage costs except to motor vehicles.

OCCUPATIONAL
Time Lost Due to Work-Related Injuries

                                                                           Days lost
TOTAL TIME LOST IN 2015 ....**100,000,000**
Due to injuries in 2015 ....**65,000,000**
Includes primarily the actual time lost during the year from disabling injuries, except it does not include time lost on the day of the injury or time required for further medical treatment or check-up following the injured person's return to work.

    Fatalities are included at an average loss of 150 days per case, and permanent impairments are included at actual days lost plus an allowance for lost efficiency resulting from the impairment.

    Not included is time lost by people with nondisabling injuries or other people directly or indirectly involved in the incidents.

                                                                             Days lost
Due to injuries in prior years **35,000,000**
Represents productive time lost in 2015 due to permanently disabling injuries that occurred in prior years.

TIME LOST IN FUTURE YEARS   **Days lost**
FROM 2015 INJURIES **50,000,000**
Includes time lost in future years due to on-the-job deaths and permanently disabling injuries that occurred in 2015.

OCCUPATIONAL
Worker Deaths and Injuries On and Off the Job

More than nine out of 10 deaths and about 77% of the medically consulted injuries[a] suffered by workers in 2015 occurred off the job. While over 15 times the number of deaths occur off the job compared to on the job (15.2 to 1), over three times as many medically consulted injuries occur off the job (3.5 to 1).

Production time lost due to off-the-job injuries totaled about 295,000,000 days in 2015, compared with 65,000,000 days lost by workers injured on the job.

Production time lost in future years due to off-the-job injuries in 2015 will total an estimated 625,000,000 days, over 12 times the 50,000,000 days lost in future years from 2015's on-the-job injuries.

Off-the-job injuries to workers cost the nation at least $358.3 billion in 2015 compared with $142.5 billion for on-the-job injuries.

Workers' on- and off-the-job deaths and injuries, United States, 2015

	Deaths		Medically consulted injuries[a]	
Place	Number	Rate[b]	Number	Rate[b]
On and off the job	67,990	0.015	19,800,000	4.5
On the job	4,190	0.003	4,400,000	2.7
Off the job	63,800	0.022	15,400,000	5.4
Motor vehicle	19,500	0.065	2,200,000	7.3
Public non-motor vehicle	11,300	0.024	4,000,000	8.6
Home	33,000	0.016	9,200,000	4.4

Source: National Safety Council estimates. Procedures for allocating time spent on and off the job were revised for the 1990 edition. Rate basis changed to 200,000 hours for the 1998 edition. Death and injury rates are not comparable to rate estimates prior to the 1998 edition.
[a] Medically consulted injuries are not comparable to estimates provided in earlier editions that used the definition of disabling injury. Please see the Technical Appendix for more information on medically consulted injuries.
[b] Per 200,000 hours exposure by place.

Workers' on- and off-the-job deaths and injuries, United States, 2015

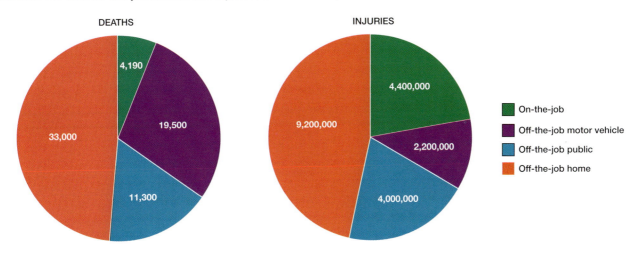

Workers' off-the-job fatalities by event, 2015

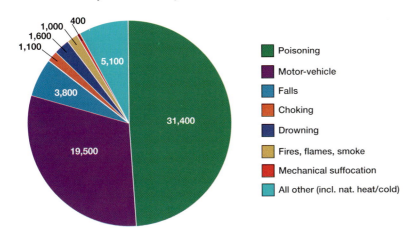

INJURY FACTS® 2017 EDITION   NATIONAL SAFETY COUNCIL®   ■   **63**

OCCUPATIONAL

Workers' Compensation Cases

According to the National Academy of Social Insurance, an estimated $62.3 billion, including benefits under deductible provisions, was paid out under workers' compensation in 2014 (the latest year for which data were available) – a decrease of 0.3% from 2013. Of this total, $30.9 billion was for income benefits and $31.4 billion was for medical and hospitalization costs. Private carriers paid about $34.3 billion of the total workers' compensation benefits in 2014. In 2014, approximately 132.7 million workers were covered by workers' compensation – an increase of 1.9% from 2013.

The table below shows the trend in the number of compensated or reported cases in each reporting state. Due to the differences in population, industries, and coverage of compensation laws, comparisons among states should not be made.

Workers' compensation cases, 2013-2015

State	Deaths[a] 2015	Deaths[a] 2014	Deaths[a] 2013	Cases[a] 2015	Cases[a] 2014	Cases[a] 2013	2014 compensation paid ($000)
Alabama[b]	31	19	16	12,814	13,290	13,471	636,575
Alaska	20	23	17	19,909	18,686	19,140	214,995
Connecticut	28	22	32	57,472	58,924	57,111	886,015
Dist. of Columbia	5	8	5	10,739	11,185	11,207	101,207
Florida[c]	108	110	112	53,949	57,986	57,684	3,147,769
Georgia	85	96	98	38,214	39,212	33,729	1,433,242
Hawaii	27	29	22	20,805	20,693	20,721	270,720
Indiana	70	94	95	53,862	56,678	56,983	589,225
Iowa[b]	44	50	50	15,541	17,661	17,286	649,719
Kansas	42	50	51	49,520	52,782	55,269	379,413
Kentucky[b]	—	36	41	—	35,695	36,495	656,611
Maryland	67	58	56	23,778	24,171	23,297	955,474
Michigan	46	80	56	20,924	23,306	21,935	1,034,772
Minnesota[d]	—	28	60	—	96,300	94,900	1,079,263
Missouri	86	96	105	102,159	102,943	103,394	853,094
Montana	20	36	32	24,853	26,255	25,475	245,909
Nebraska	54	50	35	39,457	40,285	40,411	325,263
Nevada[e]	—	136	—	—	48,627	—	369,396
New Hampshire	15	13	18	38,864	39,425	38,998	210,224
New Mexico	33	51	38	41,592	43,806	44,050	262,383
Ohio	185	158	156	93,936	97,572	97,041	2,027,964
Oregon[e]	27	31	30	19,572	19,724	18,633	655,971
Pennsylvania	65	75	72	166,102	177,316	110,300	3,010,790
South Dakota	4	13	6	21,905	22,433	22,160	98,266
Tennessee	57	30	45	99,738	97,276	98,469	710,062
Texas	—	—	253	—	91,584	92,637	1,548,645
Utah	—	54	37	54,601	51,353	51,720	271,969
Vermont	10	11	7	16,449	17,047	16,533	152,749
Virginia	74	83	49	135,328	134,834	133,242	933,059
West Virginia	12	24	34	32,000	33,568	34,777	423,527
Wisconsin[f]	—	97[g]	97	30,029	31,748	31,760	1,163,372

Source: Deaths and Cases–State workers' compensation authorities for calendar or fiscal year. States not listed did not respond to the survey. Compensation paid– Baldwin, M. L. & McLaren, C.F. (2016 October). Workers' compensation: benefits, coverage, and costs, (2014 data). Washington, DC: National Academy of Social Insurance.
Note: Dash (—) indicates data not available.

Definitions
Reported case: A reported case may or may not be work-related and may not receive compensation.
Compensated case: A case determined to be work-related and for which compensation was paid.

[a] Reported cases involving medical and indemnity benefits, unless otherwise noted.
[b] Reported cases involving indemnity benefits only.
[c] Lost-time only cases involving medical and indemnity benefits.
[d] Includes reported and closed or compensated cases involving medical and indemnity benefits.
[e] Closed or compensated cases only involving medical and indemnity benefits.
[f] Includes all claims reported.
[g] Preliminary.

OCCUPATIONAL
Transportation

Transportation-related events represent 41% of occupational fatalities and 5% of non-fatal injuries involving days away from work. Events categorized as transportation involve transportation vehicles, animals used for transportation purposes, and powered industrial vehicles or powered mobile industrial equipment in which at least one vehicle (or mobile equipment) is in normal operation and the injury or illness was due to collision or other type of traffic incident; loss of control; or a sudden stop, start, or jolting of a vehicle regardless of the location where the event occurred.

Transportation related occupational fatalities and nonfatal injuries involving days away from work, United States, 2011-2014

	2011	2012	2013	2014
Fatalities (all industries)				
Total Transportation	1,937	1,923	1,865	1,984
Roadway incidents involving motorized land vehicle	1,103	1,153	1,099	1,157
Collision with other vehicle	525	565	564	611
Collision with object other than vehicle	313	338	332	317
Noncollision incident	262	247	201	228
Pedestrian vehicular incident	316	293	294	318
Struck by vehicle in work zone	63	65	48	53
Struck by vehicle in roadway	73	73	83	75
Struck by vehicle on side of road	50	54	49	67
Struck by vehicle in nonroadway area	116	96	106	106
Nonroadway incident involving motorized land vehicle	222	233	227	248
Collision with other vehicle	8	9	11	9
Collision with object other than vehicle	42	44	34	48
Noncollision incident	169	175	181	191
Aircraft incidents	145	127	136	135
Pedestrian struck by aircraft or propeller	—	—	—	1
Aircraft crash during takeoff or landing	44	38	48	62
Explosion or fire on aircraft	—	—	3	3
Aircraft crash due to low-altitude entanglement	5	10	7	7
Other in-flight crash	82	74	59	53
Parachuting incident	7	3	12	7
Rail vehicle incidents	50	38	41	57
Collision between rail vehicle and another vehicle	42	34	28	43
Fall or jump from and struck by rail vehicle	—	—	1	—
Pedestrian struck by rail vehicle	4	2	9	10
Water vehicle incidents	72	63	60	55
Water vehicle collisions	8	4	8	—
Explosion or fire on water vehicle	—	—	1	—
Capsized or sinking of water vehicle	21	18	10	17
Fall or jump from water vehicle	22	21	24	21
Machinery or equipment incident on water vehicle	4	5	12	7
Fall on water vehicle	6	5	3	2
Animal and other non-motorized vehicle transportation incidents	29	15	8	14
Nonfatal injuries involving days away from work (private industries)				
Total Transportation	41,140	42,610	44,410	47,320
Roadway incidents involving motorized land vehicle	26,350	28,650	30,840	32,930
Collision with other vehicle	17,240	19,400	21,510	22,150
Collision with object other than vehicle	1,630	1,430	1,580	2,040
Noncollision incident	4,270	4,510	4,850	5,280
Pedestrian vehicular incident	5,440	4,750	5,480	5,510
Struck by vehicle in work zone	1,160	840	790	1,140
Struck by vehicle in roadway	1,030	590	350	660
Struck by vehicle on side of road	140	70	150	90
Struck by vehicle in nonroadway area	2,820	2,890	3,530	3,030
Nonroadway incident involving motorized land vehicle	6,460	6,830	5,900	6,810
Collision with other vehicle	1,570	1,550	1,960	1,480
Collision with object other than vehicle	1,610	1,900	1,150	1,830
Noncollision incident	3,070	3,120	2,510	3,200
Aircraft incidents	560	560	680	600
Aircraft crash during takeoff or landing	—	—	—	20
Fall on aircraft during transport	230	310	490	260
Rail vehicle incidents	410	430	250	270
Collision between rail vehicle and another vehicle	260	310	130	150
Derailment	30	30	40	20
Fall on rail vehicle	20	—	—	—
Water vehicle incidents	400	310	210	190
Water vehicle or propeller struck person	—	—	30	—
Water vehicle collisions	50	—	—	—
Fall or jump from water vehicle	30	20	80	—
Machinery or equipment incident on water vehicle	—	—	30	—
Fall on water vehicle	270	120	20	100
Animal and other non-motorized vehicle transportation incidents	470	490	380	330

Source: Bureau of Labor Statistics
Note: Dash (—) indicates no data reported or data that do not meet Bureau of Labor Statistics publication criteria.

INJURY FACTS® 2017 EDITION NATIONAL SAFETY COUNCIL® ■ 65

OCCUPATIONAL

Workers' Compensation Claims Costs, 2013-2014

■ *Head injuries are the most costly workers' compensation claims.*

The data in the graphs on this and the next page are from the National Council on Compensation Insurance's (NCCI) Workers Compensation Statistical Plan (WCSP) database.[a] WCSP reflects claims experience on workers' compensation insurance policies issued in states in which NCCI collects such data. The aggregate unit statistical data were valued 30 months after the inception date of the policy (as of the second report). The average cost for all claims combined in 2013-2014 was $38,617.

NCCI data that appeared in *Injury Facts* prior to the 2011 edition were sourced to NCCI's Detailed Claim Information file, which was a stratified random sample of lost-time claims in 42 states. Workers' compensation estimates provided in this edition are not comparable to estimates provided in editions prior to 2011.

Cause of injury. The most costly lost-time workers' compensation claims by cause of injury, according to NCCI data, are for those resulting from motor-vehicle crashes. These injuries averaged $74,499 per workers' compensation claim filed in 2013 and 2014. The only other causes with above-average costs were burns ($48,241) and falls or slips ($45,016).

Nature of injury. The most costly lost-time workers' compensation claims by nature of injury are for those resulting from amputation. These injuries averaged $85,426 per workers' compensation claim filed in 2013 and 2014. The next highest costs were for injuries resulting in fracture, crush, or dislocation ($55,886); other trauma ($49,185); and burns ($42,849).

Part of body. The most costly lost-time workers' compensation claims are for those involving the head or central nervous system. These injuries averaged $87,086 per claim filed in 2013 and 2014. The next highest costs were for injuries involving multiple body parts ($62,386) and the neck ($57,700). Injuries to the hip, thigh, and pelvis; leg; arm or shoulders; and chest or organs also had above-average costs.

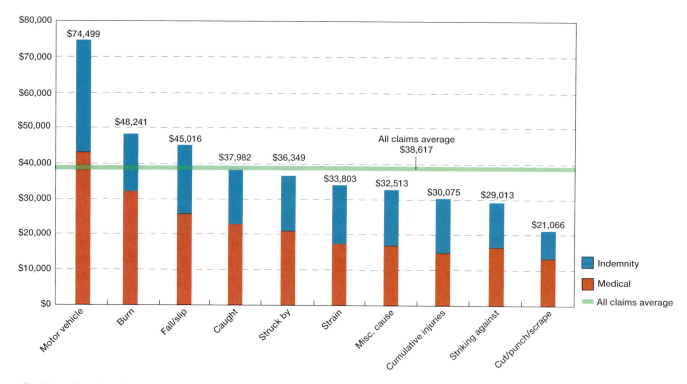

Average total incurred costs per claim by cause of injury, 2013-2014

[a] The National Council on Compensation Insurance makes no representations or warranties of any kind nor assumes any responsibility for the accuracy of the underlying data or any third-party use of the data on this and the following page.

OCCUPATIONAL

Workers' Compensation Claims Costs, 2013-2014 (cont.)

Average total incurred costs per claim by nature of injury, 2013-2014

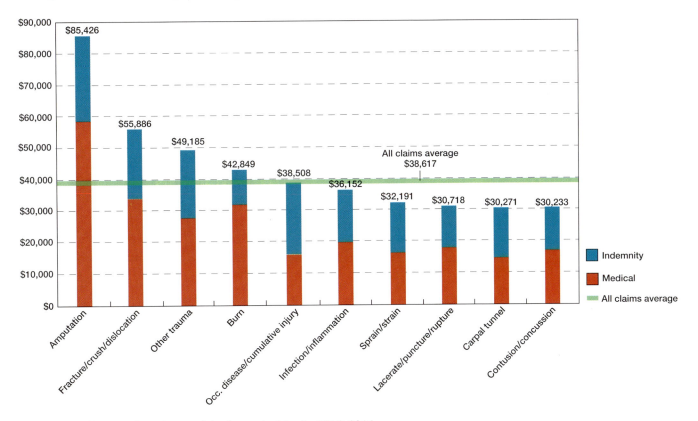

Average total incurred costs per claim by part of body, 2013-2014

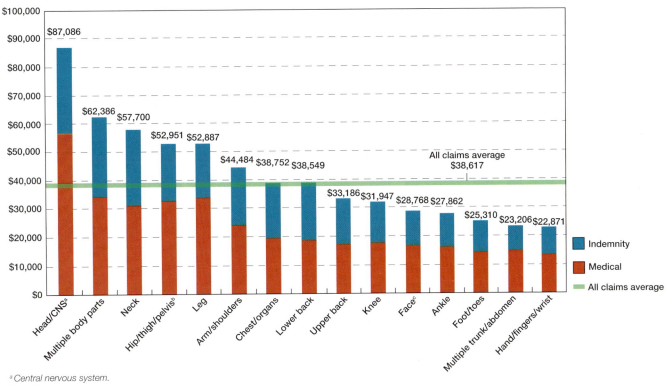

[a] Central nervous system.
[b] Includes sacrum and coccyx.
[c] Includes teeth, mouth, and eyes.

OCCUPATIONAL
Forklifts

Beginning with 2011 data, occupational injury data from the Bureau of Labor Statistics are based on the revised Occupational Injury and Illness Classification System (OIICS) 2.01 and are not comparable to the data for prior years in the tables below. The total of fatal occupational injuries in private industry with a forklift as the primary source of injury numbered 71 in 2015, a 9% increase from 2014. There were an additional 25 fatal occupational injuries with a forklift as the secondary source of injury in 2015, up 4% from 2014. Forklift fatalities are most prevalent in the trade, transportation, and utilities; manufacturing; and construction industries.

The rate of nonfatal forklift injuries involving days away from work was 0.7 per 10,000 full-time workers in 2015, down 12% from 0.8 in 2014. Trade, transportation, and utilities and manufacturing had the highest rates of nonfatal forklift injuries, followed by construction.

Number of fatal occupational injuries with a forklift as the source of injury, private industry, United States, 2012-2015

Industry division	2012 Forklift as primary[b] source	2012 Forklift as secondary[c] source	2013 Forklift as primary[b] source	2013 Forklift as secondary[c] source	2014 Forklift as primary[b] source	2014 Forklift as secondary[c] source	2015 Forklift as primary[b] source	2015 Forklift as secondary[c] source
All Industries	67	27	69	20	65	24	71	25
Natural resources and mining[d]	6	4	5	4	6	—	4	—
Construction	9	5	9	1	9	—	9	5
Manufacturing	18	8	17	4	18	—	23	7
Trade, transportation, and utilities	28	10	27	8	24	16	27	11
Information	—	—	—	—	—	—	—	—
Financial activities	—	—	—	—	—	—	—	—
Professional and business services	—	—	5	—	3	1	4	—
Education and health services	—	—	—	—	—	—	—	—
Leisure and hospitality	—	—	—	—	1	—	2	—
Other services[d]	3	—	5	2	—	—	1	—

Source: Bureau of Labor Statistics (BLS) Occupational Injuries and Illnesses and Fatal Injuries Profiles, accessed October 26, 2016. Available at http://data.bls.gov/gqt/InitialPage. Data may not add to totals because of rounding or exclusion of data that do not meet publication guidelines.
Dashes (—) indicate no data reported or data that do not meet publication guidelines.
[a] Data for 2012-2015 are based on the revised BLS Occupational Injury and Illness Classification System (OIICS) 2.01 and not compatable to data for prior years.
[b] The primary source of a fatal occupational injury is the object, substance, person, bodily motion, or exposure that most directly led to, produced, or inflicted the injury or illness.
[c] The secondary source of a fatal occupational injury is the object, substance, person, or exposure other than the source (if any) that most actively generated the source or contributed to the injury or illness.
[d] "Natural resources" includes agriculture, forestry, fishing, and hunting and excludes farms with fewer than 11 employees. "Mining" includes oil and gas extraction. "Other services" excludes public administration.

Incidence rates[a] of nonfatal occupational injuries and illnesses involving days away from work[b] with a forklift as the source of injury or illness, private industry, United States, 2009-2015

Industry division	All sources rate[a] 2015	2009	2010	2011[c]	2012[c]	2013[c]	2014[c]	2015[c]
All industries	93.9	0.9	0.8	0.7	0.8	0.7	0.8	0.7
Natural resources and mining[d]	126.8	0.6	1.1	0.9	2.5	1.3	0.8	1.3
Construction	134.8	0.8	0.7	0.6	0.8	0.6	0.9	0.5
Manufacturing	99.0	1.5	1.9	1.5	1.6	1.6	1.8	1.7
Trade, transportation, and utilities	124.5	2.3	2	1.6	1.9	1.7	1.9	1.7
Information	56.3	0.2	0.2	0.1	0.1	0.2	0.3	0.3
Financial activities	41.3	0.2	0[e]	0[e]	0[e]	0.1	0.2	0.1
Professional and business services	44.5	0.4	0.3	0.2	0.2	0.2	0.2	0.1
Education and health services	106.8	0.1	0[e]	0[e]	0[e]	0[e]	0[e]	0[e]
Leisure and hospitality	96.2	0[e]	0[e]	0[e]	0[e]	0[e]	0[e]	0[e]
Other services[d]	75.9	0.1	0.3	0.2	0.2	1.1	0.3	0.1

Source: Bureau of Labor Statistics (BLS) Occupational Injuries and Illnesses and Fatal Injuries Profiles, accessed December 15, 2016. Available at http://data.bls.gov/gqt/InitialPage.
Dashes (—) indicate no data reported or data that do not meet publication guidelines.
[a] Incidence rates represent the number of injuries and illnesses per 10,000 full-time workers and were calculated as: (N/EH) x 20,000,000, where N = number of injuries and illnesses, EH = total hours worked by all employees during the calendar year, and 20,000,000 = base for 10,000 full-time equivalent workers (working 40 hours per week, 50 weeks per year).
[b] Days away from work include those that result in days away from work with or without restricted work activity.
[c] Data for 2011-2015 are based on the revised BLS Occupational Injury and Illness Classification System (OIICS) 2.01 and not compatable to data for prior years.
[d] "Natural resources" includes agriculture, forestry, fishing, and hunting and excludes farms with fewer than 11 employees. "Mining" includes oil and gras extraction. "Other services" excludes public administration.
[e] Rounded to zero.

OCCUPATIONAL
Workplace Falls

Following highway crashes, falls to a lower level is the second leading unintentional fatal workplace event and the fifth leading event resulting in cases with days away from work. In 2014, 660 workers died while an additional 49,210 were injured. The 2014 fatality count represents about an 11% increase from 2013, while the nonfatal injuries count increased nearly 4.5%. From 2005, fall-to-a-lower-level fatalities have decreased 0.6%, while nonfatal cases with days away from work have decreased by 38%.

Fatal falls to a lower level typically involve injuries to the head or multiple body parts, while nonfatal injuries most often involve the lower extremities, multiple body parts, upper extremities, or trunk. The most common nonfatal injuries include sprains, strains, or tears, followed by fractures. Falls to a lower level result in dramatically more days away from work than typical injury events. Fall-to-a-lower-level cases result in a median of 20 days away from work compared with nine days across all injury events. In fact, more than 42% of the fall-to-a-lower-level cases involving days away from work result in 31 or more lost workdays. Falls to a lower level resulting in days away from work most often occur on floors, walkways, or ground surfaces (34%), closely followed by ladders (28%). New employees are disproportionably represented, with 35% of nonfatal injuries involving workers with less than one year of service.

As shown on the accompanying pie chart, fully 12% of fatal falls to a lower level occur from heights of less than six feet. Overall about half of fall to a lower level deaths occur at heights of 20 feet or less while 16% occur at heights of greater than 30 feet.

By far, construction is the industry most at risk from falls to a lower level. In 2014, 345 workers in the construction industry died as a result of falls to a lower level, representing 52% of all fall-to-a-lower-level fatalities. The fall-to-a-lower-level fatality rate in the construction industry is 3.8 per 100,000 workers, nearly eight times the general industry rate of 0.48. Falls to a lower level also represent the single most dangerous injury event within the construction industry, representing 38% of all construction fatalities. In 2014 the construction industry also experiences the most nonfatal cases involving days away from work, representing 20% of all nonfatal fall-to-a-lower-level cases with 9,940.

Compared to falls to a lower level, falls on the same level tend to result in less severe but more frequent injuries. In 2014, there were 155,480 fall-on-the-same-level cases involving days away from work and 138 fatalities. In 2014, the rate for cases involving days away from work was 16.6 per 10,000 workers compared with 5.3 for falls to a lower level. Transportation and warehousing has the highest fall-on-the-same-level rate with 30.4 per 10,000 workers, followed by education and health services (25.5) and leisure and hospitality (22.6).

The following two pages provide injury profiles for both falls to a lower level and falls on the same level.

Fall to a lower level deaths by height of fall, United States, 2014

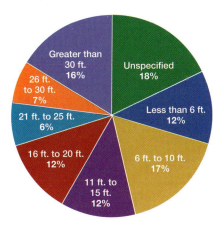

Workplace falls to a lower level, United States, 2004-2014

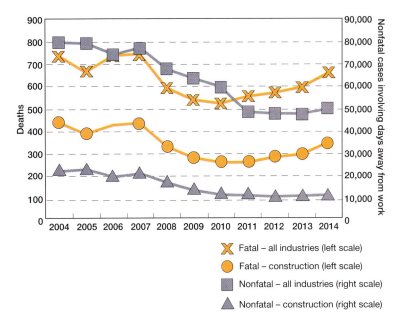

Source: This research was conducted with restricted access to Bureau of Labor Statistics (BLS) data. The views expressed here do not necessarily reflect the views of BLS.

OCCUPATIONAL

Fall to Lower Level

"Fall to lower level" applies to instances in which the injury was produced by impact between the injured person and another surface of lower elevation – the motion producing the contact being that of the person – under the following circumstances:
- The motion of the person and the force of impact were generated by gravity.
- The point of contact with the source of injury was lower than the surface supporting the person at the inception of the fall.

Fall to lower level ranks second behind highway crashes in number of workplace fatalities, and is the fifth leading event resulting in cases involving days away from work.

Fall-to-lower-level nonfatal occupational injuries and illnesses involving days away from work[a] and fatal occupational injuries by selected worker and case characteristics, United States, 2014

Characteristic	Private industry[b,c] nonfatal cases	All industries fatalities
Total	49,210	660
Sex		
Men	37,620	642
Women	11,570	18
Age		
Younger than 16	—	—
16 to 19	770	—
20 to 24	3,370	21
25 to 34	8,920	84
35 to 44	9,810	101
45 to 54	13,560	167
55 to 64	9,670	171
65 and older	2,170	116
Occupation		
Management, business, and financial	2,310	45
Professional and related	2,700	—
Service	7,230	82
Sales and related	2,670	15
Office and administrative support	2,370	9
Farming, fishing, and forestry	1,210	10
Construction and extractive	9,230	329
Installation, maintenance, and repair	6,580	73
Production	3,390	29
Transportation and material moving	11,500	64
Military occupations	—	—
Race or ethnic origin[d]		
White, non-Hispanic	23,380	442
Black, non-Hispanic	2,800	28
Hispanic	7,700	161
Other, multiple, and not reported	15,330	29
Nature of injury or illness		
Fractures	12,920	12
Sprains, strains, or tears	12,920	—
Amputations	—	—
Cuts, lacerations, or punctures	1,210	—
Bruises or contusions	4,930	—
Chemical burns and corrosions	—	—
Heat (thermal) burns	—	—
Multiple traumatic injuries	3,130	254
Soreness or pain	9,610	—
Carpal tunnel syndrome	—	—
Tendonitis	—	—
All other	4,490	387

Characteristic	Private industry[b,c] nonfatal cases	All industries fatalities
Part of body affected		
Head	2,550	277
Eye	40	—
Neck	460	31
Trunk	8,880	58
Back	5,330	9
Upper extremities	11,140	—
Shoulder	3,940	—
Arm	2,970	—
Wrist	2,630	—
Hand	990	—
Lower extremities	15,830	10
Knee	4,900	—
Ankle	4,410	—
Foot or toe	2,080	—
Body systems	60	21
Multiple	9,910	263
All other	390	—
Industry		
Agriculture, Forestry, Fishing, and Hunting	1,420	40
Mining	460	14
Construction	9,940	345
Manufacturing	4,900	35
Wholesale Trade	3,410	21
Retail Trade	4,610	21
Transportation and Warehousing	5,790	24
Utilities	210	—
Information	1,210	7
Financial Activities	2,420	15
Professional and Business Services	4,660	80
Education and Health Services	4,710	6
Leisure and Hospitality	3,800	13
Other Services	1,670	20
Government	N/A	18

Source: This research was conducted with restricted access to Bureau of Labor Statistics (BLS) data. The views expressed here do not necessarily reflect the views of BLS.
Note: Because of rounding and data exclusion of nonclassifiable responses, data may not sum to the totals. Dashes (—) indicate data that do not meet publication guidelines. "N/A" means not applicable.
[a]Days away from work include those that result in days away from work with or without restricted work activity or job transfer.
[b]Excludes farms with fewer than 11 employees.
[c]Data for mining operators in coal, metal, and nonmetal mining and for employees in railroad transportation are provided to BLS by the Mine Safety and Health Administration, U.S. Department of Labor; and the Federal Railroad Administration, U.S. Department of Transportation. Independent mining contractors are excluded from the coal, metal, and nonmetal mining industries. MSHA and FRA data do not reflect the changes in OSHA recordkeeping requirements in 2002.
[d]In the fatalities column, non-Hispanic categories include cases with Hispanic origin not reported.

OCCUPATIONAL

Fall on Same Level

"Fall on same level" applies to instances in which the injury was produced by impact between the injured person and another surface without elevation – the motion producing the contact being that of the person – under the following circumstances:

- The motion of the person was generated by gravity following the employee's loss of equilibrium (the person was unable to maintain an upright position).
- The point of contact with the source of injury was at the same level or above the surface supporting the person at the inception of the fall.

Fall on same level ranks second behind overexertion in the number of nonfatal injuries involving days away from work, but generally is not one of the top 10 events resulting in fatalities.

Fall-on-same-level nonfatal occupational injuries and illnesses involving days away from work[a] and fatal occupational injuries by selected worker and case characteristics, United States, 2014

Characteristic	Private industry[b,c] nonfatal cases	All industries fatalities
Total	155,480	138
Sex		
Men	67,500	101
Women	87,890	37
Age		
Younger than 16	30	—
16 to 19	2,070	—
20 to 24	8,880	—
25 to 34	22,230	6
35 to 44	27,300	11
45 to 54	38,100	24
55 to 64	41,210	33
65 and older	13,300	62
Occupation		
Management, business, and financial	8,210	18
Professional and related	19,010	6
Service	46,470	41
Sales and related	11,710	10
Office and administrative support	15,020	8
Farming, fishing, and forestry	1,550	—
Construction and extractive	7,740	10
Installation, maintenance, and repair	9,050	13
Production	12,030	9
Transportation and material moving	24,510	20
Military occupations	—	—
Race or ethnic origin[d]		
White, non-Hispanic	64,450	108
Black, non-Hispanic	12,550	13
Hispanic	18,830	14
Other, multiple, and not reported	59,650	—
Nature of injury or illness		
Fractures	27,490	24
Sprains, strains, or tears	43,030	—
Amputations	20	—
Cuts, lacerations, or punctures	4,260	—
Bruises or contusions	23,910	—
Chemical burns and corrosions	—	—
Heat (thermal) burns	250	—
Multiple traumatic injuries	9,830	5
Soreness or pain	31,590	—
Carpal tunnel syndrome	—	—
Tendonitis	20	—
All other	15,070	104

Characteristic	Private industry[b,c] nonfatal cases	All industries fatalities
Part of body affected		
Head	10,500	85
Eye	160	—
Neck	980	11
Trunk	27,120	11
Back	16,160	—
Upper extremities	37,570	—
Shoulder	12,490	—
Arm	9,670	—
Wrist	7,970	—
Hand	4,580	—
Lower extremities	47,820	19
Knee	24,170	—
Ankle	10,950	8
Foot or toe	3,330	—
Body systems	340	—
Multiple	30,210	8
All other	950	—
Industry		
Agriculture, Forestry, Fishing, and Hunting	2,030	7
Mining	770	—
Construction	8,280	9
Manufacturing	13,980	12
Wholesale Trade	7,470	9
Retail Trade	19,930	11
Transportation and Warehousing	12,820	17
Utilities	560	—
Information	2,900	—
Financial Activities	7,170	—
Professional and Business Services	14,360	12
Education and Health Services	39,260	14
Leisure and Hospitality	21,090	10
Other Services	4,860	9
Government	N/A	20

Source: This research was conducted with restricted access to Bureau of Labor Statistics (BLS) data. The views expressed here do not necessarily reflect the views of BLS.
Note: Because of rounding and data exclusion of nonclassifiable responses, data may not sum to the totals. Dashes (–) indicate data that do not meet publication guidelines. "N/A" means not applicable.
[a]Days away from work include those that result in days away from work with or without restricted work activity or job transfer.
[b]Excludes farms with fewer than 11 employees.
[c]Data for mining operators in coal, metal, and nonmetal mining and for employees in railroad transportation are provided to BLS by the Mine Safety and Health Administration, U.S. Department of Labor; and the Federal Railroad Administration, U.S. Department of Transportation. Independent mining contractors are excluded from the coal, metal, and nonmetal mining industries. MSHA and FRA data do not reflect the changes in OSHA recordkeeping requirements in 2002.
[d]In the fatalities column, non-Hispanic categories include cases with Hispanic origin not reported.

OCCUPATIONAL
Fatigue

It is well understood that the leading cause of occupational fatalities is motor-vehicle crashes, while the leading cause of non-fatal injuries is overexertion and bodily reaction. What is less well understood is the role fatigue plays as a contributing factor in occupational injuries and death. Fatigue is a general term used to describe feelings of tiredness, reduced energy, and the increased effort needed to perform tasks effectively and avoid errors (Dinges, 2001). Although fatigue has long been a safety concern, the current occupational injury surveillance systems managed by the Bureau of Labor Statistics do not track the prevalence of fatigue-related incidents. Instead, fatigue-related injury estimates are based upon a body of research using a variety of methods conducted throughout the world. A systematic review conducted by Uehli (2014) of 27 research studies found that workers with sleep problems have a 1.62 times higher risk of being injured than workers without sleep problems. The study also estimated that approximately 13% of work injuries can be attributed to sleep problems. Applying this estimate to the Bureau of Labor Statistics 2014 estimate of 3,675,800 total recordable occupational cases, it is possible that 478,000 occupational injuries in 2014 were attributable to sleep problems.

Analysis of National Health Interview Survey data by Luckhaupt (2010) assessed the prevalence of short sleep duration by industry. This analysis found that on average 30% of civilian employed workers from 2004 to 2007 received six or less hours of sleep a day. Short sleep duration was most prevalent among management companies and enterprises (40%), followed by transportation and warehousing (37%). Concerningly, the prevalence of short sleep duration appears to be getting worse. In a combined sample from 1985 and 1990, only 24% of workers reported short sleep duration.

Weighted prevalence of short sleep duration by major industry sector, 1985 and 1990 compared to 2004-2007

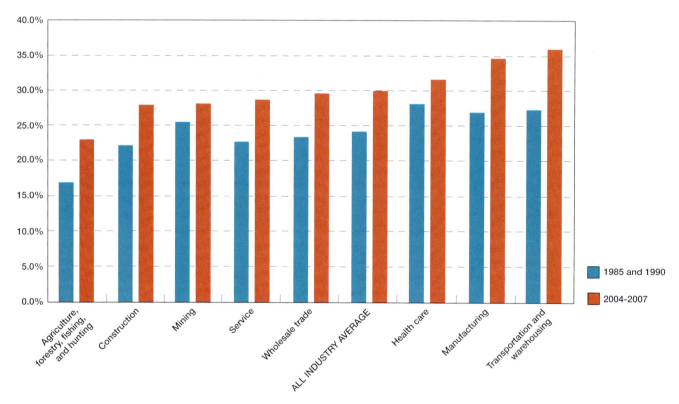

A review of research by Williamson (2011) found that although injury prevalence peaks at around midnight, self-ratings of sleepiness increase over most of the night shift. The risk of injury increases 15% on the afternoon shift and 28% on the night shift compared to the morning shift. However, a review of research by Niu (2011) concluded that fixed shift is preferable over rotating shifts because fixed shifts allow workers to better maintain circadian rhythm. If rotating shift work is necessary, the easiest and most adaptable way is forward shifts, moving from days to evenings to nights.

Williamson also found consistent evidence that obstructive sleep apnea syndrome (OSAS) is linked to increased crash risk. Depending on the study, crash risk has been found increase from 100% to 600%. Studies have also found that crash risk goes back to normal levels when OSAS is treated with nasal continuous positive airway pressure.

Sources:
Luckhaupt, S.E., Tak, S., & Calvert, G.M. (2010). The prevalence of short duration by industry and occupation in the National Health Interview Survey. Sleep, 33(2).
Niu, S., Chung, M., et.al. (2011). The effect of shift rotation on employee cortisol profile, sleep quality, fatigue, and attention level: a systematic review. Journal of Nursing Research, 19(1).
Uehli, K, Mehta, A., et.al. (2014). Sleep problems and work injuries: A systematic review and meta-analysis. Sleep Medicine Reviews, 18.
Williamson, A., Lombardi, D.A., et.al. (2011). The link between fatigue and safety. Accident Analysis and Prevention, 43.

Occupational Health

■ *More than 28,000 new cases of skin diseases or disorders were diagnosed in 2015.*

Approximately 187,900 occupational illnesses were recognized or diagnosed by employers in 2015, according to the Bureau of Labor Statistics (BLS). The all-industry illness data published by BLS now includes data for state and local governments in addition to the private sector. The overall incidence rate of occupational illness for all industries was 16.9 per 10,000 full-time workers. The highest overall incidence rate for all illnesses was for manufacturing – 32.9 cases per 10,000 full-time workers – nearly double the all industries rate.

Workers in agriculture, forestry, fishing, and hunting had the highest overall incidence rates for skin diseases or disorders, respiratory conditions, and poisoning. Manufacturing had the highest overall rate for hearing loss and also had the highest rate within private industry for "all other occupational illnesses."

State and local government, manufacturing, and education and health services accounted for about 67% of all new illness cases in 2015. Skin diseases or disorders were the most common illness with 28,300 new cases, followed by hearing loss with 19,500, respiratory conditions with 17,200, and poisonings with 2,500.

The table below shows the number of occupational illnesses and the incidence rate per 10,000 full-time workers as measured by the 2015 BLS survey. To convert these to incidence rates per 100 full-time workers, which are comparable to other published BLS rates, divide the rates in the table by 100. The BLS survey records illnesses only for the year in which they are recognized or diagnosed as work-related. Because only recognized cases are included, the figures underestimate the incidence of occupational illness.

Nonfatal occupational illness incidence rates and number of illnesses by type of illness and industry sector, 2015

Industry sector	All illnesses	Skin diseases or disorders	Respiratory conditions	Poisoning	Hearing loss	All other occupational illnesses
Incidence rate per 10,000 full-time workers						
All industries, including state and local government[a]	16.9	2.6	1.5	0.2	1.8	10.9
Private industry[a]	14.6	2.3	1.3	0.2	1.8	9.2
Goods producing[a]	24.6	3.3	1.3	0.2	6.9	12.9
Agriculture, forestry, fishing, and hunting[a]	31.2	10.0	3.9	1.6	1.2	14.5
Mining[b,c]	7.5	(d)	2.1	(d)	2.0	3.2
Construction	8.6	2.3	0.8	0.2	0.1	5.2
Manufacturing	32.9	3.4	1.3	0.2	10.9	17.1
Service providing	12.0	2.0	1.2	0.2	0.4	8.2
Wholesale trade	7.9	1.4	0.5	0.1	0.7	5.2
Retail trade	9.2	1.4	0.7	0.1	0.1	6.9
Transportation and warehousing	16.7	0.9	1.2	0.2	3.3	11.1
Utilities	18.6	4.8	(d)	(d)	8.5	5.0
Information	7.8	0.8	0.3	(d)	0.7	6.0
Finance, insurance, and real estate	4.9	0.5	0.4	(d)	(d)	4.0
Professional and business services	7.8	2.1	0.8	0.2	0.1	4.6
Educational and health services	23.6	3.7	3.0	0.1	0.1	16.7
Leisure, entertainment, and hospitality	10.8	2.4	1.2	0.3	0.1	6.8
Other services (except public administration)	7.0	1.6	0.7	(d)	0.1	4.0
State and local government[a]	32.0	4.3	3.4	0.5	1.8	21.9
Number of Illnesses (in thousands)						
All industries, including state and local government[a]	187.9	28.3	17.2	2.5	19.5	120.4
Private industry[a]	140.5	21.9	12.1	1.7	16.8	88.0
Goods producing[a]	49.7	6.6	2.7	0.5	13.8	26.0
Agriculture, forestry, fishing, and hunting[a]	3.1	1.0	0.4	0.2	0.1	1.4
Mining[b,c]	0.7	(d)	0.2	(d)	0.2	0.3
Construction	5.1	1.4	0.5	0.1	0.1	3.1
Manufacturing	40.8	4.2	1.7	0.2	13.5	21.2
Service providing	90.9	15.4	9.3	1.2	3.0	61.9
Wholesale trade	4.5	0.8	0.3	0.1	0.4	3.0
Retail trade	10.8	1.6	0.8	0.1	0.1	8.1
Transportation and warehousing	7.4	0.4	0.5	0.1	1.5	5.0
Utilities	1.0	0.3	(d)	(d)	0.5	0.3
Information	1.9	0.2	0.1	(d)	0.2	1.5
Finance, insurance, and real estate	3.6	0.3	0.3	(d)	(d)	2.9
Professional and business services	11.8	3.1	1.3	0.2	0.1	7.0
Educational and health services	37.3	5.8	4.7	0.2	0.1	26.4
Leisure, entertainment, and hospitality	10.4	2.4	1.2	0.3	0.1	6.5
Other services (except public administration)	2.2	0.5	0.2	(d)	(d)	1.2
State and local government[a]	47.4	6.4	5.1	0.8	2.7	32.4

Source: Bureau of Labor Statistics. Components may not add to totals due to rounding.
[a]Excludes farms with fewer than 11 employees.
[b]Data for mining do not reflect the changes OSHA made to its recordkeeping requirements effective Jan. 1, 2002; therefore, estimates for this industry are not comparable with estimates for other industries.
[c]Mining includes quarrying and oil and gas extraction.
[d]Data do not meet publication guidelines/too small to be displayed.

OCCUPATIONAL
Nature of Injury

According to the Bureau of Labor Statistics, sprains, strains, or tears were the most common type of injury involving days away from work in 2014, accounting for 36% of the total 916,440 injuries in private industry. Soreness or pain was the second most common type of injury, followed by cuts, lacerations, or punctures. Overall, the education and health services, manufacturing, and retail trade industry sectors had the greatest number of injuries, combining to make up 46% of the total.

Number of nonfatal occupational injuries and illnesses involving days away from work[a] by nature of injury and industry sector, private industry, United States, 2014

		Industry sector								
Nature of injury	Private sector[b,c,d]	Education and health services	Manufacturing	Retail trade	Transportation and warehousing[d]	Leisure and hospitality	Professional and business services	Construction	Wholesale trade	All other sectors[b,d,e]
Total[c]	916,440	175,900	125,990	120,640	95,040	90,920	77,720	74,460	59,240	96,530
Fractures	80,160	10,650	12,210	9,410	7,440	6,340	7,830	9,050	7,080	10,150
Sprains, strains, or tears	331,180	77,990	38,580	45,670	45,070	25,900	24,360	20,340	22,900	30,370
Amputations	4,250	160	2,110	360	140	270	150	280	430	350
Cuts, lacerations, or punctures	84,840	6,420	15,420	13,440	4,530	12,870	7,520	11,410	4,830	8,400
Cuts or lacerations	71,100	4,560	13,340	12,280	3,850	12,180	5,080	9,020	3,880	6,910
Punctures (except gunshot wounds)	13,740	1,870	2,080	1,160	680	690	2,430	2,390	950	1,490
Bruises or contusions	74,140	15,870	9,360	13,410	7,770	7,920	5,000	3,760	4,370	6,680
Chemical burns and corrosions	3,440	330	970	340	160	550	220	550	140	180
Heat (thermal) burns	12,890	1,480	2,080	1,150	170	6,330	480	400	220	580
Multiple traumatic injuries	26,680	5,390	3,180	2,820	2,770	2,440	2,870	2,430	1,530	3,250
With sprains and other injuries	11,980	2,900	930	1,290	1,250	1,180	1,310	520	640	1,960
With fractures and other injuries	5,540	610	1,050	490	440	450	500	1,210	400	390
Soreness or pain	150,180	33,790	16,050	16,430	14,820	15,110	14,170	12,910	9,450	17,450
Carpal tunnel syndrome	6,800	650	2,360	390	520	160	790	120	290	1,520
Tendonitis	1,930	410	660	200	180	160	90	—	80	150
All other	139,940	22,760	23,000	17,040	11,480	12,860	14,240	13,200	7,910	17,450

Source: Bureau of Labor Statistics Occupational Injuries/Illnesses and Fatal Injuries Profiles, accessed August 9, 2016 from http://data.bls.gov/gqt/InitialPage.
[a]Days-away-from-work cases include those that result in days away from work with or without job transfer or restriction.
[b]Excludes farms with fewer than 11 employees.
[c]Data may not sum to row and column totals because of rounding and exclusion of nonclassifiable responses.
[d]Data for transportation and mining do not reflect the changes OSHA made to its recordkeeping requirements effective Jan. 1, 2002; therefore, estimates for these industries are not comparable with estimates for other industries.
[e]Includes agriculture, forestry, fishing, and hunting; financial activities; information; mining (including oil and gas extraction); other services (except public administration); and utilities.

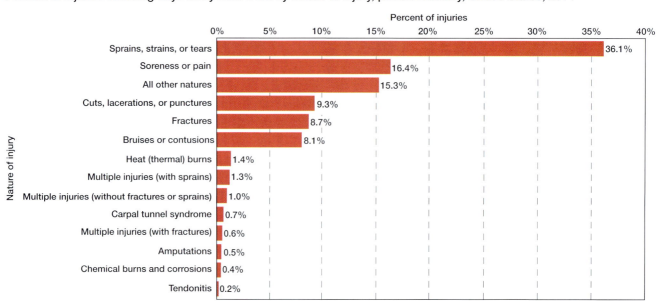

Percent of injuries involving days away from work by nature of injury, private industry, United States, 2014

- Sprains, strains, or tears: 36.1%
- Soreness or pain: 16.4%
- All other natures: 15.3%
- Cuts, lacerations, or punctures: 9.3%
- Fractures: 8.7%
- Bruises or contusions: 8.1%
- Heat (thermal) burns: 1.4%
- Multiple injuries (with sprains): 1.3%
- Multiple injuries (without fractures or sprains): 1.0%
- Carpal tunnel syndrome: 0.7%
- Multiple injuries (with fractures): 0.6%
- Amputations: 0.5%
- Chemical burns and corrosions: 0.4%
- Tendonitis: 0.2%

OCCUPATIONAL
Part of Body

According to the Bureau of Labor Statistics, the back was the body part most frequently affected in injuries involving days away from work in 2014, accounting for 18% of the total 916,440 injuries in private industry. Hand injuries were the second most common, followed by injuries to multiple body parts. Overall, the education and health services, manufacturing, and retail trade industry sectors had the highest number of injuries, combining to make up 46% of the total.

Number of nonfatal occupational injuries and illnesses involving days away from work[a] by part of body affected and industry sector, private industry, United States, 2014

Part of body affected	Private sector[b,c,d]	Education and health services	Manufacturing	Retail trade	Transportation and warehousing[d]	Leisure and hospitality	Professional and business services	Construction	Wholesale trade	All other sectors[b,d,e]
Total[c]	916,440	175,900	125,990	120,640	95,040	90,920	77,720	74,460	59,240	96,530
Head	68,940	11,560	10,200	11,900	5,550	7,150	5,050	6,620	4,050	6,860
Eye	20,910	1,890	4,900	2,470	1,150	1,880	1,530	3,530	1,610	1,950
Neck	12,410	3,440	1,410	1,350	1,740	730	660	1,110	680	1,290
Trunk	218,560	51,440	26,330	29,270	24,740	16,840	17,010	17,180	15,510	20,240
Back	162,720	42,530	18,090	22,240	18,930	11,290	12,640	11,590	10,810	14,600
Upper extremities	288,240	42,760	53,850	37,960	26,450	33,970	22,560	24,010	17,210	29,470
Shoulder	72,200	13,610	10,870	9,480	10,510	5,370	4,860	4,950	4,860	7,690
Arm	44,290	6,510	6,640	5,800	4,690	4,840	4,840	3,200	2,960	4,810
Wrist	36,540	7,160	6,610	4,730	3,450	3,900	3,100	2,060	1,690	3,840
Hand	119,810	11,810	27,340	16,520	6,440	17,780	8,650	13,080	6,790	11,400
Lower extremities	211,990	35,590	24,320	29,240	25,250	21,640	17,860	18,140	15,700	24,250
Knee	79,850	15,230	8,750	11,050	10,450	8,550	6,540	6,080	4,520	8,680
Ankle	47,950	9,020	4,800	5,560	5,930	4,690	3,940	4,500	3,510	6,000
Foot	43,460	5,310	5,800	8,320	4,270	4,220	3,500	3,620	4,000	4,420
Body systems	17,340	5,190	1,480	2,030	980	1,410	2,730	880	490	2,150
Multiple parts	89,490	24,390	7,720	8,310	9,760	8,060	8,690	5,940	5,270	11,350
All other	9,470	1,530	690	590	570	1,120	3,150	570	340	910

Source: Bureau of Labor Statistics Occupational Injuries/Illnesses and Fatal Injuries Profiles, accessed August 9, 2016 from http://data.bls.gov/gqt/InitialPage.
[a]Days-away-from-work cases include those that result in days away from work with or without job transfer or restriction.
[b]Excludes farms with fewer than 11 employees.
[c]Data may not sum to row and column totals because of rounding and exclusion of nonclassifiable responses.
[d]Data for transportation and mining do not reflect the changes OSHA made to its recordkeeping requirements effective Jan. 1, 2002; therefore, estimates for these industries are not comparable with estimates for other industries.
[e]Includes agriculture, forestry, fishing, and hunting; financial activities; information; mining (including oil and gas extraction); other services (except public administration); and utilities.

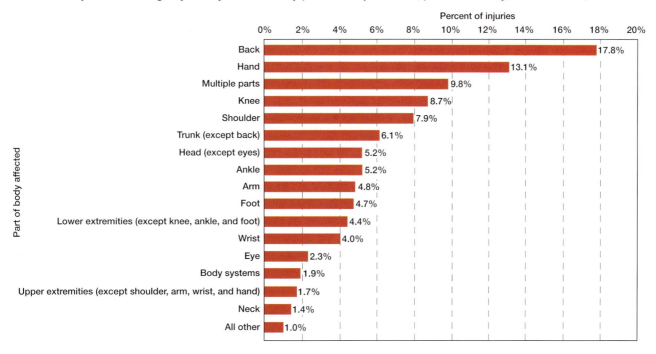

Percent of injuries involving days away from work by part of body affected, private industry, United States, 2014

OCCUPATIONAL
Benchmarking Incidence Rates

Safety professionals in business and industry often want to compare, or benchmark, the occupational injury and illness incidence rates of their establishments with the national average rates compiled by the Bureau of Labor Statistics (BLS) through its annual Survey of Occupational Injuries and Illnesses.[a] The incidence rates published on the following pages are for 2015 and were compiled under the revised Occupational Safety and Health Administration (OSHA) recordkeeping requirements that went into effect in 2002.

Step 1

The first step in benchmarking is to calculate the incidence rates for the establishment. The basic formula for computing incidence rates is *(N x 200,000)/EH*, or the number of cases *(N)* multiplied by 200,000 then divided by the number of hours worked *(EH)* by all employees during the time period, where *200,000* is the base for 100 full-time workers (working 40 hours per week, 50 weeks per year). Because BLS rates are based on reports from entire establishments, both the OSHA 300 log and the number of hours worked should cover the whole establishment being benchmarked. The hours worked and the log also should cover the same time period (e.g., a month, quarter, or full year). The following rates may be calculated.

Total cases – The incidence rate of total OSHA recordable cases per 200,000 hours worked. For this rate, *N* is the total number of cases on the OSHA 300 log.

Cases with days away from work or job transfer or restriction – The incidence rate of cases with days away from work, job transfer, or restriction. *N* is the count of cases with a check in column H or column I of the OSHA 300 log.

Cases with days away from work – The incidence rate of cases with days away from work. *N* is the count of cases with a check in column H of the OSHA 300 log.

Cases with job transfer or restriction – The incidence rate of cases with job transfer or restriction, but no days away from work. *N* is the count of cases with a check in column I of the OSHA 300 log.

Other recordable cases – The incidence rate of recordable cases without days away from work or job transfer or restriction. *N* is the count of cases with a check in column J of the OSHA 300 log.

In the flow chart on the opposite page, post the number of cases to each box in the top row and the number of employee hours worked in its box. Then use the formula to calculate the rates and write them in the last row of boxes in Step 1.

An alternative approach is to use the Incidence Rate Calculator and Comparison Tool available on BLS's website at *http://data.bls.gov/iirc*. This tool will calculate your rate and provide a report comparing your rate to your industry.

Step 2

After computing one or more of the rates, the next step is to determine the North American Industry Classification System (NAICS) code for the establishment.[b] (NAICS replaced the Standard Industrial Classification [SIC] code beginning in 2003.) This code is used to find the appropriate BLS rate for comparison. NAICS codes can be found at *www.census.gov/eos/www/naics*. The website also contains a crosswalk between NAICS and SIC codes. Otherwise, call a regional BLS office for assistance.

Write the establishment's NAICS code in the box in Step 2 of the flow chart.

Step 3

Once the NAICS code is known, the national average incidence rates may be found by (a) consulting the table of rates on pages 80-82, (b) visiting BLS's website, or (c) by calling a regional BLS office. Note that some tables on the website provide incidence rates by size of establishment and rate quartiles within each NAICS code. These rates may be useful for a more precise comparison. Note that the incidence rates for 2001 and earlier years were compiled under the old OSHA recordkeeping requirements in effect at that time. Caution must be used in comparing rates computed for 2002 and later years with earlier years – keeping in mind the differences in recordkeeping requirements.

In the flow chart on the opposite page, post the rates from the BLS survey to the boxes in Step 3. Now compare these with the rates calculated in Step 1.

An alternative way of benchmarking is to compare the current incidence rates for an establishment to its own prior historical rates to determine if the rates are improving and if progress is satisfactory (using criteria set by the organization).

[a]*Bureau of Labor Statistics. (1997). BLS Handbook of Methods. Washington, DC: U.S. Government Printing Office (Or at* www.bls.gov/opub/hom/home.htm).
[b]*Executive Office of the President, Office of Management and Budget. (2002).* North American Industry Classification System, United States, 2002. *Springfield, VA: National Technical Information Service.*

OCCUPATIONAL
Benchmarking Flow Chart

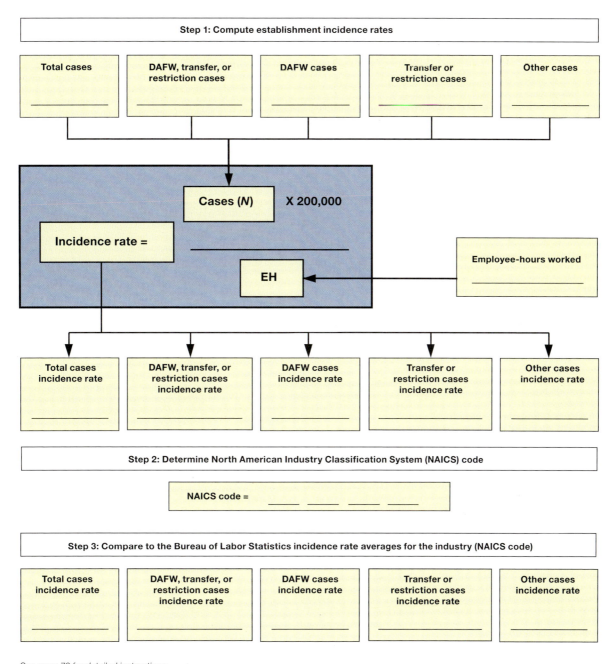

See page 76 for detailed instructions.
DAFW = Days away from work.

OCCUPATIONAL

Trends in Occupational Incidence Rates

■ *Total recordable incidence rate continues steady decrease in 2015.*

Four of the five private-sector occupational injury and illness incidence rates published by the Bureau of Labor Statistics (BLS) for 2015 decreased from 2014, while the remaining incidence rate was unchanged. The incidence rate for total recordable cases was 3.0 per 100 full-time workers in 2015, down 6% from the 2014 rate of 3.2. The incidence rate for cases with days away from work, job transfer, or restriction was 1.6 in 2015, down nearly 6% from 2014. The incidence rate for cases with days away from work decreased 10%, from 1.0 in 2014 to 0.9 in 2015. The incidence rate for other recordable cases was 1.4 in 2015, down about 7% from 2014. The incidence rate for cases with job transfer or restriction was unchanged from 2014 at 0.7.

There have been several changes that affect comparability of incidence rates from year to year. The North American Industry Classification System replaced the Standard Industrial Classification system beginning with the 2003 survey of occupational injuries and illnesses. Revisions to the Occupational Safety and Health Administration's occupational injury and illness recordkeeping requirements went into effect in 2002. Beginning with 1992, BLS revised its annual survey to include only nonfatal cases and stopped publishing the incidence rate of lost workdays.

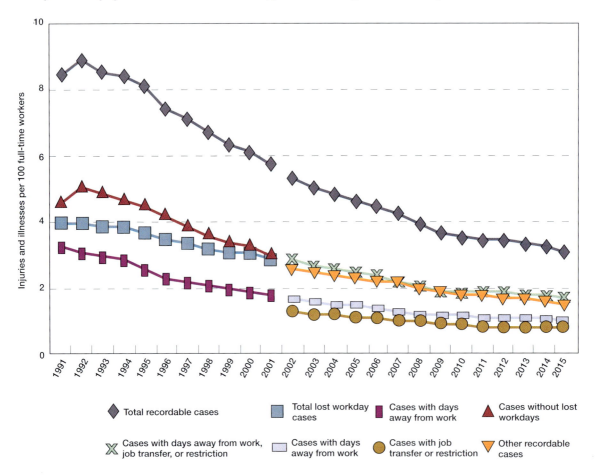

Occupational injury and illness incidence rates, private industry, United States, 1991-2015

Source: Bureau of Labor Statistics.
Note: Beginning in 1992, all rates are for nonfatal cases only. Changes in OSHA recordkeeping requirements in 2002 affect comparison with earlier years.

OCCUPATIONAL
Occupational Injuries and Illnesses

The tables below and on pages 80-82 present the results of the 2015 Survey of Occupational Injuries and Illnesses conducted by the Bureau of Labor Statistics (BLS). The survey collects data on injuries and illnesses (from the OSHA 300 log) and employee-hours worked from a nationwide sample of about 230,000 private-industry establishments, as well as state and local governments. The survey excludes private households, the self-employed, and farms with fewer than 11 employees. The incidence rates give the number of cases per 100 full-time workers per year using 200,000 employee-hours as the equivalent. Definitions of the terms are given in the Glossary on page 207.

Beginning with 1992 data, BLS revised its annual survey to include only nonfatal cases and stopped publishing incidence rates of lost workdays. Beginning with 2003 data, BLS adopted the North American Industry Classification System for publication of the incidence rates by industry.

Bureau of Labor Statistics estimates of nonfatal occupational injury and illness incidence rates and number of injuries and illnesses by industry sector, 2015

Industry sector[a]	Total recordable cases	Cases with days away from work, job transfer, or restriction — Total	Cases with days away from work	Cases with job transfer or restriction	Other recordable cases
Incidence rate per 100 full-time workers[c]					
All industries, including state and local government[d]	3.3	1.7	1.0	0.7	1.6
Private sector[d]	3.0	1.6	0.9	0.7	1.4
Goods producing[d]	3.7	2.1	1.1	1.0	1.5
Agriculture, forestry, fishing, and hunting[d]	5.7	3.5	1.9	1.6	2.2
Mining[e]	1.4	0.9	0.6	0.3	0.6
Construction	3.5	2.0	1.3	0.6	1.5
Manufacturing	3.8	2.2	1.0	1.2	1.6
Service providing	2.9	1.5	0.9	0.6	1.3
Wholesale trade	3.1	2.0	1.1	0.9	1.1
Retail trade	3.5	2.0	1.1	0.9	1.5
Transportation and warehousing	4.5	3.3	2.0	1.2	1.3
Utilities	2.2	1.2	0.7	0.5	0.9
Information	1.3	0.8	0.6	0.2	0.5
Financial, insurance, and real estate	1.1	0.6	0.4	0.2	0.5
Professional and business services	1.4	0.7	0.4	0.2	0.7
Education and health services	4.0	1.9	1.1	0.8	2.2
Leisure, entertainment, and hospitality	3.5	1.5	1.0	0.6	1.9
Other services	2.3	1.2	0.8	0.4	1.2
State and local government[d]	5.1	2.4	1.7	0.7	2.7
Number of injuries and illnesses (in thousands)					
All industries, including state and local government[d]	3,658.5	1,923.8	1,153.5	770.3	1,734.6
Private sector[d]	2,905.9	1,571.9	902.2	669.8	1,333.9
Goods producing[d]	740.1	428.0	226.3	201.7	312.1
Agriculture, forestry, fishing, and hunting[d]	56.1	34.4	18.7	15.7	21.7
Mining[e]	12.8	7.7	5.2	2.6	5.0
Construction	204.7	116.0	79.9	36.2	88.7
Manufacturing	466.5	269.9	122.6	147.2	196.6
Service providing	2,165.8	1,143.9	675.8	468.1	1,021.9
Wholesale trade	174.6	113.8	60.3	53.4	60.9
Retail trade	410.4	232.8	123.8	109.0	177.6
Transportation and warehousing	201.6	145.2	91.0	54.2	56.4
Utilities	12.0	6.8	4.1	2.8	5.2
Information	32.9	19.4	14.1	5.4	13.5
Financial, insurance, and real estate	79.0	43.0	30.1	12.9	36.0
Professional and business services	213.6	104.2	67.3	36.8	109.4
Education and health services	636.9	295.5	168.9	126.3	341.6
Leisure, entertainment, and hospitality	332.7	147.3	92.7	54.6	185.4
Other services	72.2	36.3	23.6	12.7	35.9
State and local government[d]	752.6	351.9	251.3	100.6	400.7

Source: Bureau of Labor Statistics.
[a]Industry sector and two- and three-digit NAICS code totals on pages 80-82 include data for industries not shown separately.
[b]North American Industry Classification System–United States, 2007, for industries shown on pages 80-82.
[c]Incidence rate = $\dfrac{\text{Number of injuries and illnesses} \times 200{,}000}{\text{Total hours worked by all employees during period covered}}$

where 200,000 is the base for 100 full-time workers (working 40 hours per week, 50 weeks per year). The "Total recordable cases" rate is based on the number of cases with check marks in columns (G), (H), (I), and (J) of the OSHA 300 log. The "Cases with days away from work, job transfer, or restriction – total" rate is based on columns (H) and (I). The "Cases with days away from work" rate is based on column (H). The "Cases with job transfer or restriction" rate is based on column (I). The "Other recordable cases" rate is based on column (J).
[d]Excludes farms with fewer than 11 employees.
[e]These data do not reflect the changes the Occupational Safety and Health Administration made to its recordkeeping requirements effective January 1, 2002; therefore, estimates for these industries are not comparable to estimates in other industries.
[f]Data do not meet publication guidelines/too small to be displayed.

OCCUPATIONAL

Occupational Injuries and Illnesses (cont.)

Bureau of Labor Statistics estimates of nonfatal occupational injury and illness incidence rates for selected industries, 2015

Industry[a]	NAICS code[b]	Total recordable cases	Total	Cases with days away from work	Cases with job transfer or restriction	Other recordable cases
All industries, including state and local government[d]		3.3	1.7	1.0	0.7	1.6
Private sector[d]		3.0	1.6	0.9	0.7	1.4
Goods producing[d]		3.7	2.1	1.1	1.0	1.5
Natural resources and mining[d, e]		3.7	2.2	1.3	1.0	1.4
Agriculture, forestry, fishing, and hunting[d]	11	5.7	3.5	1.9	1.6	2.2
Crop production[d]	111	5.7	3.5	1.9	1.7	2.2
Animal production and aquaculture[d]	112	6.9	4.1	2.5	1.6	2.8
Forestry and logging	113	2.3	1.5	1.4	0.1	0.8
Support activities for agriculture and forestry	115	5.4	3.4	1.6	1.7	2.1
Mining[e]	21	1.4	0.9	0.6	0.3	0.6
Oil and gas extraction	211	0.7	0.4	0.2	0.1	0.3
Mining (except oil and gas)[e]	212	2.6	1.7	1.3	0.4	0.9
Coal mining[e]	2121	3.6	2.3	2.1	0.2	1.3
Metal ore mining[e]	2122	2.1	1.4	0.8	0.6	0.7
Nonmetallic mineral mining and quarrying[e]	2123	2.1	1.4	0.9	0.6	0.7
Support activities for mining	213	1.2	0.7	0.4	0.3	0.5
Construction		3.5	2.0	1.3	0.6	1.5
Construction of buildings	236	3.1	1.8	1.3	0.5	1.3
Residential building construction	2361	3.9	2.4	1.9	(f)	1.6
Nonresidential building construction	2362	2.4	1.3	0.8	0.5	1.1
Heavy and civil engineering construction	237	2.8	1.7	1.0	0.7	1.1
Utility system construction	2371	2.4	1.4	0.8	0.6	1.0
Land subdivision	2372	2.7	1.7	1.6	0.1	1.0
Highway, street, and bridge construction	2373	3.6	2.2	1.2	1.0	1.4
Other heavy and civil engineering construction	2379	2.5	1.6	1.0	0.6	0.9
Specialty trade contractors	238	3.7	2.1	1.5	0.6	1.6
Foundation, structure, and building exterior contractors	2381	4.9	2.9	2.0	1.0	2.0
Building equipment contractors	2382	3.5	1.8	1.3	0.5	1.7
Building finishing contractors	2383	3.6	2.0	1.5	0.5	1.6
Other specialty trade contractors	2389	3.1	1.9	1.4	(f)	1.2
Manufacturing		3.8	2.2	1.0	1.2	1.6
Food manufacturing	311	4.7	3.1	1.3	1.8	1.6
Animal food manufacturing	3111	3.8	2.4	1.6	0.8	1.4
Grain and oilseed milling	3112	3.2	1.7	0.9	0.8	1.5
Sugar and confectionery product manufacturing	3113	4.5	2.9	1.2	1.7	1.6
Fruit and vegetable preserving and specialty food manufacturing	3114	4.5	2.8	1.3	1.5	1.7
Dairy product manufacturing	3115	4.8	3.0	1.5	1.5	1.8
Animal slaughtering and processing	3116	5.4	3.7	1.0	2.7	1.7
Seafood product preparation and packaging	3117	7.3	4.6	3.1	1.5	2.6
Bakeries and tortilla manufacturing	3118	4.3	2.8	1.6	1.3	1.5
Other food manufacturing	3119	4.1	2.6	1.3	1.3	1.5
Beverage and tobacco product manufacturing	312	5.3	3.8	1.4	2.4	1.5
Beverage manufacturing	3121	5.5	3.9	1.4	2.5	1.5
Tobacco manufacturing	3122	2.4	1.5	1.0	0.5	0.9
Textile mills	313	3.4	2.1	0.8	1.2	1.3
Fiber, yarn, and thread mills	3131	3.2	2.0	0.9	1.1	1.2
Fabric mills	3132	3.5	2.0	0.9	1.1	1.4
Textile and fabric finishing and fabric coating mills	3133	3.3	2.1	0.5	1.6	1.2
Textile product mills	314	3.4	1.9	0.9	1.1	1.5
Textile furnishings mills	3141	3.3	2.2	1.0	1.2	1.1
Other textile product mills	3149	3.5	1.7	0.8	0.9	1.8
Apparel manufacturing	315	2.2	1.1	0.4	0.7	1.0
Apparel knitting mills	3151	2.4	1.4	0.6	0.8	1.1
Cut and sew apparel manufacturing	3152	2.1	1.1	0.4	0.7	1.0
Apparel accessories and other apparel manufacturing	3159	2.4	1.5	0.4	1.0	1.0
Leather and allied product manufacturing	316	4.6	3.2	1.7	1.5	1.4
Footwear manufacturing	3162	4.4	2.6	1.5	1.1	1.9
Other leather and allied product manufacturing	3169	5.2	4.2	2.4	1.9	1.0
Wood product manufacturing	321	6.3	3.5	1.9	1.6	2.7
Sawmills and wood preservation	3211	6.9	3.9	2.3	1.6	3.0
Veneer, plywood, and engineered wood product manufacturing	3212	4.9	2.7	1.3	1.4	2.2
Other wood product manufacturing	3219	6.5	3.6	1.9	1.7	2.8
Paper manufacturing	322	2.8	1.6	0.8	0.9	1.2
Pulp, paper, and paperboard mills	3221	2.1	1.1	0.7	0.4	1.0
Converted paper product manufacturing	3222	3.1	1.8	0.8	1.0	1.2
Printing and related support activities	323	2.3	1.2	0.7	0.6	1.1
Petroleum and coal products manufacturing	324	1.2	0.8	0.4	0.4	0.4
Chemical manufacturing	325	2.1	1.2	0.6	0.6	0.8
Basic chemical manufacturing	3251	1.5	0.9	0.4	0.4	0.7
Resin, synthetic rubber, and artificial and synthetic fibers and filaments manufacturing	3252	1.9	1.1	0.5	0.6	0.8
Pesticide, fertilizer, and other agricultural chemical manufacturing	3253	2.6	1.4	0.6	0.8	1.2
Pharmaceutical and medicine manufacturing	3254	1.9	1.2	0.5	0.7	0.7
Paint, coating, and adhesive manufacturing	3255	2.4	1.3	0.4	0.9	1.1
Soap, cleaning compound, and toilet preparation manufacturing	3256	2.4	1.4	0.8	0.6	1.0
Other chemical product and preparation manufacturing	3259	2.8	1.7	0.9	0.8	1.1

See source and footnotes on page 79.

OCCUPATIONAL
Occupational Injuries and Illnesses (cont.)

Bureau of Labor Statistics estimates of nonfatal occupational injury and illness incidence rates for selected industries, 2015 (cont.)

Industry[a]	NAICS code[b]	Total recordable cases	Cases with days away from work, job transfer, or restriction — Total	Cases with days away from work	Cases with job transfer or restriction	Other recordable cases
Plastics and rubber products manufacturing	326	4.3	2.6	1.1	1.5	1.7
Plastics product manufacturing	3261	4.3	2.6	1.1	1.5	1.7
Rubber product manufacturing	3262	4.5	2.7	1.1	1.6	1.8
Nonmetallic mineral product manufacturing	327	4.7	2.9	1.4	1.5	1.8
Clay product and refractory manufacturing	3271	5.2	2.5	1.0	1.5	2.7
Glass and glass product manufacturing	3272	4.7	2.6	1.0	1.6	2.1
Cement and concrete product manufacturing	3273	5.0	3.4	1.9	1.5	1.6
Lime and gypsum product manufacturing	3274	2.9	1.4	0.4	1.0	1.5
Other nonmetallic mineral product manufacturing	3279	4.2	2.6	1.3	1.3	1.6
Primary metal manufacturing	331	5.1	2.8	1.3	1.5	2.3
Iron and steel mills and ferroalloy manufacturing	3311	3.5	2.0	1.0	1.0	1.6
Steel product manufacturing from purchased steel	3312	5.2	2.7	1.3	1.4	2.5
Alumina and aluminum production and processing	3313	4.0	2.2	1.1	1.0	1.9
Nonferrous metal (except aluminum) production and processing	3314	4.8	2.9	1.1	1.8	1.9
Foundries	3315	6.7	3.7	1.8	1.9	3.1
Fabricated metal product manufacturing	332	4.5	2.3	1.2	1.1	2.2
Forging and stamping	3321	5.3	3.0	1.4	1.6	2.3
Cutlery and hand tool manufacturing	3322	4.3	2.4	1.3	1.1	1.9
Architectural and structural metals manufacturing	3323	5.6	2.8	1.4	1.4	2.8
Boiler, tank, and shipping container manufacturing	3324	4.9	2.3	1.3	1.0	2.7
Hardware manufacturing	3325	4.5	2.4	0.9	1.5	2.1
Spring and wire product manufacturing	3326	5.0	2.4	1.3	1.1	2.6
Machine shops; turned product; and screw, nut, and bolt manufacturing	3327	4.0	1.7	1.0	(f)	2.3
Coating, engraving, heat treating, and allied activities	3328	4.0	2.6	1.3	1.3	1.4
Other fabricated metal product manufacturing	3329	3.5	1.9	0.9	1.0	1.6
Machinery manufacturing	333	3.6	1.9	0.9	1.0	1.7
Agriculture, construction, and mining machinery manufacturing	3331	3.5	1.9	1.0	0.9	1.6
Industrial machinery manufacturing	3332	3.3	1.7	0.9	0.8	1.6
Commercial and service machinery manufacturing	3333	2.7	1.6	0.6	1.1	1.1
Ventilation, heating, air conditioning, and commercial refrigeration equipment manufacturing	3334	4.2	2.2	0.8	1.4	2.0
Metalworking machinery manufacturing	3335	4.1	2.1	1.0	1.1	2.0
Engine, turbine, and power transmission equipment manufacturing	3336	3.0	1.5	0.7	0.8	1.4
Other general purpose machinery manufacturing	3339	3.6	1.9	0.8	1.0	1.7
Computer and electronic product manufacturing	334	1.1	0.6	0.3	0.3	0.5
Computer and peripheral equipment manufacturing	3341	0.8	0.5	0.2	0.2	0.3
Communications equipment manufacturing	3342	0.9	0.5	0.2	0.3	0.4
Audio and video equipment manufacturing	3343	1.7	0.9	0.3	0.5	0.8
Semiconductor and other electronic component manufacturing	3344	1.3	0.6	0.3	0.3	0.7
Navigational, measuring, electromedical, and control instruments manufacturing	3345	1.1	0.6	0.3	0.3	0.5
Manufacturing and reproducing magnetic and optical media	3346	2.0	1.2	0.5	0.7	0.8
Electrical equipment, appliance, and component manufacturing	335	3.0	1.6	0.8	0.8	1.4
Electric lighting equipment manufacturing	3351	2.5	1.6	1.0	0.6	0.9
Household appliance manufacturing	3352	3.6	2.0	0.9	1.1	1.6
Electrical equipment manufacturing	3353	2.7	1.4	0.7	0.6	1.3
Other electrical equipment and component manufacturing	3359	3.3	1.8	0.8	1.0	1.5
Transportation equipment manufacturing	336	4.6	2.7	1.1	1.6	1.9
Motor vehicle manufacturing	3361	6.6	3.8	1.5	2.3	2.8
Motor vehicle body and trailer manufacturing	3362	7.9	4.1	1.7	2.4	3.8
Motor vehicle parts manufacturing	3363	4.4	2.6	1.0	1.6	1.9
Aerospace product and parts manufacturing	3364	2.7	1.7	0.6	1.1	1.0
Ship and boat building	3366	6.3	3.9	1.9	2.0	2.4
Other transportation equipment manufacturing	3369	3.0	1.4	0.7	0.7	1.6
Furniture and related product manufacturing	337	4.9	2.9	1.4	1.6	2.0
Household and institutional furniture and kitchen cabinet manufacturing	3371	4.7	2.7	1.2	1.5	2.0
Office furniture (including fixtures) manufacturing	3372	5.3	3.0	1.6	1.4	2.3
Other furniture-related product manufacturing	3379	5.8	4.7	2.0	2.7	1.1
Miscellaneous manufacturing	339	2.6	1.5	0.7	0.8	1.1
Medical equipment and supplies manufacturing	3391	2.2	1.2	0.5	0.7	1.0
Other miscellaneous manufacturing	3399	3.2	1.9	0.9	0.9	1.3
Service providing		**2.9**	**1.5**	**0.9**	**0.6**	**1.3**
Trade, transportation, and utilities		**3.6**	**2.2**	**1.2**	**1.0**	**1.3**
Wholesale trade	42	3.1	2.0	1.1	0.9	1.1
Merchant wholesalers, durable goods	423	2.9	1.7	0.9	0.7	1.2
Merchant wholesalers, nondurable goods	424	3.9	2.8	1.5	1.4	1.0
Retail trade	44-45	3.5	2.0	1.1	0.9	1.5
Motor vehicle and parts dealers	441	3.4	1.7	1.0	0.7	1.7
Furniture and home furnishings stores	442	3.5	2.4	1.6	0.8	1.1
Electronics and appliance stores	443	1.0	0.6	0.4	0.2	0.5

See source and footnotes on page 79.

OCCUPATIONAL

Occupational Injuries and Illnesses (cont.)

Bureau of Labor Statistics estimates of nonfatal occupational injury and illness incidence rates for selected industries, 2015 (cont.)

Industry[a]	NAICS code[b]	Total recordable cases	Total	Cases with days away from work	Cases with job transfer or restriction	Other recordable cases
Building material and garden equipment and supplies dealers	444	4.7	3.0	1.4	1.6	1.6
Food and beverage stores	445	4.2	2.6	1.4	1.2	1.6
Health and personal care stores	446	2.2	0.9	0.7	0.2	1.3
Gasoline stations	447	2.8	1.1	0.7	0.4	1.6
Clothing and clothing accessories stores	448	2.1	0.8	0.5	0.3	1.2
Sporting goods, hobby, book, and music stores	451	2.7	1.2	0.6	0.6	1.5
General merchandise stores	452	4.5	2.7	1.1	1.5	1.9
Miscellaneous store retailers	453	3.1	1.8	0.9	0.9	1.4
Nonstore retailers	454	2.2	1.4	0.8	0.5	0.9
Transportation and warehousing	48-49	4.5	3.3	2.0	1.2	1.3
Air transportation	481	6.2	5.1	3.6	1.4	1.1
Rail transportation	482	2.0	1.5	1.3	0.1	0.5
Water transportation	483	2.0	1.4	1.0	0.5	0.6
Truck transportation	484	4.3	2.9	2.1	0.9	1.4
Transit and ground passenger transportation	485	4.5	3.0	2.2	0.8	1.5
Pipeline transportation	486	1.3	0.3	0.2	0.1	0.9
Scenic and sightseeing transportation	487	4.2	2.2	1.4	0.7	2.0
Support activities for transportation	488	3.4	2.3	1.4	0.9	1.1
Couriers and messengers	492	6.9	5.3	3.0	2.4	1.6
Warehousing and storage	493	5.0	3.7	1.7	2.1	1.3
Utilities	22	2.2	1.2	0.7	0.5	0.9
Electric power generation, transmission, and distribution	2211	1.9	0.9	0.6	0.4	0.9
Natural gas distribution	2212	2.4	1.7	1.1	0.6	0.7
Water, sewage, and other systems	2213	4.1	2.6	1.2	1.4	1.5
Information		1.3	0.8	0.6	0.2	0.5
Publishing industries (except Internet)	511	0.8	0.4	0.3	0.1	0.4
Motion picture and sound recording industries	512	2.0	0.5	0.4	0.1	1.5
Broadcasting (except Internet)	515	1.3	0.7	0.5	0.2	0.6
Telecommunications	517	2.2	1.6	1.2	0.4	0.5
Other information services	519	0.3	0.1	0.1	(f)	0.2
Finance, insurance, and real estate		1.1	0.6	0.4	0.2	0.5
Finance and insurance	52	0.5	0.2	0.2	(f)	0.3
Credit intermediation and related activities	522	0.6	0.2	0.2	(f)	0.4
Insurance carriers and related activities	524	0.6	0.2	0.2	0.1	0.4
Real estate and rental and leasing	53	2.7	1.7	1.1	0.6	1.0
Real estate	531	2.4	1.5	1.0	0.5	0.9
Rental and leasing services	532	3.4	2.2	1.5	0.7	1.3
Lessors of nonfinancial intangible assets (except copyrighted works)	533	0.6	0.3	0.2	(f)	0.3
Professional and business services		1.4	0.7	0.4	0.2	0.7
Professional, scientific, and technical services	54	0.9	0.3	0.2	0.1	0.5
Management of companies and enterprises	55	1.0	0.5	0.3	0.2	0.5
Administrative and support and waste management and remediation services	56	2.4	1.3	0.9	0.5	1.1
Administrative and support services	561	2.3	1.2	0.8	0.4	1.1
Waste management and remediation services	562	4.5	3.0	1.9	1.2	1.5
Educational and health services		4.0	1.9	1.1	0.8	2.2
Educational services	61	2.1	0.8	0.6	0.3	1.2
Health care and social assistance	62	4.3	2.0	1.1	0.9	2.3
Ambulatory health care services	621	2.4	0.9	0.6	0.3	1.6
Hospitals	622	6.0	2.4	1.4	1.0	3.6
Nursing and residential care facilities	623	6.8	4.2	2.0	2.2	2.6
Social assistance	624	2.9	1.5	1.0	0.5	1.4
Leisure, entertainment, and hospitality		3.5	1.5	1.0	0.6	1.9
Arts, entertainment, and recreation	71	4.1	2.0	1.1	1.0	2.1
Accommodation and food services	72	3.3	1.5	0.9	0.5	1.9
Accommodation	721	4.9	2.8	1.5	1.3	2.1
Food services and drinking places	722	3.0	1.2	0.8	0.3	1.8
Other services, except public administration		2.3	1.2	0.8	0.4	1.2
Repair and maintenance	811	2.6	1.3	0.9	0.4	1.3
Personal and laundry services	812	2.2	1.3	0.8	0.5	0.9
Religious, grantmaking, civic, professional, and similar organizations	813	2.1	0.9	0.6	0.2	1.2
State and local government[d]		5.1	2.4	1.7	0.7	2.7
State government[d]		3.7	1.9	1.5	0.4	1.8
Local government[d]		5.6	2.5	1.8	0.8	3.0

See source and footnotes on page 79.

OCCUPATIONAL
Occupational Injuries and Illnesses (cont.)

Bureau of Labor Statistics estimates of nonfatal occupational injury and illness incidence rates[a] for selected industries, 2015

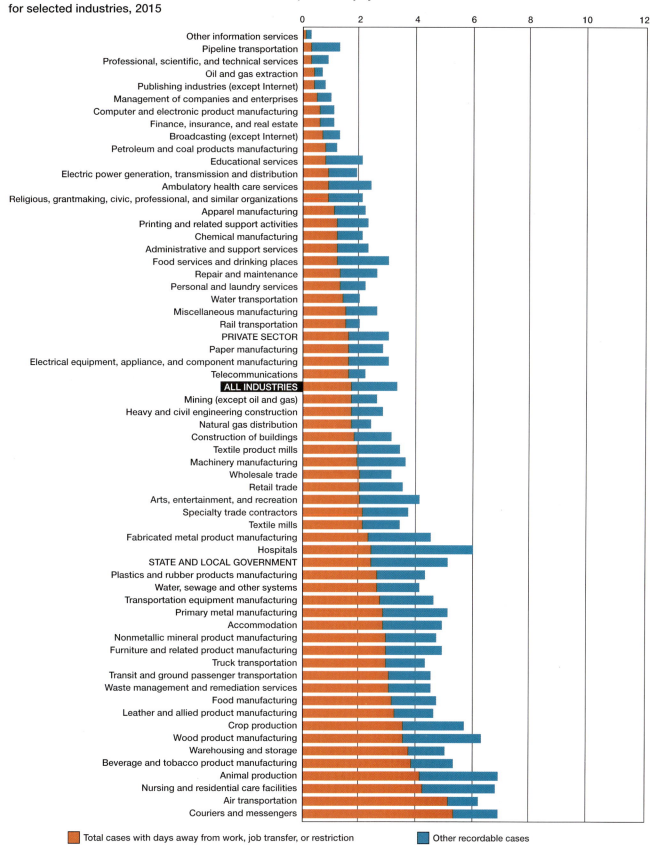

■ Total cases with days away from work, job transfer, or restriction   ■ Other recordable cases

Note: Industries are shown at the two-, three-, or four-digit NAICS level.
[a]Total cases with days away from work, job transfer, or restriction plus other recordable cases equals total recordable cases per 200,000 hours worked.

OCCUPATIONAL

Causes of Work-Related Deaths and Injuries

Roadway incidents involving motorized land vehicles are the leading cause of work-related deaths, followed by falls, slips, or trips and contact with objects and equipment. For nonfatal cases with days away from work, events involving overexertion and bodily reaction are the leading cause, followed by contact with objects and equipment and falls, slips, or trips.

Work-related deaths and injuries by event or exposure, United States, 2014

Event or exposure	Deaths[a]	Cases with days away from work[b]
Total, all events or exposures	**4,821**	**916,440**
Violence and other injuries by persons or animals	765	37,750
Intentional injury by person	689	16,110
Homicides (Intentional injury by other person)	409	15,980
Suicides (Self-inflicted injury–intentional)	280	—
Injury by person–unintentional or intent unknown	35	10,270
Injury by other person–unintentional or intent unknown	29	9,550
Self-inflicted injury–unintentional or intent unknown	6	80
Animal and insect related incidents	41	11,210
Transportation incidents	1,984	47,320
Aircraft incidents	135	600
Rail vehicle incidents	57	270
Animal and other non-motorized vehicle transportation incidents	14	330
Pedestrian vehicular incidents	318	5,510
Water vehicle incidents	55	190
Roadway incidents involving motorized land vehicle	1,157	32,930
Nonroadway incident involving motorized land vehicles	248	6,810
Fires and explosions	137	1,320
Fires	53	590
Explosions	84	720
Falls, slips, trips	818	247,120
Falls to lower level	660	49,210
Falls on same level	138	155,480
Exposure to harmful substances or environments	390	37,150
Exposure to electricity	154	1,850
Exposure to temperature extremes	26	14,990
Exposure to other harmful substances	182	15,820
Exposure to oxygen deficiency, n.e.c.[c]	27	40
Contact with objects and equipment	715	224,840
Struck by object or equipment	503	129,440
Struck against object or equipment	3	49,120
Caught in or compressed by equipment or objects	132	34,440
Struck, caught, or crushed in collapsing structure, equipment, or material	74	190
Overexertion and bodily reaction	10	312,200
Overexertion involving outside sources	5	205,920
Overexertion involving lifting, lowering	3	99,990
Overexertion in lifting–single episode	3	77,040
Repetitive motions involving microtasks	—	25,120
Nonclassifiable	—	8,730

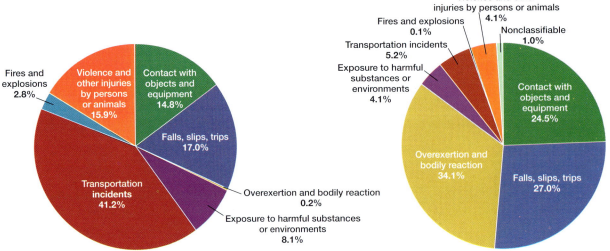

Deaths[a] by event or exposure, United States, 2014

- Fires and explosions 2.8%
- Violence and other injuries by persons or animals 15.9%
- Contact with objects and equipment 14.8%
- Falls, slips, trips 17.0%
- Transportation incidents 41.2%
- Overexertion and bodily reaction 0.2%
- Exposure to harmful substances or environments 8.1%

Cases with days away from work[b] by event or exposure, United States, 2014

- Violence and other injuries by persons or animals 4.1%
- Fires and explosions 0.1%
- Nonclassifiable 1.0%
- Transportation incidents 5.2%
- Exposure to harmful substances or environments 4.1%
- Contact with objects and equipment 24.5%
- Overexertion and bodily reaction 34.1%
- Falls, slips, trips 27.0%

Source: Bureau of Labor Statistics.
[a]Includes deaths among all workers.
[b]Includes cases with days away from work among private-sector wage and salary workers. Excludes government employees, the self-employed, and unpaid family workers.
[c]"n.e.c." means "not elsewhere classified."

OCCUPATIONAL

Benchmarking Case and Demographic Characteristics

The tables on pages 86-101 present data on the characteristics of injured and ill workers and the injuries and illnesses that affected them. These data indicate how many workers died from on-the-job injuries and how many were affected by nonfatal injuries and illnesses. The data may be used to help set priorities for occupational safety and health programs and for benchmarking.

The fatality information covers only deaths due to injuries and comes from the Bureau of Labor Statistics (BLS) Census of Fatal Occupational Injuries. The data are for calendar year 2014 and include wage and salary workers, the self-employed, and unpaid family workers in all types of businesses and industries.

The data on nonfatal cases cover both occupational injuries and illnesses and come from the BLS Survey of Occupational Injuries and Illnesses for 2014. The survey also is used to produce the incidence rates shown on the preceding pages. The estimates on the following pages are the number of cases involving days away from work (with or without days of restricted work activity). The nonfatal cases presented on pages 86-100 do not cover the self-employed; unpaid family workers; or federal, state, or local government employees. Nonfatal cases involving state and local government employees are presented on page 101.

Data are presented for the sex, age, occupation, and race or ethnic origin of the worker and for the nature of the injury or illness, the part of body affected, the source of the injury or illness, and the event or exposure that produced the injury or illness.

The text at the top of each page describes the kind of establishments that are included in the industry sector and gives the total number of workers in the industry in 2014 and the number working in the private sector.

How to benchmark

Incidence rates, percent distributions, or ranks may be used for benchmarking purposes. The results of the calculations described here may be compared to similar rates, percent distributions, and rankings based on data for a company.

For nonfatal incidence rates, multiply the number of cases by 1,000 and then divide by the private-sector employment given in the text at the top of the page. This will give the number of cases with days away from work per 1,000 employees per year. For fatality rates, multiply the number of fatalities by 100,000 then divide by the total employment given at the top of the page. This will give the number of deaths per 100,000 employees per year.

To compute percent distributions, divide the number of cases for each characteristic by the total number of cases found on the first line of the table. Multiply the quotient by 100 and round to one decimal place. Percent distributions may not add to 100% because of unclassifiable cases not shown.

Ranks are determined by arranging the characteristics from largest to smallest within each group and then numbering consecutively starting with one for the largest.

Industry sectors

Page 86 shows nonfatal injury and illness data for the private sector of the economy (excluding government entities) and fatal injury data for all industries (including government). Pages 87-100 present the data for industry sectors based on the North American Industry Classification System. Page 101 presents the fatal injury data for all government and nonfatal cases for state and local government (the BLS survey does not cover federal government entities).

OCCUPATIONAL
Private Sector/All Industries

The nonfatal occupational injury and illness data cover only private sector employees and exclude employees in federal, state, and local government entities and the self-employed. The fatal injury data cover all workers in both the private sector and government.

There were 147,533,000 people employed in 2014, of which 126,116,000 worked in the private sector.

Number of nonfatal occupational injuries and illnesses involving days away from work[a] and fatal occupational injuries by selected worker and case characteristics, private industry, United States, 2014

Characteristic	Private industry[b,c] nonfatal cases	All industries fatalities
Total	916,440	4,821
Sex		
Men	560,970	4,454
Women	348,720	367
Age		
Younger than 16	130	8
16 to 19	21,520	56
20 to 24	88,460	292
25 to 34	195,090	753
35 to 44	188,490	860
45 to 54	216,280	1,161
55 to 64	155,410	1,007
65 and older	32,250	684
Occupation		
Management, business, and financial	27,070	469
Professional and related	82,590	70
Service	218,820	770
Sales and related	55,460	239
Office and administrative support	70,750	100
Farming, fishing, and forestry	14,780	259
Construction and extractive	73,460	902
Installation, maintenance, and repair	81,730	408
Production	104,980	212
Transportation and material moving	182,800	1,354
Military occupations	—	38
Race or ethnic origin[d]		
White, non-Hispanic	358,210	3,329
Black, non-Hispanic	72,280	474
Hispanic	124,280	804
Other, multiple, and not reported	361,670	214
Nature of injury or illness		
Fractures	80,160	50
Sprains, strains, or tears	331,180	13
Amputations	4,250	20
Cuts, lacerations, or punctures	84,840	72
Bruises or contusions	74,140	—
Chemical burns and corrosions	3,440	7
Heat (thermal) burns	12,890	89
Multiple traumatic injuries	26,680	1,790
Soreness or pain	150,180	—
Carpal tunnel syndrome	6,800	—
Tendonitis	1,930	—
All other	139,940	2,778
Part of body affected		
Head	68,940	1,040
Eye	20,910	—
Neck	12,410	238
Trunk	218,560	715
Back	162,720	50
Upper extremities	288,240	10
Shoulder	72,200	6
Arm	44,290	—
Wrist	36,540	—
Hand	119,810	—
Lower extremities	211,990	80
Knee	79,850	9
Ankle	47,950	12
Foot or toe	43,460	—
Body systems	17,340	684
Multiple	89,490	2,032
All other	9,470	—

Characteristic	Private industry[b,c] nonfatal cases	All industries fatalities
Source of injury or illness		
Chemicals or chemical products	11,790	200
Containers	104,730	65
Furniture or fixtures	38,140	25
Machinery	50,480	392
Parts and materials	77,860	184
Worker motion or position	135,110	7
Health care patient	43,920	—
Floors, walkways, or ground surfaces	158,730	196
Handtools	38,790	30
Ladders	19,050	165
Vehicles	93,970	2,134
All other	143,870	1,420
Event or exposure		
Violence and other injuries by persons or animals	37,750	765
Intentional injury by other person	15,980	409
Injury by person unintentional or intent unknown	10,270	35
Transportation incidents	47,320	1,984
Roadway incidents involving motorized land vehicles	32,930	1,157
Fires or explosions	1,320	137
Falls, slips, or trips	247,120	818
Slips or trips without fall	37,020	—
Fall on same level	155,480	138
Fall to lower level	49,210	660
Exposed to harmful substances or environments	37,150	390
Contact with object or equipment	224,840	715
Struck by object	129,440	503
Struck against object	49,120	—
Caught in object, equipment, or material	34,440	132
Overexertion and bodily reaction	312,200	10
Overexertion in lifting or lowering	99,990	—
Repetitive motion involving microtasks	25,120	—
All other	8,730	—

Source: This research was conducted with restricted access to Bureau of Labor Statistics (BLS) data. The views expressed here do not necessarily reflect the views of BLS.

Note: Because of rounding and data exclusion of nonclassifiable responses, data may not sum to the totals. Dashes (—) indicate data that do not meet publication guidelines.

[a]Days away from work include those that result in days away from work with or without restricted work activity or job transfer.

[b]Excludes farms with fewer than 11 employees.

[c]Data for mining operators in coal, metal, and nonmetal mining and for employees in railroad transportation are provided to BLS by the Mine Safety and Health Administration (MSHA), U.S. Department of Labor; and the Federal Railroad Administration (FRA), U.S. Department of Transportation. Independent mining contractors are excluded from the coal, metal, and nonmetal mining industries. MSHA and FRA data do not reflect the changes in OSHA recordkeeping requirements in 2002.

[d]In the fatalities column, non-Hispanic categories include cases with Hispanic origin not reported.

OCCUPATIONAL

Agriculture, Forestry, Fishing, and Hunting

The Agriculture, Forestry, Fishing and Hunting industry sector includes growing crops; raising animals; harvesting timber; harvesting fish and other animals from a farm, ranch, or their natural habitats; and agricultural support services.

Employment in Agriculture, Forestry, Fishing, and Hunting totaled 2,237,000 in 2014, of which 2,181,000 were private sector employees.

Number of nonfatal occupational injuries and illnesses involving days away from work[a] and fatal occupational injuries by selected worker and case characteristics, private industry, United States, Agriculture, Forestry, Fishing, and Hunting, 2014

Characteristic	Nonfatal cases[b]	Fatalities
Total	17,050	584
Sex		
Men	13,260	557
Women	3,750	27
Age		
Younger than 16	40	—
16 to 19	590	14
20 to 24	2,270	29
25 to 34	4,460	67
35 to 44	3,670	75
45 to 54	3,170	87
55 to 64	1,940	108
65 and older	520	200
Occupation		
Management, business, and financial	160	271
Professional and related	240	—
Service	520	8
Sales and related	90	—
Office and administrative support	160	—
Farming, fishing, and forestry	13,320	247
Construction and extractive	30	—
Installation, maintenance, and repair	720	13
Production	410	—
Transportation and material moving	1,390	39
Military occupations	—	—
Race or ethnic origin[c]		
White, non-Hispanic	3,840	479
Black, non-Hispanic	290	21
Hispanic	9,110	68
Other, multiple, and not reported	3,810	16
Nature of injury or illness		
Fractures	1,570	5
Sprains, strains, or tears	4,610	—
Amputations	60	—
Cuts, lacerations, or punctures	1,880	—
Bruises or contusions	1,580	—
Chemical burns and corrosions	110	—
Heat (thermal) burns	80	9
Multiple traumatic injuries	580	213
Soreness or pain	2,960	—
Carpal tunnel syndrome	—	—
Tendonitis	—	—
All other	3,620	352
Part of body affected		
Head	1,850	94
Eye	870	—
Neck	140	26
Trunk	3,810	123
Back	2,450	8
Upper extremities	4,780	—
Shoulder	1,020	—
Arm	730	—
Wrist	400	—
Hand	2,330	—
Lower extremities	4,360	10
Knee	1,400	—
Ankle	860	—
Foot or toe	890	—
Body systems	410	105
Multiple	1,570	225
All other	130	—

Characteristic	Nonfatal cases[b]	Fatalities
Source of injury or illness		
Chemicals or chemical products	360	7
Containers	1,340	8
Furniture or fixtures	210	—
Machinery	820	84
Parts and materials	1,410	7
Worker motion or position	2,620	—
Health care patient	—	—
Floors, walkways, or ground surfaces	1,950	13
Handtools	890	—
Ladders	750	—
Vehicles	1,570	293
All other	5,130	166
Event or exposure		
Violence and other injuries by persons or animals	1,880	43
Intentional injury by other person	20	6
Injury by person unintentional or intent unknown	50	—
Transportation incidents	1,110	273
Roadway incidents involving motorized land vehicles	600	80
Fires or explosions	—	11
Falls, slips, or trips	4,340	48
Slips or trips without fall	780	—
Fall on same level	2,030	7
Fall to lower level	1,420	40
Exposed to harmful substances or environments	770	18
Contact with object or equipment	4,860	190
Struck by object	3,040	145
Struck against object	860	—
Caught in object, equipment, or material	620	27
Overexertion and bodily reaction	3,970	—
Overexertion in lifting or lowering	940	—
Repetitive motion involving microtasks	310	—
All other	120	—

Source: This research was conducted with restricted access to Bureau of Labor Statistics (BLS) data. The views expressed here do not necessarily reflect the views of BLS.

Note: Because of rounding and data exclusion of nonclassifiable responses, data may not sum to the totals. Dashes (—) indicate data that do not meet publication guidelines.

[a]Days away from work include those that result in days away from work with or without restricted work activity or job transfer.

[b]Excludes farms with less than 11 employees.

[c]In the fatalities column, non-Hispanic categories include cases with Hispanic origin not reported.

OCCUPATIONAL
Mining

The Mining industry sector includes extraction of naturally occurring mineral solids, such as coal and ores; liquid minerals, such as crude petroleum; and gases, such as natural gas. It also includes quarrying, well operations, beneficiating, other preparation customarily performed at the site, and mining support activities.

Mining employment in 2014 totaled 1,088,000 workers of which 1,085,000 were private sector employees.

Number of nonfatal occupational injuries and illnesses involving days away from work[a] and fatal occupational injuries by selected worker and case characteristics, private industry, United States, Mining, 2014

Characteristic	Nonfatal cases[b]	Fatalities
Total	7,680	183
Sex		
Men	7,410	181
Women	280	—
Age		
Younger than 16	—	—
16 to 19	160	5
20 to 24	1,060	19
25 to 34	2,280	62
35 to 44	1,330	35
45 to 54	1,450	29
55 to 64	1,170	27
65 and older	100	6
Occupation		
Management, business, and financial	20	5
Professional and related	90	—
Service	—	—
Sales and related	—	—
Office and administrative support	30	—
Farming, fishing, and forestry	—	—
Construction and extractive	4,210	104
Installation, maintenance, and repair	800	12
Production	470	—
Transportation and material moving	2,020	52
Military occupations	—	—
Race or ethnic origin[c]		
White, non-Hispanic	2,010	111
Black, non-Hispanic	160	7
Hispanic	860	62
Other, multiple, and not reported	4,650	—
Nature of injury or illness		
Fractures	1,680	—
Sprains, strains, or tears	2,410	—
Amputations	80	—
Cuts, lacerations, or punctures	570	—
Bruises or contusions	540	—
Chemical burns and corrosions	20	—
Heat (thermal) burns	170	8
Multiple traumatic injuries	160	79
Soreness or pain	420	—
Carpal tunnel syndrome	20	—
Tendonitis	—	—
All other	1,600	93
Part of body affected		
Head	550	37
Eye	90	—
Neck	—	7
Trunk	1,530	32
Back	930	—
Upper extremities	2,700	—
Shoulder	730	—
Arm	310	—
Wrist	160	—
Hand	1,420	—
Lower extremities	2,060	—
Knee	770	—
Ankle	420	—
Foot or toe	280	—
Body systems	160	18
Multiple	620	88
All other	40	—

Characteristic	Nonfatal cases[b]	Fatalities
Source of injury or illness		
Chemicals or chemical products	120	7
Containers	440	10
Furniture or fixtures	80	—
Machinery	1,110	37
Parts and materials	1,070	18
Worker motion or position	560	—
Health care patient	—	—
Floors, walkways, or ground surfaces	1,060	—
Handtools	560	—
Ladders	70	—
Vehicles	960	87
All other	1,650	16
Event or exposure		
Violence and other injuries by persons or animals	50	—
Intentional injury by other person	—	—
Injury by person unintentional or intent unknown	—	—
Transportation incidents	470	81
Roadway incidents involving motorized land vehicles	400	68
Fires or explosions	90	18
Falls, slips, or trips	1,560	17
Slips or trips without fall	290	—
Fall on same level	770	—
Fall to lower level	460	14
Exposed to harmful substances or environments	310	13
Contact with object or equipment	3,250	52
Struck by object	1,710	35
Struck against object	630	—
Caught in object, equipment, or material	870	10
Overexertion and bodily reaction	1,870	—
Overexertion in lifting or lowering	600	—
Repetitive motion involving microtasks	40	—
All other	70	—

Source: This research was conducted with restricted access to Bureau of Labor Statistics (BLS) data. The views expressed here do not necessarily reflect the views of BLS.

Note: Because of rounding and data exclusion of nonclassifiable responses, data may not sum to the totals. Dashes (—) indicate data that do not meet publication guidelines.

[a]Days away from work include those that result in days away from work with or without restricted work activity or job transfer.

[b]Data for mining operators in coal, metal, and nonmetal mining are provided to BLS by the Mine Safety and Health Administration (MSHA), Department of Labor. Independent mining contractors are excluded from the coal, metal, and nonmetal mining industries. MSHA data do not reflect the changes in OSHA recordkeeping requirements in 2002.

[c]In the fatalities column, non-Hispanic categories include cases with Hispanic origin not reported.

OCCUPATIONAL

Construction

The Construction industry sector includes establishments engaged in construction of buildings, heavy construction other than buildings, and specialty trade contractors such as plumbing, electrical, carpentry, etc.

In 2014, employment in the Construction industry totaled 9,813,000 workers, of which 9,390,000 were private sector employees.

Number of nonfatal occupational injuries and illnesses involving days away from work[a] and fatal occupational injuries by selected worker and case characteristics, private industry, United States, Construction, 2014

Characteristic	Nonfatal cases	Fatalities
Total	**74,460**	**899**
Sex		
Men	72,270	895
Women	2,170	—
Age		
Younger than 16	—	—
16 to 19	1,540	10
20 to 24	7,120	58
25 to 34	19,740	165
35 to 44	18,480	193
45 to 54	15,640	222
55 to 64	9,070	173
65 and older	1,080	76
Occupation		
Management, business, and financial	1,210	20
Professional and related	330	—
Service	1,000	10
Sales and related	200	—
Office and administrative support	420	—
Farming, fishing, and forestry	—	—
Construction and extractive	56,010	697
Installation, maintenance, and repair	9,780	80
Production	1,720	13
Transportation and material moving	3,610	77
Military occupations	—	—
Race or ethnic origin[b]		
White, non-Hispanic	39,550	579
Black, non-Hispanic	2,470	58
Hispanic	15,800	233
Other, multiple, and not reported	16,640	29
Nature of injury or illness		
Fractures	9,050	—
Sprains, strains, or tears	20,340	—
Amputations	280	—
Cuts, lacerations, or punctures	11,410	13
Bruises or contusions	3,760	—
Chemical burns and corrosions	550	—
Heat (thermal) burns	400	7
Multiple traumatic injuries	2,430	344
Soreness or pain	12,910	—
Carpal tunnel syndrome	120	—
Tendonitis	—	—
All other	13,200	527
Part of body affected		
Head	6,620	237
Eye	3,530	—
Neck	1,110	37
Trunk	17,180	96
Back	11,590	9
Upper extremities	24,010	—
Shoulder	4,950	—
Arm	3,200	—
Wrist	2,060	—
Hand	13,080	—
Lower extremities	18,140	9
Knee	6,080	—
Ankle	4,500	—
Foot or toe	3,620	—
Body systems	880	160
Multiple	5,940	359
All other	570	—

Characteristic	Nonfatal cases	Fatalities
Source of injury or illness		
Chemicals or chemical products	980	34
Containers	2,380	8
Furniture or fixtures	1,630	7
Machinery	4,920	92
Parts and materials	14,510	69
Worker motion or position	9,820	—
Health care patient	—	—
Floors, walkways, or ground surfaces	9,560	28
Handtools	5,930	10
Ladders	5,050	90
Vehicles	6,420	240
All other	13,260	321
Event or exposure		
Violence and other injuries by persons or animals	950	46
Intentional injury by other person	130	11
Injury by person unintentional or intent unknown	—	—
Transportation incidents	4,050	244
Roadway incidents involving motorized land vehicles	2,550	136
Fires or explosions	230	14
Falls, slips, or trips	22,330	359
Slips or trips without fall	3,320	—
Fall on same level	8,280	9
Fall to lower level	9,940	345
Exposed to harmful substances or environments	2,560	122
Contact with object or equipment	24,880	114
Struck by object	15,930	73
Struck against object	4,030	—
Caught in object, equipment, or material	2,650	12
Overexertion and bodily reaction	19,070	—
Overexertion in lifting or lowering	6,210	—
Repetitive motion involving microtasks	560	—
All other	400	—

Source: This research was conducted with restricted access to Bureau of Labor Statistics (BLS) data. The views expressed here do not necessarily reflect the views of BLS.
Note: Because of rounding and data exclusion of nonclassifiable responses, data may not sum to the totals. Dashes (—) indicate data that do not meet publication guidelines.
[a]Days away from work include those that result in days away from work with or without restricted work activity or job transfer.
[b]In the fatalities column, non-Hispanic categories include cases with Hispanic origin not reported.

OCCUPATIONAL

Manufacturing

The Manufacturing industry sector includes establishments engaged in the mechanical or chemical transformation of materials, substances, or components into new products. It includes durable and nondurable goods such as food, textiles, apparel, lumber, wood products, paper and paper products, printing, chemicals and pharmaceuticals, petroleum and coal products, rubber and plastics products, metals and metal products, machinery, electrical equipment, and transportation equipment.

Manufacturing employment in 2014 was 15,101,000 workers, of which 15,014,000 were private sector employees.

Number of nonfatal occupational injuries and illnesses involving days away from work[a] and fatal occupational injuries by selected worker and case characteristics, private industry, United States, Manufacturing, 2014

Characteristic	Nonfatal cases	Fatalities
Total	125,990	349
Sex		
Men	99,380	330
Women	26,520	19
Age		
Younger than 16	—	—
16 to 19	2,370	—
20 to 24	10,890	26
25 to 34	25,660	51
35 to 44	26,610	65
45 to 54	32,310	97
55 to 64	23,020	75
65 and older	3,140	35
Occupation		
Management, business, and financial	1,440	12
Professional and related	1,710	16
Service	2,240	7
Sales and related	730	—
Office and administrative support	3,920	—
Farming, fishing, and forestry	560	5
Construction and extractive	4,470	15
Installation, maintenance, and repair	9,290	54
Production	78,830	141
Transportation and material moving	22,710	93
Military occupations	—	—
Race or ethnic origin[b]		
White, non-Hispanic	59,470	239
Black, non-Hispanic	9,500	36
Hispanic	21,310	64
Other, multiple, and not reported	35,710	10
Nature of injury or illness		
Fractures	12,210	5
Sprains, strains, or tears	38,580	—
Amputations	2,110	—
Cuts, lacerations, or punctures	15,420	6
Bruises or contusions	9,360	—
Chemical burns and corrosions	970	—
Heat (thermal) burns	2,080	19
Multiple traumatic injuries	3,180	107
Soreness or pain	16,050	—
Carpal tunnel syndrome	2,360	—
Tendonitis	660	—
All other	23,000	204
Part of body affected		
Head	10,200	77
Eye	4,900	—
Neck	1,410	18
Trunk	26,330	44
Back	18,090	—
Upper extremities	53,850	—
Shoulder	10,870	—
Arm	6,640	—
Wrist	6,610	—
Hand	27,340	—
Lower extremities	24,320	9
Knee	8,750	—
Ankle	4,800	—
Foot or toe	5,800	—
Body systems	1,480	58
Multiple	7,720	141
All other	690	—

Characteristic	Nonfatal cases	Fatalities
Source of injury or illness		
Chemicals or chemical products	2,700	30
Containers	14,900	11
Furniture or fixtures	4,050	5
Machinery	15,980	70
Parts and materials	20,410	20
Worker motion or position	21,890	—
Health care patient	—	—
Floors, walkways, or ground surfaces	14,110	15
Handtools	8,090	—
Ladders	1,710	8
Vehicles	7,750	100
All other	14,400	86
Event or exposure		
Violence and other injuries by persons or animals	670	41
Intentional injury by other person	110	14
Injury by person unintentional or intent unknown	170	—
Transportation incidents	2,760	87
Roadway incidents involving motorized land vehicles	1,130	45
Fires or explosions	260	23
Falls, slips, or trips	23,290	49
Slips or trips without fall	3,930	—
Fall on same level	13,980	12
Fall to lower level	4,900	35
Exposed to harmful substances or environments	6,390	46
Contact with object or equipment	45,870	101
Struck by object	21,940	38
Struck against object	8,530	—
Caught in object, equipment, or material	12,780	55
Overexertion and bodily reaction	46,040	—
Overexertion in lifting or lowering	13,720	—
Repetitive motion involving microtasks	7,810	—
All other	730	—

Source: This research was conducted with restricted access to Bureau of Labor Statistics (BLS) data. The views expressed here do not necessarily reflect the views of BLS.

Note: Because of rounding and data exclusion of nonclassifiable responses, data may not sum to the totals. Dashes (—) indicate data that do not meet publication guidelines.

[a]Days away from work include those that result in days away from work with or without restricted work activity or job transfer.

[b]In the fatalities column, non-Hispanic categories include cases with Hispanic origin not reported.

OCCUPATIONAL

Wholesale Trade

Establishments in Wholesale Trade generally sell merchandise to other businesses. The merchandise includes the outputs of agriculture, mining, manufacturing, and certain information industries, such as publishing.

Wholesale Trade employed 3,642,000 people in 2014, of which 3,629,000 were private sector employees.

Number of nonfatal occupational injuries and illnesses involving days away from work[a] and fatal occupational injuries by selected worker and case characteristics, private industry, United States, Wholesale Trade, 2014

Characteristic	Nonfatal cases	Fatalities
Total	59,240	191
Sex		
Men	50,380	183
Women	8,730	8
Age		
Younger than 16	—	—
16 to 19	930	—
20 to 24	4,500	10
25 to 34	13,590	22
35 to 44	12,540	33
45 to 54	13,420	49
55 to 64	11,050	45
65 and older	1,640	31
Occupation		
Management, business, and financial	1,950	10
Professional and related	800	—
Service	600	—
Sales and related	4,140	36
Office and administrative support	6,950	6
Farming, fishing, and forestry	580	5
Construction and extractive	650	—
Installation, maintenance, and repair	6,890	22
Production	5,820	8
Transportation and material moving	30,730	97
Military occupations	—	—
Race or ethnic origin[b]		
White, non-Hispanic	27,270	137
Black, non-Hispanic	4,160	16
Hispanic	8,620	30
Other, multiple, and not reported	19,190	8
Nature of injury or illness		
Fractures	7,080	—
Sprains, strains, or tears	22,900	—
Amputations	430	—
Cuts, lacerations, or punctures	4,830	—
Bruises or contusions	4,370	—
Chemical burns and corrosions	140	—
Heat (thermal) burns	220	5
Multiple traumatic injuries	1,530	76
Soreness or pain	9,450	—
Carpal tunnel syndrome	290	—
Tendonitis	80	—
All other	7,910	105
Part of body affected		
Head	4,050	46
Eye	1,610	—
Neck	680	16
Trunk	15,510	19
Back	10,810	—
Upper extremities	17,210	—
Shoulder	4,860	—
Arm	2,960	—
Wrist	1,690	—
Hand	6,790	—
Lower extremities	15,700	—
Knee	4,520	—
Ankle	3,510	—
Foot or toe	4,000	—
Body systems	490	21
Multiple	5,270	86
All other	340	—

Characteristic	Nonfatal cases	Fatalities
Source of injury or illness		
Chemicals or chemical products	650	5
Containers	11,200	10
Furniture or fixtures	1,660	—
Machinery	2,630	19
Parts and materials	7,450	—
Worker motion or position	8,760	—
Health care patient	—	—
Floors, walkways, or ground surfaces	8,250	11
Handtools	1,900	—
Ladders	700	6
Vehicles	11,230	99
All other	4,810	34
Event or exposure		
Violence and other injuries by persons or animals	350	21
Intentional injury by other person	40	7
Injury by person unintentional or intent unknown	20	—
Transportation incidents	5,380	86
Roadway incidents involving motorized land vehicles	3,700	63
Fires or explosions	160	11
Falls, slips, or trips	14,360	30
Slips or trips without fall	3,030	—
Fall on same level	7,470	9
Fall to lower level	3,410	21
Exposed to harmful substances or environments	1,230	8
Contact with object or equipment	16,090	35
Struck by object	9,850	28
Struck against object	3,330	—
Caught in object, equipment, or material	2,280	5
Overexertion and bodily reaction	21,100	—
Overexertion in lifting or lowering	8,370	—
Repetitive motion involving microtasks	1,050	—
All other	560	—

Source: This research was conducted with restricted access to Bureau of Labor Statistics (BLS) data. The views expressed here do not necessarily reflect the views of BLS.

Note: Because of rounding and data exclusion of nonclassifiable responses, data may not sum to the totals. Dashes (—) indicate data that do not meet publication guidelines.

[a]Days away from work include those that result in days away from work with or without restricted work activity or job transfer.

[b]In the fatalities column, non-Hispanic categories include cases with Hispanic origin not reported.

OCCUPATIONAL
Retail Trade

Establishments in Retail Trade generally sell merchandise in small quantities for personal or household consumption. This sector includes both store and nonstore retailers.

Retail Trade employed 16,609,000 people in 2014, of which 16,518,000 were private sector employees.

Number of nonfatal occupational injuries and illnesses involving days away from work[a] and fatal occupational injuries by selected worker and case characteristics, private industry, United States, Retail Trade, 2014

Characteristic	Nonfatal cases	Fatalities
Total	120,640	272
Sex		
Men	68,780	225
Women	51,830	47
Age		
Younger than 16	—	—
16 to 19	4,180	—
20 to 24	16,600	23
25 to 34	25,520	40
35 to 44	21,030	38
45 to 54	26,010	61
55 to 64	19,420	65
65 and older	5,850	42
Occupation		
Management, business, and financial	2,490	10
Professional and related	1,890	—
Service	12,830	11
Sales and related	42,090	159
Office and administrative support	19,990	16
Farming, fishing, and forestry	130	—
Construction and extractive	790	—
Installation, maintenance, and repair	12,910	21
Production	6,170	—
Transportation and material moving	21,200	48
Military occupations	—	—
Race or ethnic origin[b]		
White, non-Hispanic	42,870	172
Black, non-Hispanic	4,810	34
Hispanic	9,490	21
Other, multiple, and not reported	63,470	45
Nature of injury or illness		
Fractures	9,410	—
Sprains, strains, or tears	45,670	—
Amputations	360	—
Cuts, lacerations, or punctures	13,440	6
Bruises or contusions	13,410	—
Chemical burns and corrosions	340	—
Heat (thermal) burns	1,150	—
Multiple traumatic injuries	2,820	49
Soreness or pain	16,430	—
Carpal tunnel syndrome	390	—
Tendonitis	200	—
All other	17,040	210
Part of body affected		
Head	11,900	89
Eye	2,470	—
Neck	1,350	21
Trunk	29,270	63
Back	22,240	—
Upper extremities	37,960	—
Shoulder	9,480	—
Arm	5,800	—
Wrist	4,730	—
Hand	16,520	—
Lower extremities	29,240	—
Knee	11,050	—
Ankle	5,560	—
Foot or toe	8,320	—
Body systems	2,030	17
Multiple	8,310	77
All other	590	—

Characteristic	Nonfatal cases	Fatalities
Source of injury or illness		
Chemicals or chemical products	1,470	6
Containers	23,360	—
Furniture or fixtures	8,200	—
Machinery	7,290	—
Parts and materials	9,580	9
Worker motion or position	16,400	—
Health care patient	—	—
Floors, walkways, or ground surfaces	18,930	12
Handtools	5,710	—
Ladders	3,460	14
Vehicles	12,480	69
All other	13,760	156
Event or exposure		
Violence and other injuries by persons or animals	2,570	146
Intentional injury by other person	1,390	106
Injury by person unintentional or intent unknown	450	—
Transportation incidents	4,740	59
Roadway incidents involving motorized land vehicles	3,050	39
Fires or explosions	260	8
Falls, slips, or trips	29,530	34
Slips or trips without fall	4,550	—
Fall on same level	19,930	11
Fall to lower level	4,610	21
Exposed to harmful substances or environments	3,400	9
Contact with object or equipment	36,920	15
Struck by object	22,680	13
Struck against object	8,730	—
Caught in object, equipment, or material	4,100	—
Overexertion and bodily reaction	42,720	—
Overexertion in lifting or lowering	18,490	—
Repetitive motion involving microtasks	2,510	—
All other	500	—

Source: This research was conducted with restricted access to Bureau of Labor Statistics (BLS) data. The views expressed here do not necessarily reflect the views of BLS.

Note: Because of rounding and data exclusion of nonclassifiable responses, data may not sum to the totals. Dashes (—) indicate data that do not meet publication guidelines.

[a]Days away from work include those that result in days away from work with or without restricted work activity or job transfer.

[b]In the fatalities column, non-Hispanic categories include cases with Hispanic origin not reported.

OCCUPATIONAL

Transportation and Warehousing

This industry sector includes transportation of cargo and passengers, warehousing and storage of goods, scenic and sightseeing transportation, and support activities related to transportation by rail, highway, air, water, or pipeline.

Employment in the Transportation and Warehousing industry sector totaled 6,377,000 in 2014, of which 5,381,000 were private sector employees.

Number of nonfatal occupational injuries and illnesses involving days away from work[a] and fatal occupational injuries by selected worker and case characteristics, private industry, United States, Transportation and Warehousing, 2014

Characteristic	Nonfatal cases	Fatalities
Total	95,040	766
Sex		
Men	71,380	731
Women	20,360	35
Age		
Younger than 16	—	—
16 to 19	820	6
20 to 24	5,510	21
25 to 34	14,410	78
35 to 44	20,570	140
45 to 54	27,610	224
55 to 64	20,790	213
65 and older	3,850	84
Occupation		
Management, business, and financial	330	9
Professional and related	90	—
Service	1,240	6
Sales and related	340	—
Office and administrative support	13,530	10
Farming, fishing, and forestry	—	—
Construction and extractive	770	6
Installation, maintenance, and repair	5,680	16
Production	1,510	5
Transportation and material moving	71,390	713
Military occupations	—	—
Race or ethnic origin[c]		
White, non-Hispanic	27,510	521
Black, non-Hispanic	7,450	120
Hispanic	6,930	84
Other, multiple, and not reported	53,150	41
Nature of injury or illness		
Fractures	7,440	—
Sprains, strains, or tears	45,070	—
Amputations	140	—
Cuts, lacerations, or punctures	4,530	8
Bruises or contusions	7,770	—
Chemical burns and corrosions	160	—
Heat (thermal) burns	170	23
Multiple traumatic injuries	2,770	396
Soreness or pain	14,820	—
Carpal tunnel syndrome	520	—
Tendonitis	180	—
All other	11,480	333
Part of body affected		
Head	5,550	117
Eye	1,150	—
Neck	1,740	20
Trunk	24,740	100
Back	18,930	5
Upper extremities	26,450	—
Shoulder	10,510	—
Arm	4,690	—
Wrist	3,450	—
Hand	6,440	—
Lower extremities	25,250	6
Knee	10,450	—
Ankle	5,930	—
Foot or toe	4,270	—
Body systems	980	81
Multiple	9,760	440
All other	570	—

Characteristic	Nonfatal cases	Fatalities
Source of injury or illness		
Chemicals or chemical products	660	33
Containers	19,510	—
Furniture or fixtures	2,400	—
Machinery	1,790	6
Parts and materials	9,110	11
Worker motion or position	14,730	—
Health care patient	40	—
Floors, walkways, or ground surfaces	13,970	18
Handtools	1,130	—
Ladders	870	—
Vehicles	23,190	611
All other	7,640	80
Event or exposure		
Violence and other injuries by persons or animals	1,220	71
Intentional injury by other person	510	47
Injury by person unintentional or intent unknown	200	—
Transportation incidents	10,560	548
Roadway incidents involving motorized land vehicles	6,950	394
Fires or explosions	30	9
Falls, slips, or trips	23,780	43
Slips or trips without fall	3,810	—
Fall on same level	12,820	17
Fall to lower level	5,790	24
Exposed to harmful substances or environments	1,550	39
Contact with object or equipment	18,150	55
Struck by object	9,790	50
Struck against object	4,790	—
Caught in object, equipment, or material	2,590	—
Overexertion and bodily reaction	38,960	—
Overexertion in lifting or lowering	13,000	—
Repetitive motion involving microtasks	1,510	—
All other	800	—

Source: This research was conducted with restricted access to Bureau of Labor Statistics (BLS) data. The views expressed here do not necessarily reflect the views of BLS.

Note: Because of rounding and data exclusion of nonclassifiable responses, data may not sum to the totals. Dashes (—) indicate data that do not meet publication guidelines.

[a]Days away from work include those that result in days away from work with or without restricted work activity or job transfer.

[b]Data for employees in railroad transportation are provided to BLS by the Federal Railroad Administration (FRA), U.S. Department of Transportation. FRA data do not reflect the changes in OSHA recordkeeping requirements in 2002.

[c]In the fatalities column, non-Hispanic categories include cases with Hispanic origin not reported.

OCCUPATIONAL

Utilities

The Utilities sector includes establishments that provide electric power generation, transmission, and distribution; natural gas distribution; steam supply; water treatment and distribution; and sewage collection, treatment, and disposal.

The Utilities sector employed 1,204,000 people in 2014, of which 928,000 were private sector employees.

Number of nonfatal occupational injuries and illnesses involving days away from work[a] and fatal occupational injuries by selected worker and case characteristics, private industry, United States, Utilities, 2014

Characteristic	Nonfatal cases	Fatalities
Total	3,780	17
Sex		
Men	3,410	17
Women	370	—
Age		
Younger than 16	—	—
16 to 19	—	—
20 to 24	250	—
25 to 34	560	—
35 to 44	860	—
45 to 54	1,160	6
55 to 64	800	—
65 and older	70	—
Occupation		
Management, business, and financial	60	—
Professional and related	110	—
Service	100	—
Sales and related	—	—
Office and administrative support	360	—
Farming, fishing, and forestry	—	—
Construction and extractive	570	—
Installation, maintenance, and repair	2,000	8
Production	330	—
Transportation and material moving	220	—
Military occupations	—	—
Race or ethnic origin[b]		
White, non-Hispanic	1,580	15
Black, non-Hispanic	160	—
Hispanic	190	—
Other, multiple, and not reported	1,850	—
Nature of injury or illness		
Fractures	340	—
Sprains, strains, or tears	1,790	—
Amputations	—	—
Cuts, lacerations, or punctures	230	—
Bruises or contusions	160	—
Chemical burns and corrosions	—	—
Heat (thermal) burns	30	—
Multiple traumatic injuries	100	8
Soreness or pain	500	—
Carpal tunnel syndrome	—	—
Tendonitis	—	—
All other	590	9
Part of body affected		
Head	240	—
Eye	50	—
Neck	90	—
Trunk	1,000	—
Back	780	—
Upper extremities	940	—
Shoulder	420	—
Arm	160	—
Wrist	70	—
Hand	250	—
Lower extremities	1,010	—
Knee	530	—
Ankle	160	—
Foot or toe	180	—
Body systems	50	5
Multiple	430	10
All other	20	—

Characteristic	Nonfatal cases	Fatalities
Source of injury or illness		
Chemicals or chemical products	20	—
Containers	270	—
Furniture or fixtures	30	—
Machinery	200	—
Parts and materials	570	7
Worker motion or position	810	—
Health care patient	—	—
Floors, walkways, or ground surfaces	640	—
Handtools	250	—
Ladders	40	—
Vehicles	370	5
All other	580	—
Event or exposure		
Violence and other injuries by persons or animals	80	—
Intentional injury by other person	—	—
Injury by person unintentional or intent unknown	—	—
Transportation incidents	290	5
Roadway incidents involving motorized land vehicles	200	—
Fires or explosions	—	—
Falls, slips, or trips	1,000	—
Slips or trips without fall	190	—
Fall on same level	560	—
Fall to lower level	210	—
Exposed to harmful substances or environments	160	7
Contact with object or equipment	650	—
Struck by object	310	—
Struck against object	110	—
Caught in object, equipment, or material	140	—
Overexertion and bodily reaction	1,580	—
Overexertion in lifting or lowering	460	—
Repetitive motion involving microtasks	60	—
All other	20	—

Source: This research was conducted with restricted access to Bureau of Labor Statistics (BLS) data. The views expressed here do not necessarily reflect the views of BLS.
Note: Because of rounding and data exclusion of nonclassifiable responses, data may not sum to the totals. Dashes (—) indicate data that do not meet publication guidelines.
[a]Days away from work include those that result in days away from work with or without restricted work activity or job transfer.
[b]In the fatalities column, non-Hispanic categories include cases with Hispanic origin not reported.

OCCUPATIONAL
Information

The Information sector includes establishments that produce and distribute information and cultural products, provide the means to transmit or distribute these products as well as data or communications, and process data. Included are both traditional and Internet publishing and broadcasting, motion pictures and sound recordings, telecommunications, Internet service providers, Web search portals, data processing, and information services.

The Information sector employed 3,114,000 people in 2014, of which 2,928,000 were private sector employees.

Number of nonfatal occupational injuries and illnesses involving days away from work[a] and fatal occupational injuries by selected worker and case characteristics, private industry, United States, Information, 2014

Characteristic	Nonfatal cases	Fatalities
Total	15,730	35
Sex		
Men	12,200	29
Women	3,510	6
Age		
Younger than 16	—	—
16 to 19	120	—
20 to 24	890	—
25 to 34	3,270	6
35 to 44	3,980	6
45 to 54	4,090	8
55 to 64	2,670	9
65 and older	280	—
Occupation		
Management, business, and financial	490	—
Professional and related	1,400	—
Service	660	6
Sales and related	830	—
Office and administrative support	1,450	—
Farming, fishing, and forestry	—	—
Construction and extractive	260	—
Installation, maintenance, and repair	9,010	15
Production	580	—
Transportation and material moving	1,040	11
Military occupations	—	—
Race or ethnic origin[b]		
White, non-Hispanic	2,880	30
Black, non-Hispanic	610	—
Hispanic	550	—
Other, multiple, and not reported	11,690	—
Nature of injury or illness		
Fractures	1,200	—
Sprains, strains, or tears	7,030	—
Amputations	30	—
Cuts, lacerations, or punctures	980	—
Bruises or contusions	1,070	—
Chemical burns and corrosions	—	—
Heat (thermal) burns	20	—
Multiple traumatic injuries	580	17
Soreness or pain	1,920	—
Carpal tunnel syndrome	200	—
Tendonitis	50	—
All other	2,630	17
Part of body affected		
Head	950	6
Eye	120	—
Neck	240	—
Trunk	3,220	6
Back	2,710	—
Upper extremities	3,710	—
Shoulder	1,030	—
Arm	850	—
Wrist	540	—
Hand	1,140	—
Lower extremities	4,730	—
Knee	1,550	—
Ankle	1,400	—
Foot or toe	850	—
Body systems	370	—
Multiple	2,350	18
All other	140	—

Characteristic	Nonfatal cases	Fatalities
Source of injury or illness		
Chemicals or chemical products	50	—
Containers	620	—
Furniture or fixtures	430	—
Machinery	510	—
Parts and materials	990	—
Worker motion or position	3,970	—
Health care patient	—	—
Floors, walkways, or ground surfaces	3,070	—
Handtools	270	—
Ladders	1,760	6
Vehicles	1,630	20
All other	2,430	—
Event or exposure		
Violence and other injuries by persons or animals	450	—
Intentional injury by other person	40	—
Injury by person unintentional or intent unknown	30	—
Transportation incidents	1,360	18
Roadway incidents involving motorized land vehicles	1,240	17
Fires or explosions	—	—
Falls, slips, or trips	5,280	10
Slips or trips without fall	940	—
Fall on same level	2,900	—
Fall to lower level	1,210	7
Exposed to harmful substances or environments	410	—
Contact with object or equipment	2,570	—
Struck by object	1,240	—
Struck against object	800	—
Caught in object, equipment, or material	270	—
Overexertion and bodily reaction	5,450	—
Overexertion in lifting or lowering	930	—
Repetitive motion involving microtasks	510	—
All other	220	—

Source: This research was conducted with restricted access to Bureau of Labor Statistics (BLS) data. The views expressed here do not necessarily reflect the views of BLS.

Note: Because of rounding and data exclusion of nonclassifiable responses, data may not sum to the totals. Dashes (—) indicate data that do not meet publication guidelines.

[a]Days away from work include those that result in days away from work with or without restricted work activity or job transfer.

[b]In the fatalities column, non-Hispanic categories include cases with Hispanic origin not reported.

OCCUPATIONAL

Financial Activities

Financial Activities includes the Finance and Insurance sector and the Real Estate and Rental and Leasing sector. Included are banks and other savings institutions; securities and commodities brokers, dealers, exchanges, and services; insurance carriers, brokers, and agents; real estate operators, developers, agents, and brokers; and establishments that rent and lease goods, such as automobiles, computers, and household and industrial machinery and equipment.

Financial Activities had 9,871,000 workers in 2014, of which 9,635,000 were private sector employees.

Number of nonfatal occupational injuries and illnesses involving days away from work[a] and fatal occupational injuries by selected worker and case characteristics, private industry, United States, Financial Activities, 2014

Characteristic	Nonfatal cases	Fatalities
Total	26,350	117
Sex		
Men	14,880	92
Women	11,470	25
Age		
Younger than 16	—	—
16 to 19	200	—
20 to 24	1,370	—
25 to 34	4,890	16
35 to 44	5,560	16
45 to 54	6,530	29
55 to 64	6,510	29
65 and older	1,040	24
Occupation		
Management, business, and financial	4,020	32
Professional and related	730	—
Service	4,630	9
Sales and related	2,240	26
Office and administrative support	6,120	10
Farming, fishing, and forestry	—	—
Construction and extractive	740	—
Installation, maintenance, and repair	5,550	14
Production	90	—
Transportation and material moving	2,220	20
Military occupations	—	—
Race or ethnic origin[b]		
White, non-Hispanic	9,520	83
Black, non-Hispanic	2,210	8
Hispanic	4,610	20
Other, multiple, and not reported	10,010	6
Nature of injury or illness		
Fractures	2,230	—
Sprains, strains, or tears	6,820	—
Amputations	30	—
Cuts, lacerations, or punctures	1,710	6
Bruises or contusions	2,060	—
Chemical burns and corrosions	30	—
Heat (thermal) burns	60	—
Multiple traumatic injuries	1,020	36
Soreness or pain	6,980	—
Carpal tunnel syndrome	1,000	—
Tendonitis	70	—
All other	4,350	72
Part of body affected		
Head	1,550	29
Eye	400	—
Neck	630	9
Trunk	4,980	21
Back	4,000	—
Upper extremities	8,010	—
Shoulder	2,140	—
Arm	1,040	—
Wrist	1,890	—
Hand	2,390	—
Lower extremities	6,580	—
Knee	2,870	—
Ankle	1,340	—
Foot or toe	1,130	—
Body systems	600	13
Multiple	3,920	43
All other	80	—

Characteristic	Nonfatal cases	Fatalities
Source of injury or illness		
Chemicals or chemical products	230	—
Containers	1,480	—
Furniture or fixtures	1,200	—
Machinery	1,440	7
Parts and materials	1,160	6
Worker motion or position	5,410	—
Health care patient	20	—
Floors, walkways, or ground surfaces	8,130	7
Handtools	890	—
Ladders	990	—
Vehicles	2,100	38
All other	3,300	52
Event or exposure		
Violence and other injuries by persons or animals	420	44
Intentional injury by other person	90	21
Injury by person unintentional or intent unknown	40	—
Transportation incidents	1,180	42
Roadway incidents involving motorized land vehicles	860	31
Fires or explosions	—	—
Falls, slips, or trips	10,610	19
Slips or trips without fall	860	—
Fall on same level	7,170	—
Fall to lower level	2,420	15
Exposed to harmful substances or environments	690	6
Contact with object or equipment	4,600	—
Struck by object	2,910	—
Struck against object	1,150	—
Caught in object, equipment, or material	210	—
Overexertion and bodily reaction	8,730	—
Overexertion in lifting or lowering	1,960	—
Repetitive motion involving microtasks	2,340	—
All other	110	—

Source: This research was conducted with restricted access to Bureau of Labor Statistics (BLS) data. The views expressed here do not necessarily reflect the views of BLS.

Note: Because of rounding and data exclusion of nonclassifiable responses, data may not sum to the totals. Dashes (—) indicate data that do not meet publication guidelines.

[a] Days away from work include those that result in days away from work with or without restricted work activity or job transfer.

[b] In the fatalities column, non-Hispanic categories include cases with Hispanic origin not reported.

OCCUPATIONAL
Professional and Business Services

The Professional and Business Services sector includes legal, accounting, architectural, engineering, computer, consulting, research, advertising, photographic, translation and interpretation, veterinary, and other professional scientific and technical services. Also included are business management and administrative and support activities and waste management and remediation services.

Professional and Business Services employed 17,005,000 people in 2014, of which 16,571,000 were private sector employees.

Number of nonfatal occupational injuries and illnesses involving days away from work[a] and fatal occupational injuries by selected worker and case characteristics, private industry, United States, Professional and Business Services, 2014

Characteristic	Nonfatal cases	Fatalities
Total	77,720	425
Sex		
Men	50,450	396
Women	24,750	29
Age		
Younger than 16	—	—
16 to 19	1,210	—
20 to 24	6,510	28
25 to 34	17,460	81
35 to 44	16,280	83
45 to 54	18,790	107
55 to 64	10,350	85
65 and older	2,900	37
Occupation		
Management, business, and financial	2,980	21
Professional and related	7,630	27
Service	29,900	224
Sales and related	1,880	7
Office and administrative support	8,010	13
Farming, fishing, and forestry	80	—
Construction and extractive	3,390	27
Installation, maintenance, and repair	4,370	14
Production	2,910	15
Transportation and material moving	14,000	76
Military occupations	—	—
Race or ethnic origin[b]		
White, non-Hispanic	29,880	258
Black, non-Hispanic	5,880	53
Hispanic	13,260	104
Other, multiple, and not reported	28,700	10
Nature of injury or illness		
Fractures	7,830	5
Sprains, strains, or tears	24,360	—
Amputations	150	—
Cuts, lacerations, or punctures	7,520	9
Bruises or contusions	5,000	—
Chemical burns and corrosions	220	—
Heat (thermal) burns	480	—
Multiple traumatic injuries	2,870	154
Soreness or pain	14,170	—
Carpal tunnel syndrome	790	—
Tendonitis	90	—
All other	14,240	251
Part of body affected		
Head	5,050	72
Eye	1,530	—
Neck	660	25
Trunk	17,010	74
Back	12,640	—
Upper extremities	22,560	—
Shoulder	4,860	—
Arm	4,840	—
Wrist	3,100	—
Hand	8,650	—
Lower extremities	17,860	8
Knee	6,540	—
Ankle	3,940	—
Foot or toe	3,500	—
Body systems	2,730	73
Multiple	8,690	173
All other	3,150	—

Characteristic	Nonfatal cases	Fatalities
Source of injury or illness		
Chemicals or chemical products	760	16
Containers	7,470	7
Furniture or fixtures	2,410	—
Machinery	4,240	31
Parts and materials	4,530	13
Worker motion or position	11,520	—
Health care patient	390	—
Floors, walkways, or ground surfaces	14,370	19
Handtools	3,720	7
Ladders	1,430	15
Vehicles	8,810	156
All other	18,070	159
Event or exposure		
Violence and other injuries by persons or animals	4,390	71
Intentional injury by other person	470	40
Injury by person unintentional or intent unknown	440	—
Transportation incidents	5,860	145
Roadway incidents involving motorized land vehicles	4,750	80
Fires or explosions	130	—
Falls, slips, or trips	23,140	94
Slips or trips without fall	3,690	—
Fall on same level	14,360	12
Fall to lower level	4,660	80
Exposed to harmful substances or environments	2,690	41
Contact with object or equipment	15,020	72
Struck by object	8,640	58
Struck against object	3,570	—
Caught in object, equipment, or material	2,050	11
Overexertion and bodily reaction	23,410	—
Overexertion in lifting or lowering	7,560	—
Repetitive motion involving microtasks	2,780	—
All other	3,090	—

Source: This research was conducted with restricted access to Bureau of Labor Statistics (BLS) data. The views expressed here do not necessarily reflect the views of BLS.
Note: Because of rounding and data exclusion of nonclassifiable responses, data may not sum to the totals. Dashes (—) indicate data that do not meet publication guidelines.
[a]Days away from work include those that result in days away from work with or without restricted work activity.
[b]In the fatalities column, non-Hispanic categories include cases with Hispanic origin not reported.

OCCUPATIONAL
Educational and Health Services

Educational Services includes instruction and training through schools, colleges, universities, and training centers. Health Services includes ambulatory health care facilities, hospitals, nursing and residential care facilities, and social assistance for individuals, families, and communities.

Educational and Health Services employed 32,830,000 people in 2014, of which 22,647,000 were private sector employees.

Number of nonfatal occupational injuries and illnesses involving days away from work[a] and fatal occupational injuries by selected worker and case characteristics, private industry, United States, Educational and Health Services, 2014

Characteristic	Nonfatal cases	Fatalities
Total	**175,900**	**146**
Sex		
Men	36,420	96
Women	139,250	50
Age		
Younger than 16	30	—
16 to 19	2,350	—
20 to 24	14,880	9
25 to 34	36,650	34
35 to 44	36,410	14
45 to 54	42,720	38
55 to 64	32,960	20
65 and older	7,270	30
Occupation		
Management, business, and financial	6,100	11
Professional and related	62,480	—
Service	89,620	96
Sales and related	570	—
Office and administrative support	7,410	5
Farming, fishing, and forestry	—	—
Construction and extractive	790	—
Installation, maintenance, and repair	3,820	—
Production	1,240	—
Transportation and material moving	3,580	25
Military occupations	—	—
Race or ethnic origin[b]		
White, non-Hispanic	69,070	107
Black, non-Hispanic	25,390	17
Hispanic	14,250	16
Other, multiple, and not reported	67,190	6
Nature of injury or illness		
Fractures	10,650	6
Sprains, strains, or tears	77,990	—
Amputations	160	—
Cuts, lacerations, or punctures	6,420	—
Bruises or contusions	15,870	—
Chemical burns and corrosions	330	—
Heat (thermal) burns	1,480	—
Multiple traumatic injuries	5,390	58
Soreness or pain	33,790	—
Carpal tunnel syndrome	650	—
Tendonitis	410	—
All other	22,760	73
Part of body affected		
Head	11,560	24
Eye	1,890	—
Neck	3,440	7
Trunk	51,440	14
Back	42,530	—
Upper extremities	42,760	—
Shoulder	13,610	—
Arm	6,510	—
Wrist	7,160	—
Hand	11,810	—
Lower extremities	35,590	11
Knee	15,230	—
Ankle	9,020	—
Foot or toe	5,310	—
Body systems	5,190	23
Multiple	24,390	65
All other	1,530	—

Characteristic	Nonfatal cases	Fatalities
Source of injury or illness		
Chemicals or chemical products	2,330	15
Containers	7,680	—
Furniture or fixtures	8,890	—
Machinery	2,930	—
Parts and materials	2,170	—
Worker motion or position	21,970	—
Health care patient	43,410	—
Floors, walkways, or ground surfaces	38,870	17
Handtools	1,800	—
Ladders	570	—
Vehicles	9,700	71
All other	35,580	35
Event or exposure		
Violence and other injuries by persons or animals	21,120	32
Intentional injury by other person	11,920	15
Injury by person unintentional or intent unknown	7,590	—
Transportation incidents	5,970	73
Roadway incidents involving motorized land vehicles	5,180	30
Fires or explosions	60	—
Falls, slips, or trips	51,150	21
Slips or trips without fall	6,770	—
Fall on same level	39,260	14
Fall to lower level	4,710	6
Exposed to harmful substances or environments	7,560	17
Contact with object or equipment	20,470	—
Struck by object	11,680	—
Struck against object	5,830	—
Caught in object, equipment, or material	2,000	—
Overexertion and bodily reaction	68,720	—
Overexertion in lifting or lowering	17,560	—
Repetitive motion involving microtasks	3,050	—
All other	850	—

Source: This research was conducted with restricted access to Bureau of Labor Statistics (BLS) data. The views expressed here do not necessarily reflect the views of BLS.

Note: Because of rounding and data exclusion of nonclassifiable responses, data may not sum to the totals. Dashes (—) indicate data that do not meet publication guidelines.

[a] Days away from work include those that result in days away from work with or without restricted work activity.

[b] In the fatalities column, non-Hispanic categories include cases with Hispanic origin not reported.

OCCUPATIONAL
Leisure and Hospitality

The Leisure sector includes establishments that provide arts, entertainment, and recreation experiences such as theatre, dance, music, and spectator sports, museums, zoos, amusement and theme parks, casinos, golf courses, ski areas, marinas, and fitness and sports centers. The Hospitality sector includes hotels and other traveler accommodations, food services, and drinking places.

The Leisure and Hospitality sector employed 13,490,000 people in 2014, of which 13,077,000 were private sector employees.

Number of nonfatal occupational injuries and illnesses involving days away from work[a] and fatal occupational injuries by selected worker and case characteristics, private industry, United States, Leisure and Hospitality, 2014

Characteristic	Nonfatal cases	Fatalities
Total	90,920	216
Sex		
Men	44,070	184
Women	46,820	32
Age		
Younger than 16	30	—
16 to 19	6,420	8
20 to 24	14,080	18
25 to 34	21,380	37
35 to 44	15,560	38
45 to 54	17,440	50
55 to 64	11,760	29
65 and older	3,080	34
Occupation		
Management, business, and financial	4,930	40
Professional and related	3,910	—
Service	69,470	124
Sales and related	1,900	—
Office and administrative support	1,430	6
Farming, fishing, and forestry	30	—
Construction and extractive	470	—
Installation, maintenance, and repair	2,930	12
Production	1,560	—
Transportation and material moving	4,200	28
Military occupations	—	—
Race or ethnic origin[b]		
White, non-Hispanic	29,730	140
Black, non-Hispanic	7,190	22
Hispanic	16,110	38
Other, multiple, and not reported	37,890	16
Nature of injury or illness		
Fractures	6,340	—
Sprains, strains, or tears	25,900	—
Amputations	270	—
Cuts, lacerations, or punctures	12,870	10
Bruises or contusions	7,920	—
Chemical burns and corrosions	550	—
Heat (thermal) burns	6,330	5
Multiple traumatic injuries	2,440	44
Soreness or pain	15,110	—
Carpal tunnel syndrome	160	—
Tendonitis	160	—
All other	12,860	152
Part of body affected		
Head	7,150	57
Eye	1,880	—
Neck	730	17
Trunk	16,840	43
Back	11,290	—
Upper extremities	33,970	—
Shoulder	5,370	—
Arm	4,840	—
Wrist	3,900	—
Hand	17,780	—
Lower extremities	21,640	—
Knee	8,550	—
Ankle	4,690	—
Foot or toe	4,220	—
Body systems	1,410	33
Multiple	8,060	63
All other	1,120	—

Characteristic	Nonfatal cases	Fatalities
Source of injury or illness		
Chemicals or chemical products	1,230	14
Containers	12,050	—
Furniture or fixtures	6,170	—
Machinery	5,300	12
Parts and materials	2,160	—
Worker motion or position	13,020	—
Health care patient	—	—
Floors, walkways, or ground surfaces	20,620	13
Handtools	6,260	—
Ladders	1,320	—
Vehicles	4,430	70
All other	18,360	98
Event or exposure		
Violence and other injuries by persons or animals	2,720	79
Intentional injury by other person	1,160	49
Injury by person unintentional or intent unknown	1,090	—
Transportation incidents	1,950	68
Roadway incidents involving motorized land vehicles	1,020	25
Fires or explosions	90	8
Falls, slips, or trips	29,150	23
Slips or trips without fall	3,950	—
Fall on same level	21,090	10
Fall to lower level	3,800	13
Exposed to harmful substances or environments	8,460	20
Contact with object or equipment	25,140	18
Struck by object	15,720	12
Struck against object	5,660	—
Caught in object, equipment, or material	2,900	—
Overexertion and bodily reaction	22,510	—
Overexertion in lifting or lowering	7,210	—
Repetitive motion involving microtasks	1,770	—
All other	900	—

Source: This research was conducted with restricted access to Bureau of Labor Statistics (BLS) data. The views expressed here do not necessarily reflect the views of BLS.

Note: Because of rounding and data exclusion of nonclassifiable responses, data may not sum to the totals. Dashes (—) indicate data that do not meet publication guidelines.

[a]Days away from work include those that result in days away from work with or without restricted work activity or job transfer.

[b]In the fatalities column, non-Hispanic categories include cases with Hispanic origin not reported.

OCCUPATIONAL
Other Services

The Other Services sector includes repair and maintenance of equipment and machinery and personal and household goods; personal care and laundry services; and religious, grant making, civic, professional, and similar organizations.

The Other Services sector employed 7,169,000 people in 2014, of which 7,132,000 were private sector employees.

Number of nonfatal occupational injuries and illnesses involving days away from work[a] and fatal occupational injuries by selected worker and case characteristics, private industry, United States, Other Services (except Public Administration), 2014

Characteristic	Nonfatal cases	Fatalities
Total	**25,940**	**186**
Sex		
Men	16,670	163
Women	8,920	23
Age		
Younger than 16	—	—
16 to 19	590	—
20 to 24	2,550	7
25 to 34	5,230	23
35 to 44	5,600	39
45 to 54	5,920	45
55 to 64	3,910	36
65 and older	1,440	35
Occupation		
Management, business, and financial	900	10
Professional and related	1,160	—
Service	6,000	46
Sales and related	440	—
Office and administrative support	960	—
Farming, fishing, and forestry	30	—
Construction and extractive	300	—
Installation, maintenance, and repair	7,970	96
Production	3,360	5
Transportation and material moving	4,490	19
Military occupations	—	—
Race or ethnic origin[b]		
White, non-Hispanic	13,030	130
Black, non-Hispanic	2,000	24
Hispanic	3,190	25
Other, multiple, and not reported	7,720	7
Nature of injury or illness		
Fractures	3,130	5
Sprains, strains, or tears	7,680	—
Amputations	140	—
Cuts, lacerations, or punctures	3,020	—
Bruises or contusions	1,260	—
Chemical burns and corrosions	40	—
Heat (thermal) burns	230	—
Multiple traumatic injuries	830	46
Soreness or pain	4,650	—
Carpal tunnel syndrome	280	—
Tendonitis	—	—
All other	4,670	129
Part of body affected		
Head	1,730	49
Eye	410	—
Neck	170	13
Trunk	5,700	30
Back	3,730	—
Upper extremities	9,320	—
Shoulder	2,350	—
Arm	1,710	—
Wrist	790	—
Hand	3,880	—
Lower extremities	5,510	—
Knee	1,560	—
Ankle	1,800	—
Foot or toe	1,090	—
Body systems	570	30
Multiple	2,450	60
All other	490	—

Characteristic	Nonfatal cases	Fatalities
Source of injury or illness		
Chemicals or chemical products	210	18
Containers	2,020	—
Furniture or fixtures	780	—
Machinery	1,310	9
Parts and materials	2,760	7
Worker motion or position	3,650	—
Health care patient	30	—
Floors, walkways, or ground surfaces	5,200	14
Handtools	1,390	—
Ladders	330	8
Vehicles	3,330	65
All other	4,930	62
Event or exposure		
Violence and other injuries by persons or animals	890	51
Intentional injury by other person	80	25
Injury by person unintentional or intent unknown	170	—
Transportation incidents	1,650	45
Roadway incidents involving motorized land vehicles	1,310	24
Fires or explosions	—	12
Falls, slips, or trips	7,600	29
Slips or trips without fall	910	—
Fall on same level	4,860	9
Fall to lower level	1,670	20
Exposed to harmful substances or environments	980	14
Contact with object or equipment	6,360	34
Struck by object	3,990	30
Struck against object	1,090	—
Caught in object, equipment, or material	990	—
Overexertion and bodily reaction	8,090	—
Overexertion in lifting or lowering	2,990	—
Repetitive motion involving microtasks	800	—
All other	370	—

Source: This research was conducted with restricted access to Bureau of Labor Statistics (BLS) data. The views expressed here do not necessarily reflect the views of BLS.

Note: Because of rounding and data exclusion of nonclassifiable responses, data may not sum to the totals. Dashes (—) indicate data that do not meet publication guidelines.

[a]Days away from work include those that result in days away from work with or without restricted work activity or job transfer.

[b]In the fatalities column, non-Hispanic categories include cases with Hispanic origin not reported.

OCCUPATIONAL
Government

Government includes public employees at all levels from federal (civilian and military) to state, county, and municipal.

Total government employment was 21,417,000 in 2014, of which 16,745,000 were state and local government employees.

Number of nonfatal occupational injuries and illnesses involving days away from work[a] and fatal occupational injuries by selected worker and case characteristics, United States, Government, 2014

Characteristic	State and local government nonfatal cases[b]	All government fatalities
Total	240,970	435
Sex		
Men	138,500	375
Women	97,560	60
Age		
Younger than 16	50	—
16 to 19	1,350	—
20 to 24	9,210	37
25 to 34	39,090	70
35 to 44	56,210	81
45 to 54	70,210	109
55 to 64	46,330	89
65 and older	9,350	46
Occupation		
Management, business, and financial	6,090	17
Professional and related	50,630	12
Service	115,240	219
Sales and related	440	—
Office and administrative support	11,000	25
Farming, fishing, and forestry	380	—
Construction and extractive	15,460	36
Installation, maintenance, and repair	12,700	28
Production	3,150	5
Transportation and material moving	20,380	55
Military occupations	—	38
Race or ethnic origin[c]		
White, non-Hispanic	86,390	328
Black, non-Hispanic	16,200	57
Hispanic	13,830	34
Other, multiple, and not reported	124,550	16
Nature of injury or illness		
Fractures	15,390	11
Sprains, strains, or tears	89,690	6
Amputations	650	—
Cuts, lacerations, or punctures	9,830	—
Bruises or contusions	22,940	—
Chemical burns and corrosions	310	—
Heat (thermal) burns	1,230	—
Multiple traumatic injuries	9,360	163
Soreness or pain	47,690	—
Carpal tunnel syndrome	1,170	—
Tendonitis	510	—
All other	42,210	251
Part of body affected		
Head	15,810	105
Eye	2,820	—
Neck	3,650	20
Trunk	50,720	70
Back	37,520	6
Upper extremities	57,930	—
Shoulder	16,780	—
Arm	9,040	—
Wrist	7,440	—
Hand	17,630	—
Lower extremities	56,870	—
Knee	24,240	—
Ankle	12,880	—
Foot or toe	8,610	—
Body systems	7,100	44
Multiple	42,420	184
All other	6,460	—

Characteristic	State and local government nonfatal cases[b]	All government fatalities
Source of injury or illness		
Chemicals or chemical products	2,050	12
Containers	13,800	—
Furniture or fixtures	9,000	—
Machinery	5,390	21
Parts and materials	8,460	9
Worker motion or position	39,530	—
Health care patient	14,180	—
Floors, walkways, or ground surfaces	48,880	23
Handtools	5,570	—
Ladders	2,190	5
Vehicles	22,420	210
All other	69,500	147
Event or exposure		
Violence and other injuries by persons or animals	35,660	112
Intentional injury by other person	15,400	67
Injury by person unintentional or intent unknown	16,830	12
Transportation incidents	14,920	210
Roadway incidents involving motorized land vehicles	12,040	121
Fires or explosions	660	18
Falls, slips, or trips	69,530	41
Slips or trips without fall	11,060	—
Fall on same level	48,000	20
Fall to lower level	9,240	18
Exposed to harmful substances or environments	8,860	27
Contact with object or equipment	32,090	22
Struck by object	15,860	15
Struck against object	10,370	—
Caught in object, equipment, or material	3,410	—
Overexertion and bodily reaction	72,050	5
Overexertion in lifting or lowering	19,420	—
Repetitive motion involving microtasks	4,320	—
All other	7,200	—

Source: This research was conducted with restricted access to Bureau of Labor Statistics (BLS) data. The views expressed here do not necessarily reflect the views of BLS.

Note: Because of rounding and data exclusion of nonclassifiable responses, data may not sum to the totals. Dashes (—) indicate data that do not meet publication guidelines.

[a]Days away from work include those that result in days away from work with or without restricted work activity.

[b]Data for government entities is only collected for state and local governments in the BLS National Survey of Occupational Injuries and Illnesses.

[c]In the fatalities column, non-Hispanic categories include cases with Hispanic origin not reported.

Motor Vehicle

Motor Vehicle Highlights

Costs — pg. 109

Alcohol — pgs. 114-115

Speeding — pg. 117

NEW! Assistive safety technology — pg. 119

Young drivers — pg. 124

NEW! ATV — pg. 125

NEW! Impact of recession — pg. 127

INJURY FACTS® 2017

Assistive Safety Technology — pg. 119

Assistive or advanced safety technologies like adaptive headlights, forward collision prevention, lane departure warning, and back-up cameras are becoming increasingly available in new automobiles. Back-up cameras will be a required safety feature starting in May 2018, while most major automobile makers have voluntarily committed to providing forward collision warning and emergency braking systems in new cars by the 2023 model year. These new assistive safety technologies have the potential of preventing or mitigating many crashes. *The Insurance Institute for Highway Safety* estimates that lane departure warning, adaptive headlights, forward collision warning, and side view assist have the collective potential of preventing or mitigating over 10,000 fatal crashes a year.

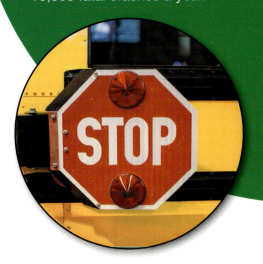 

MOTOR VEHICLE

Motor Vehicle, 2015

Between 1912 and 2015, motor-vehicle deaths per 10,000 registered vehicles decreased 96%, from 33 to 1.44. In 1912, 3,100 fatalities occurred when the number of registered vehicles totaled only 950,000. In 2015, 37,757 fatalities occurred, but registrations soared to 263 million. While mileage data were not available in 1912, the 2015 mileage death rate of 1.21 per 100,000,000 vehicle miles was up 3% from the revised 2014 rate of 1.17.

A refinement of the medically consulted injury estimate was made for the 2016 edition of *Injury Facts* that makes comparison of medically consulted injuries to previous years inappropriate. Medically consulted injuries reported in this edition are also not comparable to previous disabling injury estimates. Please see the Technical Appendix for a detailed description of this change. Medically consulted injuries in motor-vehicle incidents totaled 4,300,000 in 2015, and total motor vehicle costs were estimated at $385.3 billion. Costs include wage and productivity losses, medical expenses, administrative expenses, motor-vehicle property damage, and employer costs. Major revisions were made to the National Safety Council (NSC) cost model for the 2016 edition that took advantage of data sources not previously available. Because of the changes made to the cost model, cost estimates provided in this edition are not comparable to those published prior to the 2016 edition.

Motor-vehicle deaths increased 7% from 2014 to 2015 following an increase of less than 0.5% from 2013 to 2014. Miles traveled was up 3%, the number of registered vehicles increased 1%, and the population increased 1%. As a result, the mileage rate was up 3% while the vehicle and population death rates were each up 6% from 2014 to 2015.

Compared to 2006, 2015 motor-vehicle deaths decreased by about 17%. Mileage, registration, and population death rates also were sharply lower in 2015 compared with 2006 (see chart on next page).

The National Safety Council avoids using the word "accident." To some people, the word "accident" may imply a sense of inevitability. In contrast, the safety practice continually strives to decrease and ultimately prevent all unintentional injuries. NSC uses the terms "collision" and "crashes" in place of the word "accident."

Deaths	37,757
Medically consulted injuries	4,300,000
Cost	$385.3 billion
Motor-vehicle mileage	3,131 billion
Registered vehicles in the United States	262,800,000
Licensed drivers in the United States	214,800,000
Death rate per 100,000,000 vehicle miles	1.21
Death rate per 10,000 registered vehicles	1.44
Death rate per 100,000 population	11.75

Motor-vehicle crash outcomes, United States, 2015

Severity	Deaths or injuries	Crashes	Drivers (vehicles) involved
Fatal (within 1 year)	37,757	34,600	52,300
Medically consulted injury	4,300,000	3,000,000	5,500,000
Property damage (including unreported) and nondisabling injury		9,800,000	17,300,000
Total		12,800,000	22,900,000
Fatal (within 30 days)	35,092	32,166	48,613
Injury (disabling and nondisabling)	2,443,000	1,715,000	3,171,000
Police-reported property damage		4,548,000	8,032,000
Total		6,296,000	11,252,000

Source: National Highway Traffic Safety Administration for deaths, injuries, and total crashes in bottom half of table. All other figures are National Safety Council estimates.

MOTOR VEHICLE
Motor Vehicle, 2015 (cont.)

Travel, deaths, and death rates, United States, 1925-2015

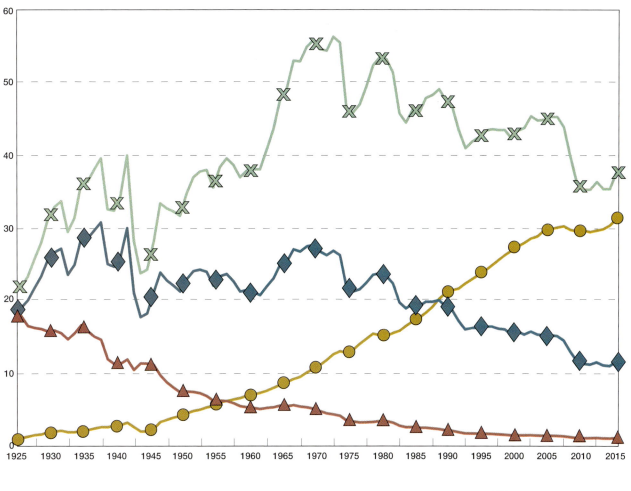

INJURY FACTS® 2017 EDITION

MOTOR VEHICLE

Deaths Due to Motor-Vehicle Crashes, 2015

Type of crash and age of victim

All motor-vehicle crashes

Includes deaths involving mechanically or electrically powered highway-transport vehicles in motion (except those on rails), both on and off the highway or street.

	Total	Change from 2014	Death rate[a]
Deaths	37,757	+7%	11.7
Nonfatal injuries[b]	4,300,000		

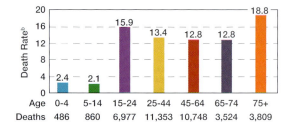

Collision between motor vehicles

Includes deaths from collisions of two or more motor vehicles. Motorized bicycles and scooters, trolley buses, and farm tractors or road machinery traveling on highways are motor vehicles.

	Total	Change from 2014	Death rate[a]
Deaths	15,300	+10%	4.8
Nonfatal injuries[b]	3,340,000		

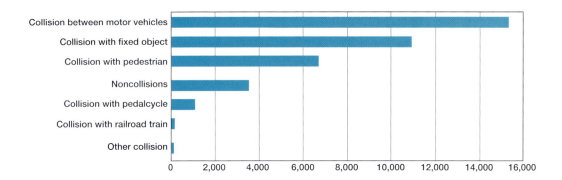

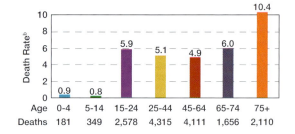

Collision with fixed object

Includes deaths from collisions in which the first harmful event is the striking of a fixed object such as a guardrail, abutment, impact attenuator, etc.

	Total	Change from 2014	Death rate[a]
Deaths	10,900	+2%	3.4
Nonfatal injuries[b]	540,000		

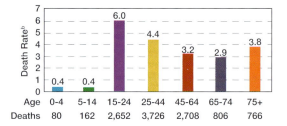

Collision with pedestrian

Includes all deaths of people struck by motor vehicles, either on or off a street or highway, regardless of the circumstances of the incident.

	Total	Change from 2014	Death rate[a]
Deaths	6,700	+6%	2.1
Nonfatal injuries[b]	160,000		

See footnotes on page 107.

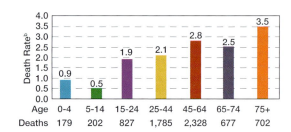

MOTOR VEHICLE
Deaths Due to Motor-Vehicle Crashes, 2015 (cont.)

Type of crash and age of victim

Noncollisions
Includes deaths from noncollisions in which the first injury or damage-producing event was an overturn, jackknife, or other type of noncollision.

	Total	Change from 2014	Death rate[a]
Deaths	3,500	+6%	1.1
Nonfatal injuries[b]	135,000		

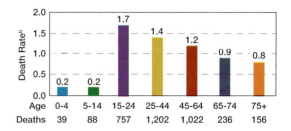

Collision with pedalcycle
Includes deaths of pedalcyclists and motor-vehicle occupants from collisions between pedalcycles and motor vehicles on streets, highways, private driveways, parking lots, etc.

	Total	Change from 2014	Death rate[a]
Deaths	1,100	+10%	0.3
Nonfatal injuries[b]	110,000		

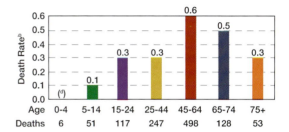

Collision with railroad train
Includes deaths from collisions of motor vehicles (moving or stalled) and railroad vehicles at public or private grade crossings. In other types of incidents, classification requires motor vehicle to be in motion.

	Total	Change from 2014	Death rate[a]
Deaths	110	-24%	[d]
Nonfatal injuries[b]	1,000		

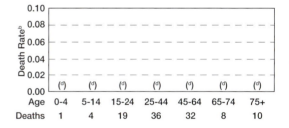

Other collision
Includes deaths from motor-vehicle collisions not specified in other categories above. Most of the deaths arose from collisions involving animals or animal-drawn vehicles.

	Total	Change from 2014	Death rate[a]
Deaths	100	0%	[d]
Nonfatal injuries[b]	14,000		

Note: Procedures and benchmarks for estimating deaths by type of incident and age were changed in 1990. Estimates for 1987 and later years are not comparable to earlier years. The noncollision and fixed-object categories were most affected by the changes.

[a] Deaths per 100,000 population.
[b] Nonfatal injury is defined as medically consulted injuries and is not comparable to estimates provided in earlier editions that used the definition of disabling injury. A refinement of the medically consulted injury estimate was made for the 2016 edition of Injury Facts that makes comparison of medically consulted injuries to previous years inappropriate. Please see the Technical Appendix for more information regarding medically consulted injuries.
[c] Deaths per 100,000 population in each age group.
[d] Death rate was less than 0.05.

MOTOR VEHICLE
Motor-Vehicle Safety Issues

Motor-vehicle crashes were the leading cause of death for people in the 1 to 24 age group in 2014. Motor-vehicle crashes also were the leading cause of unintentional-injury-related death for people at age 1 and for each single year of age from 3 to 23 and from ages 64 to 69. This is a summary of the most important issues that affect traffic safety.

Occupant protection. Safety belt use reached a record-high 90.1% overall in 2016, a statistically significant increase from the 88.5% use rate observed in 2015. Forty-nine states and the District of Columbia have mandatory safety belt use laws in effect, with laws in 34 of the states and the District of Columbia allowing standard (primary) enforcement. In 2015, safety belt use was significantly higher in states with standard (primary) enforcement (92.1%) than in states with secondary enforcement or no safety belt use law (83.0%). Nearly half (48%) of the passenger vehicle occupants killed in 2015 were unrestrained. Use of Department of Transportation (DOT)-compliant helmets by all motorcyclists was 60.7% in 2015, a statistically insignificant decrease from 64.3% in 2014. Observed use of DOT-compliant helmets in states with universal helmet laws was significantly higher than in states with weaker or no helmet laws at 79.8% versus 42.9%. Safety belts saved an estimated 13,941 lives in 2015 among passenger vehicle occupants older than 4. Child passenger restraints saved an additional 266 lives, while air bags saved approximately 2,573 lives.

Alcohol. From 2014 to 2015, traffic fatalities in alcohol-impaired crashes as a percentage of total traffic fatalities decreased by 1% to 29%. Overall, 10,265 people were killed in alcohol-impaired crashes in 2015, an increase of 3.2% from 9,943 in 2014. Passenger car drivers (+193 or 5%) and SUV drivers (+35 or 2.3%) were the only driver groups that showed increases in the number of alcohol-impaired-drivers involved in fatal crashes from 2014 to 2015. Males continue to comprise the majority – 79% in 2015 – of all drivers involved in fatal crashes with a BAC of 0.08 g/dL or higher.

Speeding. Excessive speed was a factor in 27% of all traffic fatalities in 2015, killing an average of 26 people per day for a total of 9,557 speeding-related fatalities. The impact of speeding is most severe among young drivers, with 35% of the speeding-related fatalities involving young drivers age 15-19 compared to 26% of fatalities involving drivers older than 19. It has been estimated that speeding-related crashes cost the nation nearly $52 billion annually.

Distracted driving. Over the last three years the prevalence of drivers using hand-held or hands-free cell phones at any given daylight moment has decreased from 9% of drivers in 2012 to 6.9% in 2015. The percentage of drivers likely to be on either hand-held or hands-free cell phones decreased from 11% in 2007 and 2008 down to 9% starting in 2009 and continuing through 2012. The corresponding hand-held cell phone use estimate has also dropped from 5.2% of drivers in 2012 to 3.8% of drivers in 2015. The drop in hand-held cell phone use occurred among the 16 to 24 and 25 to 69 age groups, with the decrease most pronounced among younger drivers. The percent of young drivers, 16 to 24 years of age, using hand-held cell phones has decreased 44% from 10.4% in 2005 down to 5.85% in 2014.

A very different trend is apparent regarding the prevalence of drivers observed manipulating hand-held electronic devices. The percent of drivers manipulating hand-held electronic devices has increased 1,000% from 0.2% in 2005 to 2.2% in 2014. Among other activities, this observation would include text messaging as well as manipulating devices such as MP3 players. This increase has been driven by younger drivers and middle aged drivers.

Large trucks. In 2015, 4,067 fatalities resulted from traffic crashes involving a large truck (gross vehicle weight rating greater than 10,000 pounds), a 4.2% increase from 3,903 in 2014. The majority of these deaths (74%) were occupants of vehicles other than the large truck. Fatalities among non-occupants in large truck crashes increased 5.4% from 2014 to 2015, while fatalities among truck occupants increased about 1.5% and fatalities among other vehicle occupants increased 4.7%. Large trucks are more likely to be involved in a multiple-vehicle fatal crash than passenger vehicles – 80% versus 37%, respectively, in 2015.

Motorcycles. Fatalities among motorcycle riders and passengers increased nearly 3% between 2006 and 2015, driven largely by an 8% increase in 2015. In contrast to the fatality increase, nonfatal injuries decreased 4% in 2015 to 88,000. The latest available mileage data show that motorcycle travel has increased nearly 91% from 2005 to 2014, increasing from 10.4 billion miles to 20.0 billion over this period. As a result, the death rate from 2005 to 2014 has decreased 48%, from 43.77 to 22.96 deaths per 100 million miles traveled. In 2014, 29% of motorcycle operators involved in fatal crashes were alcohol-impaired (blood-alcohol content greater than or equal to 0.08 g/dL), compared with 22% for passenger cars and light trucks, and 2% for large trucks.

Young drivers. There were 4,702 fatalities in crashes involving young drivers ages 15-20 in 2013, a 10% increase from 2010, the first increase in 11 years. Motor-vehicle crashes are the number one cause of death for U.S. teens now totaling 2,358 in 2015. One of the important components of state graduated driver licensing programs is a restriction on nighttime driving. While only about 10.4% of trips driven by 16 and 17 year olds occur between 9 p.m. and 6 a.m., over 30% of their fatal crashes occur at this time. Unfortunately, most state GDL programs currently allow some nighttime driving. Currently only five states (Idaho, Kansas, New York, North Carolina, and North Dakota) prohibit provisional license holders to drive after 9 at night.

Pedestrians. About 6,700 pedestrian deaths and 160,000 medically consulted injuries due to motor-vehicle incidents occurred in 2015. About 17% of these deaths occurred when pedestrians improperly cross roadways or intersections. Lack of visibility because of lack of lighting or dark clothing accounted for about 15% of the deaths, while being in the roadway improperly (either standing, lying, working or playing) contributed to about 13% of the deaths. No improper action or circumstance was reported for about a quarter of the pedestrian deaths. Pedestrian traffic fatality data shows a general decline in the number of pedestrian fatalities from 1994 through 2009. Since 2009, pedestrian fatalities have been trending sharply up.

MOTOR VEHICLE
Estimating Motor-Vehicle Crash Costs

The National Safety Council cost estimate procedures were extensively updated starting with the 2016 edition of *Injury Facts* and are not comparable to estimates provided in earlier editions. Two methods are commonly used to measure the costs of motor-vehicle crashes. One is the economic cost framework and the other is the comprehensive cost framework.

Economic costs may be used by a community or state to estimate the economic impact of motor-vehicle crashes that occurred within its jurisdiction in a given time period. It is a measure of the productivity lost and expenses incurred because of the crashes. Economic costs, however, should not be used for a cost-benefit analysis because they do not reflect what society is willing to pay to prevent a statistical fatality or injury.

There are five economic cost components: (1) wage and productivity losses, which include wages, fringe benefits, household production, and travel delay; (2) medical expenses, including emergency service costs; (3) administrative expenses, which include the administrative cost of private and public insurance plus police and legal costs; (4) motor-vehicle damage, including the value of damage to property; and (5) uninsured employer costs for crashes involving workers.

The information below shows the average economic costs in 2015 per death (not per fatal crash), per injury (not per injury crash), and per property damage crash.

Economic costs, 2015
Death	$1,550,000
Disabling injury	$90,000
Evident injury	$26,000
Possible injury	$21,000
No Injury Observed	$11,400
Property damage only	$4,200

Comprehensive costs include not only the economic cost components, but also a measure of the value of lost quality of life associated with the deaths and injuries – that is, what society is willing to pay to prevent them. The values of lost quality of life were obtained through empirical studies of what people actually pay to reduce their safety and health risks, such as through the purchase of air bags or smoke detectors. Comprehensive costs should be used for a cost-benefit analysis, but because the lost quality of life represents only a dollar equivalence of intangible qualities, they do not represent real economic losses and should not be used to determine the economic impact of past crashes.

The information below shows the average comprehensive costs in 2015 on a per-person basis.

Comprehensive costs, 2015
Death	$10,080,000
Disabling injury	$1,100,000
Evident injury	$304,000
Possible injury	$140,000
No injury observed	$46,500
Property damage only	$8,500

Note: The National Safety Council's cost-estimating procedures were extensively revised for the 1993 edition, for the 2005-2006 edition, and again for the 2016 edition. The costs are not comparable to those of prior years.

MOTOR VEHICLE
State Laws

No state has passed a total ban on cell phone use while driving, although 14 states and the District of Columbia have bans on handheld devices. Mandatory breath alcohol ignition interlock device laws are in effect in 28 states and four California counties for first-time DUI convictions. Mandatory safety belt use laws are in effect in 49 states and the District of Columbia, of which 21 states and the District of Columbia have primary enforcement for all seating positions. Graduated Driver Licensing is in effect in some form in all states and the District of Columbia, yet relatively few have optimum laws. Please see page 124 for further details regarding young driver issues.

State laws

	Distracted driving laws			Alcohol law	Mandatory safety belt use law		Graduated Driver Licensing laws				
State	Total cell phone ban	Total text messaging ban	Additional novice driver restrictions[c]	Mandatory alcohol ignition interlock device[e]	Enforcement	Seating positions covered by law	Minimum instructional permit period[k]	Minimum hours of supervised driving[l]	No passengers younger than 20	10 p.m. or earlier nighttime driving restriction	Unrestricted license minimum age[m]
Alabama	no	yes	cell phone[b]	yes	primary	front	6 mo.	none	no	no	17 yrs.
Alaska	no	yes	no	yes	primary	all	6 mo.	40/10	no	no	16 yrs., 6 mo.
Arizona	no	no	no	yes	secondary	front[j]	6 mo.	none	no	no	16 yrs., 6 mo.
Arkansas	no	yes	cell phone[b]	yes	primary	front	6 mo.	none	no	no	18 yrs.
California	no[a]	yes[d]	cell phone[b]	yes[h]	primary	all	6 mo.	50/10	yes	no	17 yrs.
Colorado	no	yes	cell phone	yes	secondary	front	12 mo.	50/10	yes	no	17 yrs.
Connecticut	no[a]	yes	cell phone	yes	primary	front	4 mo.	40/–	yes	no	18 yrs.
Delaware	no[a]	yes	cell phone	yes	primary	all	6 mo.	50/10	no	yes	17 yrs.
District of Columbia	no[a]	yes	cell phone	no	primary	all	6 mo.	40/10	yes	no	18 yrs.
Florida	no	yes[b]	no	yes[f, g]	primary	front[j]	12 mo.	50/10	no	no	18 yrs.
Georgia	no	yes	cell phone	yes[g, i]	primary	front[j]	12 mo.	40/6	yes	no	18 yrs.
Hawaii	no[a]	yes	cell phone	yes	primary	all	6 mo.	50/10	no	no	17 yrs.
Idaho	no	yes	no	yes[g]	secondary	all	6 mo.	50/10	no	yes	16 yrs.
Illinois	no[a]	yes	cell phone	yes	primary	all	9 mo.	50/10	no	no	18 yrs.
Indiana	no	yes	cell phone	no	primary	all	6 mo.	50/10	yes	yes	18 yrs.
Iowa	no	yes[b]	cell phone	yes[f, g]	primary	front	12 mo.	20/2	no	no	17 yrs.
Kansas	no	yes	cell phone	yes	primary	all	12 mo.	50/10	no	yes	16 yrs., 6 mo.
Kentucky	no	yes	cell phone	yes[f, g]	primary	all	6 mo.	60/10	no	no	17 yrs.
Louisiana	no	yes	cell phone	yes	primary	all	6 mo.	50/15	no	no	17 yrs.
Maine	no	yes	cell phone	yes	primary	all	6 mo.	70/10	yes	no	16 yrs., 9 mo.
Maryland	no[a]	yes	cell phone	yes	primary	all	9 mo.	60/10	no	no	18 yrs.
Massachusetts	no	yes	cell phone	yes[g]	secondary	all	6 mo.	40/–	no	no	18 yrs.
Michigan	no	yes	cell phone[d]	yes[f, g]	primary	front	6 mo.	50/10	no	yes	17 yrs.
Minnesota	no	yes	cell phone	yes[f, g]	primary	all	6 mo.	40/15	no	no	17 yrs.
Mississippi	no	yes	no	yes	primary	front	12 mo.	none	no	no	16 yrs., 6 mo.
Missouri	no	no	texting	yes	secondary	front	6 mo.	40/10	no	no	17 yrs., 11 mo.
Montana	no	no	no	no	secondary	all	6 mo.	50/10	no	no	16 yrs.
Nebraska	no	yes[b]	cell phone[b]	yes	secondary	front	6 mo.	none	no	no	17 yrs.
Nevada	no[a]	yes	no	yes[f]	secondary	all	6 mo.	50/10	no	yes	18 yrs.
New Hampshire	no[a]	yes	cell phone	yes	no law	no law	none	40/10	no	no	18 yrs.
New Jersey	no[a]	yes	cell phone	yes[f, g]	primary	all	6 mo.	none	no	no	18 yrs.
New Mexico	no	yes	cell phone	yes	primary	all	6 mo.	50/10	no	no	16 yrs., 6 mo.
New York	no[a]	yes	no	yes	primary	front	6 mo.	50/15	no	yes	17 yrs.
North Carolina	no	yes	cell phone	yes[f, g]	primary	all	12 mo.	72/16	no	yes	16 yrs., 6 mo.
North Dakota	no	yes	cell phone	no	secondary	front	6 mo.	none	no	yes	16 yrs.
Ohio	no	yes[b]	cell phone	yes[g]	secondary	front[j]	6 mo.	50/10	no	no	18 yrs.
Oklahoma	no	yes	handheld and texting	yes[f, g]	primary	front	6 mo.	50/10	no	yes	16 yrs., 6 mo.
Oregon	no[a]	yes	cell phone	yes	primary	all	6 mo.	50/–	yes	no	17 yrs.
Pennsylvania	no	yes	no	yes[f, g]	secondary	front[j]	6 mo.	65/10	no	no	17 yrs.
Rhode Island	no	yes	cell phone	yes	primary	all	6 mo.	50/10	no	no	17 yrs., 6 mo.
South Carolina	no	yes	no	yes[f, g]	primary	all	6 mo.	40/10	no	yes	16 yrs., 6 mo.
South Dakota	no	yes	cell phone[b]	no	secondary	front	3 mo.	none	no	yes	16 yrs.
Tennessee	no	yes	cell phone	yes	primary	front	6 mo.	50/10	no	no	17 yrs.
Texas	no	no	cell phone and texting	yes	primary	all	6 mo.	30/10	no	no	18 yrs.
Utah	no	yes	cell phone	yes	primary	all	6 mo.	40/10	yes	no	17 yrs.
Vermont	no[a]	yes	cell phone	yes	secondary	all	12 mo.	40/10	yes	no	16 yrs., 6 mo.
Virginia	no	yes	cell phone[b]	yes	secondary	front	9 mo.	45/15	no	no	18 yrs.
Washington	no[a]	yes	cell phone	yes	primary	all	6 mo.	50/10	yes	no	17 yrs.
West Virginia	no[a]	yes	cell phone	yes	primary	front[j]	6 mo.	none	yes	yes	17 yrs.
Wisconsin	no	yes	cell phone	yes[f, g]	primary	all	6 mo.	30/10	no	no	16 yrs., 9 mo.
Wyoming	no	yes	no	yes[f, g]	secondary	all	10 days	50/10	no	no	16 yrs., 6 mo.

Source: Insurance Institute for Highway Safety data retrieved from www.iihs.org on August 15, 2016.
[a]Statewide handheld ban.
[b]Secondary enforcement.
[c]Restrictions specific to novice drivers in addition to any other all-driver ban.
[d]Integrated voice-operated systems excepted.
[e]Instruments designed to prevent drivers from starting their cars when breath-alcohol content is at or above a set point. Mandatory in Maryland effective 10/1/16.
[f]Mandatory with a conviction for a BAC of at least .15 versus the lower limit of .08 found in other mandatory states. Effective 8/25/17 for Pennsylvania. Mandatory for high BAC offenders and offenders convicted of a felony regardless of BAC in Nevada.
[g]Mandatory with repeat convictions or upon reinstatement.
[h]Mandatory for all offenders in four counties.
[i]Mandatory unless waived due to financial hardship.
[j]Required for certain ages at all seating positions.
[k]Minimum instructional periods often include time spent in driver education classes.
[l]Figures shown as follows: Total hours/nighttime hours. For example, 25/5 means 25 hours of supervised driving, 5 of which must be at night. When states (Alabama, Arizona, Connecticut, Nebraska, Oregon, South Dakota, and West Virginia) have lower requirements if driver education is taken, the lower requirement is reflected in the table. Pennsylvania additionally requires 5 of the total hours of supervised driving to be during inclement weather.
[m]Minimum age to obtain unrestricted license provided driver is crash and violation free. Alcohol restrictions still apply at least until age 21.

MOTOR VEHICLE
Occupant Protection Use

Seat belt reached a record-high 90.1% overall in 2016, a statistically significant increase from the 88.5% use rate observed in 2015. Significant increases in seat belt use from 2015 to 2016 were identified for occupants travelling in vans and SUVs (90.3% to 92.3%), pickup trucks (80.8% to 83.2%), in the Midwest (81.7% to 85.5%), and in rural areas (86.8% to 89.5%). Overall, seat belt use has shown an increasing trend since 2000 that has been accompanied by a steady decline in the percentage of unrestrained passenger vehicle occupant fatalities during the daytime (see graph below). These results are from the National Occupant Protection Use Survey (NOPUS) that is conducted annually by the National Highway Traffic Safety Administration. NOPUS includes the observation of drivers and right-front passengers of passenger vehicles with no commercial or governmental markings.

Safety belt use by state in 2015 ranged from 69.5% in New Hampshire to 97.3% in California and Georgia. Nineteen states and the District of Columbia achieved use rates of 90% or higher, including California, Georgia, Oregon, Illinois, Washington, Minnesota, New Mexico, Alabama, Iowa, Maryland, Michigan, Hawaii, New York, Nevada, Indiana, South Carolina, New Jersey, Texas, and Delaware. Jurisdictions with stronger safety belt laws continue to exhibit generally higher use rates than those with weaker laws.

Results from the 2014 NOPUS Controlled Intersection Study showed no significant changes in belt use among front seat occupants in passenger vehicles from 2013 to 2014, with the overall use rate remaining at 87%. However, significant decreases in belt use during this period were observed among rear seat occupants, including all passengers (78% to 73%), female passengers (82% to 75%), passengers age 16 to 24 (78% to 68%), passengers age 25 to 69 (73% to 64%), white occupants (80% to 73%), and passengers in states with laws requiring belt use in the front seat only (74% to 66%). In 2014, female occupants (89%) had higher use rates than male occupants (84%), members of other races (93%) had higher use rates than whites (87%) and blacks (80%), drivers with at least one passenger (89%) had higher use rates than drivers with no passengers (86%), and drivers age 16 to 24 with all passengers age 16-24 (88%) had higher use rates than drivers age 16 to 24 with no passengers (83%) or at least one passenger not age 16-24 (86%). Occupants age 25 to 69 had the highest use rates among all age groups (87%), while occupants age 16 to 24 had the lowest use rates (84%). Drivers with a mixture of passengers under age 8 and 8 years of age or older (90%), drivers with passengers all age 8 and older (89%), and with passengers all under age 8 (89%) had higher use rates than did drivers with no passengers (86%).

Child restraint use. Restraint use for child passengers younger than 8 was 91% in 2014, up an insignificant 2 percentage points from the 89% use rate observed in 2013. From 2013 to 2014, significant increases in belt use were observed for child passengers driven by a male driver (87% to 91%) and drivers age 25 to 69 (89% to 92%). Other significant increases in belt use from 2013 to 2014 were observed among child passengers traveling in slow traffic (85% to 93%), in vans and SUVs (91% to 94%), in the South (81% to 88%), in suburban areas (91% to 94%), and traveling during weekdays (89% to 92%).

Safety belt use by the driver strongly influences the restraint status of child passengers. When the driver was belted, a significantly high 93% of child passengers younger than 8 were restrained in 2014, compared to a significantly low 72% of children when the driver was unbelted.

Children ages 4-7 should be restrained in a front-facing safety seat or booster seat, depending on the child's height and weight. The results from the 2015 National Survey of the Use of Booster Seats showed a non-significant decline in booster seat use among 4- to 7-year-old from 46.3% in 2013 to 44.5% in 2015. Restraint use for all children under 13 also decreased slightly to 89.2% in 2015 from 91.1% in 2013. This was not a statistically significant change. The results also indicate that premature graduation continues to be a problem, with some decreases in the use of appropriate restraint types noted from 2013 to 2015.

Source: Pickrell, T.M., & Li, R. (2016, November). Seat belt use in 2016–Overall Results. Traffic Safety Facts Research Note (DOT HS 812 351). Washington, DC: National Highway Traffic Safety Administration.
Hongying, L., Pickrell, T.M., & Shova, KC. (2016, September). The 2015 National Survey of the Use of Booster Seats (DOT HS 812 309). Washington, DC: National Highway Traffic Safety Administration.
Chen, Y.Y., & Webb, C. (2016, May; Rev. 2016, June). Seat belt use in 2015–use rates in the States and Territories. Traffic Safety Facts Crash Stats (DOT HS 812 274). Washington, DC: National Highway Traffic Safety Administration.
Pickrell, T.M., Choi, E.-H., & Shova, KC. (2016, February). Occupant Restraint Use in 2014–Results from the National Occupant Protection Use Survey Controlled Intersection Study (DOT HS 812 244). Washington, DC: National Highway Traffic Safety Administration.

Safety belt use rate and daytime percent of unrestrained passenger vehicle occupant fatalities, United States, 2000-2016

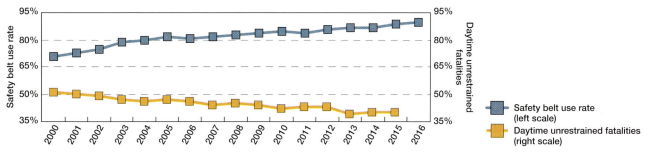

MOTOR VEHICLE
Occupant Protection

Safety belts

- When used properly, lap/shoulder safety belts reduce the risk of fatal injury to front-seat passenger car occupants by 45% and reduce the risk of moderate-to-critical injury by 50%.
- For light-truck occupants, safety belts reduce the risk of fatal injury by 60% and moderate-to-critical injury by 65%.
- Forty-nine states and the District of Columbia have mandatory safety belt use laws in effect, the only exception being New Hampshire. Sixteen of the states with safety belt use laws in effect in 2016 specified secondary enforcement (i.e., police officers are permitted to write a citation only after a vehicle is stopped for some other traffic infraction). Thirty-four states and the District of Columbia had laws that allowed primary enforcement, enabling officers to stop vehicles and write citations whenever they observe violations of the safety belt law. (See page 110 for additional information on state laws.)
- Safety belts saved an estimated 13,941 lives in 2015 among passenger vehicle occupants older than 4. An additional 2,804 lives could have been saved in 2015 if all passenger vehicle occupants older than 4 wore safety belts. From 1975 through 2015, an estimated 344,447 lives were saved by safety belts (see table on following page).
- A total of 22,441 occupants of passenger vehicles (cars, pickup trucks, vans, and SUVs) were killed in motor-vehicle traffic crashes in 2015, 64% of the total traffic fatalities reported for the year. Of those for whom restraint use was known, 9,874 (48%) were unrestrained. In contrast, among passenger vehicle occupants who survived fatal crashes, only 4,993 (14%) were unrestrained. The table below shows the number of passenger vehicle occupants involved in crashes by restraint use, survival status, and time of day for 2014 and 2015.

Passenger vehicle[a] occupants involved in fatal crashes by restraint use, survival status, and time of day, 2014 and 2015

	\multicolumn{6}{c	}{Passenger vehicle occupants killed}		\multicolumn{6}{c}{Passenger vehicle occupants who survived}
	2014	2015	Change	% Change	2014	2015		2014	2015	Change	% Change	2014	2015
					\multicolumn{2}{c	}{Restraint use percent based on known use}						\multicolumn{2}{c}{Restraint use percent based on known use}
Total[b]	21,050	22,441	+1,391	+6.6%			**Total[b]**	34,120	38,152	+4,032	+11.8%		
Restraint used	9,961	10,635	+674	+6.8%	51%	52%	Restraint used	26,397	29,703	+3,306	+12.5%	85%	86%
Restraint not used	9,410	9,874	+464	+4.9%	49%	48%	Restraint not used	4,743	4,993	+250	+5.3%	15%	14%
Unknown	1,679	1,932	+253	+15.1%			Unknown	2,890	3,456	+476	+16.0%		
\multicolumn{7}{c	}{Time of day}	\multicolumn{7}{c}{Time of day}
Daytime	10,789	11,645	+856	+7.9%			**Daytime**	17,353	19,478	+2,125	+12.2%		
Restraint used	5,972	6,500	+528	+8.8%	59%	60%	Restraint used	14,143	15,894	+1,751	+12.4%	87%	88%
Restraint not used	4,100	4,335	+235	+5.7%	41%	40%	Restraint not used	2,045	2,215	+170	+8.3%	13%	12%
Unknown	717	810	+93	+13.0%			Unknown	1,165	1,369	+204	+17.5%		
Nighttime	10,089	10,622	+533	+5.3%			**Nighttime**	16,732	18,613	+1,881	+11.2%		
Restraint used	3,936	4,084	+148	+3.8%	43%	43%	Restraint used	12,239	13,780	+1,541	+12.6%	82%	83%
Restraint not used	5,211	5,436	+225	+4.3%	57%	57%	Restraint not used	2,690	2,764	+74	+2.8%	18%	17%
Unknown	942	1,102	+160	+17.0%			Unknown	1,803	2,069	+266	+14.8%		

Source: National Center for Statistics and Analysis. (2016, August). Traffic Safety Facts Research Note — 2015 Motor Vehicle Crashes: Overview (DOT HS 812 318). Washington, DC: National Highway Traffic Safety Administration
[a]Passenger vehicles include cars, pickup trucks, vans, and SUVs
[b]Daytime and nighttime totals do not add up to total killed or total survived. Total includes unknown time of day.

Air bags

- Air bags, combined with lap/shoulder belts, offer the best available protection for passenger vehicle occupants. Analyses indicate a fatality-reducing effectiveness for frontal air bags of 14% when no safety belt was used and 11% when a safety belt was used in conjunction with air bags.
- Lap/shoulder belts should always be used, even in a vehicle with an air bag. Air bags are a supplemental form of protection, and most are designed to deploy only in moderate-to-severe frontal crashes.
- Children in rear-facing child seats should not be placed in the front seat of vehicles equipped with passenger-side air bags. The impact of the deploying air bag could result in serious injury to the child.
- An estimated 2,573 lives were saved by frontal air bags in 2015, and a total of 44,869 lives were saved from 1987 through 2015 (see table on following page).
- Since 1999, driver and passenger-side air bags have been required in all cars, light trucks, and vans.

MOTOR VEHICLE
Occupant Protection (cont.)

Child restraints
- Child restraints saved an estimated 266 lives in 2015 among children younger than 5.
- All states and the District of Columbia have had child restraint use laws in effect since 1985.
- Research has shown that child safety seats reduce fatal injury in passenger cars by 71% for infants (younger than 1) and by 54% for toddlers (1-4 years old). For infants and toddlers in light trucks, the corresponding reductions are 58% and 59%, respectively.
- In 2014, there were 183 occupant fatalities among children younger than 4. Of the 167 fatalities among children younger than 4 for which restraint use was known, 36 (22%) were completely unrestrained.
- An estimated total of 10,940 lives have been saved by child restraints from 1975 through 2015 (see table below).

Estimated number of lives saved by restraint systems, 1975-2015

Restraint type	1975-2005	2006	2007	2008	2009	2010	2011	2012	2013	2014	2015	Total
Seat belts	211,184	15,458	15,223	13,312	12,757	12,670	12,071	12,386	12,644	12,801	13,941	344,447
Child restraints	7,900	427	388	286	307	303	262	285	263	253	266	10,940
Air bags	19,670[a]	2,824	2,800	2,557	2,481	2,403	2,341	2,422	2,398	2,400	2,573	44,869

Source: National Center for Statistics and Analysis. (2016, August). Traffic Safety Facts Crash Stats: Lives Saved in 2015 by Restraint Use and Minimum-Drinking-Age Laws (DOT HS 812 319). Washington, DC: National Highway Traffic Safety Administration.
[a]Total is from 1987 to 2005. Frontal air bags did not exist prior to 1987.

Motorcycle helmets
- Motorcycle helmets are estimated to be 37% effective in preventing fatal injuries to motorcycle operators and 41% effective for motorcycle passengers.
- It is estimated that motorcycle helmets saved the lives of 1,772 motorcyclists in 2015. An additional 740 lives could have been saved in 2015 if all motorcyclists had worn helmets.
- According to the National Occupant Protection Use Survey, use of Department of Transportation (DOT)-compliant helmets by all motorcyclists (riders and passengers) was 60.7% in 2015, a statistically insignificant decrease from 64.3% in 2014. Observed use of DOT-compliant helmets in states with universal helmet laws was significantly higher than in states with weaker or no helmet laws at 79.8% vs. 42.9%.
- Reported helmet use rates for fatally injured motorcyclists in 2014 were 62% for operators and 53% for passengers, compared with the corresponding rates of 60% and 49%, respectively, in 2013.
- As of September 2016, 19 states and the District of Columbia required helmet use by all motorcycle operators and passengers. Twenty-eight states only required helmet use by a subset of motorcyclists (typically motorcyclists under age 18) and 3 states (Illinois, Iowa, and New Hampshire) do not require helmet use by motorcyclists of any age. In states without universal helmet laws, 58% of motorcyclists killed in 2014 were not wearing helmets, as compared to 8% in states with universal helmet laws.
- The economic cost savings due to helmet use was approximately $2,986 million in 2014, and an additional $1,214 million could have been saved if all motorcyclists had worn helmets.

Source: Chen, Y.Y., & Webb, C. (2016, May; Rev. 2016, June). Seat belt use in 2015—Use rates in the States and Territories (Traffic Safety Facts Crash•Stats. Report No. DOT HS 812 274). Washington, DC: National Highway Traffic Safety Administration.
National Center for Statistics and Analysis. (2016, August). Lives saved in 2015 by restraint use and minimum-drinking-age laws (Traffic Safety Facts Crash•Stats. Report No. DOT HS 812 319). Washington, DC: National Highway Traffic Safety Administration.
National Center for Statistics and Analysis. (2016, August). 2015 motor vehicle crashes: Overview. (Traffic Safety Facts Research Note. Report No. DOT HS 812 318). Washington, DC: National Highway Traffic Safety Administration.
National Center for Statistics and Analysis. (2016, July). Lives and costs saved by motorcycle helmets, 2014 (Report No. DOT HS 812 295). Washington, DC: National Highway Traffic Safety Administration.
National Center for Statistics and Analysis. (2016, June). Motorcycles: 2014 data. (Traffic Safety Facts. Report No. DOT HS 812 292). Washington, DC: National Highway Traffic Safety Administration.
National Center for Statistics and Analysis. (2016, April). Occupant protection in passenger vehicles: 2014 data. (Traffic Safety Facts. Report No. DOT HS 812 262). Washington, DC: National Highway Traffic Safety Administration.
Pickrell, T.M., & Li, R. (2016, May). Motorcycle helmet use in 2015—Overall results. (Traffic Safety Facts Research Note. Report No. DOT HS 812 275). Washington, DC: National Highway Traffic Safety Administration.
Current status of safety belt and motorcycle helmet use laws downloaded September 29, 2016, from the Insurance Institute for Highway Safety at http://www.iihs.org/iihs/topics.

MOTOR VEHICLE
Alcohol

According to the National Highway Traffic Safety Administration, about 10,265 people were killed in alcohol-impaired crashes in 2015, an increase of 3.2% from the 9,943 fatalities in 2014. Alcohol-impaired driving crashes involve at least one driver or motorcycle operator with a blood alcohol concentration (BAC) of 0.08 grams per deciliter (g/dL) or higher. The following data summarize the extent of alcohol involvement in motor-ehicle crashes with at least one alcohol-impaired driver or motorcycle operator:

- The cost of alcohol-related motor-vehicle crashes in 2010 was estimated by the National Highway Traffic Safety Administration at $201.1 billion.
- Traffic fatalities in alcohol-impaired driving crashes as a percentage of total traffic fatalities decreased by nearly 4% to 29.3% from 2014 to 2015 and decreased by over 7% from 2006 to 2015 (see corresponding chart on bottom of page). However, research shows impairment starts to occur well before the legal 0.08 BAC threshold. Fully 34% of fatalities in 2015 involved drivers with BACs of 0.01 g/dL or greater.
- The 10,265 fatalities in alcohol-impaired driving crashes in 2015 represent an average of one alcohol-impaired driving fatality every 51 minutes.
- Since July 1988, all states and the District of Columbia have had a minimum legal drinking age of 21. The impact these laws had on alcohol-related fatalities was dramatic. Among fatally injured drivers 16-20 years old, the percentage with positive BACs declined from 61% in 1982 to 31% in 1995, a larger decline than for older age groups. These declines occurred among the ages directly affected by increasing the drinking age (ages 18-20) and among young teens not directly affected (ages 16-17).
- In 2015, while people ages 21-24 constituted 10% of all drivers involved in fatal crashes, they were overrepresented among the drivers with a BAC of 0.08 g/dL or higher, comprising 28% of such drivers involved in fatal crashes. Drivers 25-34 years old were similarly overrepresented, accounting for 20% of drivers in fatal crashes and 27% of those with a BAC of 0.08 g/dL or higher. The 35-44 age group also was slightly overrepresented, making up 16% of drivers in fatal crashes and 23% of those with a BAC of 0.08 g/dL or higher.
- Males continue to comprise the majority – 79% in 2015 – of all drivers involved in fatal crashes with a BAC of 0.08 g/dL or higher. Male drivers showed a 3% decrease while female drivers showed a 1% decrease in the proportion of drivers involved in fatal crashes who were alcohol-impaired from 2006 to 2015.
- A recent study estimated the injury prevention impact and cost savings associated with the installation of alcohol interlock devices in all new vehicles. Fatal and nonfatal injuries associated with drinking driver vehicle crashes were identified from the Fatality Analysis Reporting System and the General Estimates System data sets from 2006-2010 and the impact of universal interlock installation was derived using and estimate of the proportion of alcohol-related crashes that were preventable in vehicles <1 year-old. Extending this analysis over a 15-year implementation period produced an estimated 85% reduction in crash fatalities and an 84% to 88% reduction in nonfatal injuries, saving an estimated $342 billion in injury-related costs. The greatest injury and cost benefit was observed among recently legal drinking drivers (see corresponding chart on page 115).
- In 2015, the percentage of alcohol-impaired-driving fatalities by state varied from a low of 16% in Utah to a high of 43% in Rhode Island (see corresponding chart on page 115).
- In 2015, all states and the District of Columbia had by law created a threshold making it illegal to drive with a BAC of 0.08 g/dL or higher.

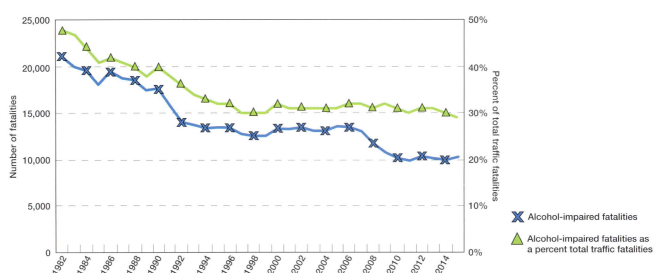

Number of alcohol-impaired driving fatalities and alcohol-impaired fatalities as a percent of total traffic fatalities, 1982-2015

MOTOR VEHICLE
Alcohol (cont.)

15-year estimated fatalities and injuries prevented through installation of alcohol interlocks in all new vehicles by drinking driver age group, United States

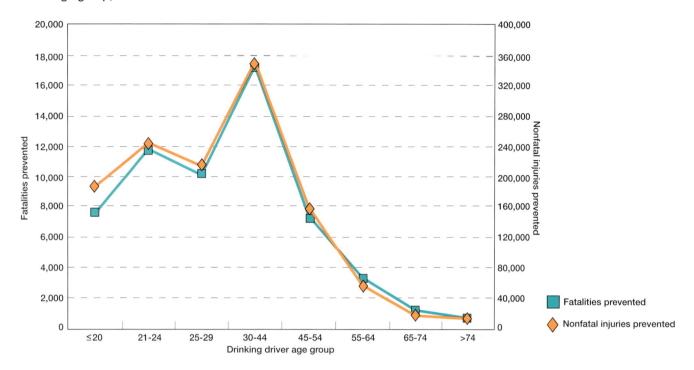

Percent of fatalities involved in fatal crashes with BAC of 0.08+, by state, 2015

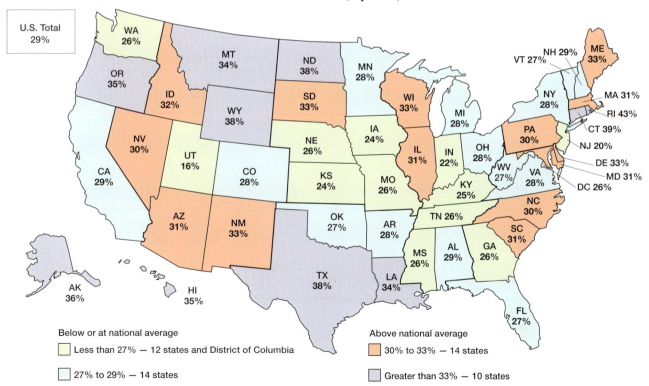

Below or at national average
- Less than 27% — 12 states and District of Columbia
- 27% to 29% — 14 states

Above national average
- 30% to 33% — 14 states
- Greater than 33% — 10 states

Source: National Center for Statistics and Analysis. (2016, August). Traffic Safety Facts Research Note: 2015 Motor Vehicle Crashes: Overview (DOT HS 812 318). Washington, DC: National Highway Traffic Safety Administration.
National Center for Statistics and Analysis. (2016, December). Traffic Safety Facts Research 2015 Data: Alcohol-Impaired Driving (DOT HS 812 350). Washington, DC: National Highway Traffic Safety Administration.
Carter, P.M., Flannagan, C.A.C., Bingham, C.R., Cunningham, R.M., & Rupp, J.D. (2015, May). Modeling the injury prevention impact of mandatory alcohol ignition interlock installation in all U.S. vehicles. *American Journal of Public Health, 105* (5), 1028-1035.

MOTOR VEHICLE
Type of Motor-Vehicle Crash

Although motor-vehicle deaths occur more often in collisions between motor vehicles than any other type of incident, this type represents only about 40% of the total. Collisions between a motor vehicle and a fixed object were the next most common type, with about 29% of deaths, followed by pedestrian incidents and noncollisions (rollovers, etc.).

While collisions between motor vehicles accounted for less than half of motor-vehicle fatalities, this crash type represented 78% of injuries, 73% of injury crashes, and 71% of all incidents. Single-vehicle crashes involving collisions with fixed objects, pedestrians, and noncollisions, on the other hand, accounted for a greater proportion of fatalities and fatal crashes compared to less-serious crashes. These three crash types made up 56% of fatalities and 59% of fatal crashes, but only 24% or less of injuries, injury crashes, or all crashes.

Of collisions between motor vehicles, angle collisions cause the greatest number of deaths, about 7,000 in 2015, and also the greatest number of fatal crashes. The table below shows the estimated number of deaths, injuries, fatal crashes, injury crashes, and all crashes for various types of motor-vehicle crashes.

Motor-vehicle deaths, injuries, and number of crashes by type of crash, 2015

Type of crash	Deaths	Nonfatal injuries[a]	Fatal crashes	Injury crashes	All crashes
Total	37,757	4,300,000	34,600	3,000,000	12,800,000
Collision with…					
Pedestrian	6,700	160,000	6,400	150,000	160,000
Other motor vehicle	15,300	3,340,000	13,100	2,180,000	9,150,000
Angle collision	7,000	1,330,000	6,200	827,000	2,700,000
Head-on collision	4,400	231,000	3,500	128,000	290,000
Rear-end collision	2,700	1,498,000	2,400	1,013,000	4,340,000
Sideswipe and other two-vehicle collisions	1,200	281,000	1,000	212,000	1,820,000
Railroad train	110	1,000	100	1,000	2,000
Pedalcycle	1,100	110,000	1,000	100,000	110,000
Animal, animal-drawn vehicle	100	14,000	100	11,000	570,000
Fixed or other object	10,900	540,000	10,600	450,000	2,590,000
Noncollision	3,500	135,000	3,300	108,000	218,000

Source: National Safety Council estimates, based on data from the National Highway Traffic Safety Administration Fatality Analysis Reporting System and General Estimates System. Procedures for estimating the number of incidents by type were changed for the 1998 edition and are not comparable to estimates in previous editions (see Technical Appendix).

[a]Nonfatal injury is defined as medically consulted injuries and is not comparable to estimates provided in earlier editions that used the definition of disabling injury. A refinement of the medically consulted injury estimate was also made in the 2016 edition of Injury Facts that makes comparison of medically consulted injuries to previous years inappropriate. Please see the Technical Appendix for more information regarding medically consulted injuries.

MOTOR VEHICLE

Speeding

Speeding is one of the major factors contributing to the occurrence of deaths, injuries, and property damage related to motor-vehicle crashes. The role of speeding in crash causation can be described in terms of its effect on the driver, the vehicle, and the road. Excessive-speed driving reduces the amount of time the driver has to react in a dangerous situation to avoid a crash. Speeding increases vehicle stopping distance and also reduces the ability of road safety structures such as guardrails, impact attenuators, crash cushions, median dividers, and concrete barriers to protect vehicle occupants in a crash.

The National Highway Traffic Safety Administration (NHTSA) estimates that speeding-related crashes[a] cost the nation $51,964 million in 2010, or 21% of the entire cost of motor-vehicle crashes in the United States. This economic loss is equivalent to $142 million per day or $5.9 million per hour.

Speeding was a factor in 27% of all traffic fatalities in 2015, killing an average of 26 people per day for a total of 9,557 speeding-related fatalities. The total number of fatal motor-vehicle crashes attributable to speeding was 8,558. Among young drivers, the impact of speeding is even more severe. Thirty-five percent of fatalities involving young drivers (ages 15-19) are speeding-related, compared with 26% of fatalities involving drivers older than 19. The speeding-related percentage of total traffic fatalities varied widely by state, ranging from 11% in Florida to 49% in New Hampshire.

Speeding-related percentage of total traffic fatalities, by state, 2015

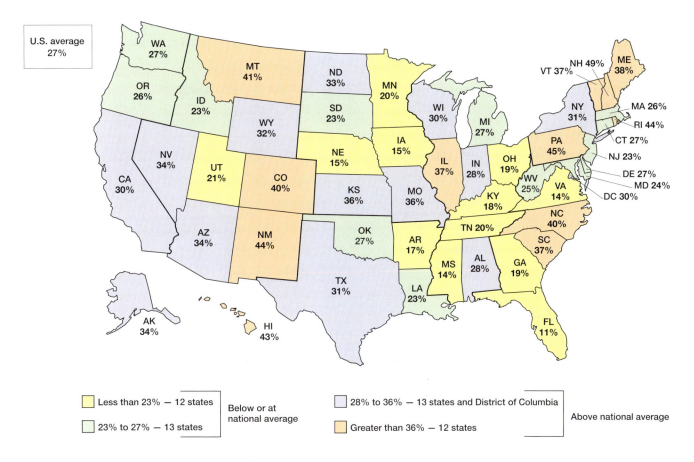

Source: National Safety Council analysis of NHTSA FARS data.
Blincoe, L.J., Miller, T.R., Zaloshnja, E., & Lawrence, B.A. (2015). The economic and societal impact of motor vehicle crashes, 2010. (Revised) (Report No. DOT HS812 013). Washington, DC: National Highway Traffic Safety Administration.
[a]A crash is considered speeding-related if the driver was charged with a speeding-related offense or if racing, driving too fast for conditions, or exceeding the posted speed limit was indicated as a contributing factor in the crash.

MOTOR VEHICLE
Distracted Driving

Distracted driving can be from electronic sources, such as cell phones or navigation devices, or more conventional distractions such as interacting with passengers and eating. Distracting tasks can affect drivers in different ways, and can be categorized into visual, manual, and cognitive distraction.

Cell phone Driving Prevalence

Over the last three years the prevalence of drivers using hand-held or hands-free cell phones at any given daylight moment has decreased from 9% of drivers in 2012 to 6.9% in 2015. This figure from the National Occupant Protection Use Survey (NOPUS) conducted by the National Highway Traffic Safety Administration is the only national estimate of driver cell phone use based on actual driver observations. As shown in the graph below, the percentage of drivers likely to be on either hand-held or hands-free cell phones decreased from 11% in 2007 and 2008 down to 9% starting in 2009 and continuing through 2012. The corresponding hand-held cell phone use estimate has also dropped from 5.2% of drivers in 2012 to 3.8% drivers in 2015.

The percent of drivers manipulating hand-held electronic devices has increased 1,000% from 0.2% in 2005 to 2.2% in 2014 and 2015. Among other activities, this observation would include text messaging as well as manipulating devices such as MP3 players. This increase has been driven by younger drivers and middle aged drivers. The percent of younger drivers observed to be manipulating hand-held devices has increased over 1,500% since 2005, while usage among middle age drivers 25 to 69 years old has increased 2,000%.

Driver use of cell phones 2002-2015

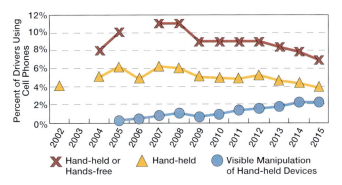

An observational study conducted in 2015 by the Minnesota Department of Public Safety found that overall about 30% of drivers are distracted at any given daylight moment. Distracted driving was most prevalent on Saturdays (34.5% of drivers) closely followed by Mondays (33.7%) and least distracted on Tuesdays (24.2%). Distracted driving also appears to be least prevalent in the morning, between 7 and 9 a.m. (24.8%), and most prevalent between 5 and 6 p.m. (32.6%). Similar to the NHTSA NOPUS findings, drivers 16 to 29 were most frequently observed to be distracted (36.1%).

Cell phone Driving Risk

A recent study assessed crash risk through analyzing 905 injury and property damage crash events from the Second Strategic Highway Research Program Naturalistic Driving Study (SHRP 2 NDS). Results show that driver-related factors such as driver error, impairment, fatigue, and distraction was present in almost 90% of the crashes studied. Although the study did not assess the risk of hands-free cell phone use, results did show that distraction increased crash risk and that hand-held electronic devices use was frequently observed and associated with elevated crash risk.

Driver visibly manipulating hand-held devices by age, 2005-2015

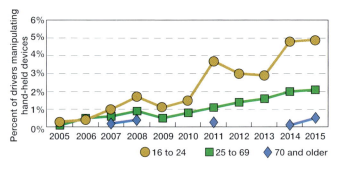

A National Safety Council review of 33 cell phone driving studies published representing a total sample size of approximately 2,000 participants revealed the following:

- Cell phone conversation while driving increases driver reaction time. The total mean increase in reaction time is 0.25 sec.
- Use of hand-held and hands-free phones results in similar increases in reaction time.

State Laws

Although research findings indicate that there is little to no safety advantage of hands-free over hand-held cell phone use, the states that have implemented bans impacting all drivers have focused on hand-held bans. As of September 2016, 14 states and the District of Columbia ban hand-held-devices for all drivers while 46 states and the District of Columbia have passed total text ban laws. The only state laws banning any use of cell phones while driving are limited to either young drivers or bus drivers. Thirty-seven states and the District of Columbia ban young or novice drivers from using cell phones. See page 110 for additional information regarding state motor-vehicle laws.

Dingus, T.A.; Guo, F.; Lee, S.; Antin, J.F.; Perez, M.; and Buchanan-King, M. (2016). Driver crash risk factors and prevalence evaluation using naturalistic driving data. Proceedings of the National Academy of Sciences of the United States of America. 2636-2641, 113(10).

Lucas, J; Scopatz, R.; and Cook, L. (2015). Minnesota Distracted Driving Survey: 2015. Office of Traffic Safety, State of Minnesota.(job number: J1066).

National Highway Traffic Safety Administration [NHTSA]. (2002 - 2015). Traffic Safety Fact Sheets. Available at http://www-nrd.nhtsa.dot.gov/cats/index.aspx.

National Safety Council. (2010). Understanding the distracted brain, why driving while using hands-free cellphones is risky behavior. Downloaded on November 6, 2015 from: http://www.nsc.org/safety_road/Distracted_Driving/Pages/distracted_driving.aspx.

Ranney, T.A. (2008, April). Driver distraction: A review of the current state-of-knowledge (Report No. DOT HS 810 787). Washington, DC: National Highway Traffic Safety Administration.

MOTOR VEHICLE
Assistive Safety Technology

Assistive or advanced safety technologies like adaptive headlights, forward collision prevention, lane departure warning, and back-up cameras are becoming increasingly available in new automobiles. Back-up cameras will be a required safety feature starting in May 2018, while most major automobile makers have voluntarily committed to providing forward collision warning and emergency breaking systems in new cars by the 2023 model year. These new assistive safety technologies have the potential of preventing or mitigating many crashes.

These assistive safety technologies work by compensating or assisting drivers to prevent or mitigate crashes. Analysis of the National Motor Vehicle Crash Causation Survey shows that the critical reason for 94% of crashes involves the driver. The largest portion of these driver error crashes involve the driver failing to recognize hazards (including distraction). Many of the most promising assistive technologies are designed to identify and react to potential hazards faster than a human driver.

Critical reasons for crashes investigated in the National Motor Vehicle Crash Causation Survey, United States, 2005–2007

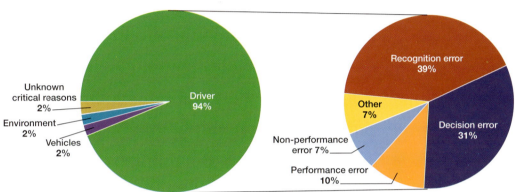

Source: NHTSA (DOT HS 812 115)

The actual real-world effectiveness of these assistive technologies is still being assessed. There are currently several obstacles slowing the evaluation of these new technologies. These obstacles primarily involve a lack of data because few cars are currently equipped with these technologies and because it can be difficult to identify which cars have these technologies when analyzing crash databases. One promising line of research is being conducted by the Insurance Loss Data institute using insurance claims data. Provided below is a summary of these findings representing several different car makes and numerous safety features. As can be seen, changes in insurance losses vary substantially depending on the make of the car and the safety feature.

Change in insurance losses by vehicle make and safety feature

	Property damage liability	Bodily injury liability
Honda Accord, 2013–2015 model years		
Forward collision warning and Lane departure warning	–10.1%[a]	–24.2%[a]
Forward collision warning, Lane departure warning, and adaptive cruise control	–13.2%[a]	–12.5%
Mazda, 2007–2014 model years		
Adaptive front lighting system	–4.6%[a]	–3.6%
Blind spot monitry	–11.1%[a]	–17.7%[a]
Back-up camera	–4.2%[a]	–4.4%
Smart City Brake Support	–13.4%[a]	–11.5%
Lane departure warning	–4.5%	
Rear cross traffic alert	–2.3%	–5.2%
Mercedes-Benz, 2004-2010 model years		
Distronic	–7.1%[a]	–4.0%
Distronic Plus	–14.3%[a]	–16.0%
High Intesity Discharge Headlights	–5.5%[a]	–4.5%
Active Curve Illumination	–4.7%[a]	–9.9%[a]
Active Cornering Lights	–1.7%	3.2%
Adaptive High Beam Assist	–5.9%	32.6%
Night View Assist/Plus	–8.1%[a]	–2.5%
Blind Spot Assist	0.4%	–3.6%
Lane Keeping Assist	10.9%	–2.8%
Parktronic	–1.8%	0.5%
Parking Guidance	–5.0%	1.6%
Back-up camera	–0.5%	10.8%
Subaru, 2013 and 2014 model years		
EyeSight	–15.1%[a]	–34.7%[a]
Rear-vision camera	–7.0%[a]	–1.6%
Volvo, 2011 - 2014 model years		
City Safety	–14.3%[a]	–27.5%[a]

Source: Insurance Institute for Highway Safety Highway Loss Data Institute: http://www.iihs.org/iihs/topics/t/automation-and-crash-avoidance/hldi-research
[a]Change is statistically significant.

INJURY FACTS® 2017 EDITION — NATIONAL SAFETY COUNCIL® — 119

MOTOR VEHICLE
Improper Driving

In most motor-vehicle crashes, factors are present relating to the driver, the vehicle, and the road, and it is the interaction of these factors that often sets up the series of events that result in a crash. The table below relates only to the driver, and shows the principal kinds of improper driving in crashes in 2015 as reported by police. The data provided in the table below reflect National Safety Council's analysis of NHTSA data and are not comparable to previous reports that relied on other data sources.

Although crash causation studies regularly find 95% of crashes involve driver related factors, police do not report driver related factors for the majority of vehicles involved in crashes. Exceeding the posted speed limit or driving at an unsafe speed was the most common primary error in fatal crashes.

While some drivers were under the influence of alcohol or other drugs, this represents the driver's physical condition – not a driving error. See page 114 for a discussion of alcohol involvement in traffic incidents.

Improper driving reported in crashes, 2015

Kind of improper driving	Vehicles in Fatal crashes
Total	100%
Improper driving	**45.7%**
Speed too fast or unsafe	18.0%
Right of way	11.0%
Failed to yield	7.1%
Disregarded signal	3.9%
Driving on wrong side of two-way road	2.0%
Made improper turn	2.0%
Followed improperly	1.0%
Improper lane usage	6.9%
Improper or erratic lane change	1.5%
Over correcting	3.8%
Eratic, reckless, careless, or neglignet vehicle operation	8.9%
Road rage/aggressive driving	0.9%
Other improper driving	5.8%
No improper driving reported	**54.3%**

Source: National Safety Council analysis of NHTSA FARS and GES data. Note: Not all driver related crash factors are collected for non-fatal crashes.

MOTOR VEHICLE
Large Trucks

In 2015, 4,067 fatalities resulted from a traffic crash involving a large truck, a 4.2% increase from 3,903 in 2014. About 74% of these deaths were occupants of vehicles other than the large truck (see figure below). Fatalities among non-occupants in large truck crashes increased by 5.4% from 2014 to 2015, while fatalities among truck occupants increased 1.5% and other vehicle occupants fatalities increased 4.7%. A large truck is one with a gross vehicle weight rating greater than 10,000 pounds.

Large trucks are more likely to be involved in a multiple-vehicle fatal crash than passenger vehicles. In 2015, 80% of large truck fatal crashes were multiple-vehicle crashes, compared with 37% of other fatal crashes.

In two-vehicle fatal crashes involving a large truck, 60% of the vehicles were struck in the front compared with 66% in two-vehicle fatal crashes not involving large trucks. During fatal truck crashes, the truck is more likely to be struck in the rear than other vehicle types involved in the crash – 22% and 6%, respectively.

Source: National Safety Council analysis of NHTSA FARS data.

Fatalities in crashes involving large trucks, United States, 2015

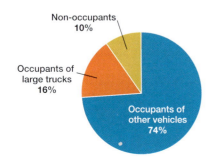

MOTOR VEHICLE
Motorcycles

Although motorcycles make up 3% of all registered vehicles and only 0.7% of all vehicle miles traveled in the United States, motorcyclists accounted for 14% of total traffic fatalities, 17% of all occupant fatalities, and 4% of all occupant injuries in 2014.

Fatalities among motorcycle riders and passengers have increased nearly 3% from 2006 to 2015 driven largely by an 8% increase in 2015. The number of motorcycle fatalities now stands at 4,976. Over the last 10 years motorcycle fatalities peaked in 2008 with 5,312 and reached a low point in 2009 with 4,469. The number of nonfatal injuries peaked in 2007 with 103,000 injuries and reached a low point in 2011 with 81,000 injuries. In contrast to the fatality increase, nonfatal injuries decreased 4% in 2015 to 88,000.

Exposure has also increased. From 2005 through 2014 (the latest year available), the number of registered motorcycles increased nearly 35% to 8.4 million from 6.2 million. Miles traveled is up 91%, from 10.4 billion to 20.0 billion in 2014 (latest available data). Consequently, the death rate from 2005 to 2014 has decreased 48%, from 43.77 to 22.96 deaths per 100 million miles traveled.

In 2014, 29% of motorcycle operators involved in fatal crashes were alcohol-impaired (blood-alcohol content greater than or equal to 0.08 g/dL), compared with 22% for passenger cars and light trucks, and 2% for large trucks.

In 2015, 1,922 motorcyclists died without a helmet on. Motorcycle helmets are estimated to be 37% effective in preventing fatal injuries to motorcycle operators and 41% effective for motorcycle passengers. The National Highway Traffic Safety Administration estimated helmets saved 1,669 motorcyclists' lives in 2014, and an additional 660 lives could have been saved if all motorcyclists wore helmets. Use of DOT-compliant helmets was 60.7% in 2015, statistically unchanged from 64.3% in 2014. The 2014 helmet use rate is substantially lower than the high of 71% achieved in 2000.

In 2015, 19 states and the District of Columbia had laws requiring helmet use by all motorcyclists. Other states either required only a subset of motorcyclists to use helmets (such as those younger than 18) or had no helmet requirement.

As shown in the table below, 53% of the 4,976 motorcycle fatalities in 2015 involved collision with another motor vehicle, while 26% involved collision with a fixed object and 18% were noncollision events. Over 30% of the motorcycle fatalities involved the motorcycle speeding, 49% of the fatalities occurred at night, 33% occurred at intersections, and 27% involved a motorcycle operator without a valid motorcycle license.

Motorcycle fatalities by type of crash and contributing factors, 2015

Contributing factors	Total	Speeding	Nighttime	Intersection	Invalid motorcyle license status
Total	4,976	1,648	2,439	1,665	1,357
Collision with...					
Other motor vehicle	2,614	627	1,190	1,349	702
Animal	95	4	66	1	11
Fixed object	1,280	609	749	130	382
Other/unknown	85	37	44	14	27
Noncollision	902	371	390	171	235

Source: National Center for Statistics and Analysis. (2016 July). Traffic Safety Facts Lives and Costs Saved by Motorcycle Helmets, 2014. (DOT HS 812 292.) Washington, DC: National Highway Traffic Safety Administration.
National Center for Statistics and Analysis. (2016 June). Traffic Safety Facts 2014 Data: Motorcycles. (DOT HS 812 292.) Washington, DC: National Highway Traffic Safety Administration.
National Center for Statistics and Analysis. (2016, May). Traffic Safety Facts Research Note – Motorcycle Helmet Use in 2015 – Overall Results (DOT HS 812 275). Washington, DC: National Highway Traffic Safety Administration.
Insurance Institute for Highway Safety. (September 2016). Motorcycle and bicycle helmet use laws. Downloaded on September 14, 2016 from http://www.iihs.org/iihs/topics/laws/helmetuse?topicName=motorcycles.

MOTOR VEHICLE
School Bus Transportation

School bus-related crashes killed 115 people nationwide in 2015, according to National Safety Council tabulations of data from the National Highway Traffic Safety Administration (NHTSA).

A school bus-related crash is defined by NHTSA to be any crash in which a vehicle, regardless of body design, used as a school bus is directly or indirectly involved, such as a crash involving school children alighting from a vehicle.

From 2007 to 2015, about 71% of the deaths in school bus-related crashes were occupants of vehicles other than the school bus and 17% were pedestrians. About 5% were school bus passengers, 4% were school bus drivers, and another 3% were pedalcyclists.

Out of the people injured in school bus-related crashes from 2007 to 2015, about 36% were school bus passengers, 6% were school bus drivers, and an additional 49% were occupants of other vehicles. The remainder were pedestrians, pedalcyclists, and other or unknown type persons.

Characteristics of school bus transportation

According to the American School Bus Council, an estimated 480,000 yellow school buses provide transportation service daily nationwide and travel approximately 5.8 billion miles each school year. Approximately 26 million elementary and secondary school children ride school buses to and from school each day throughout the United States. This compares to projections from the U.S. Department of Education of enrollments in fall 2015 in grades K-12 of about 56.5 million public school pupils and 6.0 million private school pupils nationwide.

Deaths and injuries in school bus-related crashes, United States, 2007-2015

Deaths	2007	2008	2009	2010	2011	2012	2013	2014	2015
Totals	142	152	118	130	123	131	130	120	115
School bus driver	4	4	2	6	7	6	5	4	8
School bus passenger	1	15	3	10	4	8	6	7	5
Pedestrian	19	21	21	26	21	27	22	28	11
Pedalcyclist	6	8	1	3	4	3	3	4	4
Occupant of other vehicle	112	104	91	84	86	87	92	77	87
Other non-occupants	0	0	0	1	1	0	2	0	0
Injuries									
Total	9,000	13,000	13,000	10,000	12,000	9,000	24,000	14,000	13,500
School bus driver	1,000	1,000	1,000	1,000	(a)	1,000	2,000	1,000	2,000
School bus passenger	2,000	6,000	6,000	3,000	4,000	2,000	11,000	4,000	4,000
Pedestrian	(a)	(a)	1,000	(a)	(a)	(a)	1,000	(a)	500
Pedalcyclist	(a)	(a)	(a)	(a)	(a)	(a)	(a)	(a)	(a)
Occupant of other vehicle	5,000	5,000	5,000	5,000	6,000	6,000	9,000	9,000	7,000
Other non-occupants	(a)	(a)	(a)	(a)	(a)	(a)	(a)	(a)	(a)

Source: Deaths for 2007-2014 – National Center for Statistics and Analysis. (2016). Traffic Safety Facts 2002-2014 Data – School Transportation-Related Crashes (DOT HS 811 746). Washington, DC: National Highway Traffic Safety Administration.
Fatality data for 2015 and pedalcyclist deaths are National Safety Council tabulations of Fatality Analysis Reporting System (FARS) data.
Injuries – National Center for Statistics and Analysis. (2007-2014). Traffic Safety Facts, 2007-2014 editions. Washington, DC: National Highway Traffic Safety Administration.
Injury data for 2015 are National Safety Council tabulations of General Estimates System data. School bus transportation data accessed September 8, 2016 from American School Bus Council at http://www.americanschoolbuscouncil.org/issues/environmental-benefits.
Student enrollment data from the Digest of Education Statistics: 2015, accessed September. 8, 2016 from the National Center for Education Statistics at https://nces.ed.gov/programs/digest/d15/tables/dt15_105.10.asp?current=yes.
[a]Fewer than 500.

MOTOR VEHICLE
Pedestrians

In 2015, an estimated 6,700 pedestrian deaths and 160,000 medically consulted nonfatal injuries occurred among pedestrians in motor-vehicle incidents. About 17% of these deaths occurred when pedestrians improperly cross roadways or intersections. Lack of visibility because of lack of lighting or dark clothing accounted for about 15% of the deaths, while being in the roadway improperly (either standing, lying, working, or playing) contributed to about 13% of the deaths. No improper action or circumstance was reported for about a quarter of the pedestrian deaths.

Pedestrian deaths by age and action/circumstance, United States, 2015

Action or circumstance	Total[a]	Younger than 5	5-9 years	10-15 years	16-20 years	21-24 years	25-44 years	45-64 years	65 or older
Total	126.5%	119.5%	132.9%	127.7%	130.9%	125.8%	127.8%	126.2%	125.0%
No improper action/circumstance	26.8%	28.6%	26.0%	26.5%	24.2%	27.3%	22.9%	25.3%	36.0%
Improper crossing of roadway or intersection	16.6%	10.4%	17.8%	20.5%	10.8%	11.2%	15.5%	17.9%	19.8%
Not visible (dark clothing, no lighting, etc.)	14.9%	3.9%	4.1%	6.0%	11.7%	14.8%	18.4%	14.8%	13.4%
In roadway improperly (standing, lying, working, playing)	13.2%	13.0%	8.2%	6.0%	17.0%	15.8%	18.1%	12.8%	6.0%
Failure to obey traffic signs, signals or officer	3.5%	0.0%	0.0%	1.2%	4.9%	2.9%	2.7%	3.6%	5.1%
Darting or running into roadway	2.9%	11.7%	15.1%	7.2%	6.7%	3.6%	2.3%	2.3%	2.1%
Inattentive—talking, eating, etc.	1.8%	3.9%	4.1%	3.6%	2.2%	2.4%	1.5%	1.8%	1.2%
Other action/circumstance	39.2%	39.0%	52.1%	51.8%	43.5%	40.6%	39.3%	39.2%	35.7%
Not reported/unknown	7.6%	9.1%	5.5%	4.8%	9.9%	7.1%	7.3%	8.6%	5.8%

Source: National Safety Council tabulations of National Highway Traffic Safety Administration FARS data.
[a]Totals are greater than 100% as multiple actions/circumstances may be entered for each case. Columns may not sum to totals because of rounding.

A National Safety Council analysis of pedestrian traffic fatality data shows a general decline in the number of pedestrian fatalities from 1994 through 2009. Since 2009, pedestrian fatalities have been trending sharply up, now totaling 5,376 traffic related deaths. Looking at pedestrian fatalities as a percent of all traffic fatalities, the upward trend started several years earlier in 2005. In 2004, pedestrian fatalities accounted for 10.9% of all traffic fatalities, while in 2015 pedestrian deaths accounted for 15.3% of the total (see graph below).

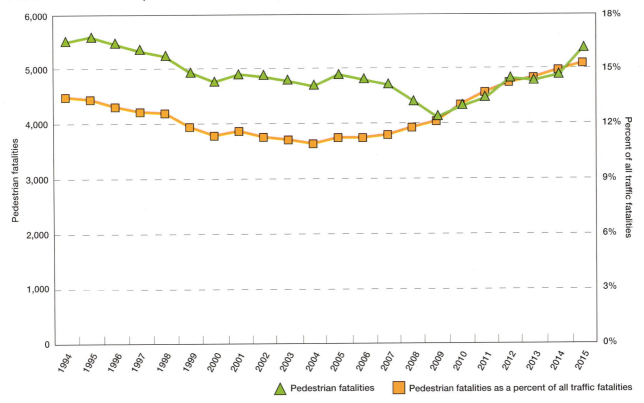

Pedestrian fatalities and pedestrian fatalities as a percent of all traffic fatalities, 1994-2015

MOTOR VEHICLE
Young Drivers

According to the latest data available from the National Highway Traffic Safety Administration, 2015 marked the second year in a row in which the number of teen motor-vehicle occupant fatalities increased in the United States, now at 2,358 compared to 2,176 in 2014. Motor-vehicle crashes continue to be the number one cause of death for U.S. teens. The total death toll, including pedestrian and bicycle incidents, among teens ages 13 to 19 was 2,715 in 2015, and is equivalent to more than seven deaths per day.

Crashes involving young drivers impact people of all ages.

In 2015, the number of people dying in crashes involving at least one young driver totaled 4,702, a 10% increase over the 2014 total of 4,272. The chart below clearly shows that young driver fatalities account for less than half of the overall fatalities associated with young driver crashes. In 2015, there were 1,886 young driver fatalities, 975 fatalities among passengers of young drivers, 1,320 fatalities to occupants of all other vehicles, and 521 non-occupant fatalities.

Historical trend of young driver-related fatalities, United States, 1982-2015

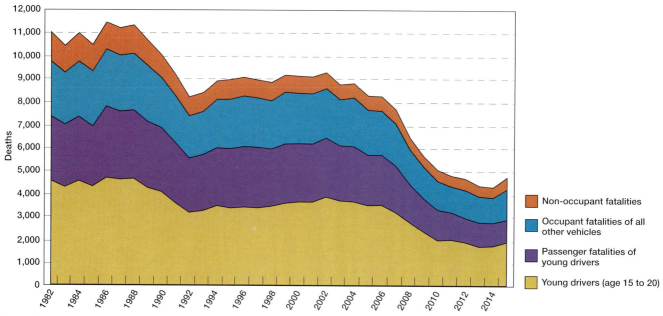

Source: National Safety Council analysis of National Highway Traffic Safety Administration data.

GDL

A strategy shown to help prevent young driver crashes is the passage and enforcement of state Graduated Driver Licensing (GDL) programs. GDL programs allow for a gradual phasing in of full driving privileges using a three-step process comprising an initial learner's permit phase; an intermediate, or provisional, license phase; and a full licensure phase.

One of the important components of GDL programs is a restriction on nighttime driving. While only about 10.4% of trips driven by 16 and 17 year olds occur between 9 p.m. and 6 a.m., over 30% of their fatal crashes occur at this time. Unfortunately, most state GDL programs currently allow some nighttime driving. Currently only five states, (Idaho, Kansas, New York, North Carolina, and North Dakota) prohibit provisional license holders to drive after 9 p.m.

Driver Education

A recent epidemiological study examined a census of all teen drivers in Nebraska during an eight year period from 2003 to 2010 to assess the impact of participating in a driver education program. Teen driver crash experiences were compared between those teens who obtained an intermediate-level provisional operators permit in a graduated driver licensing environment after completing a driver education program versus those teens who obtained a provisional permit by completing a supervised driving certification log without taking driver education. Results showed that teens participating in driver education experienced fewer crashes and violations.

Driver Behavior

A naturalistic driving study using Ltyx DrivCam in-vehicle video camera systems explored the driver behaviors associated with 1,691 young driver crashes from August 2007 through July 2013. Results found that young drivers drove too fast for conditions in 79% of single-vehicle crashes and followed too closely in 36% of rear-end crashes.

Sources: Carne, C., McGehee, D., Harland, K., Weiss, M., & Raby, M. (2015). Using naturalistic driving data to assess the prevalence of environmental factors and driver behaviors in teen driver crashes. Downloaded on November 9, 2015 from: https://www.aaafoundation.org/using-naturalistic-driving-data-assess-vehicle-vehicle-crashes-involving-fleet-drivers.
Shell, D.F., Newman, I.M., Cordova-Cazar, A.L., & Heese, J.M. (2015). Driver education and teen crashes and traffic violations in the first two years of driving in a graduated licensing system. Accident Analysis and Prevention, 82 45-52.
Shults, R.A. & Williams, A.F. (2016). Graduated Driver Licensing Night Driving Restrictions and Drivers Aged 16 or 17 Years Involved in Fatal Night Crashes – United States, 2009-2014. MMWR Morb Mortal Wkly Rep 2016; 65:725-730.

MOTOR VEHICLE
ATV Fatalities and Non-Fatal Injuries

All-terrain vehicles (ATV)s are off-road recreational vehicles that may or may not be permitted for use on public roadways depending on a wide range of State regulations. An ATV generally has three or more low-pressure tires, a straddle seat, a handlebar for steering, and hand controls for braking and acceleration. The National Highway Traffic Administration (NHTSA) tracks ATV traffic crashes on public roadways while the Consumer Product Safety Commission (CPSC) tracks ATV fatalities and injuries regardless of the location of incident.

The NHTSA traffic-related ATV fatality estimate is generally about half the CPSC total estimate. In the last year with final estimates from both NHTSA and CPSC, 2011, NHTSA reported 309 ATV-related fatalities while CPSC reported 626 fatalities. According to NHTSA estimates, about 98% of fatalities are among ATV occupants versus occupants of other vehicles or nonoccupants. As shown below, CPSC estimates show a downward fatality trend starting in 2008. CPSC estimates also indicate that about 8% of the ATV fatalities are among children younger than 12, 10% among children aged 12 to 15, and 82% of the fatalities among individuals 16 or older.

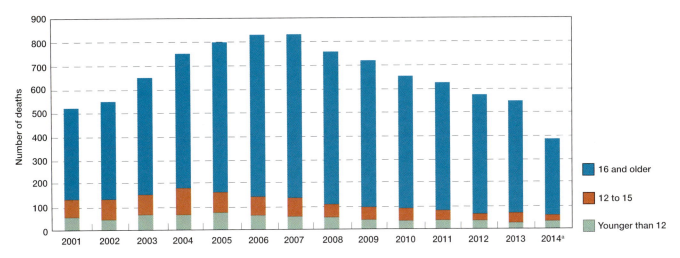

CPSC estimate of ATV-related deaths by age group, United States, 2001-2014

[a] Preliminary, fatality estimates likely to be revised upward.

CPSC estimates that the number of ATV-related emergency department visits has decreased 38% from 2007 to 2014. In 2014, a total of 93,700 emergency department visits are estimated with about 24,800 of these visits involving children younger than 16.

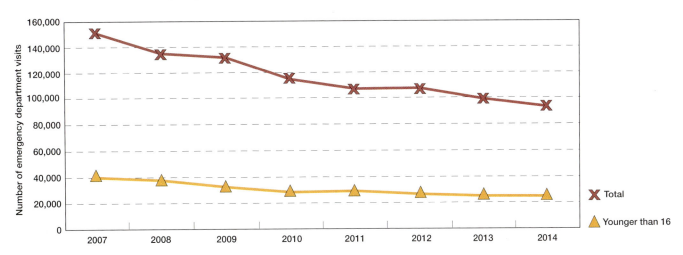

Number of ATV-related emergency department visits, United States, 2007-2014

Source: Consumer Product Safety Commission (2015). 2014 Annual Report of ATV-Related Deaths and Injuries. Downloaded on June 22, 2016 from: http://www.cpsc.gov/en/Research--Statistics/Sports--Recreation/ATVs/Injury-Statistics/
National Center for Statistics and Analysis. (2015, September). Fatalities in traffic crashes involving all-terrain vehicles (Research Note. Report No. HS 812 193). Washington, DC: National Highway Traffic Safety Administration. Downloaded on June 22, 2016 from: http://www-nrd.nhtsa.dot.gov/Pubs/812193.pdf

MOTOR VEHICLE
Age of Driver

The table below shows the total number of licensed drivers and drivers involved in crashes by selected ages and age groups. Also shown is the rate of crash involvement on the basis of the number of drivers in each age group. The fatal crash involvement rates per 100,000 licensed drivers in each age group ranged from a low of 17 for drivers in the 65-74 age group to a high of 41 for drivers age 19 and 22. The all-incident involvement rates per 100 drivers in each age group ranged from five for drivers in the 75 and older age group to 33 for drivers age 16.

On the basis of miles driven by each age group, however, involvement rates (not shown in the table) are highest for the youngest drivers. The rates of fatal crashes per mile driven for 16-19 year-olds are about three times the rates for drivers age 20 and older. Passenger vehicle drivers age 16 had the highest fatal crash involvement rate at 9.1 fatal crashes per 100 million vehicle miles traveled in 2008, more than seven times the rate of 1.2 for drivers aged 30-59.

For more details of this mileage-based analysis, please see the 2016 edition, pages 124 and 125.

Source: National Safety Council estimates based on NHTSA FARS data. Involvement rates per mile driven: McCartt, A.T., & Teoh, E.R., (March 2014). Tracking Progress in Teenage Crash Risk in the United States Since the Advent of Graduated Driver Licensing Programs. Arlington, VA: Insurance Institute for Highway Safety.

Licensed drivers and number in crashes by age of driver, United States, 2015

Age group	Licensed drivers Number	Licensed drivers Percent	Fatal crashes Number	Fatal crashes Percent	Fatal crashes Rate[a]	All crashes Number	All crashes Percent	All crashes Rate[b]
Total	214,800,000	100.0%	52,300	100.0%	24	22,900,000	100.0%	11
Younger than 16	125,000	0.1	200	0.4	([c])	270,000	1.2	([c])
16	1,019,000	0.5	400	0.8	39	340,000	1.5	33
17	1,871,000	0.9	700	1.3	37	520,000	2.3	28
18	2,517,000	1.2	1,000	1.9	40	650,000	2.8	26
19	2,921,000	1.4	1,200	2.3	41	650,000	2.8	22
19 and younger	8,453,000	3.9	3,500	6.7	41	2,430,000	10.6	29
20	3,157,000	1.5	1,200	2.3	38	650,000	2.8	21
21	3,293,000	1.5	1,300	2.5	39	630,000	2.8	19
22	3,447,000	1.6	1,400	2.7	41	680,000	3.0	20
23	3,620,000	1.7	1,400	2.7	39	660,000	2.9	18
24	3,807,000	1.8	1,300	2.5	34	590,000	2.6	15
20-24	17,324,000	8.1	6,600	12.6	38	3,210,000	14.0	19
25-34	37,614,000	17.5	11,000	21.0	29	4,970,000	21.7	13
35-44	35,663,000	16.6	8,400	16.1	24	3,860,000	16.9	11
45-54	38,962,000	18.1	8,600	16.4	22	3,450,000	15.1	9
55-64	37,314,000	17.4	7,100	13.6	19	2,780,000	12.1	7
65-74	24,692,000	11.5	4,100	7.8	17	1,430,000	6.2	6
75 and older	14,778,000	6.9	3,000	5.7	20	770,000	3.4	5

Source: National Safety Council estimates. Drivers in incidents based on data from the National Highway Traffic Safety Administration's Fatality Analysis Reporting System and General Estimates System. Total licensed drivers and age distribution estimated by the National Safety Council based on data from the Federal Highway Administration.
Note: Percents may not add to total due to rounding.
[a]Drivers in fatal incidents per 100,000 licensed drivers in each age group.
[b]Drivers in all incidents per 100 licensed drivers in each age group.
[c]Rates for drivers younger than 16 are substantially overstated due to the high proportion of unlicensed drivers involved.

MOTOR VEHICLE

Impact of Recession Periods on Motor-Vehicle Deaths and Rates

Comparing data of long-term motor-vehicle deaths and death rates to the backdrop of recession periods reveals several interesting trends. First, during recession periods the number of deaths declines and, to a lesser extent, the mileage-based death rate also tends to decline. The large decline in the number of deaths is partially a result of fewer people driving during poor economic times. As would be expected following the end of recessionary periods, the number of deaths tends to increase. The latest 2015 motor-vehicle data does indeed show a substantial increase in the number of fatalities compared to recession period levels and preliminary partial year estimates for 2016 (not included in chart) also showing a substantial increase in the number of fatalities. In contrast to the increase in the number of fatalities following recession periods, the mileage-based death rate does not typically increase substantially, but instead stabilizes or continues a slow, steady decline following recessions. However, the most recent final data does show an over 3% increase in the mileage death rate between 2014 and 2015 from 1.17 up to 1.21. Looking at the overall long term trend over the last 60 years, it appears that even after accounting for recession periods, there is a slow but steady improvement in motor-vehicle safety when measured using mileage-based death rates.

A recent study conducted by He (2016) investigating the factors contributing to the decrease in motor-vehicle fatalities during the recent Great Recession found that for each percentage point increase in the unemployment rate, motor-vehicle fatalities decrease by 2.82%. The decrease in fatalities during a recession is driven by a number of factors. For each percentage increase in the unemployment rate: fatalities involving large trucks decrease 8.4%; speeding related fatalities decrease 5.0%; drunk driving related fatalities decrease 3.6%; non-drunk driving fatalities decrease 2.5%; multi-vehicle crash fatalities decrease 4.1%; and urban crash fatalities decrease 4.6%.

Historial motor-vehicle deaths and death rates, United States, 1950-2015

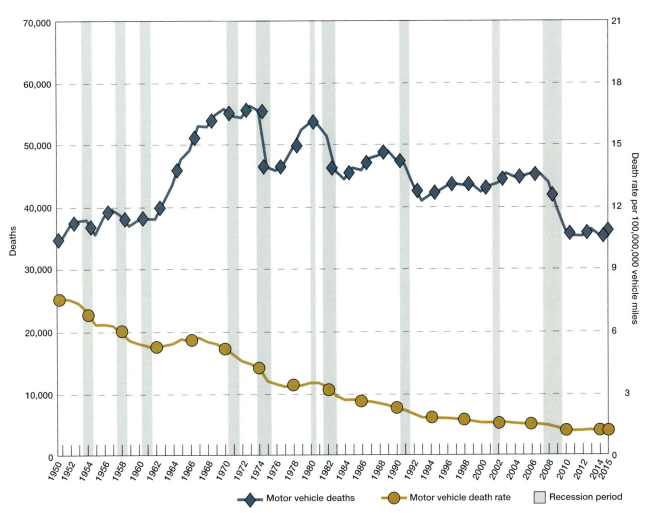

Source: Death data are from the National Center for Health Statistics except 1964, which is a National Safety Council estimate based on data from the National Highway Traffic Safety Administration's Fatality Analysis Reporting System. Motor-vehicle rates are based on mileage estimates from the Federal Highway Administration, except 2015, which is a National Safety Council estimate. Recession periods are from the National Bureau of Economic Research.
He, M.M. (2016). Driving through the great recession: why does motor vehicle fatality decrease when the economy slows down? Social Science & Medicine, 155, 1-11.

MOTOR VEHICLE
Motor-Vehicle Crashes by Time of Day and Day of Week

More fatal crashes occurred on Saturday than any other day of the week in 2015, according to data from the National Highway Traffic Safety Administration. More than 17% of fatal crashes occurred on Saturday, compared with 16% on Sundays and 15% on Fridays. For all crashes, Friday had the highest percentage with 16%, while Sunday had the lowest percentage with 10%.

Patterns by time of day for fatal crashes show peaks during afternoon rush hour for weekdays and, especially, late at night during weekends. For all crashes, primary peaks also occurred during afternoon rush hours.

Number of crashes by time of day and day of week, United States, 2015

Time of day	Fatal crashes								All crashes							
	Total	Sun.	Mon.	Tues.	Wed.	Thurs.	Fri.	Sat.	Total	Sun.	Mon.	Tues.	Wed.	Thurs.	Fri.	Sat.
All hours	32,166	5,237	3,991	3,950	4,128	4,406	4,857	5,597	6,296,000	636,000	934,384	981,533	947,930	988,524	1,017,281	779,673
Midnight to 3:59 a.m.	4,576	1,263	405	331	393	485	572	1,127	323,000	87,000	31,000	33,000	29,000	36,000	39,000	69,000
4:00 to 7:59 a.m.	4,045	578	560	559	561	584	598	605	662,000	50,000	109,000	123,000	112,000	108,000	103,000	56,000
8:00 to 11:59 a.m.	3,990	511	567	580	570	586	572	604	1,179,000	93,000	194,000	191,000	187,000	195,000	181,000	138,000
Noon to 3:59 p.m.	5,739	804	801	788	828	828	868	822	1,647,000	159,000	246,000	252,000	237,000	259,000	280,000	215,000
4:00 to 7:59 p.m.	7,086	1,077	931	942	970	1,002	1,060	1,104	1,768,000	157,000	269,000	295,000	285,000	293,000	291,000	178,000
8:00 to 11:59 p.m.	6,481	966	703	720	777	886	1,154	1,275	705,000	91,000	86,000	87,000	97,000	97,000	123,000	124,000

Source: National Safety Council analysis of data from the National Highway Traffic Safety Administration — Fatality Analysis Reporting System (FARS) and General Estimates System (GES).
Note: Column and row totals may not equal sum of parts due to rounding and unreported time of day or day of week data.

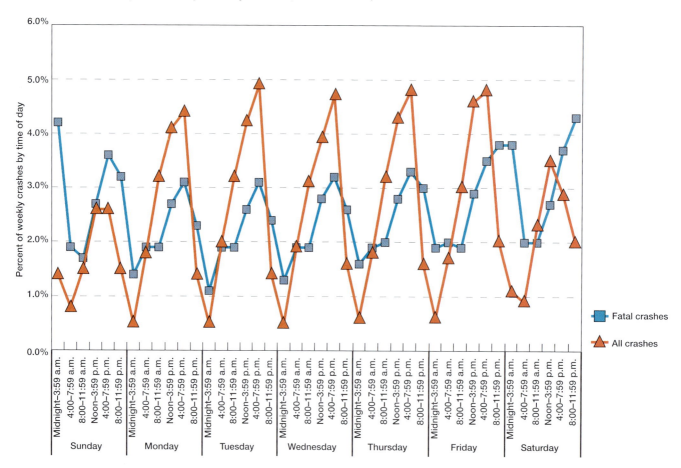

Percent of crashes by time of day and day of week, United States, 2015

128 ■ NATIONAL SAFETY COUNCIL® INJURY FACTS® 2017 EDITION

MOTOR VEHICLE
Deaths and Mileage Death Rates by Month

Motor-vehicle deaths in 2015 were at their lowest level in February and increased to their highest level in August. In 2015, the highest monthly mileage death rate of 1.32 deaths per 100,000,000 vehicle miles occurred in August. The overall rate for the year was 1.21.

Motor-vehicle deaths and mileage death rates by month, United States, 2015

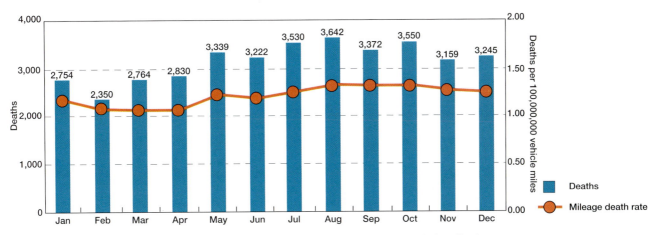

Source: Deaths – National Safety Council estimates. Mileage – Federal Highway Administration, Traffic Volume Trends.

MOTOR VEHICLE
Holidays

Holidays traditionally are a time of travel for families across the United States. Many choose the automobile – with the highest fatality rate of any of the major forms of transportation based on fatalities per passenger mile (see page 156) – as their mode of travel, therefore increasing their risk of dying in a motor-vehicle crash. In addition, holidays are often the cause for celebrations that include drinking alcohol, which is a major contributing factor to motor-vehicle crashes. Nationwide, alcohol-impaired (blood-alcohol content of 0.08 g/dL or higher) fatalities in 2015 represented over 29% of the total traffic fatalities. The table below shows the number of fatalities for each major holiday period and the percent of those fatalities that were alcohol-impaired.

Motor-vehicle deaths and percent alcohol-impaired during holiday periods, United States, 2011-2015

Year	New Year's Day Deaths[b]	Alcohol-impaired[c] (%)	Memorial Day Deaths[b]	Alcohol-impaired[c] (%)	Independence Day Deaths[b]	Alcohol-impaired[c] (%)	Labor Day Deaths[b]	Alcohol-impaired[c] (%)	Thanksgiving Day Deaths[b]	Alcohol-impaired[c] (%)	Christmas Day Deaths[b]	Alcohol-impaired[c] (%)
2011	304 (3)	43	389 (3)	40	405 (3)	37	373 (3)	37	375 (4)	32	256 (3)	36
2012	348 (3)	39	367 (3)	44	157 (1)	45	378 (3)	38	405 (4)	41	351 (4)	35
2013	343 (4)	44	334 (3)	38	461 (4)	39	371 (3)	39	360 (4)	34	88 (1)	37
2014	126 (1)	53	337 (3)	36	347 (3)	41	362 (3)	40	403 (4)	35	355 (4)	34
2015	355 (4)	—	367 (3)	—	366 (3)	—	394 (3)	—	386 (4)	—	273 (3)	—

Source: Deaths – National Safety Council tabulations of National Highway Traffic Safety Administration (NHTSA), Fatality Analysis Reporting System data. Percent alcohol impaired – NHTSA, Traffic Safety Facts, 2014 edition.
Note: Dashes indicate data not available.
[a] The length of the holiday period depends on the day of the week on which the holiday falls. Memorial Day and Labor Day are always 3.25 days; Thanksgiving is always 4.25 days; and New Year's Day, Independence Day, and Christmas are 3.25 days if the holiday falls on Friday through Monday, 4.25 days if on Tuesday or Thursday, and 1.25 days if on Wednesday.
[b] Number in parentheses refers to the number of whole days in the holiday period.
[c] Highest blood alcohol concentration (BAC) among drivers or motorcycle riders involved in the crash was 0.08 grams per deciliter (g/dL) or higher. The holiday periods used to calculate the percentages conform to the NHTSA holiday period definitions that add another quarter day to the periods noted in footnote (a).

MOTOR VEHICLE
Work Zone Deaths and Injuries

In 2015, 700 people were killed and 35,500 people were injured in work zone crashes (see table below). Of the 700 killed in work zones, 489 were in construction zones, 66 were in maintenance zones, 7 were in utility zones, and 138 were in an unknown type of work zone.

From 2006 through 2015, work zone deaths have ranged from 576 to 1,010 and averaged 695 per year.

According to the Governors Highway Safety Association, nearly all states have laws that increase the penalties for speeding or committing other traffic violations while in a construction work zone.[a] The penalties often involve doubled fines, but also can be a fixed dollar amount. In some cases, the penalty is applicable only when workers are present and/or if signs are posted. Presently, 32 states and the District of Columbia double the fine for speeding or other traffic violations in a work zone. Twenty-four states and the District of Columbia require workers to be present in the construction zone for the increased penalties to take effect.

[a]Retrieved September. 9, 2016 from www.ghsa.org/html/stateinfo/laws/sanctions_laws.html.

People killed or injured in work zones, United States, 2015

	Total	Vehicle occupants	Pedestrians	Pedalcyclists	Other nonmotorists
Killed	700	586	104	6	4
Injured	35,500	33,500	1,100	500	400

Source: National Safety Council analysis of data from National Highway Traffic Safety Administration Fatality Analysis Reporting System and General Estimates Systems.

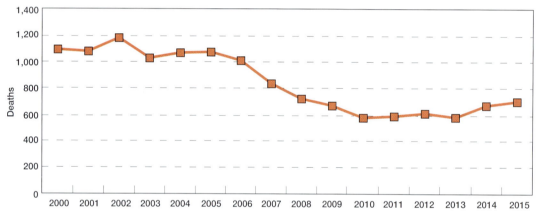

Work zone deaths, United States, 2000-2015

Source: NSC analysis of NHTSA FARS data files.

MOTOR VEHICLE
Emergency Vehicles

Crashes involving emergency vehicles, United States, 2015

	Ambulance		Fire truck/car		Police car	
	Total	Emergency use[a]	Total	Emergency use[a]	Total	Emergency use[a]
Emergency vehicles in fatal crashes	25	13	12	12	72	26
Emergency vehicles in injury crashes	1,400	1,000	500	400	7,100	2,700
Emergency vehicles in all crashes	**5,600**	**2,900**	**3,300**	**2,000**	**23,200**	**6,800**
Emergency vehicle drivers killed	1	0	0	0	20	6
Emergency vehicle passengers killed	10	6	0	0	1	0
Other vehicle occupants killed	15	10	11	11	31	13
Nonmotorists killed	2	0	1	1	23	9
Total killed in crashes	28	16	12	12	75	28
Total injured in crashes	2,200	1,200	700	600	10,500	3,200

Source: National Safety Council analysis of data from National Highway Traffic Safety Administration Fatality Analysis Reporting System and General Estimates Systems.
[a]Vehicle being used as an emergency vehicle at the time of the crash with or without the use of emergency warning equipment.

MOTOR VEHICLE
NSC and NHTSA Motor-Vehicle Fatality Statistics

The National Safety Council (NSC) and the National Highway Traffic Safety Administration (NHTSA) count motor-vehicle crash deaths using somewhat different criteria. NSC counts total motor-vehicle-related fatalities – both traffic and nontraffic – that occur within one year of the crash. This is consistent with the data compiled from death certificates by the National Center for Health Statistics (NCHS). NSC uses NCHS death certificate data less intentional fatalities as the final count of unintentional deaths from all causes.

NHTSA counts only traffic fatalities that occur within 30 days of the crash in its Fatality Analysis Reporting System (FARS). This means that the FARS count omits about 800 to 1,000 motor-vehicle-related deaths each year that occur more than 30 days after the crash. Nontraffic fatalities (those that do not occur on public highways; e.g., parking lots, private roads, and driveways), which account for 900 to 1,900 deaths annually, also are omitted. By using a 30-day cutoff, NHTSA can issue a "final" count about eight months after the reference year.

This edition of *Injury Facts* includes the 2014 and 2015 NCHS final counts by cause of death including motor-vehicle crashes. The graph below shows the NCHS death certificate counts of unintentional motor-vehicle deaths through 2015 compared to the NHTSA FARS counts of traffic deaths.

Motor-vehicle deaths: NSC and NHTSA, 1992-2015

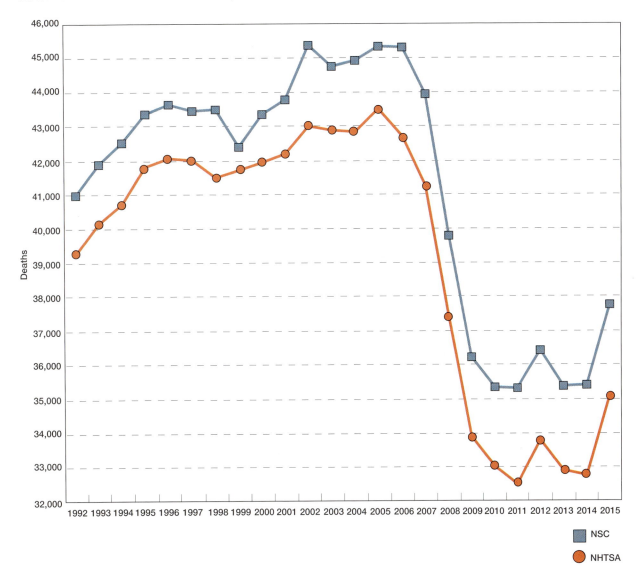

MOTOR VEHICLE

Motor-Vehicle Deaths and Rates

Motor-vehicle deaths and rates, United States, 1913-2015

Year	No. of deaths	Estimated no. of vehicles (millions)	Estimated vehicle miles (billions)	Estimated no. of drivers (millions)	Death rates Per 10,000 motor vehicles	Per 100,000,000 vehicle miles	Per 100,000 population
1913	4,200	1.3	(a)	2.0	33.38	(a)	4.4
1914	4,700	1.8	(a)	3.0	26.65	(a)	4.8
1915	6,600	2.5	(a)	3.0	26.49	(a)	6.6
1916	8,200	3.6	(a)	5.0	22.66	(a)	8.1
1917	10,200	5.1	(a)	7.0	19.93	(a)	10.0
1918	10,700	6.2	(a)	9.0	17.37	(a)	10.3
1919	11,200	7.6	(a)	12.0	14.78	(a)	10.7
1920	12,500	9.2	(a)	14.0	13.53	(a)	11.7
1921	13,900	10.5	(a)	16.0	13.25	(a)	12.9
1922	15,300	12.3	(a)	19.0	12.47	(a)	13.9
1923	18,400	15.1	85	22.0	12.18	21.65	16.5
1924	19,400	17.6	104	26.0	11.02	18.65	17.1
1925	21,900	20.1	122	30.0	10.89	17.95	19.1
1926	23,400	22.2	141	33.0	10.54	16.59	20.1
1927	25,800	23.3	158	34.0	11.07	16.33	21.8
1928	28,000	24.7	173	37.0	11.34	16.18	23.4
1929	31,200	26.7	197	40.0	11.69	15.84	25.7
1930	32,900	26.7	206	40.0	12.32	15.97	26.7
1931	33,700	26.1	216	39.0	12.91	15.60	27.2
1932	29,500	24.4	200	36.0	12.09	14.75	23.6
1933	31,363	24.2	201	35.0	12.96	15.60	25.0
1934	36,101	25.3	216	37.0	14.27	16.71	28.6
1935	36,369	26.5	229	39.0	13.72	15.88	28.6
1936	38,089	28.5	252	42.0	13.36	15.11	29.7
1937	39,643	30.1	270	44.0	13.19	14.68	30.8
1938	32,582	29.8	271	44.0	10.93	12.02	25.1
1939	32,386	31.0	285	46.0	10.44	11.35	24.7
1940	34,501	32.5	302	48.0	10.63	11.42	26.1
1941	39,969	34.9	334	52.0	11.45	11.98	30.0
1942	28,309	33.0	268	49.0	8.58	10.55	21.1
1943	23,823	30.9	208	46.0	7.71	11.44	17.8
1944	24,282	30.5	213	45.0	7.97	11.42	18.3
1945	28,076	31.0	250	46.0	9.05	11.22	21.2
1946	33,411	34.4	341	50.0	9.72	9.80	23.9
1947	32,697	37.8	371	53.0	8.64	8.82	22.8
1948	32,259	41.1	398	55.0	7.85	8.11	22.1
1949	31,701	44.7	424	59.3	7.09	7.47	21.3
1950	34,763	49.2	458	62.2	7.07	7.59	23.0
1951	36,996	51.9	491	64.4	7.13	7.53	24.1
1952	37,794	53.3	514	66.8	7.10	7.36	24.3
1953	37,956	56.3	544	69.9	6.74	6.97	24.0
1954	35,586	58.6	562	72.2	6.07	6.33	22.1
1955	38,426	62.8	606	74.7	6.12	6.34	23.4
1956	39,628	65.2	631	77.9	6.07	6.28	23.7
1957	38,702	67.6	647	79.6	5.73	5.98	22.7
1958	36,981	68.8	665	81.5	5.37	5.56	21.3
1959	37,910	72.1	700	84.5	5.26	5.41	21.5
1960	38,137	74.5	719	87.4	5.12	5.31	21.2
1961	38,091	76.4	738	88.9	4.98	5.16	20.8
1962	40,804	79.7	767	92.0	5.12	5.32	22.0
1963	43,564	83.5	805	93.7	5.22	5.41	23.1
1964	47,700	87.3	847	95.6	5.46	5.63	25.0
1965	49,163	91.8	888	99.0	5.36	5.54	25.4
1966	53,041	95.9	930	101.0	5.53	5.70	27.1
1967	52,924	98.9	962	103.2	5.35	5.50	26.8
1968	54,862	103.1	1,016	105.4	5.32	5.40	27.5
1969	55,791	107.4	1,071	108.3	5.19	5.21	27.7
1970	54,633	111.2	1,120	111.5	4.92	4.88	26.8
1971	54,381	116.3	1,186	114.4	4.68	4.57	26.3
1972	56,278	122.3	1,268	118.4	4.60	4.43	26.9
1973	55,511	129.8	1,309	121.6	4.28	4.24	26.3
1974	46,402	134.9	1,290	125.6	3.44	3.59	21.8
1975	45,853	137.9	1,330	129.8	3.33	3.45	21.3
1976	47,038	143.5	1,412	133.9	3.28	3.33	21.6

See source and footnotes on page 133.

MOTOR VEHICLE
Motor-Vehicle Deaths and Rates (cont.)

Motor-vehicle deaths and rates, United States, 1913-2015 (cont.)

Year	No. of deaths	Estimated no. of vehicles (millions)	Estimated vehicle miles (billions)	Estimated no. of drivers (millions)	Death rates Per 10,000 motor vehicles	Per 100,000,000 vehicle miles	Per 100,000 population
1977	49,510	148.8	1,477	138.1	3.33	3.35	22.5
1978	52,411	153.6	1,548	140.8	3.41	3.39	23.6
1979	53,524	159.6	1,529	143.3	3.35	3.50	23.8
1980	53,172	161.6	1,521	145.3	3.29	3.50	23.4
1981	51,385	164.1	1,556	147.1	3.13	3.30	22.4
1982	45,779	165.2	1,592	150.3	2.77	2.88	19.8
1983	44,452	169.4	1,657	154.2	2.62	2.68	19.0
1984	46,263	171.8	1,718	155.4	2.69	2.69	19.6
1985	45,901	177.1	1,774	156.9	2.59	2.59	19.3
1986	47,865	181.4	1,835	159.5	2.63	2.60	19.9
1987	48,290	183.9	1,924	161.8	2.63	2.51	19.9
1988	49,078	189.0	2,026	162.9	2.60	2.42	20.1
1989	47,575	191.7	2,107	165.6	2.48	2.26	19.3
1990	46,814	192.9	2,148	167.0	2.43	2.18	18.8
1991	43,536	192.5	2,172	169.0	2.26	2.00	17.3
1992	40,982	194.4	2,240	173.1	2.11	1.83	16.1
1993	41,893	198.0	2,297	173.1	2.12	1.82	16.3
1994	42,524	201.8	2,360	175.4	2.11	1.80	16.3
1995	43,363	205.3	2,423	176.6	2.11	1.79	16.5
1996	43,649	210.4	2,486	179.5	2.07	1.76	16.5
1997	43,458	211.5	2,562	182.7	2.05	1.70	16.2
1998	43,501	215.0	2,632	185.2	2.02	1.65	16.1
1999	42,401	220.5	2,691	187.2	1.92	1.58	15.5
2000	43,354	225.8	2,747	190.6	1.92	1.58	15.8
2001	43,788	235.3	2,797	191.3	1.86	1.57	15.4
2002	45,380	234.6	2,856	194.3	1.93	1.59	15.8
2003	44,757	236.8	2,890	196.2	1.89	1.55	15.4
2004	44,933	243.0	2,965	199.0	1.85	1.52	15.3
2005	45,343	247.4	2,989	200.5	1.83	1.52	15.3
2006	45,316	250.8	3,014	202.8	1.81	1.50	15.2
2007	43,945	254.4	3,032	205.7	1.73	1.45	14.6
2008	39,790	255.9	2,976	208.3	1.55	1.34	13.1
2009	36,216	254.2	2,957	209.6	1.42	1.22	11.8
2010	35,332	250.3	2,967	210.1	1.41	1.19	11.4
2011	35,303	253.2	2,950	211.9	1.39	1.20	11.3
2012	36,415	253.6	2,969	211.8	1.44	1.23	11.6
2013[b]	35,369	255.9	2,988	212.2	1.38	1.18	11.2
2014[b]	35,398	260.3	3,026	214.1	1.36	1.17	11.1
2015[c]	37,757	262.8	3,131	214.8	1.44	1.21	11.7
Changes							
2006 to 2015	-17%	5%	4%	6%	-20%	-19%	-23%
2014 to 2015	7%	1%	3%	[d]	6%	3%	6%

Source: Deaths from National Center for Health Statistics except 1964 which are National Safety Council estimates based on data from the National Highway Traffic Safety Administration's Fatality Analysis Reporting System. See Technical Appendix for comparability. Motor vehicle registrations, mileage, and drivers estimated by Federal Highway Administration except for 2015 registrations and drivers, which are National Safety Council estimates.
[a] Mileage data inadequate prior to 1923.
[b] Revised.
[c] Preliminary
[d] Less than 0.5%.

MOTOR VEHICLE

Motor-Vehicle Deaths by Type of Incident

Motor-vehicle deaths by type of incident, United States, 1913-2015

Year	Total deaths	Pedestrians	Other motor vehicles	Railroad trains	Streetcars	Pedalcycles	Animal-drawn vehicle or animal	Fixed objects	Deaths from noncollision incidents	Nontraffic deaths[a]
1913	4,200	(b)	(b)	(b)	(b)	(b)	(b)	(b)	(b)	(c)
1914	4,700	(b)	(b)	(b)	(b)	(b)	(b)	(b)	(b)	(c)
1915	6,600	(b)	(b)	(b)	(b)	(b)	(b)	(b)	(b)	(c)
1916	8,200	(b)	(b)	(b)	(b)	(b)	(b)	(b)	(b)	(c)
1917	10,200	(b)	(b)	(b)	(b)	(b)	(b)	(b)	(b)	(c)
1918	10,700	(b)	(b)	(b)	(b)	(b)	(b)	(b)	(b)	(c)
1919	11,200	(b)	(b)	(b)	(b)	(b)	(b)	(b)	(b)	(c)
1920	12,500	(b)	(b)	(b)	(b)	(b)	(b)	(b)	(b)	(c)
1921	13,900	(b)	(b)	(b)	(b)	(b)	(b)	(b)	(b)	(c)
1922	15,300	(b)	(b)	(b)	(b)	(b)	(b)	(b)	(b)	(c)
1923	18,400	(b)	(b)	(b)	(b)	(b)	(b)	(b)	(b)	(c)
1924	19,400	(b)	(b)	1,130	410	(b)	(b)	(b)	(b)	(c)
1925	21,900	(b)	(b)	1,410	560	(b)	(b)	(b)	(b)	(c)
1926	23,400	(b)	(b)	1,730	520	(b)	(b)	(b)	(b)	(c)
1927	25,800	10,820	3,430	1,830	520	(b)	(b)	(b)	(b)	(c)
1928	28,000	11,420	4,310	2,140	570	(b)	(b)	540	8,070	(c)
1929	31,200	12,250	5,400	2,050	530	(b)	(b)	620	9,380	(c)
1930	32,900	12,900	5,880	1,830	480	(b)	(b)	720	9,970	(c)
1931	33,700	13,370	6,820	1,710	440	(b)	(b)	870	9,570	(c)
1932	29,500	11,490	6,070	1,520	320	350	400	800	8,500	(c)
1933	31,363	12,840	6,470	1,437	318	400	310	900	8,680	(c)
1934	36,101	14,480	8,110	1,457	332	500	360	1,040	9,820	(c)
1935	36,369	14,350	8,750	1,587	253	450	250	1,010	9,720	(c)
1936	38,089	15,250	9,500	1,697	269	650	250	1,060	9,410	(c)
1937	39,643	15,500	10,320	1,810	264	700	200	1,160	9,690	(c)
1938	32,582	12,850	8,900	1,490	165	720	170	940	7,350	(c)
1939	32,386	12,400	8,700	1,330	150	710	200	1,000	7,900	(c)
1940	34,501	12,700	10,100	1,707	132	750	210	1,100	7,800	(c)
1941	39,969	13,550	12,500	1,840	118	910	250	1,350	9,450	(c)
1942	28,309	10,650	7,300	1,754	124	650	240	850	6,740	(c)
1943	23,823	9,900	5,300	1,448	171	450	160	700	5,690	(c)
1944	24,282	9,900	5,700	1,663	175	400	140	700	5,600	(c)
1945	28,076	11,000	7,150	1,703	163	500	130	800	6,600	(c)
1946	33,411	11,600	9,400	1,703	174	450	130	950	8,900	(c)
1947	32,697	10,450	9,900	1,736	102	550	150	1,000	8,800	(c)
1948	32,259	9,950	10,200	1,474	83	500	100	1,000	8,950	(c)
1949	31,701	8,800	10,500	1,452	56	550	140	1,100	9,100	838
1950	34,763	9,000	11,650	1,541	89	440	120	1,300	10,600	900
1951	36,996	9,150	13,100	1,573	46	390	100	1,400	11,200	966
1952	37,794	8,900	13,500	1,429	32	430	130	1,450	11,900	970
1953	37,956	8,750	13,400	1,506	26	420	120	1,500	12,200	1,026
1954	35,586	8,000	12,800	1,289	28	380	90	1,500	11,500	1,004
1955	38,426	8,200	14,500	1,490	15	410	90	1,600	12,100	989
1956	39,628	7,900	15,200	1,377	11	440	100	1,600	13,000	888
1957	38,702	7,850	15,400	1,376	13	460	80	1,700	11,800	1,016
1958	36,981	7,650	14,200	1,316	9	450	80	1,650	11,600	929
1959	37,910	7,850	14,900	1,202	6	480	70	1,600	11,800	948
1960	38,137	7,850	14,800	1,368	5	460	80	1,700	11,900	995
1961	38,091	7,650	14,700	1,267	5	490	80	1,700	12,200	1,065
1962	40,804	7,900	16,400	1,245	3	500	90	1,750	12,900	1,029
1963	43,564	8,200	17,600	1,385	10	580	80	1,900	13,800	990
1964	47,700	9,000	19,600	1,580	5	710	100	2,100	14,600	1,123
1965	49,163	8,900	20,800	1,556	5	680	120	2,200	14,900	1,113
1966	53,041	9,400	22,200	1,800	2	740	100	2,500	16,300	1,108
1967	52,924	9,400	22,000	1,620	3	750	100	2,350	16,700	1,165
1968	54,862	9,900	22,400	1,570	4	790	100	2,700	17,400	1,061
1969	55,791	10,100	23,700	1,495	2	800	100	3,900[d]	15,700[d]	1,155
1970	54,633	9,900	23,200	1,459	3	780	100	3,800	15,400	1,140
1971	54,381	9,900	23,100	1,378	2	800	100	3,800	15,300	1,015
1972	56,278	10,300	23,900	1,260	2	1,000	100	3,900	15,800	1,064
1973	55,511	10,200	23,600	1,194	2	1,000	100	3,800	15,600	1,164
1974	46,402	8,500	19,700	1,209	1	1,000	100	3,100	12,800	1,088
1975	45,853	8,400	19,550	979	1	1,000	100	3,130	12,700	1,033
1976	47,038	8,600	20,100	1,033	2	1,000	100	3,200	13,000	1,026

See source and footnotes on page 135.

MOTOR VEHICLE
Motor-Vehicle Deaths by Type of Incident (cont.)

Motor-vehicle deaths by type of incident, United States, 1913-2015 (cont.)

Year	Total deaths	Pedestrians	Other motor vehicles	Railroad trains	Streetcars	Pedalcycles	Animal-drawn vehicle or animal	Fixed objects	Deaths from noncollision incidents	Nontraffic deaths[a]
1977	49,510	9,100	21,200	902	3	1,100	100	3,400	13,700	1,053
1978	52,411	9,600	22,400	986	1	1,200	100	3,600	14,500	1,074
1979	53,524	9,800	23,100	826	1	1,200	100	3,700	14,800	1,271
1980	53,172	9,700	23,000	739	1	1,200	100	3,700	14,700	1,242
1981	51,385	9,400	22,200	668	1	1,200	100	3,600	14,200	1,189
1982	45,779	8,400	19,800	554	1	1,100	100	3,200	12,600	1,066
1983	44,452	8,200	19,200	520	1	1,100	100	3,100	12,200	1,024
1984	46,263	8,500	20,000	630	0	1,100	100	3,200	12,700	1,055
1985	45,901	8,500	19,900	538	2	1,100	100	3,200	12,600	1,079
1986	47,865	8,900	20,800	574	2	1,100	100	3,300	13,100	998
1987	48,290	7,500[e]	20,700	554	1	1,000[e]	100	13,200[e]	5,200[e]	993
1988	49,078	7,700	20,900	638	2	1,000	100	13,400	5,300	1,054
1989	47,575	7,800	20,300	720	2	900	100	12,900	4,900	989
1990	46,814	7,300	19,900	623	2	900	100	13,100	4,900	987
1991	43,536	6,600	18,200	541	1	800	100	12,600	4,700	915
1992	40,982	6,300	17,600	521	2	700	100	11,700	4,100	997
1993	41,893	6,400	18,300	553	3	800	100	11,500	4,200	994
1994	42,524	6,300	18,900	549	1	800	100	11,500	4,400	1,017
1995	43,363	6,400	19,000	514	(c)	800	100	12,100	4,400	1,032
1996	43,649	6,100	19,600	373	(c)	800	100	12,100	4,600	1,127
1997	43,458	5,900	19,900	371	(c)	800	100	12,000	4,400	1,118
1998	43,501	5,900	19,700	309	(c)	700	100	12,200	4,600	1,310
1999	42,401	6,100	18,600	314	1	800	100	11,800	4,700	1,436
2000	43,354	5,900	19,100	321	(c)	800	100	12,300	4,800	1,360
2001	43,788	6,100	18,800	324	3	800	100	12,800	4,900	1,345
2002	45,380	6,100	19,200	283	(c)	800	100	13,600	5,300	1,315
2003	44,757	6,000	19,300	245	(c)	800	100	13,100	5,200	1,417
2004	44,933	6,000	19,600	253	(c)	900	100	13,000	5,100	1,501
2005	45,343	6,100	19,000	250	(c)	1,000	100	13,600	5,300	1,676
2006	45,316	6,200	18,500	264	(c)	1,000	100	13,900	5,400	1,652
2007	43,945	6,000	17,700	211	(c)	900	100	13,800	5,200	1,914
2008	39,790	5,600	15,500	199	(c)	900	100	12,900	4,600	1,805
2009	36,216	5,300	14,100	154	(c)	800	100	11,700	4,100	1,731
2010	35,332	5,500	13,600	139	(c)	800	100	11,300	3,900	1,645
2011	35,303	5,700	13,500	139	(c)	900	100	11,200	3,800	1,520
2012	36,415	6,100	13,900	132	(c)	1,000	100	11,500	3,700	1,480
2013[f]	35,369	6,000	13,700	136	(c)	1,000	100	11,000	3,400	1,565
2014[f]	35,398	6,300	13,900	144	(c)	1,000	100	10,700	3,300	1,662
2015	37,757	6,700	15,300	110	(c)	1,100	100	10,900	3,500	1,596
Changes in deaths										
2006 to 2015	-17%	8%	-17%	-58%	—	10%	0%	-22%	-35%	-3%
2014 to 2015	7%	6%	10%	-24%	—	10%	0%	2%	6%	-4%

Source: Total deaths from National Center for Health Statistics except 1964 which are National Safety Council estimates based on data from the National Highway Traffic Safety Administration's Fatality Analysis Reporting System. Most totals by type are estimated and may not add to the total deaths. See Technical Appendix for comparability.

[a] See definition, page 206. Nontraffic deaths are included in appropriate incident-type totals in the table. In 2014, 36% of the nontraffic deaths were pedestrians, while in 2015 pedestrians accounted for 33% of nontraffic deaths.
[b] Insufficient data for approximations.
[c] Data not available.
[d] 1969 through 1986 totals are not comparable to previous years.
[e] Procedures and benchmarks for estimating deaths for certain types of incidents were changed for the 1990 edition. Estimates for 1987 and later years are not comparable to earlier years.
[f] Revised.

MOTOR VEHICLE
Motor-Vehicle Deaths by Age

Motor-vehicle deaths by age, United States, 1913-2015

Year	All ages	Younger than 5 years	5-14 years	15-24 years	25-44 years	45-64 years	65-74 years	75 and older[a]
1913	4,200	300	1,100	600	1,100	800	300	
1914	4,700	300	1,200	700	1,200	900	400	
1915	6,600	400	1,500	1,000	1,700	1,400	600	
1916	8,200	600	1,800	1,300	2,100	1,700	700	
1917	10,200	700	2,400	1,400	2,700	2,100	900	
1918	10,700	800	2,700	1,400	2,500	2,300	1,000	
1919	11,200	900	3,000	1,400	2,500	2,100	1,300	
1920	12,500	1,000	3,300	1,700	2,800	2,300	1,400	
1921	13,900	1,100	3,400	1,800	3,300	2,700	1,600	
1922	15,300	1,100	3,500	2,100	3,700	3,100	1,800	
1923	18,400	1,200	3,700	2,800	4,600	3,900	2,200	
1924	19,400	1,400	3,800	2,900	4,700	4,100	2,500	
1925	21,900	1,400	3,900	3,600	5,400	4,800	2,800	
1926	23,400	1,400	3,900	3,900	5,900	5,200	3,100	
1927	25,800	1,600	4,000	4,300	6,600	5,800	3,500	
1928	28,000	1,600	3,800	4,900	7,200	6,600	3,900	
1929	31,200	1,600	3,900	5,700	8,000	7,500	4,500	
1930	32,900	1,500	3,600	6,200	8,700	8,000	4,900	
1931	33,700	1,500	3,600	6,300	9,100	8,200	5,000	
1932	29,500	1,200	2,900	5,100	8,100	7,400	4,800	
1933	31,363	1,274	3,121	5,649	8,730	7,947	4,642	
1934	36,101	1,210	3,182	6,561	10,232	9,530	5,386	
1935	36,369	1,253	2,951	6,755	10,474	9,562	5,374	
1936	38,089	1,324	3,026	7,184	10,807	10,089	5,659	
1937	39,643	1,303	2,991	7,800	10,877	10,475	6,197	
1938	32,582	1,122	2,511	6,016	8,772	8,711	5,450	
1939	32,386	1,192	2,339	6,318	8,917	8,292	5,328	
1940	34,501	1,176	2,584	6,846	9,362	8,882	5,651	
1941	39,969	1,378	2,838	8,414	11,069	9,829	6,441	
1942	28,309	1,069	1,991	5,932	7,747	7,254	4,316	
1943	23,823	1,132	1,959	4,522	6,454	5,996	3,760	
1944	24,282	1,203	2,093	4,561	6,514	5,982	3,929	
1945	28,076	1,290	2,386	5,358	7,578	6,794	4,670	
1946	33,411	1,568	2,508	7,445	8,955	7,532	5,403	
1947	32,697	1,502	2,275	7,251	8,775	7,468	5,426	
1948	32,259	1,635	2,337	7,218	8,702	7,190	3,173	2,004
1949	31,701	1,667	2,158	6,772	8,892	7,073	3,116	2,023
1950	34,763	1,767	2,152	7,600	10,214	7,728	3,264	2,038
1951	36,996	1,875	2,300	7,713	11,253	8,276	3,444	2,135
1952	37,794	1,951	2,295	8,115	11,380	8,463	3,472	2,118
1953	37,956	2,019	2,368	8,169	11,302	8,318	3,508	2,271
1954	35,586	1,864	2,332	7,571	10,521	7,848	3,247	2,203
1955	38,426	1,875	2,406	8,656	11,448	8,372	3,455	2,214
1956	39,628	1,770	2,640	9,169	11,551	8,573	3,657	2,268
1957	38,702	1,785	2,604	8,667	11,230	8,545	3,560	2,311
1958	36,981	1,791	2,710	8,388	10,414	7,922	3,535	2,221
1959	37,910	1,842	2,719	8,969	10,358	8,263	3,487	2,272
1960	38,137	1,953	2,814	9,117	10,189	8,294	3,457	2,313
1961	38,091	1,891	2,802	9,088	10,212	8,267	3,467	2,364
1962	40,804	1,903	3,028	10,157	10,701	8,812	3,696	2,507
1963	43,564	1,991	3,063	11,123	11,356	9,506	3,786	2,739
1964	47,700	2,120	3,430	12,400	12,500	10,200	4,150	2,900
1965	49,163	2,059	3,526	13,395	12,595	10,509	4,077	3,002
1966	53,041	2,182	3,869	15,298	13,282	11,051	4,217	3,142
1967	52,924	2,067	3,845	15,646	12,987	10,902	4,285	3,192
1968	54,862	1,987	4,105	16,543	13,602	11,031	4,261	3,333
1969	55,791	2,077	4,045	17,443	13,868	11,012	4,210	3,136
1970	54,633	1,915	4,159	16,720	13,446	11,099	4,084	3,210
1971	54,381	1,885	4,256	17,103	13,307	10,471	4,108	3,251
1972	56,278	1,896	4,258	17,942	13,758	10,836	4,138	3,450
1973	55,511	1,998	4,124	18,032	14,013	10,216	3,892	3,236
1974	46,402	1,546	3,332	15,905	11,834	8,159	3,071	2,555
1975	45,853	1,576	3,286	15,672	11,969	7,663	3,047	2,640
1976	47,038	1,532	3,175	16,650	12,112	7,770	3,082	2,717

See source and footnotes on page 137.

MOTOR VEHICLE
Motor-Vehicle Deaths by Age (cont.)

Motor-vehicle deaths by age, United States, 1913-2015 (cont.)

Year	All ages	Younger than 5 years	5-14 years	15-24 years	25-44 years	45-64 years	65-74 years	75 and older[a]
1977	49,510	1,472	3,142	18,092	13,031	8,000	3,060	2,713
1978	52,411	1,551	3,130	19,164	14,574	8,048	3,217	2,727
1979	53,524	1,461	2,952	19,369	15,658	8,162	3,171	2,751
1980	53,172	1,426	2,747	19,040	16,133	8,022	2,991	2,813
1981	51,385	1,256	2,575	17,363	16,447	7,818	3,090	2,836
1982	45,779	1,300	2,301	15,324	14,469	6,879	2,825	2,681
1983	44,452	1,233	2,241	14,289	14,323	6,690	2,827	2,849
1984	46,263	1,138	2,263	14,738	15,036	6,954	3,020	3,114
1985	45,901	1,195	2,319	14,277	15,034	6,885	3,014	3,177
1986	47,865	1,188	2,350	15,227	15,844	6,799	3,096	3,361
1987	48,290	1,190	2,397	14,447	16,405	7,021	3,277	3,553
1988	49,078	1,220	2,423	14,406	16,580	7,245	3,429	3,775
1989	47,575	1,221	2,266	12,941	16,571	7,287	3,465	3,824
1990	46,814	1,123	2,059	12,607	16,488	7,282	3,350	3,905
1991	43,536	1,076	2,011	11,664	15,082	6,616	3,193	3,894
1992	40,982	1,020	1,904	10,305	14,071	6,597	3,247	3,838
1993	41,893	1,081	1,963	10,500	14,283	6,711	3,116	4,239
1994	42,524	1,139	2,026	10,660	13,966	7,097	3,385	4,251
1995	43,363	1,004	2,055	10,600	14,618	7,428	3,300	4,358
1996	43,649	1,035	1,980	10,576	14,482	7,749	3,419	4,408
1997	43,458	933	1,967	10,208	14,167	8,134	3,370	4,679
1998	43,501	921	1,868	10,026	14,095	8,416	3,410	4,765
1999	42,401	834	1,771	10,128	13,516	8,342	3,276	4,534
2000	43,354	819	1,772	10,560	13,811	8,867	3,038	4,487
2001	43,788	770	1,686	10,725	14,020	9,029	2,990	4,568
2002	45,380	733	1,614	11,459	14,169	9,701	3,113	4,591
2003	44,757	766	1,642	10,972	13,794	10,032	2,967	4,584
2004	44,933	778	1,653	10,987	13,699	10,369	2,974	4,473
2005	45,343	763	1,447	10,908	13,987	10,851	3,110	4,277
2006	45,316	728	1,339	11,015	14,025	11,133	2,916	4,160
2007	43,945	675	1,285	10,568	13,457	10,889	2,940	4,131
2008	39,790	566	1,027	8,946	12,242	10,457	2,826	3,726
2009	36,216	574	974	7,688	10,953	9,777	2,693	3,557
2010	35,332	528	890	7,250	10,491	9,727	2,676	3,770
2011	35,303	520	881	7,105	10,352	9,866	2,913	3,666
2012	36,415	531	820	7,062	10,933	10,270	3,112	3,687
2013	35,369	493	852	6,692	10,567	10,030	3,066	3,669
2014	35,398	473	829	6,709	10,518	10,024	3,153	3,692
2015	37,757	486	860	6,977	11,353	10,748	3,524	3,809
Changes in deaths								
2006 to 2015	-17%	-33%	-36%	-37%	-19%	-3%	21%	-8%
2014 to 2015	7%	3%	4%	4%	8%	7%	12%	3%

Source: 1913 to 1932 calculated from National Center for Health Statistics (NCHS) data for registration states; 1933 to 1963 and 1965 to 2015 are NCHS totals. All other figures are National Safety Council estimates. See Technical Appendix for comparability.
[a] Includes "age unknown." In 2014, these deaths numbered 7 and in 2015 they numbered 5.

MOTOR VEHICLE

Motor-Vehicle Death Rates by Age

Motor-vehicle death rates[a] by age, United States, 1913-2015

Year	All ages	Younger than 5 years	5-14 years	15-24 years	25-44 years	45-64 years	65-74 years	75 and older
1913	4.4	2.3	5.5	3.1	3.8	5.3	8.5	
1914	4.8	2.5	5.7	3.5	4.1	6.2	9.3	
1915	6.6	3.5	7.3	5.0	5.6	8.8	13.5	
1916	8.1	4.7	8.6	6.0	7.0	10.7	15.8	
1917	10.0	5.6	10.6	7.4	8.6	12.6	18.6	
1918	10.3	6.9	12.3	7.7	8.3	13.7	21.2	
1919	10.7	7.5	13.9	7.5	8.1	12.4	24.1	
1920	11.7	8.6	14.6	8.7	8.8	13.5	27.0	
1921	12.9	9.0	14.5	9.2	10.2	15.4	31.0	
1922	13.9	9.2	15.0	10.8	11.1	17.2	34.9	
1923	16.5	9.7	15.6	13.4	13.6	21.0	40.5	
1924	17.1	11.1	16.1	14.3	13.7	21.8	43.7	
1925	19.1	11.0	15.6	17.2	15.8	25.0	48.9	
1926	20.1	11.0	15.9	18.6	17.1	26.3	51.4	
1927	21.8	12.8	16.0	20.0	18.8	28.9	56.9	
1928	23.4	12.7	15.5	21.9	20.2	32.4	62.2	
1929	25.7	13.4	15.6	25.6	22.3	35.6	68.6	
1930	26.7	13.0	14.7	27.4	23.9	37.0	72.5	
1931	27.2	13.3	14.5	27.9	24.8	37.4	70.6	
1932	23.6	11.3	12.0	22.6	22.0	32.9	63.6	
1933	25.0	12.0	12.7	24.8	23.4	34.7	63.1	
1934	28.6	11.7	13.0	28.6	27.2	40.7	71.0	
1935	28.6	12.3	12.2	29.2	27.6	39.9	68.9	
1936	29.7	13.2	12.6	30.8	28.2	41.3	70.5	
1937	30.8	13.0	12.7	33.2	28.2	42.0	75.1	
1938	25.1	11.0	10.8	25.4	22.5	34.3	64.1	
1939	24.7	11.2	10.4	26.5	22.6	32.2	60.2	
1940	26.1	11.1	11.5	28.7	23.5	33.9	62.1	
1941	30.0	12.7	12.6	35.7	27.5	37.0	68.6	
1942	21.1	9.5	8.8	25.8	19.2	26.9	44.5	
1943	17.8	9.4	8.6	20.6	16.1	21.9	37.6	
1944	18.3	9.6	9.1	22.5	16.6	21.6	38.2	
1945	21.2	10.0	10.3	27.8	19.7	24.2	44.1	
1946	23.9	11.9	10.8	34.4	21.1	26.4	49.6	
1947	22.8	10.5	9.7	32.8	20.3	25.7	48.2	
1948	22.1	11.0	9.8	32.5	19.8	24.3	39.6	55.4
1949	21.3	10.7	9.0	30.7	19.9	23.4	37.8	53.9
1950	23.0	10.8	8.8	34.5	22.5	25.1	38.8	52.4
1951	24.1	10.9	9.2	36.0	24.7	26.5	39.5	53.0
1952	24.3	11.3	8.7	38.6	24.7	26.7	38.5	50.8
1953	24.0	11.5	8.5	39.1	24.5	25.8	37.7	52.6
1954	22.1	10.4	8.1	36.2	22.6	24.0	33.9	49.0
1955	23.4	10.2	8.0	40.9	24.5	25.2	35.1	47.1
1956	23.7	9.4	8.4	42.9	24.6	25.3	36.2	46.4
1957	22.7	9.2	8.0	39.7	23.9	24.8	34.4	45.5
1958	21.3	9.1	8.1	37.0	22.3	22.6	33.5	42.3
1959	21.5	9.1	7.9	38.2	22.2	23.2	32.3	41.8
1960	21.2	9.6	7.9	37.7	21.7	22.9	31.3	41.1
1961	20.8	9.2	7.6	36.5	21.8	22.5	30.7	40.5
1962	22.0	9.3	8.1	38.4	22.9	23.7	32.2	41.7
1963	23.1	9.8	8.0	40.0	24.3	25.2	32.6	44.3
1964	25.0	10.5	8.8	42.6	26.8	26.6	35.5	45.2
1965	25.4	10.4	8.9	44.2	27.0	27.0	34.6	45.4
1966	27.1	11.4	9.7	48.7	28.5	27.9	35.4	46.2
1967	26.8	11.2	9.5	48.4	27.8	27.1	35.6	45.4
1968	27.5	11.1	10.1	49.8	28.8	27.0	35.1	46.0
1969	27.7	12.0	9.9	50.7	29.1	26.6	34.3	42.0
1970	26.8	11.2	10.2	46.7	27.9	26.4	32.7	42.2
1971	26.3	10.9	10.5	45.7	27.4	24.7	32.4	41.3
1972	26.9	11.1	10.7	47.1	27.4	25.3	32.0	42.6
1973	26.3	11.9	10.5	46.3	27.2	23.6	29.4	39.1
1974	21.8	9.4	8.6	40.0	22.4	18.8	22.6	30.1
1975	21.3	9.8	8.6	38.7	22.1	17.5	21.9	30.1
1976	21.6	9.8	8.4	40.3	21.8	17.6	21.6	30.1

See source and footnotes on page 139.

MOTOR VEHICLE
Motor-Vehicle Death Rates by Age (cont.)

Motor-vehicle death rates[a] by age, United States, 1913-2015 (cont.)

Year	All ages	Younger than 5 years	5-14 years	15-24 years	25-44 years	45-64 years	65-74 years	75 and older
1977	22.5	9.5	8.5	43.3	22.7	18.1	20.9	29.3
1978	23.6	9.9	8.6	45.4	24.6	18.2	21.5	28.7
1979	23.8	9.1	8.3	45.6	25.6	18.4	20.7	28.1
1980	23.4	8.7	7.9	44.8	25.5	18.0	19.1	28.0
1981	22.4	7.4	7.5	41.1	25.2	17.6	19.4	27.5
1982	19.8	7.5	6.7	36.8	21.5	15.5	17.5	25.2
1983	19.0	7.0	6.6	34.8	20.6	15.0	17.2	26.0
1984	19.6	6.4	6.7	36.4	21.0	15.6	18.2	27.7
1985	19.3	6.7	6.9	35.7	20.5	15.4	17.9	27.5
1986	19.9	6.6	7.0	38.5	21.0	15.2	18.1	28.3
1987	19.9	6.6	7.1	37.1	21.3	15.7	18.8	29.1
1988	20.1	6.7	7.1	37.8	21.2	15.9	19.5	30.2
1989	19.3	6.6	6.5	34.6	20.8	15.9	19.4	29.8
1990	18.8	6.0	5.8	34.2	20.4	15.7	18.5	29.7
1991	17.3	5.6	5.6	32.1	18.3	14.2	17.5	28.9
1992	16.1	5.2	5.2	28.5	17.1	13.6	17.6	27.8
1993	16.3	5.5	5.3	29.1	17.3	13.5	16.7	30.0
1994	16.3	5.8	5.4	29.5	16.8	13.9	18.1	29.4
1995	16.5	5.1	5.4	29.3	17.5	14.2	17.6	29.4
1996	16.5	5.4	5.2	29.2	17.3	14.4	18.3	29.0
1997	16.2	4.9	5.1	27.9	17.0	14.7	18.2	29.9
1998	16.1	4.9	4.8	26.9	16.9	14.7	18.5	29.8
1999	15.5	4.4	4.5	26.8	16.3	14.1	18.0	27.8
2000	15.7	4.3	4.5	27.5	16.8	14.5	16.7	27.0
2001	15.4	4.0	4.1	26.8	16.5	14.0	16.3	26.8
2002	15.8	3.7	3.9	28.2	16.8	14.6	17.0	26.5
2003	15.4	3.9	4.0	26.6	16.4	14.6	16.2	26.0
2004	15.3	3.9	4.1	26.4	16.3	14.7	16.1	25.1
2005	15.3	3.8	3.6	25.9	16.6	14.9	16.7	23.6
2006	15.2	3.6	3.3	26.1	16.8	14.9	15.4	22.7
2007	14.6	3.3	3.2	24.9	16.1	14.2	15.2	22.2
2008	13.1	2.7	2.5	20.8	14.7	13.4	14.0	20.0
2009	11.8	2.7	2.4	17.8	13.2	12.3	13.0	18.9
2010	11.4	2.5	2.2	16.8	12.6	12.0	12.5	19.9
2011	11.3	2.6	2.1	16.2	12.6	11.9	13.0	19.4
2012	11.6	2.7	2.0	16.1	13.2	12.4	13.0	19.2
2013[b]	11.2	2.5	2.1	15.2	12.7	12.1	12.2	18.8
2014[b]	11.1	2.4	2.0	15.3	12.5	12.0	11.9	18.6
2015	11.7	2.4	2.1	15.9	13.4	12.8	12.8	18.8
Changes in rates								
2006 to 2015	-23%	-33%	-36%	-39%	-20%	-14%	-17%	-17%
2014 to 2015	6%	0%	5%	4%	7%	7%	8%	1%

Source: 1913 to 1932 calculated from National Center for Health Statistics (NCHS) data for registration states; 1933 to 1963 and 1965 to 2015 are NCHS totals. All other figures are National Safety Council estimates. See Technical Appendix for comparability.
[a] Death rates are deaths per 100,000 population in each age group that were calculated using population data from the U.S. Census Bureau.
[b] Revised.

Home and Community

Home and Community Highlights

Weather — pg. 152

NEW! Playground injuries — pg. 153

Consumer product injuries — pg. 155

Poisonings — pgs. 160–162

NEW! Fire-related fatalities and injuries — pg. 164

Firearms — pg. 168

INJURY FACTS® 2017

Playground Injuries — pg. 153

A recent study found that an average of 214,883 playground-related injuries occur each year in the United States. About 10% of these injuries or 21,101 injuries per year involved traumatic brain injury. The study analyzed Consumer Product Safety Commission emergency department data from 2001 through 2013 and included injuries to children up to age 14. The researchers found that while playground-related injuries decreased nearly 17% from 2001 to 2007, they have increased 14% since 2007. The reason for this increase is unclear.

HOME AND COMMUNITY
Home and Community, 2015

The home and community venue is the combination of the home class and the public class. Home and community, together with the occupational and transportation venues, make up the totality of unintentional injuries. Home and community includes all unintentional injuries that are not work-related and do not involve motor vehicles on streets and highways.

In 2015, an estimated 106,700 unintentional-injury-related deaths occurred in the home and community venue, or 73% of all unintentional-injury-related deaths that year. The number of deaths was up about 8% from the revised 2014 total of 98,500. An additional 32,100,000 people suffered nonfatal medically consulted injuries. The death rate per 100,000 population was 33.2 – about 7% higher than the revised 2014 rate.

About 1 out of 10 people experienced an unintentional injury in the home and community venue, and about 1 out of 3,000 people died from such an injury in 2015. About 42% of the deaths and injuries involved workers while they were away from work (off the job).

The graph on the next page shows the five leading causes of unintentional-injury-related deaths in the home and community venue and the broad age groups (children, youths and adults, and the elderly) affected by them. This is one way to prioritize issues in this venue. Below is a graph of the trend in deaths and death rates from 1999 to present. Similar graphs for the home and public classes appear on pages 144 and 148.

The National Safety Council adopted the Bureau of Labor Statistics' Census of Fatal Occupational Injuries count for work-related unintentional injuries beginning with 1992 data. Because of the lower work class total resulting from this change, adjustments were made to the home and public classes. Long-term historical comparisons for these three classes should be made with caution. Also, beginning with 1999 data, deaths are now classified according to the 10th revision of the *International Classification of Diseases*. Caution should be used in comparing data classified under the 10th revision with prior revisions. See the Technical Appendix for more information about both changes.

Deaths	106,700
Medically consulted injuries	32,100,000[a]
Death rate per 100,000 population	33.2
Costs	$387.3 billion

[a]Medically consulted injury estimate procedure was revised for the 2016 edition and is not comparable to estimates provided in earlier editions.

Home and community deaths and death rates, United States, 1999-2015

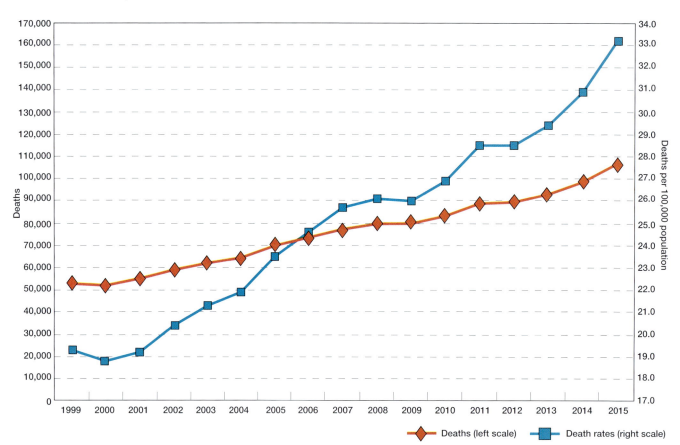

HOME AND COMMUNITY
Home and Community, 2015 (cont.)

Causes of unintentional-injury-related deaths in home and community, United States, 2015

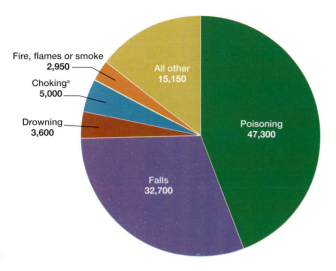

[a] Inhalation and ingestion of food or other object that obstructs breathing.

Leading causes of unintentional-injury-related deaths in home and community, United States, 2015

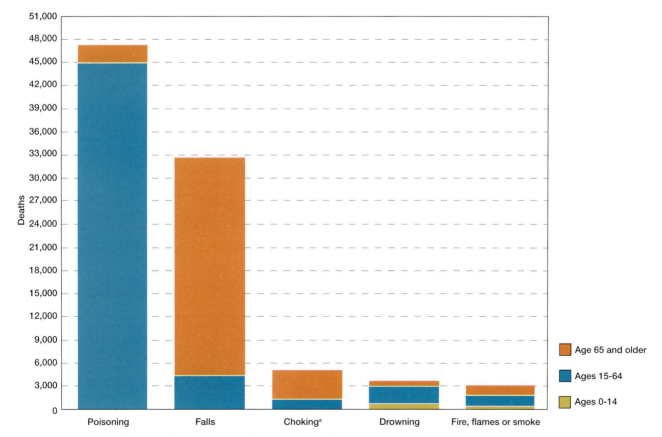

[a] Inhalation and ingestion of food or other object that obstructs breathing.

INJURY FACTS® 2017 EDITION NATIONAL SAFETY COUNCIL® 143

HOME AND COMMUNITY
Home, 2015

Between 1912 and 2015, unintentional-home-injury-related deaths per 100,000 population were reduced 17% from 28 to 23.2 (after adjusting for the 1948 classification change). In 1912, when there were 21 million households, an estimated 26,000 to 28,000 people were killed by unintentional-home-related injuries. In 2015, with 125 million households and the population tripled, home-related deaths numbered 74,600. However, the number and rate of unintentional-home-injury-related deaths has been steadily increasing since 2000. This increase in deaths is largely driven by increases in both unintentional poisonings and falls.

The injury total of 20,700,000 means that 1 person in 15 in the United States experienced an unintentional injury in the home in 2015 that was serious enough to consult with a medical professional. The number of medically consulted injuries occurring in the home is greater than the total number of medically consulted injuries that occur in public places, the workplace, and motor-vehicle crashes combined. The National Health Interview Survey estimates that about 49% of all medically attended injuries occurred at home.

The National Safety Council adopted the Bureau of Labor Statistics' Census of Fatal Occupational Injuries count for work-related unintentional injuries beginning with 1992 data. This affected long-term historical comparisons for the work, home, and public classes. Beginning with 1999 data, deaths are classified according to the 10th revision of the *International Classification of Diseases*. Caution should be used in comparing current data with data classified under prior revisions. See the Technical Appendix for more information.

Deaths	74,600
Medically consulted injuries	20,700,000[a]
Death rate per 100,000 population	23.2
Costs	$254.7 billion

[a]Medically consulted injury estimate procedure was revised for the 2016 edition and is not comparable to estimates provided in previous editions.

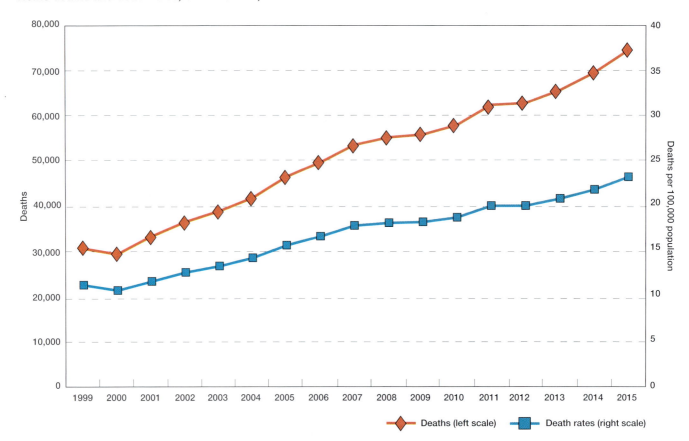

Home deaths and death rates, United States, 1999-2015

144 ■ NATIONAL SAFETY COUNCIL®   INJURY FACTS® 2017 EDITION

HOME AND COMMUNITY
Home, 2015 (cont.)

Principal types of home unintentional-injury-related deaths, United States, 1987-2015

Year	Total home	Poisoning	Falls	Fire, flames, or smoke[a]	Choking[b]	Mechanical suffocation	Drowning	Natural heat or cold	Firearms	Other
1987	21,400	4,100	6,300	3,900	2,500	600	700	(c)	800	2,500
1988	22,700	4,800	6,600	4,100	2,600	600	700	(c)	800	2,500
1989	22,500	5,000	6,600	3,900	2,500	600	700	(c)	800	2,400
1990	21,500	4,500	6,700	3,400	2,300	600	900	(c)	800	2,300
1991	22,100	5,000	6,900	3,400	2,200	700	900	(c)	800	2,200
1992	24,000	5,200	7,700	3,700	1,500	700	900	(c)	1,000	3,300
1993	26,100	6,500	7,900	3,700	1,700	700	900	(c)	1,100	3,600
1994	26,300	6,800	8,100	3,700	1,600	800	900	(c)	900	3,500
1995	27,200	7,000	8,400	3,500	1,500	800	900	(c)	900	4,200
1996	27,500	7,300	9,000	3,500	1,500	800	900	(c)	800	3,700
1997	27,700	7,800	9,100	3,200	1,500	800	900	(c)	700	3,500
1998	29,000	8,400	9,500	2,900	1,800	800	1,000	(c)	600	4,000
1999[d]	30,500	9,300	7,600	3,000	1,900	1,100	900	700	600	5,400
2000	29,200	9,800	7,100	2,700	2,100	1,000	1,000	400	500	4,600
2001	33,200	11,300	8,600	3,000	2,000	1,100	900	400	600	5,300
2002	36,400	13,900	9,700	2,800	1,900	1,100	900	400	500	5,200
2003	38,800	15,900	10,300	2,900	2,100	1,000	800	400	500	4,900
2004	41,700	17,500	11,300	2,900	2,200	1,200	900	400	400	4,900
2005	46,400	20,000	12,000	2,900	2,300	1,300	900	500	500	6,000
2006	49,600	23,300	12,800	2,800	2,300	1,400	1,000	600	400	5,000
2007	53,500	25,800	14,200	3,000	2,100	1,400	1,000	500	400	5,100
2008	55,200	26,800	15,100	2,600	2,300	1,500	900	400	400	5,200
2009	55,800	27,500	15,700	2,600	2,300	1,300	1,000	500	400	4,500
2010	57,900	28,800	16,500	2,500	2,200	1,400	1,000	600	400	4,500
2011	62,400	31,400	17,400	2,400	2,500	1,400	900	700	400	5,300
2012	62,800	31,400	17,900	2,300	2,600	1,400	1,000	500	400	5,300
2013	65,700	33,200	19,300	2,400	2,400	1,500	1,100	500	400	4,900
2014[e]	69,600	35,700	20,400	2,500	2,500	1,500	1,000	600	400	5,000
2015	74,600	39,600	21,100	2,500	2,600	1,600	1,100	500	400	5,200

Source: National Safety Council estimates based on National Center for Health Statistics (NCHS)—Mortality Data compiled from data provided by the 57 vital statistics jurisdictions through the Vital Statistics Cooperative Program. Rates are National Safety Council estimates based on data from NCHS. The Council adopted the Bureau of Labor Statistics' Census of Fatal Occupational Injuries count for work-related unintentional-injuries retroactive to 1992 data. Because of the lower work class total resulting from this change, several thousand unintentional-injury-related deaths that had been classified by the Council as work-related had to be reassigned to the home and public classes. For this reason, long-term historical comparisons for these three classes should be made with caution. See the Technical Appendix for an explanation of the methodological changes.

[a] Includes deaths resulting from conflagration, regardless of nature of injury.
[b] Inhalation and ingestion of food or other object that obstructs breathing.
[c] Included in "Other."
[d] In 1999, a revision was made in the International Classification of Diseases. See the Technical Appendix for comparability with earlier years.
[e] Revised.

Principal types of home unintentional-injury-related deaths, United States, 2015

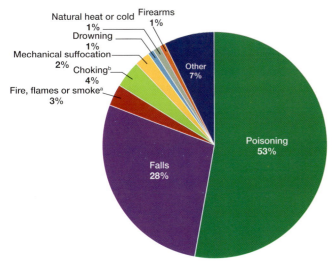

[a] Includes deaths resulting from conflagration, regardless of nature of injury.
[b] Inhalation and ingestion of food or other object that obstructs breathing.

HOME AND COMMUNITY
Deaths Due to Unintentional Home Injuries, 2015

Type of event and age of victim

All home
Includes deaths in the home and on home premises to occupants, guests, and trespassers. Also includes hired household workers but excludes other people working on home premises.

	Total	Change from 2014	Death rate[a]
Deaths	74,600	+7%	23.2

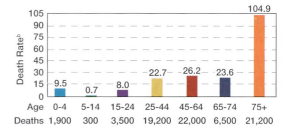

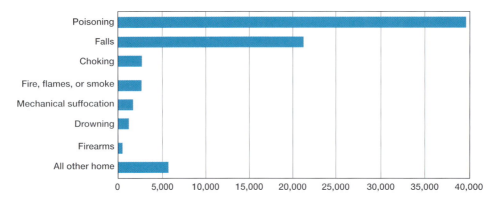

Poisoning
Includes deaths from drugs, medicines, other solid and liquid substances, and gases and vapors. Excludes poisonings from spoiled foods, *Salmonella*, etc., which are classified as disease deaths.

	Total	Change from 2014	Death rate[a]
Deaths	39,600	+11%	12.3

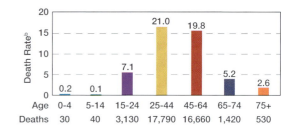

Falls
Includes deaths from falls from one level to another or on the same level in the home or on home premises.

	Total	Change from 2014	Death rate[a]
Deaths	21,100	+3%	6.6

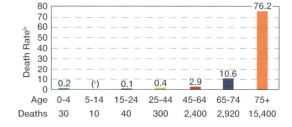

Choking
Includes deaths from unintentional ingestion or inhalation of objects or food resulting in the obstruction of respiratory passages.

	Total	Change from 2014	Death rate[a]
Deaths	2,600	+4%	0.8

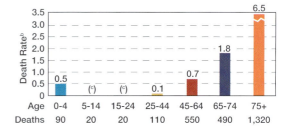

See footnotes on page 147.

HOME AND COMMUNITY

Deaths Due to Unintentional Home Injuries, 2015 (cont.)

Type of event and age of victim

Fires, flames, or smoke

Includes deaths from fires, burns, and injuries in conflagrations in the home – such as asphyxiation, falls, and struck by falling objects. Excludes burns from hot objects or liquids.

	Total	Change from 2014	Death rate[a]
Deaths	2,500	0%	0.8

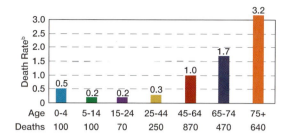

Mechanical suffocation

Includes deaths from smothering by bed clothes, thin plastic materials, etc.; suffocation by cave-ins or confinement in closed spaces; and mechanical strangulation or hanging.

	Total	Change from 2014	Death rate[a]
Deaths	1,600	7%	0.5

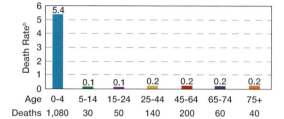

Drowning

Includes drowning of people in or on home premises – such as in swimming pools and bathtubs. Excludes drowning in floods and other cataclysms.

	Total	Change from 2014	Death rate[a]
Deaths	1,100	10%	0.3

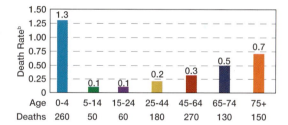

Firearms

Includes firearm injuries in or on home premises – such as while cleaning or playing with guns. Excludes deaths from explosive materials.

	Total	Change from 2014	Death rate[a]
Deaths	400	0%	0.1

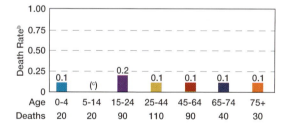

All other home

Most important types included are natural heat and cold, struck by or against objects, machinery, and electric current.

	Total	Change from 2014	Death rate[a]
Deaths	5,700	+2%	1.8

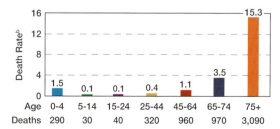

[a]Deaths per 100,000 population.
[b]Deaths per 100,000 population in each age group.
[c]Death rate less than 0.05.

INJURY FACTS® 2017 EDITION NATIONAL SAFETY COUNCIL® 147

HOME AND COMMUNITY
Public, 2015

Between 1912 and 2015, public unintentional-injury-related deaths per 100,000 population were reduced 67% from 30 to 10.0 (after adjusting for the 1948 change in classification). In 1912, an estimated 28,000 to 30,000 people died from public non-motor vehicle injuries. In 2015, with the population tripled, and travel and recreational activity greatly increased, 32,100 people died from public unintentional injuries and 11,400,000 suffered injuries serious enough to consult a medical professional. The public class excludes deaths and injuries involving motor vehicles and people at work or at home.

In 2015, the number of public unintentional-injury-related deaths was up 11.1% from the revised 2014 figure of 28,900. The 2015 death rate per 100,000 population increased 9.9% from 9.1 in 2014 to 10.0.

With an estimated 11,400,000 medically consulted unintentional injuries occurring in public places and a population of over 321 million people, on average about 1 person in 28 experienced such an injury.

The National Safety Council adopted the Bureau of Labor Statistics' Census of Fatal Occupational Injuries count for work-related unintentional-injuries beginning with 1992 data. This affected long-term historical comparisons for the work, home, and public classes. Beginning with 1999 data, deaths are classified according to the 10th revision of the *International Classification of Diseases*. Caution should be used in comparing current data with data classified under prior revisions. See the Technical Appendix for more information.

Deaths	32,100
Medically consulted injuries	11,400,000[a]
Death rate per 100,000 population	10.0
Costs	$132.6 billion

[a] Medically consulted injury estimate procedure was revised for the 2016 edition and is not comparable to estimates provided in previous editions.

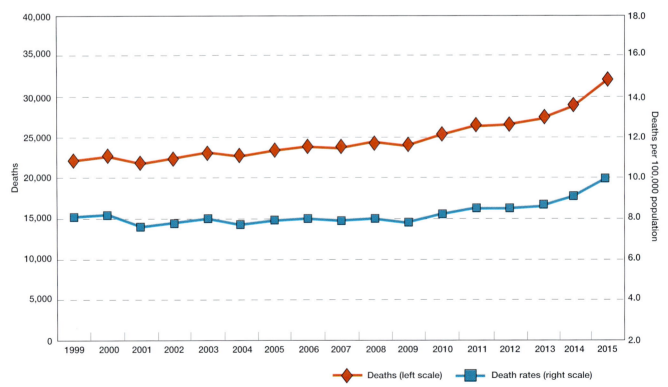

Public deaths and death rates, United States, 1999-2015

148 ■ NATIONAL SAFETY COUNCIL®

HOME AND COMMUNITY
Public, 2015 (cont.)

Principal types of public unintentional-injury-related deaths, United States, 1987-2015

Year	Total public[a]	Falls	Poisoning	Drowning	Choking[f]	Fire, flames, or smoke	Firearms	Air transport	Water transport	Rail transport[b]	Mechanical suffocation
1987	18,400	4,000	800	3,200	1,100	500	600	900	800	400	(c)
1988	18,400	4,100	900	3,100	1,100	500	600	700	800	400	(c)
1989	18,200	4,200	900	3,000	1,000	500	600	800	700	400	(c)
1990	17,400	4,300	900	2,800	1,000	400	500	700	800	400	(c)
1991	17,600	4,500	1,000	2,800	900	400	600	700	700	500	(c)
1992	19,000	4,400	1,700	2,500	1,600	200	400	700	700	600	(c)
1993	19,700	4,600	1,900	2,800	1,500	200	400	600	700	600	(c)
1994	19,600	4,700	2,100	2,400	1,500	200	400	600	600	600	(c)
1995	20,100	5,000	2,000	2,800	1,600	200	300	600	700	500	(c)
1996	21,000	5,300	2,100	2,500	1,700	200	300	700	600	500	(c)
1997	21,700	5,600	2,300	2,600	1,700	200	300	500	600	400	(c)
1998	22,600	6,000	2,300	2,900	1,700	200	300	500	600	500	(c)
1999[d]	22,200	4,800	2,800	2,600	2,000	200	300	500	600	400	500
2000	22,700	5,500	2,900	2,400	2,200	200	200	500	500	400	300
2001	21,800	5,600	2,700	2,400	2,100	200	200	700	500	400	300
2002	22,500	5,900	3,600	2,500	2,200	300	200	500	500	400	300
2003	23,200	6,300	3,400	2,400	2,200	300	200	600	500	400	300
2004	22,700	6,700	3,400	2,400	2,200	200	200	400	500	400	200
2005	23,400	6,800	3,500	2,600	2,100	(c)	(c)	400	500	400	200
2006	23,900	7,200	4,100	2,500	2,100	(c)	(c)	400	400	400	200
2007	23,700	7,600	3,900	2,400	2,200	(c)	(c)	400	400	400	200
2008	24,500	8,200	4,200	2,500	2,100	(c)	(c)	400	300	400	200
2009	24,000	8,500	4,200	2,400	2,100	(c)	(c)	400	400	300	200
2010	25,300	8,900	4,100	2,700	2,300	(c)	(c)	300	300	400	200
2011	26,400	9,400	4,700	2,600	2,200	(c)	(c)	300	500	300	200
2012	26,600	10,100	4,800	2,500	2,100	(c)	(c)	300	400	300	200
2013	27,300	10,200	5,600	2,200	2,500	(c)	(c)	300	300	400	200
2014[e]	28,900	10,800	6,100	2,400	2,300	(c)	(c)	300	300	400	200
2015	32,100	11,600	7,700	2,500	2,400	(c)	(c)	300	400	400	200

Source: National Safety Council estimates based on data from the National Center for Health Statistics. The Council adopted the Bureau of Labor Statistics' Census of Fatal Occupational Injuries count for work-related unintentional injuries retroactive to 1992 data. Because of the lower work class total resulting from this change, several thousand unintentional-injury-related deaths that had been classified by the Council as work-related had to be reassigned to the home and public classes. For this reason, long-term historical comparisons for these three classes should be made with caution. See the Technical Appendix for an explanation of the methodological changes.
[a] Includes some deaths not shown separately.
[b] Includes subways and elevateds.
[c] Estimates not available.
[d] In 1999, a revision was made in the International Classification of Diseases. See the Technical Appendix for comparability with earlier years.
[e] Revised.
[f] Inhalation and ingestion of food or other object that obstructs breathing.

Principal types of public unintentional-injury-related deaths, United States, 2015

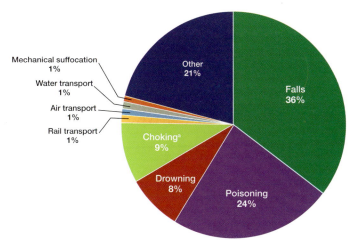

[a] Inhalation and ingestion of food or other object that obstructs breathing.

HOME AND COMMUNITY

Deaths Due to Unintentional Public Injuries, 2015

Type of event and age of victim

All public
Includes deaths in public places and not involving motor vehicles. Most sports, recreation, and transportation deaths are included. Excludes work deaths.

	Total	Change from 2014	Death rate[a]
Deaths	32,100	+11%	10.0

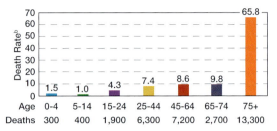

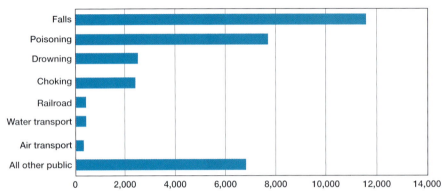

Falls
Includes deaths from falls from one level to another or on the same level in public places. Excludes deaths from falls from moving vehicles.

	Total	Change from 2014	Death rate[a]
Deaths	11,600	+7%	3.6

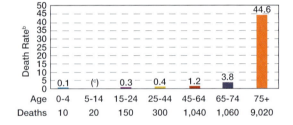

Poisoning
Includes deaths from drugs, medicines, other solid and liquid substances, and gases and vapors. Excludes poisonings from spoiled foods.

	Total	Change from 2014	Death rate[a]
Deaths	7,700	+26%	2.4

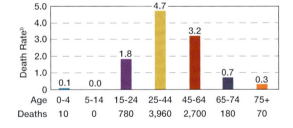

Drowning
Includes drownings of people swimming or playing in water, or falling into water, except on home premises or at work. Excludes drownings involving boats, which are included in water transportation.

	Total	Change from 2014	Death rate[a]
Deaths	2,500	+4%	0.8

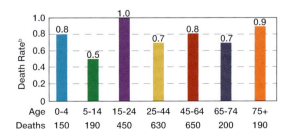

See footnotes on page 151.

HOME AND COMMUNITY

Deaths Due to Unintentional Public Injuries, 2015 (cont.)

Type of event and age of victim

Choking

Includes deaths from unintentional ingestion or inhalation of food or other objects resulting in the obstruction of respiratory passages.

	Total	Change from 2014	Death rate[a]
Deaths	2,400	4%	0.7

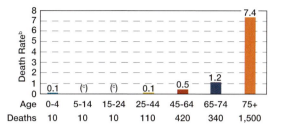

Railroad

Includes deaths arising from railroad vehicles in motion (except involving motor vehicles), subway and elevated trains, and people boarding or alighting from standing trains. Excludes crews and people traveling in the course of employment.

	Total	Change from 2014	Death rate[a]
Deaths	400	0%	0.1

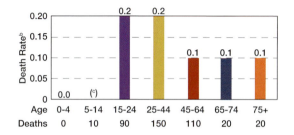

Water transport

Includes deaths in water transport incidents from falls, burns, etc., as well as drownings. Excludes crews and people traveling in the course of employment.

	Total	Change from 2014	Death rate[a]
Deaths	400	+33%	0.1

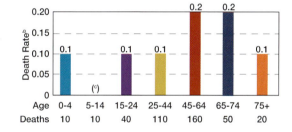

Air transport

Includes deaths in private flying, passengers in commercial aviation, and deaths of military personnel in the United States. Excludes crews and people traveling in the course of employment.

	Total	Change from 2014	Death rate[a]
Deaths	300	0%	0.1

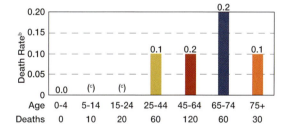

All other public

Most important types included are mechanical suffocation, excessive natural heat or cold, firearms, fires and flames, and machinery.

	Total	Change from 2014	Death rate[a]
Deaths	6,800	+8%	2.1

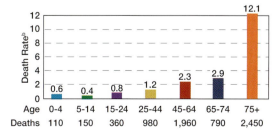

[a]Deaths per 100,000 population.
[b]Deaths per 100,000 population in each age group.
[c]Rate less than 0.05.

HOME AND COMMUNITY
Weather

■ *Weather-related deaths up 24% in 2015.*

Overall, deaths in 2015 are up 24% from 2014. A variety of weather events resulted in 676 deaths in the United States in 2015, compared with 546 deaths in 2014. Floods and temperature extremes drove the dramatic increase in weather-related deaths. Floods accounted for 28% of the deaths, temperature extremes for 18%, while snow, ice, and winter weather accounted for 15%. See page 34 for additional information on specific weather-related disasters in 2015. Even with the dramatic increase in 2015, the death toll is still far below 2011 levels with a total of 1,012 deaths dominated by 587 tornado-related deaths.

Data on weather-related deaths were compiled by the National Climatic Data Center (NCDC), which is part of the National Oceanic and Atmospheric Administration. NCDC data may differ from data based on death certificates that appear elsewhere in *Injury Facts*.

Weather-related deaths, United States, 2015

Event	Total	Jan.	Feb.	March	April	May	June	July	Aug.	Sept.	Oct.	Nov.	Dec.
Total	676	66	79	42	36	95	51	76	46	47	18	26	94
Flood	192	3	0	11	8	50	14	19	4	25	12	6	40
Temperature extremes	120	13	39	2	0	0	12	32	13	8	0	0	1
Snow, ice, winter weather	104	31	33	12	1	0	0	0	0	0	0	8	19
Thunderstorm/heavy rain/high winds	92	3	1	2	14	17	10	12	15	3	3	9	3
Ocean/lake surf/rip current	56	5	4	5	2	13	5	7	6	4	2	1	2
Tornado	36	0	0	1	2	7	0	0	0	0	0	0	26
Lightning	27	0	0	0	2	5	10	5	4	1	0	0	0
Fog	23	10	1	4	6	0	0	0	0	0	0	0	2
Avalanche and debris flow/mudslide	12	1	1	3	0	2	0	0	3	0	0	1	1
Wildfire	10	0	0	1	1	0	0	1	1	6	0	0	0
Dust storm/smoke	4	0	0	1	0	1	0	0	0	0	1	1	0

Source: National Safety Council analysis of National Climatic Data Center data.

Weather-related fatalities by month, United States, 2015

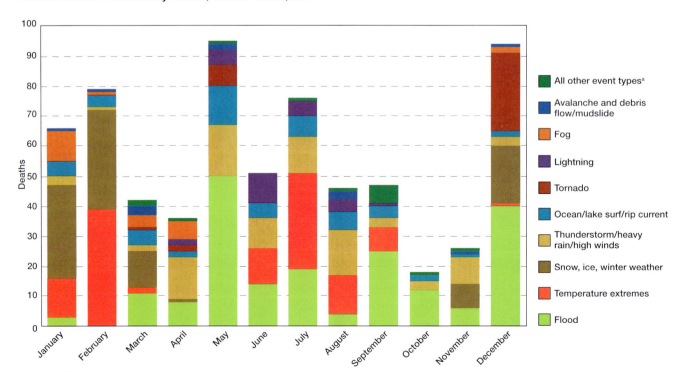

[a] Includes wildfires, dust storms, and heavy smoke.

HOME AND COMMUNITY

Playground Injuries

A recent study found that an average of 214,883 playground-related injuries occur each year in the United States[a]. About 10% of these injuries or 21,101 injuries per year involved traumatic brain injury. The study analyzed Consumer Product Safety Commission emergency department data from 2001 through 2013 and included injuries to children up to age 14. The researchers found that, while playground-related injuries decreased nearly 17% from 2001 to 2007, they have increased 14% since 2007. The reason for this increase is unclear.

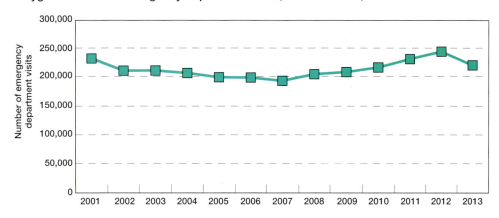

Playground-related emergency department visits, United States, 2001-2013

The majority of injuries involve children from 5 to 9 years of age and they occur on monkey bars and swing sets. While this study found that only 17% of the playground-related injuries occurred at home, a previous study conducted in Canada found that playground injuries occurring at home are more likely to be serious than injuries occurring at public playgrounds[b]. It is speculated that the more serious injuries occur at home playgrounds because they are less likely to have appropriate landing material than those at public playgrounds.

[a]Cheng, T.A., Bell, J.M., et.al. (2016). Nonfatal playground-related Traumatic Brain Injuries Among Children. Pediatrics, 137(6).

[b]Kaeys, G. & Skinner, R. (2012). Playground equipment injuries at home versus those in public setting: differences in severity. Injury Prevention 18.

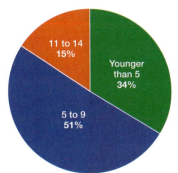

Age distribution of playground-related injuries, United States, 2001–2013

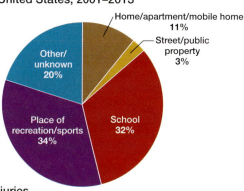

Location of playground-related injuries, United States, 2001–2013

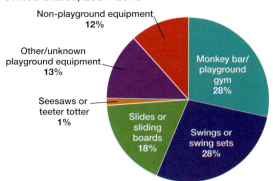

Equipment involved in playground-related injuries, United States, 2001–2013

HOME AND COMMUNITY
Sports and Recreational Injuries

■ *In the United States in 2015, basketball and bicycle riding injuries each resulted in nearly a half a million emergency department visits.*

The table below shows estimates of the number of injuries treated in hospital emergency departments associated with various sports and recreational activities. Because this list of sports is not complete and the frequency and duration of participation is not known, no inference should be made concerning the relative hazard of these sports or rank with respect to risk of injury. Since currently available sports participation estimates do not provide a valid estimate of exposure risk, they are inappropriate for use in rate calculations. Because of this limitation, they are not included in the table below.

Sports and recreational injuries resulting in emergency department visits, United States, 2015

Sport or activity	Injuries	% Males	% Concussion related[a]	Younger than 5	5–14	14–24	25–64	65 and older
Archery	4,506	81%	<0.5%	22	755	825	2,484	420
Baseball	120,234	85%	5%	3,248	61,215	33,958	20,266	1,547
Basketball	493,011	81%	3%	1,736	172,998	225,560	91,529	1,158
Bicycle riding	488,123	71%	3%	20,085	147,916	87,869	195,576	36,646
Biking–mountain	9,011	82%	5%	16	454	1,582	6,653	306
Billiards, pool	3,299	60%	2%	126	752	314	1,601	506
Bowling	17,680	51%	1%	1,501	2,118	3,451	8,496	2,113
Boxing	16,897	86%	4%	49	2,259	7,483	7,075	30
Cheerleading	40,843	2%	6%	98	22,861	17,467	417	—
Dancing	58,160	26%	1%	2,124	14,521	16,531	19,856	5,128
Exercise[b]	361,551	50%	1%	5,696	36,947	75,015	196,445	47,432
Fishing	66,529	81%	<0.5%	1,330	10,023	11,103	35,556	8,518
Football	399,873	94%	8%	990	204,795	158,315	35,294	479
Golf[c]	37,369	78%	<0.5%	855	3,958	1,982	12,964	17,610
Gymnastics[d]	35,063	17%	2%	686	27,657	5,019	1,680	16
Handball	4,103	72%	2%	—	1,302	1,469	1,045	287
Hockey–Ice	19,283	91%	12%	38	6,296	7,583	4,999	367
Hockey–street, roller, field	5,901	60%	6%	17	1,766	2,635	1,483	—
Hockey–unspecified	21,339	88%	4%	140	7,100	7,703	6,365	32
Horseback riding	56,727	29%	7%	754	9,268	14,402	28,055	4,248
Lacrosse	15,999	72%	8%	—	5,691	9,579	729	—
Martial arts	26,949	71%	3%	181	7,351	7,823	11,451	143
Mountain climbing	5,186	61%	2%	91	315	1,874	2,877	31
Racquetball, squash & paddleball	4,354	78%	<0.5%	6	392	1,108	2,081	767
Rugby	11,101	70%	7%	—	255	9,186	1,660	—
Skateboarding	125,145	81%	3%	1,150	40,488	63,375	19,877	239
Skating–Ice	21,701	46%	6%	287	9,438	5,910	5,637	429
Skating–roller[e]	57,192	35%	<0.5%	380	30,586	8,755	16,735	736
Skating–unspecified	6,828	36%	<0.5%	16	4,484	1,042	1,237	49
Snowboarding	25,452	74%	10%	43	6,292	13,367	5,622	128
Snowmobiling	9,561	74%	6%	81	733	2,404	5,974	370
Soccer	227,732	66%	6%	2,064	104,167	84,972	36,122	407
Softball	95,285	34%	4%	203	31,311	30,036	32,429	1,306
Surfing	13,832	75%	1%	17	3,138	3,327	7,065	286
Swimming[f]	191,396	51%	2%	18,089	79,312	32,309	51,537	10,133
Tennis	23,609	59%	2%	121	3,254	3,352	10,078	6,804
Track & field	32,237	51%	2%	114	12,821	14,347	4,719	237
Trampolines	107,123	49%	2%	16,636	68,323	13,399	8,592	173
Volleyball	57,067	27%	4%	196	19,304	25,434	11,429	704
Water skiing	7,335	68%	4%	—	544	2,535	3,946	311
Water tubing	5,280	41%	9%	—	1,205	1,336	2,690	49
Weight lifting	107,655	77%	1%	3,160	8,921	34,833	56,535	4,206
Wrestling	39,775	94%	7%	—	15,483	21,641	2,651	—

Source: NSC analysis of Consumer Product Safety Commission NEISS data; figures include only injuries treated in hospital emergency departments.
Note: Sum of injuries by age group may not equal injury total.
[a] Concussion listed as primary diagnosis.
[b] Includes exercise equipment (64,093 injuries) and exercise activity (297,458 injuries).
[c] Excludes golf carts (17,754 injuries).
[d] Excludes trampolines.
[e] Includes roller skating (46,469 injuries) and in-line skating (10,723 injuries).
[f] Includes injuries associated with swimming, swimming pools, diving or diving boards, and swimming pool equipment.

HOME AND COMMUNITY

Injuries Associated with Consumer Products

■ *Nearly 1.2 million injury-related emergency department visits each year are associated with stairs and steps.*

The following list of items found in and around the home was selected from the Consumer Product Safety Commission's National Electronic Injury Surveillance System (NEISS) for 2015. NEISS estimates are calculated from a statistically representative sample of hospitals in the United States. Injury totals represent estimates of the number of hospital emergency department-treated cases nationwide associated with various products. However, product involvement may or may not be the cause of the injury.

Consumer product-related injuries treated in hospital emergency departments, 2015
(excluding most sports and sports equipment; also see page 154)

Description	Injuries
Home workshop equipment	
Hammers	29,835
Tools, not specified	26,025
Workshop grinders, buffers or polishers	20,493
Hoists, lifts, jacks or jack stands	16,392
Packaging & Containers, Household	
Paper products	28,995
Cardboard products	15,789
Buckets or pails	15,730
Housewares	
Knives	334,780
Drinking glasses	65,259
Waste containers, trash baskets, etc.	44,324
Manual cleaning equipment (excl. buckets)	37,586
Slicers and choppers	24,718
Home Furnishing, Fixtures and Accessories	
Tables, n.e.c.[a]	343,810
Sofas, couches, davenports, divans, etc.	195,814
Cabinets, racks, room dividers	160,070
Desks, dressers, bureaus, chests, buffets, etc.	131,453
Toilets	125,073
Beds	38,224
Benches	36,415
Sinks	34,015
Chairs	29,010
Mirrors or mirror glass	26,311
Rugs and carpets	23,460
Stools	20,975
Ladders	14,757
Light bulbs	14,331
Home structures or construction materials	
Floors or flooring materials	1,792,878
Stairs or steps	1,195,154
Ceilings and walls	363,500
Porches, balconies, open-side floors	149,825
Nails, screws, tacks or bolts	124,431
Fences or fence posts	116,999
Door sills or frames	67,450
Counters or countertops	61,163
Handrails, railings or banisters	54,220
Poles	42,902
Glass doors	28,001
Cabinet or door hardware	22,564
Ramps or landings	19,098
Garage doors (excl. automatic garage doors)	16,814
House repair and construction materials	15,227
General Household Appliances	
Refrigerators	42,802
Ranges or ovens, not specified	33,058
Vacuum cleaners	19,778
Heating, Cooling, and Ventilating Equipment	
Pipes (excluding smoking pipes)	28,352
Fans	17,845
Air conditioners	15,958

Description	Injuries
Home Communication and Entertainment Equipment	
Televisions	45,744
Telephones or telephone accessories	25,808
Computers (equip. & electronic games)	24,525
Television tables or stands	13,595
Personal Use Items	
Footwear	203,374
Jewelry	103,925
Daywear	79,972
Coins	35,613
Razors and shavers	34,687
Manicuring devices	22,662
Other clothing[b]	22,397
Luggage	18,382
Yard and Garden Equipment	
Manual snow or ice removal tools	35,249
Other unpowered garden tools[c]	25,079
Chainsaws	24,917
Greenhouse or gardening supplies	18,795
Garden hoses, nozzles or sprinklers	16,981
Decorative yard equipment, excl. water feature	14,336
Recreation	
Monkey bars or other playground climbing equipment	82,436
Swings or swing sets	56,937
Scooters (unpowered)	52,393
Slides or sliding boards	46,192
Other playground equipment[d]	26,165
Bleachers	19,751
Mopeds or power-assisted cycles	15,613
Sleds	15,599
Gas, air, or spring operated guns	14,370
Miscellaneous Products	
Hot water	47,061
Carts	36,357
Baby strollers	14,808
Fireworks	12,011
Household Chemicals	
Soaps (excl. laundry soaps or detergents)	25,207
Bleaches (noncosmetic)	20,313
Paints, varnishes, shellacs	15,811
General purpose household cleaners	14,781

Source: NSC analysis of U.S. Consumer Product Safety Commission NEISS data.
Note: Products are listed above if the estimate was greater than 11,000 cases. "n.e.c." = not elsewhere classified.
[a] Excludes baby changing tables (3,951 injuries), billiard or pool tables (3,299 injuries), and television tables or stands (13,595 injuries).
[b] Excludes costumes or mask (2,108 injuries); day wear (79,972 injuries); footwear (203,374 injuries); nightwear (5,744 injuries); and outerwear (6,507 injuries).
[c] Includes cultivators, hoes, pitchforks, rakes, shovels, spades, and trowels.
[d] Excludes monkey bars (82,436 injuries), see-saws (3,161 injuries), slides (46,192 injuries), and swings (56,937 injuries).

HOME AND COMMUNITY
Transportation Mode Comparisons

Overall, passenger transportation incidents account for about 1 out of 6 unintentional-injury-related deaths. But the risk of death for the passenger, expressed on a per-mile basis, varies greatly by transportation mode. Highway travel by personal vehicle presents the greatest risk; air, rail, and bus travel have much lower death rates. The tables below show the latest information on passenger transportation deaths and death rates.

In recognition of the current use of vans, sport utility vehicles (SUVs), pickups, and other light trucks as passenger vehicles, the Federal Highway Administration (FHWA) reclassified these vehicles and passenger automobiles as "light duty vehicles" beginning in 2009. Because the data for 2007 and 2008 also meet the requirements of the new FHWA methodology, they are presented with the data for later years in the table below. The statistics for light duty vehicles shown in the tables below represent all use of such vehicles, both intercity and local. The bus data also include intercity and local (transit) bus travel. Railroad includes both intercity (Amtrak) and local commuting travel. Scheduled airlines includes both large airlines and commuter airlines, but excludes on-demand air taxis and charter operations. In comparing the four modes, drivers of light duty vehicles (except taxis) are considered passengers. Bus drivers and airline or railroad crews are not considered passengers.

Other comparisons are possibly based on passenger trips, vehicle miles, or vehicle trips, but passenger miles is the most commonly used basis for comparing the safety of various modes of travel.

Transportation incident death rates, 2012-2014

Mode of transportation	2014 Passenger deaths	2014 Passenger miles (billions)	2014 Deaths per 100,000,000 passenger miles	2012-2014 average death rate
Light duty vehicles[a]	21,014	4,526.6	0.46	0.47
Buses[b]	28	64.8	0.04	0.04
Transit buses	0	22.6	0.00	0
Intercity buses	18	42.2	0.04	0.04
Railroad passenger trains[c]	5	21.9	0.02	0.02
Scheduled airlines[d]	0	596.0	0.00	< 0.001

Source: Highway passenger deaths – Fatality Analysis Reporting System data. Railroad passenger deaths and miles – Federal Railroad Administration. Airline passenger deaths – National Transportation Safety Board. Airline passenger miles – Bureau of Transportation Statistics. Passenger miles for transit buses – American Public Transit Association. All other figures – National Safety Council estimates.
[a]Includes passenger cars, light trucks, vans, and SUVs regardless of wheelbase. Includes taxi passengers. Drivers of light duty vehicles are considered passengers.
[b]Figures exclude school buses but include "other" and "unknown" bus types.
[c]Includes Amtrak and commuter rail service.
[d]Includes large airlines and scheduled commuter airlines; excludes charter, cargo, on-demand services, and suicide/sabotage.

Passenger deaths and death rates, United States, 2007-2014

Year	Light duty vehicles[a] Deaths	Rate[b]	Buses Deaths	Rate[b]	Railroad passenger trains Deaths	Rate[b]	Scheduled airlines Deaths	Rate[b]
2007	29,075	0.66	18	0.03	5	0.03	0	0.00
2008	25,457	0.59	50	0.08	24	0.13	0	0.00
2009	23,441	0.53	21	0.04	3	0.02	49	0.01
2010	22,271	0.50	28	0.05	3	0.02	0	0.00
2011	21,221	0.48	35	0.06	6	0.03	0	0.00
2012	21,669	0.49	25	0.04	5	0.02	0	0.00
2013	21,127	0.47	29	0.05	6	0.03	5	0.001
2014	21,014	0.46	28	0.04	5	0.02	0	0.00

Source: See table above.
[a]Includes passenger cars, light trucks, vans, and SUVs regardless of wheelbase. Includes taxi passengers. Drivers of light duty vehicles are considered passengers.
[b]Deaths per 100,000,000 passenger miles.

HOME AND COMMUNITY
Transportation Mode Comparisons (cont.)

Passenger death rates, United States, 2012-2014

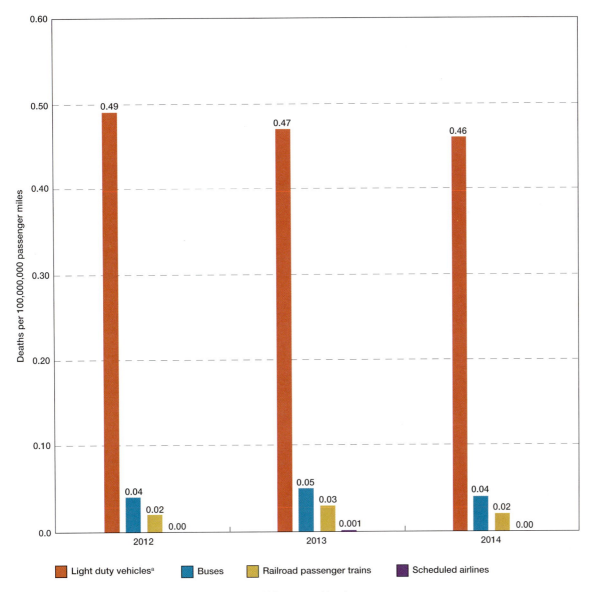

[a] With the exception of taxi drivers, drivers of these vehicles are considered passengers.

HOME AND COMMUNITY

Aviation

The total number of incidents involving United States registered civil aviation decreased slightly from 1,223 in 2014 to a preliminary estimate of 1,209 in 2015.

U.S. civil aviation incidents, deaths, and death rates, 2010-2015

| | Incidents | | | Incident rates | | | |
| | | | | Per 100,000 flight hours | | Per million miles flown | |
Year	Total	Fatal	Total deaths[a]	Total	Fatal	Total	Fatal
Large airlines[b]							
2010	28	0	0	0.162	0	0.0038	0
2011	29	0	0	0.166	0	0.0039	0
2012	26	0	0	0.151	0	0.0035	0
2013	19	0	0	0.110	0	0.0025	0
2014	28	0	0	0.162	0	0.0037	0
2015	27	0	0	0.155	0	0.0035	0
Commuter airlines[b]							
2010	6	0	0	1.907	0	0.1250	0
2011	4	0	0	1.228	0	0.0821	0
2012	5	0	0	1.551	0	0.0994	0
2013	7	2	5	2.364	0.675	0.1616	0.0462
2014	4	0	0	1.205	0	0.0827	0
2015	5	1	1	1.458	0.292	0.0991	0.0198
On-demand air taxis[b]							
2010	30	6	17	0.96	0.19	—	—
2011	50	16	41	—	—	—	—
2012	36	8	12	1.02	0.23	—	—
2013	44	10	25	1.30	0.30	—	—
2014	35	8	20	0.96	0.22	—	—
2015	38	7	27	1.07	0.20	—	—
General aviation[b]							
2010[c]	1,440	271	458	6.63	1.24	—	—
2011[c]	1,471	270	458	—	—	—	—
2012[c]	1,473	273	438	7.05	1.30	—	—
2013[c]	1,224	222	391	6.26	1.12	—	—
2014[c]	1,223	257	424	6.23	1.31	—	—
2015[c]	1,209	229	376	5.85	1.09	—	—

Source: National Transportation Safety Board: 2015 preliminary, 2010-2014 revised; exposure data for rates from the Federal Aviation Administration (FAA). Also note that the 2011 exposure estimates are not currently available for on-demand air taxis and general aviation. The FAA is engaged in re-calibration efforts.
Note: Dash (—) indicates data not available.
[a] Includes passengers, crew members, and others such as people on the ground.
[b] Civil aviation incident statistics collected by the National Transportation Safety Board are classified according to federal air regulations under which the flights were made. The classifications are (1) large airlines operating scheduled service under Title 14, Code of Federal Regulations, part 121 (14 CFR 121); (2) commuter carriers operating scheduled service under 14 CFR 135; (3) unscheduled, "on-demand" air taxis under 14 CFR 135; and (4) "general aviation," which includes incidents involving aircraft flown under rules other than 14 CFR 121 and 14 CFR 135. Not shown in the table is nonscheduled air carrier operations under 14 CFR 121 that experienced (3 incidents/2 fatalities) in 2010, (3/0) in 2011, (0/0) in 2012, (4/9) in 2013, (1/0) in 2014, and (1/0) in 2015. Since 1997, "large airlines" includes aircraft with 10 or more seats, formerly operated as commuter carriers under 14 CFR 135.
[c] Suicide/sabotage/terrorism and stolen/unauthorized cases are included in incident and fatality totals but excluded from rates –General Aviation, 2010 (3/2), 2011 (2/1), 2012 (1/1), 2013 (3/3), 2014 (0/0), and 2015 (5/4).

Civil aviation incidence rates, United States, 1991-2015

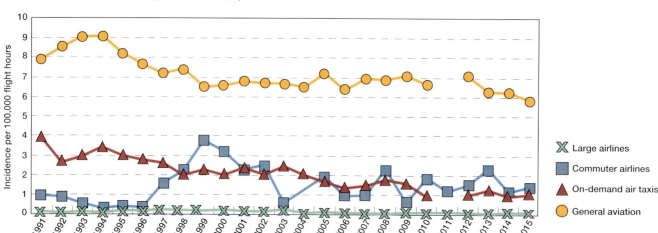

HOME AND COMMUNITY
Railroad

Railroad deaths totaled 771 in 2015, nearly unchanged from the 2014 revised total of 768 but 2% higher than the 2006-2014 average of 758. From 2014 to 2015, there was a 10% decrease in fatalities at highway-rail crossings, but a 6% increase in fatalities involving other types of incidents. The latter included 468 deaths, or 88%, to trespassers. Eleven employees were killed while on duty, a 10% increase compared to the 2014 death toll and 35% lower than the 2006-2014 average. Deaths to passengers on trains totaled 17, representing a 240% increase over the 2014 total of five deaths and a 143% increase over the 2006-2014 average.

The ratio of railroad-related deaths to nonfatal injuries and illnesses is approximately 1:11. In 2015, railroad incidents resulted in 8,767 cases of nonfatal conditions, compared to 8,669 in 2014 and the 2006-2014 average of 8,699. Eleven percent of the total, 991, was attributed to highway-rail-crossing incidents, up 15% from the 2014 total of 862 and was 3% higher than the 2006-2014 average of 960. Of the 4,327 nonfatal occupational railroad injuries and illnesses reported in 2015, 2% were attributed to highway-rail-crossing incidents.

Deaths and nonfatal cases in railroad incidents, United States, 2006-2015

Year	Total	Highway rail-crossing incident? Yes	Highway rail-crossing incident? No	Occurring in other than highway-rail crossing incident Trespassers	Occurring in other than highway-rail crossing incident Others	Employees on duty At highway-rail crossing? Yes	Employees on duty At highway-rail crossing? No	Passengers on trains[a] At highway-rail crossing? Yes	Passengers on trains[a] At highway-rail crossing? No
Deaths									
2006	903	369	534	511	23	4	12	0	2
2007	851	339	512	470	42	1	16	0	5
2008	804	290	514	457	57	3	23	0	24
2009	695	248	447	416	31	0	16	0	3
2010	735	261	474	441	33	0	20	0	3
2011	682	426	436	400	36	6	15	4	2
2012	674	231	443	410	33	1	15	0	5
2013	700	232	468	425	43	1	13	0	6
2014	768	264	504	470	34	0	10	0	5
2015	771	237	534	468	66	0	11	5	12
Nonfatal conditions									
2006	8,797	1,070	7,727	481	7,246	96	5,179	95	841
2007	9,669	1,059	8,610	407	8,203	105	5,357	72	1,444
2008	9,062	990	8,072	432	7,640	75	4,925	101	1,231
2009	8,023	743	7,280	344	6,936	72	4,432	61	1,130
2010	8,378	888	7,490	390	7,100	80	4,332	114	1,256
2011	8,437	1,048	7,389	366	7,023	72	4,156	245	1,337
2012	8,454	971	7,483	410	7,073	76	3,915	179	1,409
2013	8,730	975	7,755	434	7,321	84	4,207	109	1,586
2014	8,669	862	7,807	424	7,383	55	4,415	76	1,345
2015	8,767	991	7,776	414	7,362	80	4,247	170	1,396

Source: Federal Railroad Administration.
[a] Passenger cases include all circumstances, including getting on/off standing trains, stumbling aboard trains, assaults, train incidents, crossing incidents, etc.

Casualties at public and private highway-rail crossings, United States, 2006-2015

Year	Deaths Total	Deaths Motor vehicle-related	Deaths Pedestrians	Deaths Others	Nonfatal conditions Total	Nonfatal conditions Motor vehicle-related	Nonfatal conditions Pedestrians	Nonfatal conditions Others
2006	369	305	53	11	1,070	1,035	29	6
2007	339	265	59	15	1,059	1,018	32	9
2008	290	221	64	5	990	923	54	13
2009	248	182	59	7	743	697	38	8
2010	261	169	81	11	888	821	49	18
2011	246	168	67	11	1,048	987	43	18
2012	231	164	56	11	971	913	40	18
2013	232	162	54	16	975	902	50	23
2014	264	167	79	18	863	786	56	21
2015	237	152	68	17	992	918	53	21

Source: Federal Railroad Administration (July 1, 2016).

HOME AND COMMUNITY
Unintentional Fatal Poisonings

■ *Poisoning deaths were up 8% from 2013 to 2014.*

Deaths from unintentional poisoning numbered 42,032 in 2014, the latest year for which data are available. The death rate per 100,000 population was 13.2. Males are at greatest risk, with a death rate of 17.3 compared with 9.1 for females. Total poisoning deaths increased 8% from 38,851 in 2013 and are about 1.8 times the 2005 total. See pages 52-55 for long-term trends.

Forty percent of the poisoning deaths were classified in the "narcotics and psychodysleptics (hallucinogens), not elsewhere classified," category, which includes prescription narcotic analgesics and illegal drugs such as cocaine, heroin, cannabinol, and LSD.

A National Safety Council analysis of National Center for Health Statistics mortality data shows that the greatest number of poisoning deaths in 2014 was due to prescription drug overdoses, accounting for 19,896 deaths or over 47% of all unintentional poisoning deaths. Since 1999, total unintentional drug deaths have increased 247% while unintentional prescription drug deaths have increased 351% (see top graph on opposite page). The three drug categories associated with the fastest unintentional fatality increases are prescription opioids, heroin, and benzodiazepines. Unintentional deaths associated with these drugs have increased 448%, 480%, and 867% since 1999, respectively (see bottom graph on opposite page). In 2014 prescription opioids were involved in 15,906 unintentional deaths or 80% of all unintentional prescription drug deaths while benzodiazepines were involved in 6,544 deaths or 33% of unintentional prescription drug deaths. Please note that prescription opioids and benzodiazepines are often combined and can both be listed in association with a death.

Deaths due to alcohol poisoning increased nearly 2% from 2013 and totaled 2,283 in 2014. Alcohol poisoning deaths for males outnumbered those for females by more than 3 to 1. The number of alcohol poisoning deaths among males increased by 4% from 2013 to 2014, while the number for females decreased 5%. It should be noted that alcohol may also be present in combination with other drugs.

Carbon monoxide poisoning is included in the category of "other gases and vapors." Additional information on human poisoning exposure cases may be found on pages 162 and 191.

Unintentional poisoning deaths by type, age, and sex, United States, 2014

Type of poison	All ages	Younger than 5	5-14 years	15-19 years	20-24 years	25-44 years	45-64 years	65 or older
Both sexes								
Total poisoning deaths	42,032	37	31	567	2,925	18,450	18,022	2,000
Deaths per 100,000 population	13.2	0.2	0.1	2.7	12.8	22.0	21.6	4.3
Total drug-related poisoning deaths	38,718	22	16	513	2,795	17,322	16,420	1,630
Nonopioid analgesics, antipyretics, and antirheumatics (X40)[a]	224	1	0	1	9	83	94	36
Antiepileptic, sedative-hypnotic, antiparkinsonism, and psychotropic drugs, n.e.c. (X41)	3,069	3	1	31	108	1,118	1,671	137
Narcotics and psychodysleptics (hallucinogens), n.e.c. (X42)	16,822	12	6	246	1,491	7,950	6,610	507
Other drugs acting on the autonomic nervous system (X43)	21	0	1	0	0	6	10	4
Other and unspecified drugs, medicaments, and biological substances (X44)	18,582	6	8	235	1,187	8,165	8,035	946
Alcohol (X45)	2,283	1	0	30	65	750	1,273	164
Organic solvents and halogenated hydrocarbons and their vapors (X46)	46	0	0	0	5	20	18	3
Other gases and vapors (X47)	801	10	14	20	53	295	252	157
Pesticides (X48)	6	0	0	0	0	0	3	3
Other and unspecified chemical and noxious substances (X49)	178	4	1	4	7	63	56	43
Males								
Total poisoning deaths	27,225	20	17	402	2,165	12,603	10,939	1,079
Deaths per 100,000 population	17.3	0.2	0.1	3.7	18.4	29.9	26.8	5.3
Total drug-related poisoning deaths	24,725	11	9	365	2,069	11,728	9,715	828
Nonopioid analgesics, antipyretics, and antirheumatics (X40)	98	0	0	0	2	40	41	15
Antiepileptic, sedative-hypnotic, antiparkinsonism, and psychotropic drugs, n.e.c. (X41)	2,034	1	0	22	70	744	1,112	85
Narcotics and psychodysleptics (hallucinogens), n.e.c. (X42)	12,019	6	2	175	1,137	5,878	4,507	314
Other drugs acting on the autonomic nervous system (X43)	12	0	0	0	0	3	6	3
Other and unspecified drugs, medicaments, and biological substances (X44)	10,562	4	7	168	860	5,063	4,049	411
Alcohol (X45)	1,754	1	0	20	48	590	972	123
Organic solvents and halogenated hydrocarbons and their vapors (X46)	39	0	0	0	4	16	16	3
Other gases and vapors (X47)	591	7	7	14	39	223	197	104
Pesticides (X48)	5	0	0	0	0	0	2	3
Other and unspecified chemical and noxious substances (X49)	111	1	1	3	5	46	37	18
Females								
Total poisoning deaths	14,807	17	14	165	760	5,847	7,083	921
Deaths per 100,000 population	9.1	0.2	0.1	1.6	6.8	14.0	16.6	3.6
Total drug-related poisoning deaths	13,993	11	7	148	726	5,594	6,705	802
Nonopioid analgesics, antipyretics, and antirheumatics (X40)	126	1	0	1	7	43	53	21
Antiepileptic, sedative-hypnotic, antiparkinsonism, and psychotropic drugs, n.e.c. (X41)	1,035	2	1	9	38	374	559	52
Narcotics and psychodysleptics (hallucinogens), n.e.c. (X42)	4,803	6	4	71	354	2,072	2,103	193
Other drugs acting on the autonomic nervous system (X43)	9	0	1	0	0	3	4	1
Other and unspecified drugs, medicaments, and biological substances (X44)	8,020	2	1	67	327	3,102	3,986	535
Alcohol (X45)	529	0	0	10	17	160	301	41
Organic solvents and halogenated hydrocarbons and their vapors (X46)	7	0	0	0	1	4	2	0
Other gases and vapors (X47)	210	3	7	6	14	72	55	53
Pesticides (X48)	1	0	0	0	0	0	1	0
Other and unspecified chemical and noxious substances (X49)	67	3	0	1	2	17	19	25

Source: National Safety Council tabulations of National Center for Health Statistics–Mortality Data for 2014, as compiled from data provided by the 57 vital statistics jurisdictions through the Vital Statistics Cooperative Program.
Note: "n.e.c." means "not elsewhere classified." [a]Numbers following titles refer to external cause of injury and poisoning classifications in ICD-10.

HOME AND COMMUNITY
Unintentional Fatal Poisonings (cont.)

Unintentional poisoning deaths, United States, 1996-2014

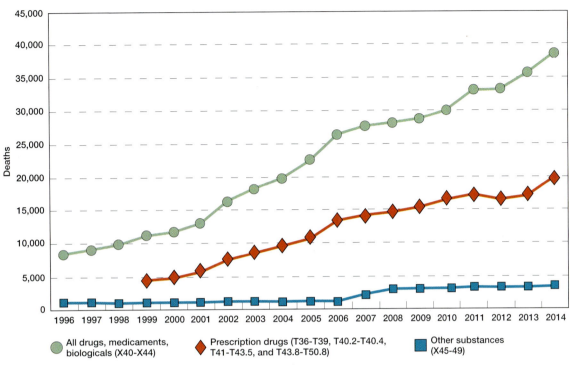

Note: Classification system changed in 1999 (see the Technical Appendix).

Unintentional poisoning deaths by selected drugs, United States, 1999-2014

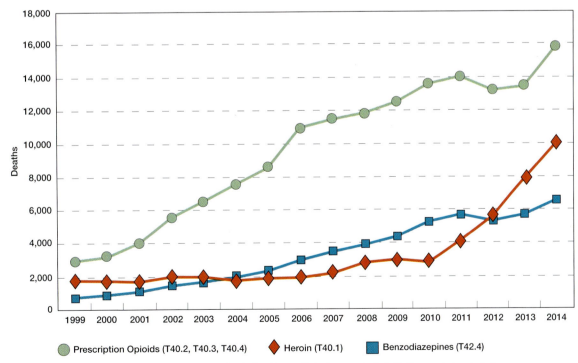

Note: Deaths by drug type are not mutually exclusive, deaths involving multiple drugs are included in the count of each drug.

HOME AND COMMUNITY

Fatal Versus Nonfatal Unintentional Poisoning

Most people think of poisoning as a childhood issue. That is true for poisonings exposures, but not for nonfatal and fatal poisonings. The pie charts below show the distribution of poisoning exposures, nonfatal poisonings, and fatal poisonings by age groups. The poisoning exposure data are from the American Association of Poison Control Centers and represent the calls received by poison control centers. The nonfatal data represent emergency department visits, while the fatality data are from death certificates.

Nonfatal exposures occur predominantly among young children, whereas nonfatal and fatal poisonings are overwhelmingly among adults. While 46% of the poisoning exposures involve children four or younger, over 90% of the nonfatal poisonings and 98% of the fatalities occur among adults 19 and older.

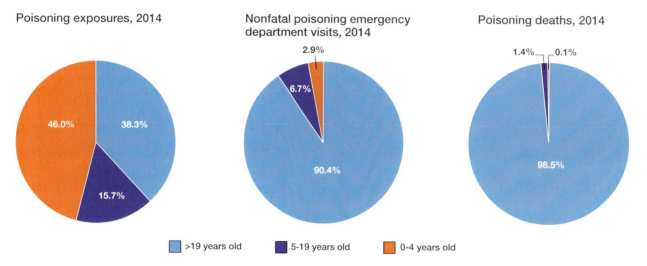

Nonfatal poisonings increased 16.6% in 2014 and now account for more than 1.2 million emergency department visits a year. Fatal poisonings continue to increase, showing over an 8% increase from 2013. The charts below illustrate the trends for both categories of poisonings starting in 2002.

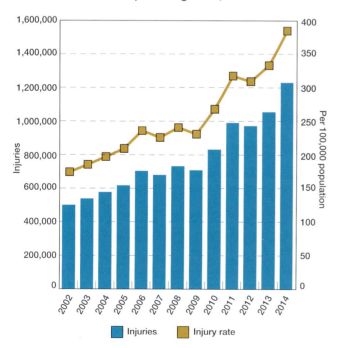

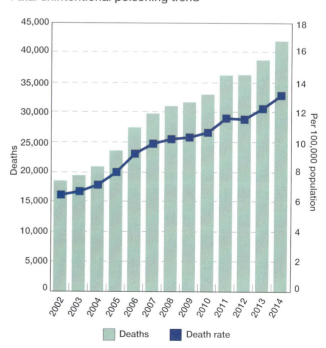

Source: Centers for Disease Control and Prevention, NEISS-AIP; Source: Centers for Disease Control and Prevention, WISQARS
[a] 2014 is the latest official data available. National Safety Council estimates for 2015 are available on pages 53 and 55.

HOME AND COMMUNITY
Older Adult Falls

The impact of unintentional falls on the older adult population has been highlighted in numerous editions of *Injury Facts* (2010-2016, 2008, 2007, etc.).

The Centers for Disease Control and Prevention (CDC) reports that, in 2011, 65% of emergency department visits among individuals 65 years and older were due to falls. Injury rates among older adults from falls steadily increase with age and peak among those aged 100 and older. Not surprisingly, research is also showing that older individuals who require mobility assistive devices like canes and walkers are at especially high risk for falls. Compared with older individuals who do not use assistive devices, users are 11 times more likely (odds ratio 12.0) to report a fall in the last three months and are six times more likely (odds ratio 7.1) to report that they limit walking outside due to concerns about falling.

A recent CDC study assessing the cost-benefit analysis of three older adult fall prevention programs identified a positive return on investment for all three programs. Otago Exercise Program, Tai Chi: Moving for Better Balance, and Stepping On demonstrated that the cost of decreased direct medical costs was greater than the costs associated with implementing the program. Two of these programs, Tai Chi: Moving for Better Balance and Otago Exercise Program, that are delivered to persons aged 80 and older both resulted in return on investments greater than 100%. A similar study found that adults who consistently participate in exercise programs such as EnhanceFitness can reduce their risk of experiencing a medically treated fall by 20 to 30%. EnhancedFitness is an evidence-based community-based group exercise intervention funded by CDC.

Looking at 2014, 27,044 fatalities occurred among adults age 65 or older. From 1999 to 2014, the number of fall-related deaths among individuals 65 or older has increased 168%, while the population death rate has increased 102%. At this same time, the number of fall deaths among individuals younger than 65 increased 60% and the death rate increased 44% (see chart below).

As reported in the 2014 edition of *Injury Facts*, it is likely that a substantial proportion of the increase in older adult fall deaths is a result of improved death certificate coding and that the more recent estimates more accurately reflect the full extent of the problem.

Source: DeGrauw, X., Annest, J.L., Stevens, J.A., Xu, L., & Coronado, V. (2016). *Unintentional injuries treated in hospital emergency department among persons aged 65 years and older, United States, 2006-2011.* Journal of Safety Research, 56, 105-109.

West, B.A., Bhat, G., Stevens, J., & Bergen, G. (2015). *Assistive device use and mobility-related factors among adults aged >= 65 years.* Journal of Safety Research, 55, 147-150.

Greenwood-Hickman, M.A., Rosenberg, D.E., Phelan, E.A., & Fitzpatrick A.L. (2015). *Participation in older adult physical activity programs and risk for falls requiring medical care, Washington State, 2005-2011.* Preventing Chronic Disease, 12: 140574.

Carande-Kulis, V., Stevens, J.A., Florence, C.S., Beattie, B.L., & Aria, I. (2015). *A cost-benefit analysis of three older adult fall prevention interventions.* Journal of Safety Research, 52, 65-70.

Fall deaths and death rates, United States, 1999-2014

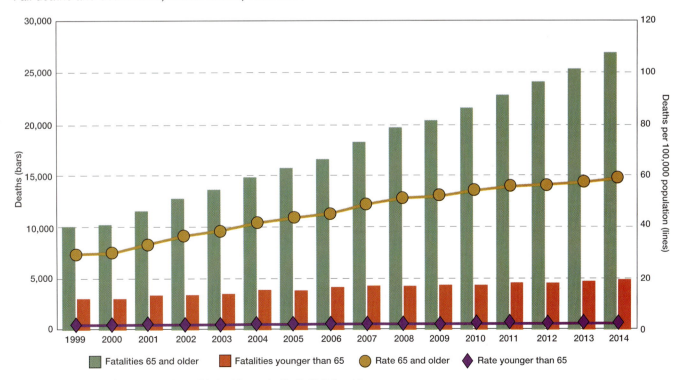

Source: National Safety Council tabulations of National Center for Health Statistics data.

HOME AND COMMUNITY

Fires

The National Fire Protection Association (NFPA) estimates that in the United States:
- One fire occurs every 24 seconds
- One civilian fire-related injury occurs every 33 minutes
- One civilian fire-related death occurs every 160 minutes

In addition to these civilian injuries and deaths, 63,350 firefighters were injured and 64 died while performing their duties in 2014.

Although the number of fire-related deaths have decreased by over half since 1977, 2014 marks the second consecutive increase from the record low number of deaths recorded by NFPA in 2012. The 2014 civilian fire death toll of 3,275 is 15% higher than the 2,855 total in 2012 and 1% higher than the 3,240 deaths in 2013. The fire death rate per million population has also shown strong long term improvement, falling 70% from 34.4 in 1977 to 10.3 in 2014. However, the population death rate has increased 14% since 2012. As can be seen in the graph below, the vast majority of these deaths resulted from home fires.

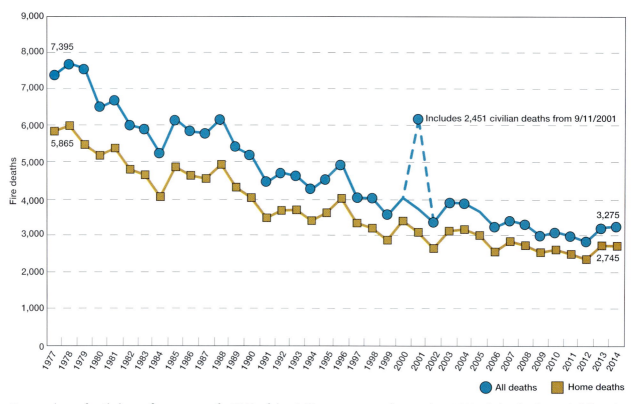

Total civilian fire deaths and home fire deaths, United States, 1977-2014

One- and two-family home fires account for 72% of the civilian deaths and 51% of the injuries. Apartment structure fires account for another 12% of the deaths and fully 24% of the injuries.

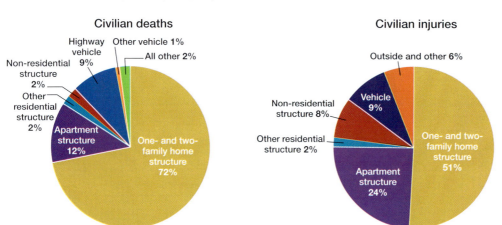

Civilian deaths and injuries by property class, United States, 2014

Source: Haynes, H.J.G. (September 2015). Fire loss in the United States During 2014. National Fire Protection Association.
Ahrens, M. (February 2016). Trends and patterns of U.S. fire loss. National Fire Protection Association.

HOME AND COMMUNITY
Pedalcycles

The estimated number of deaths from collisions between pedalcycles and motor vehicles increased from about 750 in 1940 to 1,200 in 1980, and then declined to about 1,100 in 2015.

In 2014, 623 pedalcyclists died in motor-vehicle crashes and 279 in other incidents, according to National Center for Health Statistics mortality data. Males accounted for 89% of all pedalcycle deaths, over 7 times the fatalities for females.

Emergency department-treated injuries associated with bicycles and bicycle accessories were estimated to total 510,905 in 2014 and 488,123 in 2015, according to the Consumer Product Safety Commission.

A meta-analysis of bicycle helmet efficacy by Attewell, Glase, and McFadden (2001) estimated that bicycle helmets reduce the risk of head injury by 60% and brain injury by 58%. As of March 2016, 21 states, the District of Columbia, and more than 201 localities had bicycle helmet use laws, according to the Bicycle Helmet Safety Institute.

Source: National Safety Council estimates and tabulations of National Center for Health Statistics mortality data obtained via WISQARS at www.cdc.gov/injury/wisqars/index.html. Population data for rates are from the U.S. Census Bureau. Data from Bicycle Helmet Safety Institute was retrieved August 11, 2016, from www.bhsi.org.

Attewell, R.G., Glase, K., & McFadden, M. (2001). Bicycle helmet efficacy: A meta-analysis. *Accident Analysis & Prevention, Vol. 33, No. 3,* pp. 345-352.

Pedalcycle fatalities by month, United States, 2014

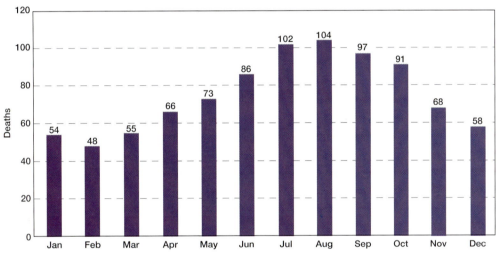

Source: National Safety Council tabulations of National Center for Health Statistics data.

Pedalcycle deaths and death rates by sex and age group, United States, 2014

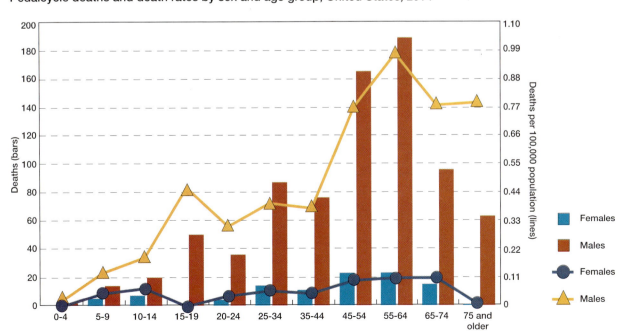

Source: National Safety Council tabulations based on U.S. Census Bureau and National Center for Health Statistics data.

HOME AND COMMUNITY
Risks by Age Group

The leading risks for unintentional injury vary with age and are different for deaths and nonfatal injuries. The tables here and on the next page list, for eight age groups, the five leading causes of unintentional-injury-related deaths and the five leading causes of hospital emergency department visits, which is one measure of nonfatal injuries.

For all ages, the five leading causes account for 86% of all unintentional-injury-related deaths and 72% of unintentional-injury-related emergency department visits. Only motor-vehicle crashes and falls are common to both lists. Motor-vehicle crashes rank second for unintentional-injury-related deaths and fourth for unintentional-injury-related emergency department visits. Falls rank third for unintentional-injury-related deaths and first for emergency department unintentional-injury-related visits.

The five leading causes of unintentional-injury-related deaths account for between 82% and 94% of such deaths depending on the age group. The leading causes of unintentional-injury-related emergency department visits account for between 67% and 89% of such hospital visits.

For deaths, poisoning; motor-vehicle crashes; falls; fire, flames, or smoke; and drowning are most often among the top five, with choking; firearms; and mechanical suffocation sometimes included. For emergency department visits, falls; struck by or against; overexertion; motor-vehicle occupant injuries; and cut or pierce injuries are most often in the top five. In the younger age groups, bites and stings (except dog bites); foreign body injuries; and struck by or against are among the leading risks.

Leading unintentional-injury risks, all ages, United States, 2014

Rank	Unintentional-injury-related deaths				Emergency department unintentional-injury-related visits			
	Event	Number	Percent	Rate[a]	Event	Number	Percent	Rate[a]
—	Total	136,053	100.0%	42.7	Total	28,728,927	100.0%	9,010
1	Poisoning	42,032	30.9%	13.2	Falls	9,163,980	31.9%	2,874
2	Motor vehicle crashes	35,398	26.0%	11.1	Struck by or against	4,083,298	14.2%	1,281
3	Falls	31,959	23.5%	10.0	Overexertion	3,132,271	10.9%	982
4	Choking[b]	4,816	3.5%	1.5	Motor vehicle occupant	2,412,109	8.4%	756
5	Drowning	3,406	2.5%	1.1	Cut or pierce	1,989,505	6.9%	624

Leading unintentional-injury risks, young children (ages 0-4), United States, 2014

Rank	Unintentional-injury-related deaths				Emergency department unintentional-injury-related visits			
	Event	Number	Percent	Rate[a]	Event	Number	Percent	Rate[a]
—	Total	2,377	100.0%	12.0	Total	2,114,717	100.0%	10,639
1	Mechanical suffocation	1,016	42.7%	5.1	Falls	948,254	44.8%	4,771
2	Motor vehicle crashes	473	19.9%	2.4	Struck by or against	346,225	16.4%	1,742
3	Drowning	417	17.5%	2.1	Bite or sting (except dog)	177,578	8.4%	893
4	Fire, flames, or smoke	130	5.5%	0.7	Foreign body	133,120	6.3%	670
5	Choking[b]	95	4.0%	0.5	Cut or pierce	83,935	4.0%	422

Leading unintentional-injury risks, children and young adolescents (ages 5-14), United States, 2014

Rank	Unintentional-injury-related deaths				Emergency department unintentional-injury-related visits			
	Event	Number	Percent	Rate[a]	Event	Number	Percent	Rate[a]
—	Total	1,480	100.0%	3.6	Total	3,594,008	100.0%	8,725
1	Motor vehicle crashes	829	56.0%	2.0	Falls	1,155,257	32.1%	2,805
2	Drowning	230	15.5%	0.6	Struck by or against	922,252	25.7%	2,239
3	Fire, flames, or smoke	117	7.9%	0.3	Overexertion	365,997	10.2%	889
4	Mechanical suffocation	44	3.0%	0.1	Cut or pierce	212,096	5.9%	515
5	Poisoning	31	2.1%	0.1	Bite or sting (except dog)	186,731	5.2%	453

Leading unintentional-injury risks, teens (ages 15-19), United States, 2014

Rank	Unintentional-injury-related deaths				Emergency department unintentional-injury-related visits			
	Event	Number	Percent	Rate[a]	Event	Number	Percent	Rate[a]
—	Total	3,736	100.0%	17.7	Total	2,251,398	100.0%	10,687
1	Motor vehicle crashes	2,515	67.3%	11.9	Struck by or against	502,280	22.3%	2,384
2	Poisoning	567	15.2%	2.7	Falls	429,614	19.1%	2,039
3	Drowning	245	6.6%	1.2	Overexertion	340,721	15.1%	1,617
4	Falls	57	1.5%	0.3	Motor vehicle occupant	243,992	10.8%	1,158
5	Firearms	56	1.5%	0.3	Cut or pierce	160,820	7.1%	763

See footnotes on page 167.

HOME AND COMMUNITY
Risks by Age Group (cont.)

Leading unintentional-injury risks, young adults (ages 20-24), United States, 2014

	Unintentional-injury-related deaths				Emergency department unintentional-injury-related visits			
Rank	Event	Number	Percent	Rate[a]	Event	Number	Percent	Rate[a]
—	Total	8,100	100.0%	35.4	Total	2,395,360	100.0%	10,455
1	Motor vehicle crashes	4,194	51.8%	18.3	Falls	403,365	16.8%	1,760
2	Poisoning	2,925	36.1%	12.8	Struck by or against	363,567	15.2%	1,587
3	Drowning	262	3.2%	1.1	Motor vehicle occupant	350,361	14.6%	1,529
4	Falls	117	1.4%	0.5	Overexertion	295,364	12.3%	1,289
5	Firearms	92	1.1%	0.4	Cut or pierce	247,228	10.3%	1,079

Leading unintentional-injury risks, adults (ages 25-44), United States, 2014

	Unintentional-injury-related deaths				Emergency department unintentional-injury-related visits			
Rank	Event	Number	Percent	Rate[a]	Event	Number	Percent	Rate[a]
—	Total	33,405	100.0%	39.8	Total	7,584,708	100.0%	9,026
1	Poisoning	18,450	55.2%	22.0	Falls	1,491,145	19.7%	1,775
2	Motor vehicle crashes	10,518	31.5%	12.5	Overexertion	1,103,258	14.5%	1,313
3	Falls	789	2.4%	0.9	Struck by or against	1,008,201	13.3%	1,200
4	Drowning	762	2.3%	0.9	Motor vehicle occupant	884,623	11.7%	1,053
5	Fire, flames, or smoke	381	1.1%	0.5	Cut or pierce	686,824	9.1%	817

Leading unintentional-injury risks, adults (ages 45-64), United States, 2014

	Unintentional-injury-related deaths				Emergency department unintentional-injury-related visits			
Rank	Event	Number	Percent	Rate[a]	Event	Number	Percent	Rate[a]
—	Total	38,640	100.0%	46.3	Total	6,474,101	100.0%	7,750
1	Poisoning	18,022	46.6%	21.6	Falls	1,944,683	30.0%	2,328
2	Motor vehicle crashes	10,024	25.9%	12.0	Overexertion	721,430	11.1%	864
3	Falls	3,898	10.1%	4.7	Struck by or against	659,417	10.2%	789
4	Choking[b]	887	2.3%	1.1	Motor vehicle occupant	586,330	9.1%	702
5	Drowning	884	2.3%	1.1	Poisoning	454,570	7.0%	544

Leading unintentional-injury risks, older adults (ages 65-74), United States, 2014

	Unintentional-injury-related deaths				Emergency department unintentional-injury-related visits			
Rank	Event	Number	Percent	Rate[a]	Event	Number	Percent	Rate[a]
—	Total	11,909	100.0%	45.1	Total	1,801,964	100.0%	6,826
1	Falls	3,938	33.1%	14.9	Falls	916,928	50.9%	3,473
2	Motor vehicle crashes	3,153	26.5%	11.9	Struck by or against	139,105	7.7%	527
3	Poisoning	1,410	11.8%	5.3	Overexertion	129,909	7.2%	492
4	Choking[b]	789	6.6%	3.0	Motor vehicle occupant	115,619	6.4%	438
5	Fire, flames, or smoke	475	4.0%	1.8	Cut or pierce	94,336	5.2%	357

Leading unintentional-injury risks, elderly (age 75 or older), United States, 2014

	Unintentional-injury-related deaths				Emergency department unintentional-injury-related visits			
Rank	Event	Number	Percent	Rate[a]	Event	Number	Percent	Rate[a]
—	Total	36,386	100.0%	183.4	Total	2,508,196	100.0%	12,639
1	Falls	23,106	63.5%	116.4	Falls	1,874,531	74.7%	9,446
2	Motor vehicle crashes	3,685	10.1%	18.6	Struck by or against	142,203	5.7%	717
3	Choking[b]	2,755	7.6%	13.9	Overexertion	92,478	3.7%	466
4	Fire, flames, or smoke	633	1.7%	3.2	Motor vehicle occupant	76,229	3.0%	384
5	Poisoning	583	1.6%	2.9	Cut or pierce	53,404	2.1%	269

Source: National Safety Council analysis of National Center for Health Statistics—Mortality Data for 2014, as compiled from data provided by the 57 vital statistics jurisdictions through the Vital Statistics Cooperative Program. Rates are National Safety Council estimates based on data from the National Center for Health Statistics and the U.S. Census Bureau. Emergency department data are from NEISS-AIP.
[a]Deaths or emergency department visits per 100,000 population.
[b]Inhalation and ingestion of food or other object obstructing breathing.

HOME AND COMMUNITY
Firearms

■ *Unintentional firearms-related deaths up 16% in 2014.*

Firearms-related deaths from unintentional, intentional, and undetermined causes totaled 33,599 in 2014, a decrease of less than 1% from 33,677 in 2013. Suicides accounted for 63.5% of deaths related to firearms, while 32.6% were homicides, and 1.7% unintentional deaths. Males dominated all categories of deaths related to firearms and accounted for 86% of the total.

The number of homicide deaths related to firearms decreased by 2.5% from 2013 to 2014 following a decrease of 3.7% from 2012 to 2013. Unintentional deaths related to firearms increased for the first time in four years with a 15.8% increase from 2013. Suicide deaths related to firearms increased by 0.7% from 2013 to 2014, marking the eighth consecutive annual increase.

Hospital emergency department surveillance data[a] indicate an estimated 15,928 nonfatal unintentional firearms-related injuries occurred in 2014. Assault was related to an estimated 60,470[b] nonfatal injuries, while the estimated total for intentionally self-inflicted nonfatal injuries was 3,320[b].

[a]Source: National Center for Injury Prevention and Control injury surveillance data using WISQARS from www.cdc.gov/injury/wisqars/nonfatal.html.
[b]Estimate is unstable because of small sample size and should be used with caution.

Deaths involving firearms by age and sex, United States, 2014

Type and sex	All ages	Younger than 5	5-14 years	15-19 years	20-24 years	25-44 years	45-64 years	65-74 years	75 or older
Total firearms deaths	33,599	78	382	2,089	4,051	11,267	9,863	3,034	2,835
Male	28,717	44	273	1,857	3,615	9,609	8,087	2,649	2,583
Female	4,882	34	109	232	436	1,658	1,776	385	252
Unintentional	586	24	26	56	92	163	140	57	28
Male	505	17	20	55	86	134	119	47	27
Female	81	7	6	1	6	29	21	10	1
Suicide	21,334	—	174	755	1,515	5,659	7,863	2,711	2,657
Male	18,335	—	136	674	1,333	4,773	6,507	2,423	2,489
Female	2,999	—	38	81	182	886	1,356	288	168
Homicide	10,945	52	173	1,230	2,357	5,095	1,670	233	135
Male	9,223	26	109	1,087	2,116	4,384	1,297	150	54
Female	1,722	26	64	143	241	711	373	83	81
Legal intervention	464	0	1	23	56	266	106	10	2
Male	440	0	1	19	56	256	96	10	2
Female	24	0	0	4	0	10	10	0	0
Undetermined[a]	270	2	8	25	31	84	84	23	13
Male	214	1	7	22	24	62	68	19	11
Female	56	1	1	3	7	22	16	4	2

Source: National Safety Council tabulation of National Center for Health Statistics--Mortality Data for 2014, as compiled from data provided by the 57 vital statistics jurisdictions through the Vital Statistics Cooperative Program.
Note: Dashes (—) indicate category not applicable.
[a]Undetermined means the intentionality of the deaths (unintentional, homicide, suicide) was not determined.

Firearms deaths by intentionality, United States, 1999-2014

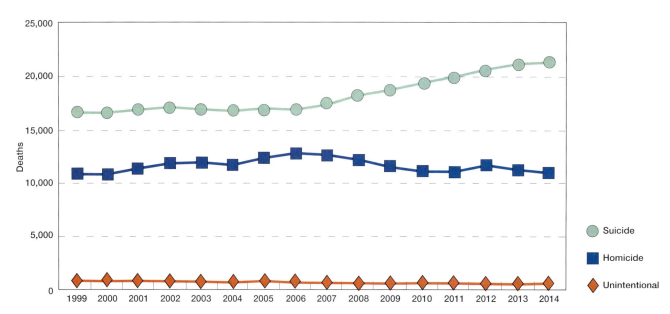

HOME AND COMMUNITY

Home and Community, 1987-2015

Principal types of home and community unintentional-injury-related deaths, United States, 1987-2015

Year	Total home and community[a]	Falls	Drowning	Poisoning	Choking[b]	Fire, flames, or smoke	Firearms	Mechanical suffocation	Air transport	Water transport	Rail transport[c]	Other
1987	39,800	10,300	3,900	4,900	3,600	4,400	1,400	[d]	900	800	400	9,200
1988	41,100	10,700	3,800	5,700	3,700	4,600	1,400	[d]	700	800	400	9,300
1989	40,700	10,800	3,700	5,900	3,500	4,400	1,400	[d]	800	700	400	9,100
1990	38,900	11,000	3,700	5,400	3,300	3,800	1,300	[d]	700	800	400	8,500
1991	39,700	11,400	3,700	6,000	3,100	3,800	1,400	[d]	700	700	500	8,400
1992	43,000	12,100	3,400	6,900	3,100	3,900	1,400	[d]	700	700	600	10,200
1993	45,800	12,500	3,700	8,400	3,200	3,900	1,500	[d]	600	700	600	10,700
1994	45,900	12,800	3,300	8,900	3,100	3,900	1,300	[d]	600	600	600	10,800
1995	47,300	13,400	3,700	9,000	3,100	3,700	1,200	[d]	600	700	500	11,400
1996	48,500	14,300	3,400	9,400	3,200	3,700	1,100	[d]	700	600	500	11,600
1997	49,400	14,700	3,500	10,100	3,200	3,400	1,000	[d]	500	600	400	12,000
1998	51,600	15,500	3,900	10,700	3,500	3,100	900	[d]	500	600	500	12,400
1999[e]	52,700	12,400	3,500	12,100	3,900	3,200	900	1,600	500	600	400	13,600
2000	51,900	12,600	3,400	12,700	4,300	2,900	800	1,300	500	500	400	12,500
2001	55,000	14,200	3,300	14,000	4,100	3,200	800	1,400	700	500	400	12,400
2002	58,700	15,600	3,400	17,500	4,100	3,100	700	1,400	500	500	400	11,500
2003	61,800	16,600	3,200	19,300	4,300	3,200	700	1,300	600	500	400	11,700
2004	64,200	18,000	3,300	20,900	4,400	3,100	600	1,400	400	500	400	11,200
2005	69,600	18,800	3,500	23,500	4,400	3,100	[d]	1,500	400	500	400	13,500
2006	73,300	20,000	3,500	27,400	4,400	3,000	[d]	1,600	400	400	400	12,200
2007	77,200	21,800	3,400	29,700	4,300	3,200	[d]	1,600	400	400	400	12,000
2008	79,700	23,300	3,400	31,000	4,400	2,800	[d]	1,700	400	300	400	12,000
2009	79,800	24,200	3,400	31,700	4,400	2,700	[d]	1,500	400	400	300	10,800
2010	83,200	25,400	3,700	32,900	4,500	2,700	[d]	1,600	300	300	400	11,400
2011	88,800	26,800	3,500	36,100	4,700	2,600	[d]	1,600	300	500	300	12,400
2012	89,400	28,000	3,500	36,200	4,700	2,700	[d]	1,600	300	400	300	11,700
2013	93,000	29,500	3,300	38,800	4,900	2,600	[d]	1,700	300	300	400	11,200
2014[f]	98,500	31,200	3,400	41,800	4,800	2,700	[d]	1,700	300	300	400	11,900
2015	106,700	32,700	3,600	47,300	5,000	2,700	[d]	1,800	300	400	400	12,500

Source: National Safety Council estimates based on data from National Center for Health Statistics and state vital statistics departments. The Council adopted the Bureau of Labor Statistics' Census of Fatal Occupational Injuries count for work-related unintentional injuries retroactive to 1992 data. Because of the lower work class total resulting from this change, several thousand unintentional-injury-related deaths that had been classified by the Council as work-related had to be reassigned to the home and public classes. For this reason, long-term historical comparisons for these three classes should be made with caution. See the Technical Appendix for an explanation of the methodological changes.
[a] Includes some deaths not shown separately.
[b] Inhalation and ingestion of food or other object that obstructs breathing.
[c] Includes subways and elevateds.
[d] Estimates for both home and public are not available.
[e] In 1999, a revision was made in the International Classification of Diseases. See the Technical Appendix for comparability with earlier years.
[f] Revised.

Leading types of home and community unintentional-injury-related deaths, United States, 2001-2015

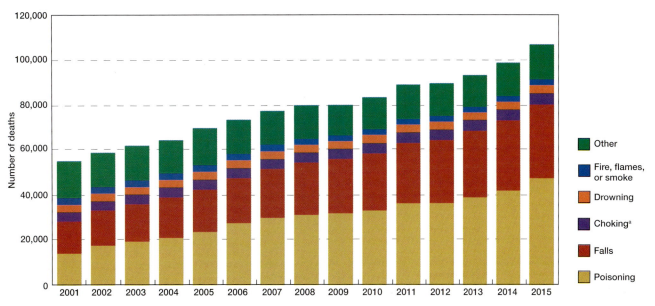

[a]Inhalation and ingestion of food or other object that obstructs breathing.

State Data

State Data Highlights

Deaths by state — pgs. 175-177

Deaths by state and event — pgs. 178-179

Fatal occupational injuries by state — pg. 181

Nonfatal occupational injuries by state — pg. 182

Motor-vehicle deaths by state — pgs. 184-185

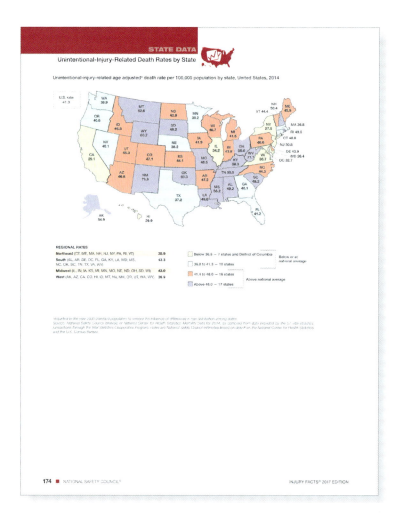

 **INJURY FACTS® 2017**

Unintentional Injuries are a Leading Cause of Death in all States!

Unintentional injuries as a whole are the fourth leading cause of death in the United States and in 22 states. Unintentional injuries are the third leading cause of death in 14 states and the District of Columbia, the fifth leading cause in 13 states, and the sixth leading cause in one state. In 2014, poisonings were the leading cause of unintentional-injury-related deaths in 24 states and the District of Columbia. Motor-vehicle crashes were the leading cause in 13 states. Falls were the leading cause in 13 states.

State Data

■ *Poisonings are the leading cause of unintentional-injury-related deaths in 24 states and the District of Columbia.*

This section on state-level data includes data for occupational and motor-vehicle injuries, as well as general injury mortality.

Death rates by state of residence for unintentional injuries can vary greatly from one type of injury to the next and from state to state. The graph on the next page shows for each state the age-adjusted death rates (per 100,000 population) for total unintentional-injury-related deaths and the four leading types of unintentional-injury-related deaths nationally – poisonings, motor-vehicle crashes, falls, and choking (inhalation or ingestion of food or other object that obstructs breathing).

The map on page 174 shows graphically the overall age-adjusted unintentional-injury-related death rates by state of residence. Rates by region were lowest in Northeast and highest in southern states.

The charts on pages 175-177 show the total unintentional-injury-related deaths by state of residence and where unintentional injuries rank as a cause of death in each state, as well as the five leading causes of unintentional-injury-related deaths in each state.

Unintentional injuries as a whole are the fourth leading cause of death in the United States and in 22 states. Unintentional injuries are the third leading cause of death in 14 states and the District of Columbia, the fifth leading cause in 13 states, and the sixth leading cause in one state.

In 2014, poisonings were the leading cause of unintentional-injury-related deaths in 24 states and the District of Columbia. Motor-vehicle crashes were the leading cause in 13 states. Falls were the leading cause in 13 states.

The second leading cause of unintentional-injury-related deaths was motor-vehicle crashes in 18 states, while poisoning was the second leading cause in 17 states. Falls were second in 15 states and the District of Columbia.

The most common third leading cause of unintentional-injury-related deaths was falls, in 22 states, while motor-vehicle crashes were the third leading cause in 19 states and the District of Columbia. Poisoning ranked third in 9 states.

Choking was the fourth leading cause of unintentional-injury-related deaths in 41 states, while the fourth ranking cause was drowning in seven states; fire, flames or smoke was the fourth ranked in the District of Columbia and Oklahoma; and mechanical suffocation was fourth in South Dakota.

Fire, flames or smoke was the fifth leading unintentional-injury-related cause of death in 19 states. Drowning was fifth in 16 states and choking ranked fifth in six states. Natural heat and cold was fifth-ranked in five states and the District of Columbia, mechanical suffocation was fifth in four states, and firearms was fifth in Tennessee.

The table on pages 178-179 shows the number of unintentional-injury-related deaths by state of occurrence for the 15 most common types of injury events. State populations also are shown to facilitate computation of detailed death rates.

The table on page 180 consists of a four-year state-by-state comparison of unintentional-injury-related deaths by state of residence and death rates for 2011 through 2014.

Page 181 shows fatal occupational injuries by state and counts of deaths for some of the principal types of events – transportation incidents, assaults or violent acts, contact with objects or equipment, falls, exposure to harmful substances or environments, and fires or explosions.

Nonfatal occupational injury and illness incidence rates for most states are shown in the table on page 182 and graphically in the map on page 183. States not shown do not have state occupational safety and health plans.

Pages 184 and 185 show motor-vehicle-related deaths and death rates by state both in tables and maps. The maps show death rates based on population, vehicle miles traveled, and registered vehicles.

STATE DATA
State Data (cont.)

Unintentional-injury-related age adjusted[a] death rates by state of residence, United States, 2014

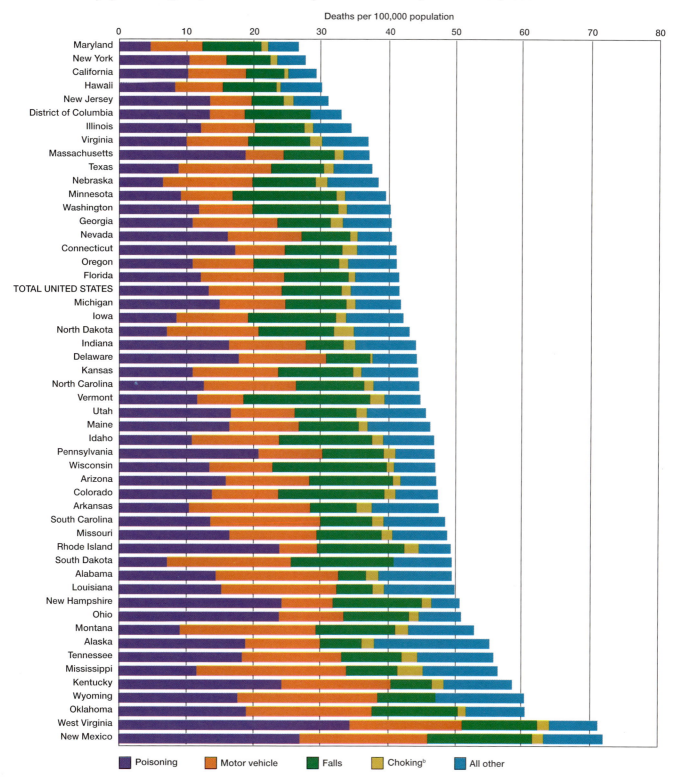

[a] Adjusted to the year 2000 standard population to remove the influence of differences in age distribution among states.
[b] Suffocation by ingestion or inhalation of food or other objects.

STATE DATA
Unintentional-Injury-Related Death Rates by State

Unintentional-injury-related age adjusted[a] death rate per 100,000 population by state, United States, 2014

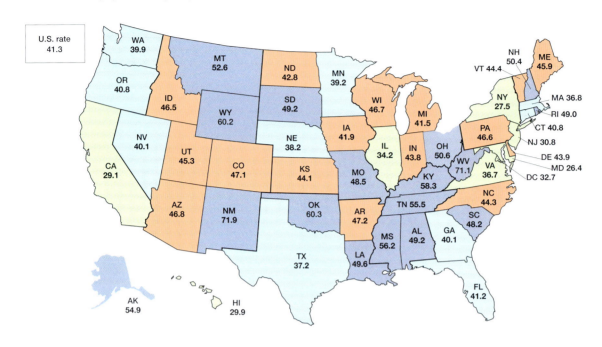

REGIONAL RATES

Region	Rate
Northeast (CT, ME, MA, NH, NJ, NY, PA, RI, VT)	35.9
South (AL, AR, DE, DC, FL, GA, KY, LA, MD, MS, NC, OK, SC, TN, TX, VA, WV)	43.3
Midwest (IL, IN, IA, KS, MI, MN, MO, NE, ND, OH, SD, WI)	43.0
West (AK, AZ, CA, CO, HI, ID, MT, NV, NM, OR, UT, WA, WY)	36.9

Legend:
- Below 36.8 — 7 states and District of Columbia (Below or at national average)
- 36.8 to 41.3 — 10 states
- 41.4 to 48.0 — 16 states (Above national average)
- Above 48.0 — 17 states

[a] Adjusted to the year 2000 standard population to remove the influence of differences in age distribution among states.
Source: National Safety Council analysis of National Center for Health Statistics–Mortality Data for 2014, as compiled from data provided by the 57 vital statistics jurisdictions through the Vital Statistics Cooperative Program. Rates are National Safety Council estimates based on data from the National Center for Health Statistics and the U.S. Census Bureau.

STATE DATA
Unintentional-Injury-Related Deaths by State

The following series of tables is a state-by-state ranking of the five leading causes of deaths due to unintentional injuries based on 2014 data. The data are classified by state of residence. The first line of each section gives the rank of unintentional-injury-related deaths among all causes of death, the total number of unintentional-injury-related deaths, and the rate of unintentional-injury-related deaths per 100,000 population in the state. The following lines list the five leading types of unintentional-injury-related deaths in the state, along with the number and rate for each type.

2014

UNITED STATES

Rank	Cause	Deaths	Rate
4	All unintentional injuries	136,053	42.7
1	Poisoning[a]	42,032	13.2
2	Motor vehicle	35,398	11.1
3	Falls	31,959	10.0
4	Choking[b]	4,816	1.5
5	Drowning[c]	3,406	1.1

ALABAMA

Rank	Cause	Deaths	Rate
5	All unintentional injuries	2,463	50.8
1	Motor vehicle	896	18.5
2	Poisoning[a]	678	14.0
3	Falls	222	4.6
4	Choking[b]	100	2.1
5	Fire, flames or smoke	85	1.8

ALASKA

Rank	Cause	Deaths	Rate
3	All unintentional injuries	379	51.4
1	Poisoning[a]	136	18.5
2	Motor vehicle	87	11.8
3	Falls	34	4.6
4	Drowning[c]	25	3.4
5	Choking[b]	14	1.9

ARIZONA

Rank	Cause	Deaths	Rate
4	All unintentional injuries	3,322	49.4
1	Poisoning[a]	1,039	15.4
2	Falls	962	14.3
3	Motor vehicle	856	12.7
4	Choking[b]	86	1.3
5	Drowning[c]	84	1.2

ARKANSAS

Rank	Cause	Deaths	Rate
5	All unintentional injuries	1,458	49.2
1	Motor vehicle	532	17.9
2	Poisoning[a]	291	9.8
3	Falls	234	7.9
4	Choking[b]	77	2.6
5	Fire, flames or smoke	57	1.9

CALIFORNIA

Rank	Cause	Deaths	Rate
6	All unintentional injuries	11,804	30.4
1	Poisoning[a]	4,139	10.7
2	Motor vehicle	3,438	8.9
3	Falls	2,318	6.0
4	Drowning[c]	399	1.0
5	Choking[b]	242	0.6

COLORADO

Rank	Cause	Deaths	Rate
3	All unintentional injuries	2,517	47.0
1	Falls	798	14.9
2	Poisoning[a]	756	14.1
3	Motor vehicle	537	10.0
4	Choking[b]	83	1.5
5	Drowning[c]	49	0.9

CONNECTICUT

Rank	Cause	Deaths	Rate
3	All unintentional injuries	1,642	45.7
1	Poisoning[a]	599	16.7
2	Falls	410	11.4
3	Motor vehicle	275	7.6
4	Choking[b]	103	2.9
5	Fire, flames or smoke	24	0.7

DELAWARE

Rank	Cause	Deaths	Rate
5	All unintentional injuries	425	45.4
1	Poisoning[a]	155	16.6
2	Motor vehicle	126	13.5
3	Falls	72	7.7
4	Choking[b]	15	1.6
5	Drowning[c]	—	—

DISTRICT OF COLUMBIA

Rank	Cause	Deaths	Rate
3	All unintentional injuries	217	32.9
1	Poisoning[a]	91	13.8
2	Falls	60	9.1
3	Motor vehicle	37	5.6
4	Fire, flames or smoke	—	—
5	Natural heat or cold	—	—

FLORIDA

Rank	Cause	Deaths	Rate
5	All unintentional injuries	9,433	47.4
1	Falls	2,819	14.2
2	Motor vehicle	2,578	13.0
3	Poisoning[a]	2,342	11.8
4	Drowning[c]	400	2.0
5	Choking[b]	274	1.4

GEORGIA

Rank	Cause	Deaths	Rate
4	All unintentional injuries	3,964	39.3
1	Motor vehicle	1,282	12.7
2	Poisoning[a]	1,097	10.9
3	Falls	710	7.0
4	Choking[b]	166	1.6
5	Drowning[c]	127	1.3

HAWAII

Rank	Cause	Deaths	Rate
4	All unintentional injuries	476	33.5
1	Falls	149	10.5
2	Poisoning[a]	118	8.3
3	Motor vehicle	108	7.6
4	Drowning[c]	38	2.7
5	Choking[b]	10	0.7

IDAHO

Rank	Cause	Deaths	Rate
4	All unintentional injuries	765	46.8
1	Falls	233	14.3
2	Motor vehicle	212	13.0
3	Poisoning[a]	165	10.1
4	Choking[b]	27	1.7
5	Drowning[c]	26	1.6

ILLINOIS

Rank	Cause	Deaths	Rate
5	All unintentional injuries	4,644	36.1
1	Poisoning[a]	1,561	12.1
2	Falls	1,070	8.3
3	Motor vehicle	1,065	8.3
4	Choking[b]	178	1.4
5	Fire, flames or smoke	109	0.8

INDIANA

Rank	Cause	Deaths	Rate
5	All unintentional injuries	2,974	45.1
1	Poisoning[a]	1,040	15.8
2	Motor vehicle	763	11.6
3	Falls	412	6.2
4	Choking[b]	122	1.8
5	Fire, flames or smoke	88	1.3

IOWA

Rank	Cause	Deaths	Rate
4	All unintentional injuries	1,517	48.8
1	Falls	554	17.8
2	Motor vehicle	340	10.9
3	Poisoning[a]	253	8.1
4	Choking[b]	59	1.9
5	Fire, flames or smoke	37	1.2

KANSAS

Rank	Cause	Deaths	Rate
4	All unintentional injuries	1,377	47.4
1	Falls	388	13.4
2	Motor vehicle	381	13.1
3	Poisoning[a]	305	10.5
4	Choking[b]	42	1.4
5	Fire, flames or smoke	31	1.1

See source and footnotes on page 177.

STATE DATA

Unintentional-Injury-Related Deaths by State (cont.)

2014

KENTUCKY

Rank	Cause	Deaths	Rate
4	All unintentional injuries	2,622	59.4
1	Poisoning[a]	1,038	23.5
2	Motor vehicle	716	16.2
3	Falls	302	6.8
4	Choking[b]	86	1.9
5	Fire, flames or smoke	71	1.6

LOUISIANA

Rank	Cause	Deaths	Rate
3	All unintentional injuries	2,344	50.4
1	Motor vehicle	804	17.3
2	Poisoning[a]	699	15.0
3	Falls	261	5.6
4	Drowning[c]	95	2.0
5	Choking[b]	79	1.7

MAINE

Rank	Cause	Deaths	Rate
4	All unintentional injuries	690	51.9
1	Poisoning[a]	204	15.3
2	Falls	165	12.4
3	Motor vehicle	143	10.8
4	Choking[b]	24	1.8
5	Fire, flames or smoke	21	1.6

MARYLAND

Rank	Cause	Deaths	Rate
5	All unintentional injuries	1,674	28.0
1	Falls	572	9.6
2	Motor vehicle	475	7.9
3	Poisoning[a]	281	4.7
4	Choking[b]	65	1.1
5	Drowning[c]	57	1.0

MASSACHUSETTS

Rank	Cause	Deaths	Rate
3	All unintentional injuries	2,692	39.9
1	Poisoning[a]	1,250	18.5
2	Falls	626	9.3
3	Motor vehicle	409	6.1
4	Choking[b]	104	1.5
5	Fire, flames or smoke	32	0.5

MICHIGAN

Rank	Cause	Deaths	Rate
5	All unintentional injuries	4,422	44.6
1	Poisoning[a]	1,447	14.6
2	Falls	1,095	11.0
3	Motor vehicle	1,006	10.2
4	Choking[b]	163	1.6
5	Mechanical suffocation	111	1.1

See source and footnotes on page 177.

MINNESOTA

Rank	Cause	Deaths	Rate
3	All unintentional injuries	2,385	43.7
1	Falls	1,026	18.8
2	Poisoning[a]	490	9.0
3	Motor vehicle	432	7.9
4	Choking[b]	80	1.5
5	Drowning[c]	50	0.9

MISSISSIPPI

Rank	Cause	Deaths	Rate
4	All unintentional injuries	1,712	57.2
1	Motor vehicle	673	22.5
2	Poisoning[a]	330	11.0
3	Falls	243	8.1
4	Choking[b]	122	4.1
5	Fire, flames or smoke	66	2.2

MISSOURI

Rank	Cause	Deaths	Rate
4	All unintentional injuries	3,110	51.3
1	Poisoning[a]	959	15.8
2	Motor vehicle	798	13.2
3	Falls	701	11.6
4	Choking[b]	113	1.9
5	Mechanical suffocation	83	1.4

MONTANA

Rank	Cause	Deaths	Rate
4	All unintentional injuries	581	56.8
1	Motor vehicle	204	19.9
2	Falls	150	14.7
3	Poisoning[a]	90	8.8
4	Choking[b]	25	2.4
5	Natural heat or cold	15	1.5

NEBRASKA

Rank	Cause	Deaths	Rate
5	All unintentional injuries	781	41.5
1	Motor vehicle	252	13.4
2	Falls	219	11.6
3	Poisoning[a]	113	6.0
4	Choking[b]	39	2.1
5	Drowning[c]	20	1.1

NEVADA

Rank	Cause	Deaths	Rate
4	All unintentional injuries	1,166	41.1
1	Poisoning[a]	475	16.7
2	Motor vehicle	316	11.1
3	Falls	201	7.1
4	Drowning[c]	34	1.2
5	Choking[b]	30	1.1

NEW HAMPSHIRE

Rank	Cause	Deaths	Rate
3	All unintentional injuries	716	54.0
1	Poisoning[a]	301	22.7
2	Falls	220	16.6
3	Motor vehicle	107	8.1
4	Choking[b]	23	1.7
5	Fire, flames or smoke	10	0.8

NEW JERSEY

Rank	Cause	Deaths	Rate
5	All unintentional injuries	2,970	33.2
1	Poisoning[a]	1,192	13.3
2	Motor vehicle	574	6.4
3	Falls	512	5.7
4	Choking[b]	156	1.7
5	Fire, flames or smoke	61	0.7

NEW MEXICO

Rank	Cause	Deaths	Rate
3	All unintentional injuries	1,534	73.6
1	Poisoning[a]	532	25.5
2	Motor vehicle	395	18.9
3	Falls	376	18.0
4	Choking[b]	38	1.8
5	Natural heat or cold	32	1.5

NEW YORK

Rank	Cause	Deaths	Rate
5	All unintentional injuries	5,945	30.1
1	Poisoning[a]	2,098	10.6
2	Falls	1,548	7.8
3	Motor vehicle	1,147	5.8
4	Choking[b]	238	1.2
5	Fire, flames or smoke	137	0.7

NORTH CAROLINA

Rank	Cause	Deaths	Rate
5	All unintentional injuries	4,558	45.8
1	Motor vehicle	1,393	14.0
2	Poisoning[a]	1,229	12.4
3	Falls	1,085	10.9
4	Choking[b]	149	1.5
5	Fire, flames or smoke	121	1.2

NORTH DAKOTA

Rank	Cause	Deaths	Rate
4	All unintentional injuries	349	47.2
1	Motor vehicle	103	13.9
2	Falls	102	13.8
3	Poisoning[a]	48	6.5
4	Choking[b]	25	3.4
5	Mechanical suffocation	—	—
5	Natural heat or cold	—	—

STATE DATA
Unintentional-Injury-Related Deaths by State (cont.)

2014

OHIO

Rank	Cause	Deaths	Rate
4	All unintentional injuries	6,178	53.3
1	Poisoning[a]	2,640	22.8
2	Falls	1,382	11.9
3	Motor vehicle	1,130	9.7
4	Choking[b]	204	1.8
5	Fire, flames or smoke	114	1.0

OKLAHOMA

Rank	Cause	Deaths	Rate
4	All unintentional injuries	2,421	62.4
1	Motor vehicle	730	18.8
2	Poisoning[a]	721	18.6
3	Falls	553	14.3
4	Fire, flames or smoke	69	1.8
4	Drowning[c]	60	1.5

OREGON

Rank	Cause	Deaths	Rate
5	All unintentional injuries	1,803	45.4
1	Falls	614	15.5
2	Poisoning[a]	435	11.0
3	Motor vehicle	378	9.5
4	Choking[b]	63	1.6
5	Drowning[c]	58	1.5

PENNSYLVANIA

Rank	Cause	Deaths	Rate
3	All unintentional injuries	6,640	51.9
1	Poisoning[a]	2,560	20.0
2	Falls	1,623	12.7
3	Motor vehicle	1,281	10.0
4	Choking[b]	288	2.3
5	Fire, flames or smoke	135	1.1

RHODE ISLAND

Rank	Cause	Deaths	Rate
3	All unintentional injuries	592	56.1
1	Poisoning[a]	251	23.8
2	Falls	190	18.0
3	Motor vehicle	62	5.9
4	Choking[b]	30	2.8
5	Drowning[c]	—	—

SOUTH CAROLINA

Rank	Cause	Deaths	Rate
4	All unintentional injuries	2,436	50.4
1	Motor vehicle	807	16.7
2	Poisoning[a]	654	13.5
3	Falls	414	8.6
4	Choking[b]	91	1.9
5	Fire, flames or smoke	83	1.7

SOUTH DAKOTA

Rank	Cause	Deaths	Rate
3	All unintentional injuries	462	54.2
1	Falls	168	19.7
2	Motor vehicle	158	18.5
3	Poisoning[a]	57	6.7
4	Mechanical suffocation	15	1.8
5	Natural heat or cold	—	—

TENNESSEE

Rank	Cause	Deaths	Rate
4	All unintentional injuries	3,781	57.7
1	Poisoning[a]	1,178	18.0
2	Motor vehicle	994	15.2
3	Falls	642	9.8
4	Choking[b]	172	2.6
5	Firearms	105	1.6

TEXAS

Rank	Cause	Deaths	Rate
4	All unintentional injuries	9,723	36.1
1	Motor vehicle	3,714	13.8
2	Poisoning[a]	2,343	8.7
3	Falls	1,846	6.8
4	Choking[b]	329	1.2
5	Drowning[c]	306	1.1

UTAH

Rank	Cause	Deaths	Rate
3	All unintentional injuries	1,167	39.7
1	Poisoning[a]	448	15.2
2	Motor vehicle	260	8.8
3	Falls	206	7.0
4	Choking[b]	35	1.2
5	Drowning[c]	33	1.1

VERMONT

Rank	Cause	Deaths	Rate
4	All unintentional injuries	322	51.4
1	Falls	154	24.6
2	Poisoning[a]	67	10.7
3	Motor vehicle	46	7.3
4	Choking[b]	13	2.1
5	Drowning[c]	—	—

VIRGINIA

Rank	Cause	Deaths	Rate
4	All unintentional injuries	3,147	37.8
1	Poisoning[a]	824	9.9
2	Falls	790	9.5
3	Motor vehicle	787	9.5
4	Choking[b]	155	1.9
5	Drowning[c]	77	0.9

WASHINGTON

Rank	Cause	Deaths	Rate
4	All unintentional injuries	2,997	42.4
1	Falls	974	13.8
2	Poisoning[a]	860	12.2
3	Motor vehicle	578	8.2
4	Choking[b]	98	1.4
5	Drowning[c]	87	1.2

WEST VIRGINIA

Rank	Cause	Deaths	Rate
4	All unintentional injuries	1,380	74.6
1	Poisoning[a]	593	32.0
2	Motor vehicle	324	17.5
3	Falls	275	14.9
4	Choking[b]	42	2.3
5	Fire, flames or smoke	22	1.2

WISCONSIN

Rank	Cause	Deaths	Rate
3	All unintentional injuries	3,015	52.4
1	Falls	1,226	21.3
2	Poisoning[a]	761	13.2
3	Motor vehicle	565	9.8
4	Choking[b]	75	1.3
5	Mechanical suffocation	46	0.8

WYOMING

Rank	Cause	Deaths	Rate
3	All unintentional injuries	361	61.8
1	Motor vehicle	124	21.2
2	Poisoning[a]	99	16.9
3	Falls	53	9.1
4	Drowning[c]	12	2.1
5	Natural heat or cold	—	—

Source: National Safety Council analysis of National Center for Health Statistics (NCHS—Mortality Data for 2014, as compiled from data provided by the 57 vital statistics jurisdictions through the Vital Statistics Cooperative Program. Rates are National Safety Council estimates based on data from NCHS and the U.S. Census Bureau. Dashes (—) indicate data values less than 10 as per NCHS publication guidelines.

[a]Solid, liquid, gas, and vapor poisoning.
[b]Inhalation or ingestion of food or other objects.
[c]Excludes transport drownings.

STATE DATA
Unintentional-Injury-Related Deaths by State and Event

Unintentional-injury-related deaths by state of occurrence and type of event, United States, 2014

State	Population (000)	Total[a]	Poisoning	Motor vehicle[b]	Falls	Choking[c]	Drowning[d]	Fire, flames, or smoke	Mechanical suffocation
Total U.S.	318,857	136,053	42,032	35,398	31,959	4,816	3,406	2,701	1,764
Alabama	4,849	2,394	662	875	197	98	78	84	18
Alaska	737	377	134	87	31	15	27	—	—
Arizona	6,731	3,309	1,048	809	966	86	92	33	33
Arkansas	2,966	1,386	294	511	206	73	39	41	16
California	38,803	11,778	4,162	3,422	2,294	240	395	136	91
Colorado	5,356	2,606	783	551	815	82	49	21	33
Connecticut	3,597	1,620	603	258	403	108	18	24	11
Delaware	936	442	163	127	74	16	—	—	—
District of Columbia	659	287	111	43	87	—	—	10	—
Florida	19,893	9,627	2,365	2,632	2,889	275	451	112	136
Georgia	10,097	3,967	1,098	1,263	715	167	121	143	66
Hawaii	1,420	521	122	113	152	10	69	—	—
Idaho	1,634	757	152	215	238	25	30	—	—
Illinois	12,881	4,355	1,535	962	974	171	88	105	67
Indiana	6,597	2,937	1,024	732	411	124	76	85	72
Iowa	3,107	1,509	264	339	536	58	25	39	17
Kansas	2,904	1,351	298	399	360	47	22	33	16
Kentucky	4,413	2,542	1,046	683	273	83	36	65	27
Louisiana	4,650	2,393	711	817	279	87	88	70	76
Maine	1,330	707	201	159	163	25	20	20	—
Maryland	5,976	1,614	231	485	560	63	60	50	12
Massachusetts	6,745	2,637	1,220	380	620	107	31	32	11
Michigan	9,910	4,319	1,427	977	1,054	162	75	108	111
Minnesota	5,457	2,363	496	420	1,025	76	45	41	46
Mississippi	2,994	1,631	307	662	226	118	42	58	36
Missouri	6,064	3,296	982	871	772	112	64	70	87
Montana	1,024	601	86	211	153	26	13	11	—
Nebraska	1,882	775	109	257	222	43	15	16	14
Nevada	2,839	1,227	496	327	229	30	33	15	20
New Hampshire	1,327	727	306	99	230	26	14	—	—
New Jersey	8,938	2,880	1,164	566	488	152	41	56	29
New Mexico	2,086	1,525	522	427	348	35	27	23	15
New York	19,746	5,769	2,096	1,077	1,487	231	94	137	52
North Carolina	9,944	4,542	1,214	1,386	1,093	149	88	125	34
North Dakota	739	445	65	145	124	30	—	—	—
Ohio	11,594	6,171	2,661	1,127	1,361	202	79	114	58
Oklahoma	3,878	2,381	714	719	546	51	59	67	25
Oregon	3,970	1,816	429	393	624	61	56	40	28
Pennsylvania	12,787	6,700	2,596	1,284	1,640	291	91	142	40
Rhode Island	1,055	646	267	72	216	28	—	—	—
South Carolina	4,832	2,407	645	829	400	91	74	58	46
South Dakota	853	490	53	166	193	—	—	—	15
Tennessee	6,549	4,111	1,194	1,109	737	188	89	112	65
Texas	26,957	9,815	2,339	3,769	1,875	332	307	166	120
Utah	2,943	1,226	455	285	218	37	32	—	11
Vermont	627	314	64	42	155	11	—	—	—
Virginia	8,326	3,070	805	758	781	144	67	69	43
Washington	7,062	2,927	857	527	965	103	80	40	44
West Virginia	1,850	1,390	594	332	282	40	13	21	13
Wisconsin	5,758	3,013	764	562	1,228	73	47	43	44
Wyoming	584	360	98	137	44	—	—	—	—

See source and footnotes on page 179.

178 ■ NATIONAL SAFETY COUNCIL® INJURY FACTS® 2017 EDITION

STATE DATA
Unintentional-Injury-Related Deaths by State and Event (cont.)

Unintentional-injury-related deaths by state of occurrence and type of event, United States, 2014

State	Natural heat or cold	Struck by or against	Machinery	Firearms	Rail transportation	Air transportation	Water transportation	Electric current	All other incidents
Total U.S.	1,174	899	605	586	455	412	393	257	9,196
Alabama	17	19	13	29	—	—	—	—	281
Alaska	—	—	—	—	—	—	14	—	30
Arizona	59	—	—	—	—	17	—	—	133
Arkansas	—	20	11	—	—	—	—	—	136
California	60	56	34	23	94	38	27	21	685
Colorado	27	12	—	—	—	32	13	—	173
Connecticut	12	—	—	—	—	—	—	—	166
Delaware	—	—	—	—	—	—	—	—	34
District of Columbia	—	—	—	—	—	—	—	—	15
Florida	27	32	19	28	20	30	36	40	535
Georgia	43	30	25	28	15	19	—	—	219
Hawaii	—	—	—	—	—	—	—	—	23
Idaho	12	—	—	—	—	—	—	—	41
Illinois	56	32	18	—	19	—	15	14	283
Indiana	36	22	—	16	—	—	—	—	308
Iowa	13	15	18	—	—	—	—	—	166
Kansas	11	13	12	—	—	—	—	—	111
Kentucky	17	19	16	13	—	—	—	—	242
Louisiana	14	19	11	19	10	11	13	—	162
Maine	—	—	—	—	—	—	—	—	91
Maryland	29	12	—	—	—	—	—	—	91
Massachusetts	—	11	—	28	—	—	—	—	173
Michigan	38	32	13	—	—	—	13	11	278
Minnesota	29	16	14	—	—	—	—	—	134
Mississippi	19	17	—	15	—	—	—	—	106
Missouri	30	25	24	15	—	—	13	—	216
Montana	15	—	—	—	—	—	—	—	62
Nebraska	—	—	—	—	—	—	—	—	65
Nevada	12	—	—	—	—	—	—	—	39
New Hampshire	—	—	—	—	—	—	—	—	21
New Jersey	16	15	—	—	—	—	—	—	333
New Mexico	35	—	—	—	—	14	—	—	59
New York	46	38	20	—	41	16	20	—	398
North Carolina	30	47	25	38	18	—	18	—	266
North Dakota	—	—	—	—	—	—	—	—	35
Ohio	45	31	26	18	12	14	13	—	403
Oklahoma	20	—	18	14	—	—	—	—	131
Oregon	17	16	—	—	13	—	—	—	114
Pennsylvania	55	48	24	15	13	—	12	10	437
Rhode Island	—	—	—	—	—	—	—	—	37
South Carolina	33	14	12	13	—	—	10	—	166
South Dakota	10	—	—	—	—	—	—	—	20
Tennessee	32	27	20	118	—	—	—	—	390
Texas	55	81	51	39	40	26	27	42	546
Utah	12	—	10	—	—	13	—	—	124
Vermont	—	—	—	—	—	—	—	—	15
Virginia	42	20	13	12	—	13	12	—	277
Washington	19	21	15	—	—	13	15	—	214
West Virginia	—	15	—	—	—	—	—	—	50
Wisconsin	40	24	22	—	12	—	—	—	134
Wyoming	—	—	—	—	—	—	—	—	28

Source: National Safety Council analysis of National Center for Heatlh Statistics (NCHS)—Mortality Data for 2014, as compiled from data provided by the 57 vital statistics jurisdictions through the Vital Statistics Cooperative Program. Dashes (—) indicate data values less than 10 as per NCHS publication guidelines.
[a]Deaths are by place of occurrence and exclude nonresident aliens.
[b]See page 184 for motor-vehicle deaths by place of residence.
[c]Suffocation by inhalation or ingestion of food or object obstructing breathing.
[d]Excludes water transport drownings.

STATE DATA
Unintentional-Injury Trends by State

Nationwide, from 2011 to 2014, unintentional-injury-related deaths increased by 8% and the death rate increased by 5%. By state, the greatest decrease in the number of unintentional-injury-related deaths and death rates occurred in Hawaii (-8% and -11%, respectively). The greatest increase in unintentional-injury-related deaths and death rates occurred in New Hampshire (+29% for each).

The table below shows the trend in unintentional-injury-related deaths and death rates by state over the most recent four years for which data are available.

Unintentional-injury-related deaths by state of residence, United States, 2011-2014

State	Deaths[a] 2014[b]	2013	2012	2011	Deaths per 100,000 population 2014[b]	2013	2012	2011
Total U.S.	136,053	130,557	127,792	126,438	42.7	41.3	40.7	40.6
Alabama	2,463	2,329	2,283	2,662	50.8	48.2	47.4	55.4
Alaska	379	353	368	385	51.4	48.0	50.4	53.2
Arizona	3,322	3,349	3,029	3,096	49.4	50.5	46.2	47.9
Arkansas	1,458	1,373	1,521	1,510	49.2	46.4	51.6	51.4
California	11,804	11,538	10,906	10,824	30.4	30.1	28.7	28.7
Colorado	2,517	2,422	2,403	2,330	47.0	46.0	46.3	45.5
Connecticut	1,642	1,582	1,392	1,339	45.7	44.0	38.8	37.3
Delaware	425	412	374	338	45.4	44.5	40.8	37.2
District of Columbia	217	216	194	185	32.9	33.4	30.6	29.9
Florida	9,433	8,736	8,770	8,901	47.4	44.7	45.4	46.6
Georgia	3,964	3,727	3,731	3,785	39.3	37.3	37.6	38.6
Hawaii	476	467	458	517	33.5	33.3	32.9	37.5
Idaho	765	776	699	710	46.8	48.1	43.8	44.8
Illinois	4,644	4,511	4,488	4,166	36.1	35.0	34.9	32.4
Indiana	2,974	2,898	2,776	2,699	45.1	44.1	42.5	41.4
Iowa	1,517	1,422	1,369	1,369	48.8	46.0	44.5	44.7
Kansas	1,377	1,359	1,319	1,333	47.4	47.0	45.7	46.5
Kentucky	2,622	2,513	2,741	2,608	59.4	57.2	62.6	59.7
Louisiana	2,344	2,333	2,362	2,091	50.4	50.4	51.3	45.7
Maine	690	644	602	574	51.9	48.5	45.3	43.2
Maryland	1,674	1,732	1,696	1,569	28.0	29.2	28.8	26.9
Massachusetts	2,692	2,393	2,195	2,224	39.9	35.8	33.0	33.7
Michigan	4,422	4,225	3,805	3,951	44.6	42.7	38.5	40.0
Minnesota	2,385	2,405	2,301	2,319	43.7	44.4	42.8	43.4
Mississippi	1,712	1,692	1,627	1,724	57.2	56.6	54.5	57.9
Missouri	3,110	2,981	3,002	3,169	51.3	49.3	49.8	52.7
Montana	581	623	572	609	56.8	61.4	56.9	61.0
Nebraska	781	703	792	678	41.5	37.6	42.7	36.8
Nevada	1,166	1,184	1,177	1,155	41.1	42.4	42.7	42.5
New Hampshire	716	619	573	553	54.0	46.8	43.4	42.0
New Jersey	2,970	3,028	2,990	2,685	33.2	34.0	33.7	30.4
New Mexico	1,534	1,245	1,351	1,336	73.6	59.7	64.8	64.3
New York	5,945	5,927	5,786	5,537	30.1	30.2	29.6	28.4
North Carolina	4,558	4,324	4,281	4,297	45.8	43.9	43.9	44.5
North Dakota	349	326	318	298	47.2	45.1	45.3	43.5
Ohio	6,178	5,497	5,420	5,275	53.3	47.5	46.9	45.7
Oklahoma	2,421	2,474	2,388	2,261	62.4	64.3	62.6	59.7
Oregon	1,803	1,755	1,709	1,722	45.4	44.7	43.8	44.5
Pennsylvania	6,640	6,359	6,334	6,216	51.9	49.8	49.6	48.8
Rhode Island	592	537	525	541	56.1	51.1	50.0	51.5
South Carolina	2,436	2,287	2,336	2,285	50.4	47.9	49.5	48.9
South Dakota	462	425	426	411	54.2	50.3	51.1	49.9
Tennessee	3,781	3,540	3,513	3,485	57.7	54.5	54.4	54.5
Texas	9,723	9,395	9,313	9,410	36.1	35.5	35.7	36.7
Utah	1,167	1,103	1,097	1,058	39.7	38.0	38.4	37.6
Vermont	322	352	333	301	51.4	56.2	53.2	48.1
Virginia	3,147	2,951	2,883	2,809	37.8	35.7	35.2	34.7
Washington	2,997	2,826	2,760	2,709	42.4	40.5	40.0	39.7
West Virginia	1,380	1,395	1,371	1,432	74.6	75.2	73.8	77.2
Wisconsin	3,015	2,969	2,825	2,680	52.4	51.7	49.3	46.9
Wyoming	361	325	308	317	61.8	55.8	53.4	55.9

Source: Deaths are from the National Center for Health Statistics (NCHS)—Mortality Data for 2011-2014, as compiled from data provided by the 57 vital statistics jurisdictions through the Vital Statistics Cooperative Program. Rates are National Safety Council estimates based on data from NCHS and the U.S. Census Bureau. See Technical Appendix for comparability.
[a]Deaths for each state are by state of residence and exclude nonresident aliens.
[b]Latest official figures.

STATE DATA
Fatal Occupational Injuries by State

In general, states with the largest number of people employed have the largest number of work-related fatalities. The four largest states – California, Texas, Florida, and New York – accounted for 29% of the total 2015 work-related fatalities in the United States. Each state's industry mix, geographic features, age of population, and other characteristics of the workforce must be considered when evaluating state fatality profiles. Overall, the six leading events or exposures accounted for all but 12 of the 4,836 total occupational fatalities in all states in 2015.

Fatal occupational injuries by state and event or exposure, United States, 2015

State	Total fatal injuries[a] Number	Total fatal injuries[a] Rate[e]	Transportation incidents[c]	Falls, slips or trips	Contact with objects and equipment	Violence and other injuries by persons or animals[d]	Exposure to harmful substances or environments	Fire and explostions
Total	4,836	3.4	2,054	800	722	703	424	121
Alabama	70	3.7	37	10	9	5	4	5
Alaska	14	4.1	5	—	6	—	—	—
Arizona	69	2.4	29	10	8	15	6	1
Arkansas	74	5.8	41	10	9	9	3	1
California	388	2.2	150	77	39	77	33	10
Colorado	75	2.9	34	20	9	8	—	3
Connecticut	44	2.6	14	7	7	10	6	—
Delaware	8	1.9	3	—	—	3	—	—
District of Columbia	8	2.4	—	3	1	3	—	—
Florida	272	3.1	127	52	28	39	21	—
Georgia	180	4.3	68	37	25	24	20	6
Hawaii	18	2.6	6	3	—	5	3	—
Idaho	36	4.8	22	—	6	—	4	—
Illinois	172	2.9	59	33	29	27	19	5
Indiana	115	3.9	55	9	18	16	14	3
Iowa	60	3.9	19	16	17	1	—	4
Kansas	60	4.4	37	7	4	8	—	1
Kentucky	99	5.5	37	9	25	15	11	—
Louisiana	112	5.8	47	14	16	18	13	—
Maine	15	2.5	5	—	3	3	—	—
Maryland	69	2.4	26	9	7	16	10	—
Massachusetts	69	2.1	26	17	6	10	8	2
Michigan	134	3.1	45	19	22	35	10	3
Minnesota	74	2.7	31	13	17	7	3	—
Mississippi	77	6.8	37	10	13	11	6	—
Missouri	117	4.3	60	14	13	13	11	6
Montana	36	7.5	16	5	10	3	—	—
Nebraska	50	5.4	23	4	11	6	—	4
Nevada	44	3.5	21	7	6	4	6	—
New Hampshire	18	2.7	—	—	4	4	6	—
New Jersey	97	2.3	37	24	11	18	7	—
New Mexico	35	4.1	24	3	—	4	—	—
New York	236	2.7	86	45	35	43	17	9
North Carolina	150	3.4	51	26	33	24	13	3
North Dakota	47	12.5	28	—	7	4	—	3
Ohio	202	3.9	92	29	29	27	23	2
Oklahoma	91	5.5	44	11	19	7	7	3
Oregon	44	2.6	22	5	8	5	—	2
Pennsylvania	173	3.0	70	36	25	22	16	4
Rhode Island	6	1.2	—	—	—	—	—	—
South Carolina	117	5.6	54	16	17	17	10	3
South Dakota	21	4.9	9	3	4	—	—	3
Tennessee	112	3.7	47	17	21	15	12	—
Texas	527	4.5	238	86	72	76	41	13
Utah	42	3.2	21	8	7	—	4	—
Vermont	9	2.9	—	1	2	1	3	—
Virginia	106	2.8	36	20	20	13	15	—
Washington	70	2.1	29	21	10	7	3	—
West Virginia	35	5.0	17	4	8	—	4	—
Wisconsin	104	3.6	46	17	18	11	11	—
Wyoming	34	12.0	17	5	3	4	3	—

Source: Bureau of Labor Statistics. National Census of Fatal Occupational Injuries in 2015 accessed December 17, 2016, from http://www.bls.gov/iif
Note: Dashes (—) indicate no data or data that do not meet publication criteria.
[a] State totals include other events and exposures, such as bodily reaction, in addition to those shown separately.
[b] Based on the BLS Occupational Injury and Illness Classification System (OIICS) 2.01, implemented for 2011 data forward.
[c] Includes highway, nonhighway, air, water, and rail fatal injuries, and fatal injuries resulting from being struck by a vehicle.
[d] Includes violence by persons, self-inflicted injuries, and attacks by animals.
[e] Fatal injury rates are per 100,000 full-time equivalent workers.

STATE DATA

Nonfatal Occupational Incidence Rates by State

Nonfatal occupational injury and illness rates[a] by state, private industry, 2014

State	Total recordable cases	Cases with days away from work[b]	Cases with job transfer or restriction	Other recordable cases
Private industry[c]	**3.2**	**1.0**	**0.7**	**1.5**
Alabama	2.9	0.8	0.7	1.4
Alaska	3.9	1.6	0.5	1.9
Arizona	3.0	0.8	0.7	1.5
Arkansas	2.6	0.6	0.6	1.3
California	3.4	1.0	1.0	1.3
Colorado	—	—	—	—
Connecticut	3.5	1.3	0.7	1.5
Delaware	2.6	0.9	0.4	1.3
District of Columbia	1.6	0.7	0.1	0.8
Florida	—	—	—	—
Georgia	2.9	0.8	0.6	1.4
Hawaii	3.7	2.0	0.3	1.5
Idaho	—	—	—	—
Illinois	2.8	1.0	0.6	1.2
Indiana	3.8	0.8	1.1	1.9
Iowa	3.9	1.0	1.0	1.9
Kansas	3.4	0.9	0.8	1.7
Kentucky	3.7	1.0	0.9	1.8
Louisiana	2.0	0.7	0.3	1.0
Maine	5.3	1.3	1.5	2.4
Maryland	3.1	1.2	0.4	1.4
Massachusetts	2.7	1.2	0.3	1.2
Michigan	3.6	0.9	0.8	1.8
Minnesota	3.6	1.0	0.8	1.8
Mississippi	—	—	—	—
Missouri	3.2	0.8	0.8	1.5
Montana	4.5	1.4	0.6	2.4
Nebraska	3.5	1.0	0.8	1.7
Nevada	4.0	1.2	1.1	1.8
New Hampshire	—	—	—	—
New Jersey	2.9	1.2	0.5	1.2
New Mexico	3.2	1.0	0.6	1.6
New York	2.5	1.2	0.1	1.1
North Carolina	2.7	0.7	0.7	1.3
North Dakota	—	—	—	—
Ohio	2.9	0.8	0.7	1.4
Oklahoma	—	—	—	—
Oregon	3.9	1.5	0.8	1.7
Pennsylvania	3.7	1.1	0.8	1.8
Rhode Island	—	—	—	—
South Carolina	2.8	0.8	0.7	1.2
South Dakota	—	—	—	—
Tennessee	3.2	0.8	0.8	1.6
Texas	2.4	0.7	0.7	1.0
Utah	3.2	0.7	0.7	1.9
Vermont	5.0	1.6	0.9	2.6
Virginia	2.7	0.9	0.6	1.3
Washington	4.6	1.5	1.0	2.0
West Virginia	4.0	1.5	0.5	2.0
Wisconsin	3.9	1.1	0.9	1.9
Wyoming	3.5	1.3	0.4	1.8

Source: Bureau of Labor Statistics, U.S. Department of Labor.
Note: Because of rounding, components may not add to totals. Dashes (—) indicate data not available.
[a]Incidence rates represent the number of injuries and illnesses per 100 full-time workers using 200,000 hours as the equivalent.
[b]Days-away-from-work cases include those that result in days away from work with or without job transfer or restriction.
[c]Data cover all 50 states.

STATE DATA

Nonfatal Occupational Incidence Rates by State (cont.)

Nonfatal occupational injury and illness incidence rates[a] for total recordable cases by state, private industry, 2014

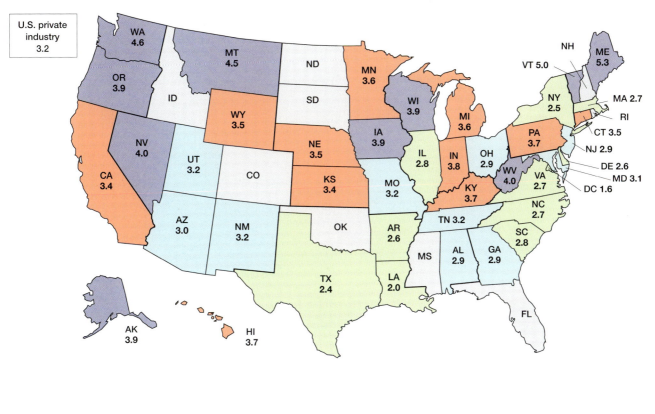

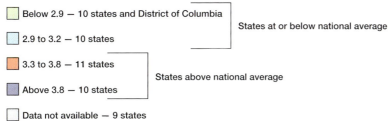

[a] Incidence rates represent the number of injuries and illnesses per 100 full-time workers using 200,000 hours as the equivalent.

INJURY FACTS® 2017 EDITION   NATIONAL SAFETY COUNCIL® ■ 183

STATE DATA
Motor-Vehicle Deaths by State

Motor-vehicle deaths by state, United States, 2014-2015

State	Motor-vehicle traffic deaths (Place of incident) Number 2015[c]	Number 2014	Mileage rate[b] 2015	Mileage rate[b] 2014	Total motor-vehicle deaths[a] (Place of residence) Number 2015[c]	Number 2014	Population rate[b] 2015	Population rate[b] 2014
Total U.S.	35,092	32,744	1.1	1.1	37,757	35,398	11.7	11.1
Alabama	849	820	1.2	1.2	962	896	19.8	18.5
Alaska	65	73	1.3	1.5	74	87	10.0	11.8
Arizona	893	773	1.4	1.2	920	856	13.5	12.7
Arkansas	531	470	1.5	1.4	593	532	19.9	17.9
California	3,176	3,102	0.9	0.9	3,721	3,438	9.5	8.9
Colorado	546	488	1.1	1.0	587	537	10.8	10.0
Connecticut	266	248	0.8	0.8	286	275	8.0	7.6
Delaware	126	124	1.3	1.3	129	126	13.6	13.5
District of Columbia	23	23	0.6	0.7	43	37	6.4	5.6
Florida	2,939	2,494	1.4	1.2	2,983	2,578	14.7	13.0
Georgia	1,430	1,164	1.2	1.0	1,471	1,282	14.4	12.7
Hawaii	94	95	0.9	0.9	105	108	7.3	7.6
Idaho	216	186	1.3	1.2	243	212	14.7	13.0
Illinois	998	924	0.9	0.9	1,108	1,065	8.6	8.3
Indiana	821	745	1.0	0.9	854	763	12.9	11.6
Iowa	320	322	1.0	1.0	352	340	11.3	10.9
Kansas	355	385	1.1	1.3	398	381	13.7	13.1
Kentucky	761	672	1.5	1.4	831	716	18.8	16.2
Louisiana	726	740	1.5	1.5	805	804	17.2	17.3
Maine	156	131	1.1	0.9	151	143	11.4	10.8
Maryland	513	442	0.9	0.8	518	475	8.6	7.9
Massachusetts	306	354	0.5	0.6	393	409	5.8	6.1
Michigan	963	901	1.0	0.9	880	1,006	8.9	10.2
Minnesota	411	361	0.7	0.6	476	432	8.7	7.9
Mississippi	677	607	1.7	1.5	769	673	25.7	22.5
Missouri	869	766	1.2	1.1	932	798	15.3	13.2
Montana	224	192	1.8	1.6	220	204	21.3	19.9
Nebraska	246	225	1.2	1.1	268	252	14.1	13.4
Nevada	325	291	1.2	1.2	365	316	12.6	11.1
New Hampshire	114	95	0.8	0.7	106	107	8.0	8.1
New Jersey	562	556	0.7	0.7	591	574	6.6	6.4
New Mexico	298	386	1.1	1.5	342	395	16.4	18.9
New York	1,121	1,041	0.8	0.8	1,189	1,147	6.0	5.8
North Carolina	1,379	1,284	1.2	1.2	1,518	1,393	15.1	14.0
North Dakota	131	135	1.2	1.3	137	103	18.1	13.9
Ohio	1,110	1,006	1.0	0.9	1,257	1,130	10.8	9.7
Oklahoma	643	669	1.3	1.4	673	730	17.2	18.8
Oregon	447	357	1.2	1.0	501	378	12.4	9.5
Pennsylvania	1,200	1,195	1.2	1.2	1,296	1,281	10.1	10.0
Rhode Island	45	51	0.6	0.7	55	62	5.2	5.9
South Carolina	977	823	1.9	1.6	985	807	20.1	16.7
South Dakota	133	136	1.4	1.5	143	158	16.7	18.5
Tennessee	958	963	1.3	1.3	988	994	15.0	15.2
Texas	3,516	3,536	1.4	1.5	3,722	3,714	13.5	13.8
Utah	276	256	1.0	0.9	282	260	9.4	8.8
Vermont	57	44	0.8	0.6	54	46	8.6	7.3
Virginia	753	703	0.9	0.9	791	787	9.4	9.5
Washington	568	462	0.9	0.8	641	578	8.9	8.2
West Virginia	268	272	1.4	1.4	304	324	16.5	17.5
Wisconsin	566	506	0.9	0.8	611	565	10.6	9.8
Wyoming	145	150	1.5	1.6	134	124	22.9	21.2

Source: 2014 and 2015 motor vehicle traffic deaths are from the National Highway Traffic Safety Administration; 2014 and 2015 total motor vehicle deaths are from the National Center for Health Statistics (also see page 178).
[a] Includes both traffic and nontraffic motor vehicle deaths. See definitions of motor vehicle traffic and nontraffic incidents on page 206.
[b] The mileage death rate is deaths per 100,000,000 vehicle miles; the population death rate is deaths per 100,000 population. Death rates are National Safety Council estimates.
[c] Latest year available. See Technical Appendix for comparability.

STATE DATA
Motor-Vehicle Deaths by State (cont.)

Mileage death rates, 2015
Motor-vehicle traffic deaths per 100,000,000 vehicle miles

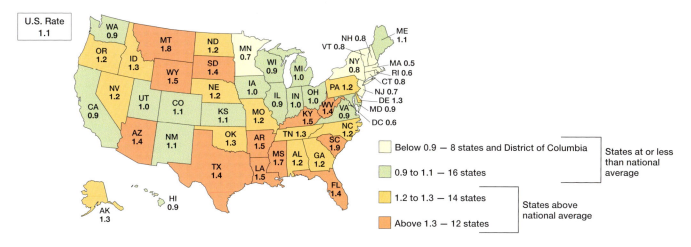

Registration death rates, 2015
Motor-vehicle traffic deaths per 10,000 motor vehicles

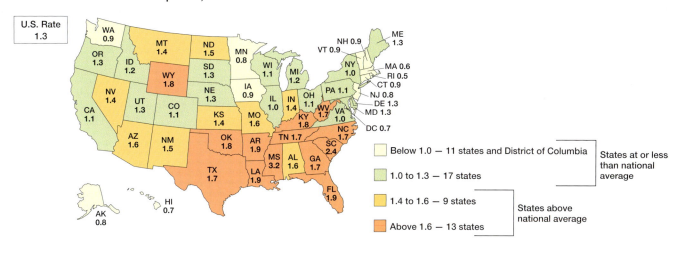

Population death rates, 2015
Motor-vehicle traffic deaths per 100,000 population

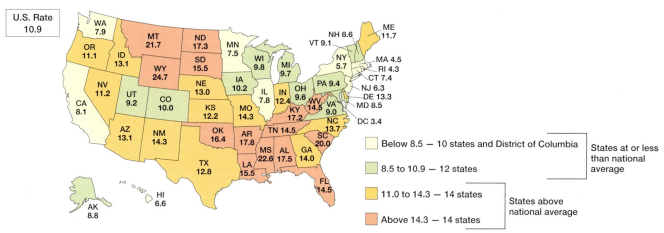

Source: Rates estimated by National Safety Council based on data from state traffic authorities, National Center for Health Statistics, Federal Highway Administration, and the U.S. Census Bureau.

International Data

International Data Highlights

Deaths and death rates by country — pgs. 189–193

Occupational deaths by country — pgs. 194–195

Occupational injuries by country — pgs. 196–197

193,000 Unintentional Poisoning Deaths in 2012!

Unintentional poisoning is also a leading cause of death in the world. In 2012, an estimated 193,000 deaths were caused by unintentional poisonings. In lower- and middle-income countries, pesticides, kerosene, household chemicals, carbon monoxide, and drugs are common poisoning causes. In high-income countries, drugs, carbon monoxide, and personal care and cleaning products are the most frequent substances involved in poisonings. In contrast to U.S. trends that have seen sharp increases in poisoning deaths, the global mortality rate attributed to unintentional poisonings decreased by 34% between 2000 and 2012. The WHO South-East and European regions drove the decrease in poisoning deaths worldwide.

 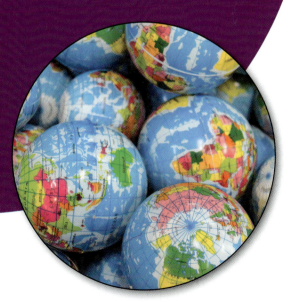

INTERNATIONAL

International Injuries and Fatalities
Introduction

■ *WHO Reports Number of Road Traffic Deaths Plateaued Since 2007.*

This section on international injury and fatalities includes data for occupational and motor-vehicle injuries, as well as general unintentional injury and mortality. The two primary data sources used in this section are the World Health Organization (WHO) and the International Labour Organization.

The WHO currently ranks road traffic injuries as the ninth leading cause of death in the world while fall deaths ranks 21st. However, by 2030 the WHO projects that road traffic injury deaths will be the 7th leading cause of death and falls will be the 17th leading cause of death in the world.

According to the WHO, around 1.25 million people died from road traffic injuries in 2013 and 20 to 50 million sustained non-fatal injuries. There are several evidence-based measures recommended to help reduce unintentional injury deaths in the world. Top measures recommended to reduce road traffic crashes include:
- Setting and enforcing laws on speeding
- Setting and enforcing laws on drinking and driving
- Setting and enforcing laws on motorcycle helmets
- Setting and enforcing laws on seat-belts
- Setting and enforcing laws on child restraint

Top measures recommended to reduce fall deaths include:
- Setting and enforcing laws requiring window guards for tall buildings
- Redesigning furniture and other products
- Establishing standards for playground equipment

Unintentional poisoning is also a leading cause of death in the world. In 2012, an estimated 193,000 deaths were caused by unintentional poisonings. In lower- and middle-income countries, pesticides, kerosene, household chemicals, carbon monoxide and drugs are common poisoning causes. In high-income countries, drugs, carbon monoxide, and personal care and cleaning products are the most frequent substances involved in poisonings. In contrast to U.S. trends that have seen sharp increases in poisoning deaths, the global mortality rate attributed to unintentional poisonings decreased by 34% between 2000 and 2012. The WHO South-East and European regions drove the decrease in poisoning deaths worldwide.

Another global unintentional injury issue that is often overlooked is drowning. A recent WHO report, *Global report on drowning: preventing a leading killer*, reports that drowning is the third most prevalent unintentional injury death event after motor vehicle and fall deaths. The WHO estimates about 372,000 drowning deaths occur every year. More than 90% of these drowning deaths take place in low- and middle-income countries.

Drowning is in the top 10 leading causes of death among children and young people in every region of the world. Over half of the drowning deaths occur among individuals under the age of 25, with children under the age of 5 at greatest risk.

Data limitations are making it hard to estimate the full extent of the drowning problem. Data collection in many low- and middle- income countries is limited. In addition, current injury coding standards exclude deaths from flood disasters and water transport incidents. Data on non-fatal drowning is often not collected at all in many parts of the developing world.

The WHO identified several risk factors associated with drowning deaths. These risk factors include:
- Lack of physical barriers controlling between people and water
- Lack of or inadequate supervision of young children
- Uncovered or unprotected water supplies and lack of safe water crossings
- Lack of water safety awareness and risky behavior around water
- Travelling on water, especially on overcrowded or poorly maintained vessels
- Flood disasters, whether from extreme rainfall, storm surges, tsunamis or cyclones.

The charts on pages 189-193 provide the unintentional-injury-related deaths and death rates for 52 countries. The most current year of mortality data available is reported for motor vehicle, poisonings, falls, drowning, and overall unintentional-injury-related deaths.

The International Labour Organization has implemented a new occupational injury database. Because of the database change, comparisons prior to 2009 are not recommended. The charts on pages 194 and 195 detail the occupational deaths and death rates by country for the past five years. Because of the wide range of recordkeeping standards used in the world, countries with similar recordkeeping practices are grouped together. Comparison among countries is not recommended even within these recordkeeping groupings.

The charts on pages 196 and 197 detail occupational injuries and injury rates by country. Because of differences in injury definitions among countries, comparisons between countries is not recommended.

Source: World Health Organization. (2016). World Health Statistics 2016, Monitoring Health for the Sustainable Development Goals. Geneva: Author. Downloaded from
http://www.who.int/gho/publications/world_health_statistics/en/ on October 20, 2016.
World Health Organization. (2015). Global Status Report on Road Safety 2015. Geneva: Author: Downloaded from: http://www.who.int/violence_injury_prevention/road_safety_status/2015/en/ on November 9, 2015.
World Health Organization. (2014). Global report on drowning: preventing a leading killer. Downloaded from: http://www.who.int/violence_injury_prevention/publications/drowning_global_report/Final_report_full_web.pdf?ua=1 on December 8, 2014.
World Health Organization. (2014). Injuries and violence the facts 2014. Geneva: Author: Downloaded from:
http://www.who.int/violence_injury_prevention/media/news/2015/Injury_violence_facts_2014/en/ on November. 9, 2015.

INTERNATIONAL

International Unintentional-Injury-Related Deaths and Death Rates

The term "Accidents and Adverse Effects" used in the International Classification of Diseases (ICD) system refers to all causes of unintentional-injury-related deaths, including transportation incidents; unintentional poisonings; falls; fires; burns; natural and environmental factors; drowning; suffocation; medical and surgical complications and misadventures; and other causes, such as those involving machinery, firearms, or electric current. The data presented in the table below are identified by codes V01-X59 and Y85-Y86 of the 10th revision of ICD (except where noted). Worldwide unintentional-injury-related deaths were a projected 3,864,259 in 2015, resulting in a projected death rate of 53 per 100,000 population.

The table below and those on pages 190 through 193 show the number of injury-related deaths and the unadjusted death rates for 52 countries for which mortality data and population estimates were obtained.

Unintentional-injury-related deaths and death rates by age group, latest year available

Country	Year	Deaths Total	% male	Deaths per 100,000 population[a] All ages	0 to 4	5 to 14	15 to 24	25 to 44	45 to 64	65 or older
Argentina	2013	11,395	72%	26.7	14.0	5.8	31.6	25.2	28.6	61.4
Austria	2014	2,444	55%	28.6	2.7	1.2	8.8	7.6	16.8	111.3
Belarus[b]	2011	13,498	79%	142.5	17.3	9.3	62.5	146.7	236.9	163.7
Brazil	2013	72,611	77%	36.1	13.7	7.3	35.8	36.6	40.7	111.0
Canada	2011	10,723	58%	31.5	4.8	2.8	17.2	18.0	21.6	111.7
Chile	2013	5,091	73%	29.6	10.2	4.2	17.9	22.9	35.0	107.0
Colombia	2012	10,329	80%	22.8	12.2	5.9	23.6	24.2	24.8	69.7
Costa Rica	2013	1,216	75%	25.9	5.6	3.1	18.4	22.2	30.6	125.4
Cuba	2013	5,066	52%	45.0	8.6	5.8	11.8	17.5	23.3	226.6
Czech Republic	2013	3,612	64%	34.4	4.0	1.8	16.9	16.9	32.9	106.7
Dominican Republic	2012	2,002	83%	19.8	8.4	4.6	28.9	22.8	22.7	35.7
Ecuador	2013	5,543	78%	35.9	25.5	10.3	35.6	39.6	40.8	97.4
Egypt	2013	18,156	82%	21.5	17.5	11.9	28.1	23.4	22.9	26.9
Finland	2013	2,548	65%	46.8	2.3	1.4	14.0	21.8	49.4	135.3
France	2011	24,889	54%	39.4	4.6	2.1	15.9	15.4	24.4	154.6
Georgia	2014	1,490	71%	40.0	7.4	12.5	29.1	36.4	40.4	94.3
Germany	2013	20,453	54%	25.4	2.3	1.4	9.2	8.0	12.4	88.6
Guatemala	2013	7,680	81%	53.4	21.4	10.8	50.2	73.5	89.6	192.8
Hungary	2013	3,642	59%	36.8	3.5	2.3	10.9	14.1	35.4	123.5
Israel	2013	1,092	64%	13.5	5.4	1.9	8.4	6.3	11.4	71.2
Italy	2012	18,460	53%	31.0	1.8	1.5	11.9	11.9	13.0	108.3
Japan	2013	42,018	58%	33.4	3.9	1.6	6.3	6.2	16.0	105.6
Kazakhstan[b]	2012	16,497	78%	98.2	32.7	17.3	69.0	135.5	149.4	130.9
Kuwait	2013	658	85%	16.9	6.6	8.6	23.3	14.7	18.8	111.5
Kyrgyzstan	2013	2,184	76%	38.2	26.8	9.0	21.6	50.5	73.7	56.1
Lithuania	2013	2,034	75%	69.1	6.6	4.8	28.6	53.7	115.9	99.7
Mexico	2013	34,657	77%	29.2	19.5	6.0	25.2	29.7	34.5	105.2
Netherlands	2013	4,353	48%	25.9	2.1	0.8	6.5	6.0	9.3	121.5
Nicaragua	2013	1,291	79%	22.3	14.8	4.8	15.7	25.6	29.4	104.4
Panama	2013	847	81%	23.8	11.4	7.9	21.1	24.2	31.2	64.2
Paraguay	2013	2,075	78%	31.3	15.9	7.2	37.0	29.9	35.7	97.1
Peru	2013	10,113	69%	33.9	33.4	7.8	21.0	29.8	41.7	140.7
Poland	2013	13,374	71%	34.7	3.8	3.4	21.5	22.1	42.9	89.9
Portugal	2013	2,037	67%	19.5	2.5	1.7	9.8	9.8	16.0	56.4
Puerto Rico	2013	1,028	73%	28.2	3.4	2.6	18.6	21.1	28.5	75.8
Republic of Korea	2013	13,252	68%	26.2	5.6	2.7	8.0	11.1	28.6	109.0
Republic of Moldova	2013	1,847	76%	51.9	25.2	7.4	21.6	35.7	95.8	97.6
Romania	2012	7,528	76%	35.3	14.4	8.8	20.8	23.3	50.5	73.2
Russian Federation[b]	2011	199,358	77%	139.4	25.6	15.4	90.0	167.0	186.9	169.1
Saudi Arabia	2012	3,174	88%	12.0	4.5	3.5	13.7	14.6	16.1	29.8
Slovakia	2014	1,771	69%	32.5	3.5	3.0	15.5	17.5	43.6	92.2
South Africa	2013	32,316	75%	60.8	37.0	15.6	54.5	88.7	71.2	115.0
Spain	2013	9,987	59%	21.4	3.3	1.7	6.7	9.5	13.5	78.0
Sweden	2013	3,035	60%	31.6	1.2	1.1	8.7	11.5	17.8	118.6
Switzerland	2013	2,624	51%	32.4	3.9	1.6	7.9	9.2	15.2	139.1
Turkey	2013	15,135	71%	19.9	12.3	6.2	14.8	14.5	21.4	87.0
Turkmenistan[b]	2013	1,561	67%	30.5	19.4	4.1	19.9	33.5	43.4	143.8
Ukraine[b]	2012	41,713	78%	91.9	21.3	10.9	55.8	98.2	129.2	115.4
United Kingdom	2013	14,875	58%	23.5	2.8	1.4	9.8	16.9	15.7	76.9
United States of America	2013	130,557	63%	41.3	12.4	3.7	26.4	37.9	45.0	102.8
Uruguay	2013	1,538	66%	46.3	15.3	5.9	39.1	34.4	42.8	141.0
Venezuela	2012	9,912	80%	33.8	22.7	7.7	44.6	40.4	35.6	65.4

Source: National Safety Council tabulations of World Health Organization (WHO) data.
[a]Population estimates based on data from WHO and the U.S. Census Bureau (International Data Base).
[b]Data include deaths due to all external causes, including self-harm and assault.

INTERNATIONAL

International Motor-Vehicle Injury-Related Deaths and Death Rates

The International Classification of Diseases (ICD) system identifies motor-vehicle traffic incidents by codes V02-V04, V09, V12-V14, V19-V79, and V86-V89 of the 10th revision of ICD. A motor vehicle is a mechanically or electrically powered device used in the transportation of people or property on a land highway. A motor-vehicle traffic incident involves a motor vehicle in transport (i.e., in motion or on a roadway) on a public highway. Worldwide road-injury-related deaths were a projected 1,423,355 in 2015, resulting in a projected death rate of 20 per 100,000 population.

Motor-vehicle injury-related deaths and death rates by age group, latest year available

Country	Year	Deaths Total	% male	All ages	0 to 4	5 to 14	15 to 24	25 to 44	45 to 64	65 or older
Argentina	2013	5,044	79%	11.8	2.4	2.5	18.5	14.5	13.5	13.7
Austria	2014	269	74%	3.1	0.5	0.4	4.3	2.3	3.5	5.2
Belarus[b]	2011	1,507	76%	15.9	1.7	2.8	17.1	20.4	19.0	13.5
Brazil	2013	34,672	82%	17.2	2.4	2.8	23.2	22.3	19.7	23.4
Canada	2011	2,158	72%	6.3	1.0	1.3	10.7	6.3	5.6	9.2
Chile	2013	1,257	81%	7.3	1.6	1.2	8.3	9.1	8.5	10.3
Colombia	2012	5,554	82%	12.3	1.8	2.1	15.6	15.3	13.0	28.6
Costa Rica	2013	535	83%	11.4	1.1	1.2	12.8	13.8	15.5	20.1
Cuba	2013	805	76%	7.2	1.3	1.8	5.9	8.1	8.2	11.2
Czech Republic	2013	587	76%	5.6	1.0	0.5	9.8	5.5	5.4	7.6
Dominican Republic	2012	1,528	86%	15.1	1.6	3.1	25.1	18.7	17.4	21.2
Ecuador	2013	1,475	82%	9.6	2.5	1.7	13.0	13.9	9.2	14.7
Egypt	2013	8,656	83%	10.2	6.2	5.2	12.5	11.1	13.6	15.1
Finland	2013	247	74%	4.5	0.7	0.8	6.1	3.9	4.4	7.9
France	2011	3,624	76%	5.7	1.1	1.0	11.0	6.8	4.8	6.9
Georgia	2014	469	77%	12.6	2.3	3.8	14.3	15.6	14.1	13.3
Germany	2013	2,892	74%	3.6	0.4	0.5	6.0	3.4	3.3	5.0
Guatemala	2013	1	100%	0.0	0.0	0.0	0.0	0.0	0.0	0.0
Hungary	2013	665	72%	6.7	0.4	0.6	5.9	6.9	8.4	9.4
Israel	2013	235	80%	2.9	1.0	0.6	6.4	2.8	3.4	3.2
Italy	2012	3,736	80%	6.3	0.5	0.8	9.3	6.7	5.5	9.0
Japan	2013	5,497	67%	4.4	0.7	0.7	3.7	2.3	3.6	9.4
Kazakhstan[b]	2012	3,181	74%	18.9	5.7	5.7	19.0	26.0	25.2	17.7
Kuwait	2013	446	87%	11.5	3.5	4.9	18.9	9.6	11.7	83.6
Kyrgyzstan	2013	657	74%	11.5	3.0	2.2	8.6	17.6	20.4	14.3
Lithuania	2013	255	75%	8.7	2.0	1.0	11.1	9.8	9.6	10.0
Mexico	2013	12,092	80%	10.2	3.1	2.2	12.7	13.2	12.1	17.9
Netherlands	2013	483	73%	2.9	0.4	0.4	4.2	2.2	2.2	6.5
Nicaragua	2013	541	85%	9.3	1.3	1.8	9.3	13.5	12.9	22.3
Panama	2013	355	82%	10.0	2.1	2.4	11.5	12.5	12.8	17.8
Paraguay	2013	1,051	84%	15.9	3.2	2.1	26.1	18.6	18.8	18.5
Peru	2013	376	77%	1.3	0.5	0.3	0.9	1.4	2.1	3.1
Poland	2013	2,929	77%	7.6	0.7	1.6	10.3	6.9	8.7	11.1
Portugal	2013	580	78%	5.5	0.6	0.6	6.0	5.6	5.7	8.7
Puerto Rico	2013	354	77%	9.7	1.5	2.1	12.8	11.6	10.3	11.8
Republic of Korea	2013	5,852	73%	11.6	1.8	1.5	6.0	6.7	13.8	37.8
Republic of Moldova	2013	353	82%	9.9	1.0	2.4	13.7	10.7	12.5	7.3
Romania	2012	1,767	76%	8.3	1.6	2.7	9.4	7.4	10.1	12.3
Russian Federation[b]	2011	29,342	74%	20.5	3.3	4.4	26.1	27.4	20.3	18.7
Saudi Arabia	2012	2,659	88%	10.0	3.1	2.9	12.3	12.3	13.4	21.1
Slovakia	2014	301	72%	5.5	0.0	1.5	8.3	5.9	5.7	7.0
South Africa	2013	5,684	74%	10.7	4.2	3.4	9.3	16.9	14.0	12.1
Spain	2013	1,883	77%	4.0	0.9	0.8	3.7	3.9	4.0	7.3
Sweden	2013	253	77%	2.6	0.2	0.5	3.5	2.5	2.9	3.9
Switzerland	2013	254	70%	3.1	1.7	0.5	3.4	2.0	3.0	6.9
Turkey	2013	1,431	79%	1.9	0.8	0.5	2.0	1.9	2.6	3.8
Turkmenistan[b]	2013	144	81%	2.8	1.7	0.6	2.2	4.3	3.7	3.3
Ukraine[b]	2012	5,905	75%	13.0	2.3	2.5	16.4	16.5	13.8	11.8
United Kingdom	2013	1,572	75%	2.5	0.3	0.4	4.2	2.6	2.2	3.6
United States of America	2013	35,369	71%	11.2	2.5	2.1	15.2	12.7	12.1	15.1
Uruguay	2013	452	77%	13.6	2.3	2.7	19.5	15.4	15.2	17.8
Venezuela	2012	4,512	83%	15.4	3.0	3.0	25.4	21.0	16.0	15.4

Source: National Safety Council tabulations of World Health Organization (WHO) data.
[a]Population estimates based on data from WHO and the U.S. Census Bureau (International Data Base).
[b]Data include deaths due to all transportation-related causes, ICD codes V01-V99.

INTERNATIONAL

International Poisoning Injury-Related Deaths and Death Rates

The International Classification of Diseases (ICD) system identifies unintentional poisonings by codes X40-X49, which include cases of accidental poisoning by drugs, medicaments, biological substances, alcohol, solvents, gases, vapors, and pesticides. Other accidental poisonings by unspecified chemicals and noxious substances also are included. Worldwide poisoning-related deaths were a projected 192,416 in 2015, resulting in a projected death rate of 3 per 100,000 population.

Unintentional poisoning injury-related deaths and death rates by age group, latest year available

Country	Year	Deaths Total	% male	All ages	0 to 4	5 to 14	15 to 24	25 to 44	45 to 64	65 or older
Argentina	2013	320	66%	0.8	0.9	0.3	0.7	0.5	0.9	1.9
Austria	2014	25	60%	0.3	0.2	0.0	0.1	0.3	0.3	0.6
Belarus	2011	898	80%	9.5	1.9	0.8	2.4	8.3	17.1	12.5
Brazil	2013	980	79%	0.5	0.1	0.0	0.8	0.6	0.5	0.5
Canada	2011	1,641	67%	4.8	0.0	0.1	2.8	7.5	7.2	2.4
Chile	2013	261	80%	1.5	0.0	0.1	0.4	1.9	2.6	2.6
Colombia	2012	217	78%	0.5	0.3	0.1	0.6	0.6	0.5	0.7
Costa Rica	2013	44	84%	0.9	0.0	0.0	0.1	1.0	2.2	2.2
Cuba	2013	96	82%	0.9	0.6	0.0	0.3	0.6	1.7	1.0
Czech Republic	2013	419	72%	4.0	0.0	0.1	1.6	3.9	7.0	4.5
Dominican Republic	2012	4	100%	0.0	0.0	0.0	0.0	0.0	0.1	0.1
Ecuador	2013	155	77%	1.0	0.5	0.2	0.9	0.9	1.7	3.1
Egypt	2013	160	51%	0.2	0.2	0.1	0.4	0.2	0.1	0.1
Finland	2013	597	74%	11.0	0.0	0.0	5.5	12.1	20.5	8.6
France	2011	2,017	55%	3.2	0.0	0.0	0.6	2.2	3.3	9.6
Georgia	2014	37	62%	1.0	0.8	1.0	0.4	0.9	1.3	1.3
Germany	2013	650	74%	0.8	0.0	0.1	0.3	1.4	0.9	0.7
Guatemala	2013	1,176	80%	8.2	1.1	0.8	6.8	12.7	20.1	19.1
Hungary	2013	103	67%	1.0	0.2	0.4	1.0	1.0	1.0	1.7
Israel	2013	1	100%	0.0	0.0	0.0	0.0	0.0	0.1	0.0
Italy	2012	504	67%	0.8	0.0	0.0	0.3	1.2	0.7	1.5
Japan	2013	694	61%	0.6	0.0	0.0	0.3	0.7	0.7	0.6
Kazakhstan	2012	2,016	76%	12.0	2.5	1.4	3.2	16.8	23.0	18.0
Kuwait	2013	12	75%	0.3	0.0	0.2	0.2	0.3	0.6	1.3
Kyrgyzstan	2013	372	83%	6.5	0.3	0.2	1.0	7.5	21.6	13.1
Lithuania	2013	437	81%	14.8	0.0	0.0	4.1	17.7	28.4	9.9
Mexico	2013	1,233	80%	1.0	0.6	0.1	0.6	1.3	1.7	2.7
Netherlands	2013	135	65%	0.8	0.0	0.0	0.5	1.4	0.9	0.8
Nicaragua	2013	57	82%	1.0	2.2	0.1	0.3	0.8	1.6	5.1
Panama	2013	15	80%	0.4	1.5	0.0	0.3	0.2	0.6	0.7
Paraguay	2013	26	65%	0.4	0.7	0.0	0.3	0.2	0.3	2.8
Peru	2013	277	63%	0.9	0.3	0.4	0.9	0.9	1.4	2.4
Poland	2013	1,337	84%	3.5	0.2	0.2	0.9	3.8	6.5	2.6
Portugal	2013	50	60%	0.5	0.2	0.0	0.1	0.5	0.5	0.9
Puerto Rico	2013	54	80%	1.5	0.0	0.0	0.8	1.9	2.3	1.8
Republic of Korea	2013	252	69%	0.5	0.0	0.0	0.1	0.4	0.8	1.3
Republic of Moldova	2013	312	73%	8.8	3.1	0.8	0.9	6.4	19.3	12.4
Romania	2012	781	68%	3.7	1.3	0.4	0.9	2.5	5.9	7.7
Russian Federation	2011	29,407	77%	20.6	2.3	1.2	6.0	26.6	33.0	17.9
Slovakia	2014	149	79%	2.7	0.3	0.2	0.9	1.9	6.2	2.4
South Africa	2013	799	57%	1.5	6.7	0.3	0.3	1.0	1.8	2.0
Spain	2013	872	71%	1.9	0.0	0.1	0.4	2.4	2.1	2.9
Sweden	2013	437	78%	4.6	0.0	0.0	3.6	6.8	6.4	3.8
Switzerland	2013	139	71%	1.7	0.0	0.1	1.4	3.0	2.3	0.4
Turkey	2013	530	71%	0.7	0.3	0.2	0.5	0.6	1.0	2.4
Turkmenistan	2013	46	67%	0.9	0.2	0.0	0.7	1.6	1.4	0.5
Ukraine	2012	6,690	79%	14.7	1.5	0.8	3.1	15.6	27.9	12.0
United Kingdom	2013	2,878	72%	4.5	0.0	0.1	2.2	9.4	5.7	1.5
United States of America	2013	38,851	65%	12.3	0.2	0.1	7.5	20.0	20.5	4.1
Uruguay	2013	24	58%	0.7	0.0	0.0	0.0	0.6	1.1	2.4
Venezuela	2012	133	62%	0.5	0.9	0.1	0.3	0.5	0.5	0.9

Source: National Safety Council tabulations of World Health Organization (WHO) data.
[a]Population estimates based on data from WHO and the U.S. Census Bureau (International Data Base).

INTERNATIONAL

International Fall Injury-Related Deaths and Death Rates

"Accidental falls" are identified by codes W00-W19 in the 10th revision of the International Classification of Diseases (ICD) system. Worldwide fall-related deaths were a projected 714,161 in 2015, resulting in a projected death rate of 10 per 100,000 population.

Unintentional fall injury-related deaths and death rates by age group, latest year available

Country	Year	Deaths Total	% male	All ages	0 to 4	5 to 14	15 to 24	25 to 44	45 to 64	65 or older
Argentina	2013	284	65%	0.7	0.2	0.1	0.2	0.2	0.8	3.5
Austria	2014	895	53%	10.5	0.7	0.0	0.4	1.2	4.4	47.9
Belarus	2011	978	77%	10.3	0.6	0.6	3.5	8.8	16.5	18.5
Brazil	2013	12,551	59%	6.2	0.8	0.3	0.8	2.2	6.4	55.2
Canada	2011	4,198	47%	12.3	0.2	0.1	0.5	0.9	3.5	69.5
Chile	2013	941	46%	5.5	0.1	0.2	0.7	1.4	3.1	43.0
Colombia	2012	1,066	76%	2.4	0.5	0.3	0.9	1.4	3.4	16.5
Costa Rica	2013	86	83%	1.8	0.0	0.1	0.6	1.0	2.5	12.9
Cuba	2013	2,137	44%	19.0	0.5	0.2	0.7	1.4	5.3	124.6
Czech Republic	2013	657	62%	6.3	0.3	0.2	1.8	1.5	5.2	24.5
Dominican Republic	2012	29	69%	0.3	0.0	0.0	0.1	0.2	0.4	2.1
Ecuador	2013	417	77%	2.7	0.5	0.4	1.2	2.1	3.5	17.1
Egypt	2013	1,398	74%	1.7	2.9	1.3	1.2	1.3	1.8	3.7
Finland	2013	1,113	54%	20.5	0.0	0.0	0.5	1.4	10.2	90.3
France	2011	6,160	47%	9.7	0.3	0.1	0.5	1.1	4.4	48.0
Georgia	2014	183	50%	4.9	0.8	0.5	2.1	2.0	1.6	25.3
Germany	2013	10,842	46%	13.4	0.2	0.1	0.4	0.8	3.4	58.5
Guatemala	2013	3	100%	0.0	0.0	0.0	0.0	0.0	0.0	0.2
Hungary	2013	1,776	47%	18.0	0.4	0.1	0.1	1.3	9.8	85.8
Israel	2013	126	60%	1.6	0.5	0.1	0.2	0.6	1.1	10.4
Italy	2012	4,178	52%	7.0	0.4	0.1	0.5	0.9	2.4	28.7
Japan	2013	7,766	58%	6.2	0.1	0.1	0.5	0.7	2.4	21.1
Kazakhstan	2012	499	73%	3.0	2.0	0.4	1.5	3.6	4.1	7.6
Kuwait	2013	60	87%	1.5	0.3	0.4	0.8	2.1	1.9	4.0
Kyrgyzstan	2013	77	79%	1.3	0.8	0.2	0.8	1.9	2.4	2.5
Lithuania	2013	378	66%	12.8	0.0	0.0	1.1	5.5	15.4	37.6
Mexico	2013	2,503	79%	2.1	0.8	0.2	0.7	1.4	3.6	12.6
Netherlands	2013	2,174	43%	12.9	0.1	0.0	0.2	0.9	2.8	69.7
Nicaragua	2013	152	55%	2.6	0.7	0.3	0.5	0.7	2.4	39.4
Panama	2013	144	74%	4.0	1.5	0.3	1.0	1.9	5.3	28.6
Paraguay	2013	83	75%	1.3	0.9	0.2	0.4	0.6	2.4	7.5
Peru	2013	240	74%	0.8	0.4	0.2	0.3	0.6	1.1	4.3
Poland	2013	4,662	56%	12.1	0.4	0.2	1.6	2.7	10.0	57.3
Portugal	2013	533	60%	5.1	0.4	0.0	0.7	0.7	3.0	20.4
Puerto Rico	2013	152	74%	4.2	0.0	0.2	0.2	0.8	4.4	17.2
Republic of Korea	2013	2,333	75%	4.6	1.0	0.3	0.5	1.4	6.1	19.4
Republic of Moldova	2013	183	73%	5.1	1.0	0.0	0.7	2.2	9.0	19.1
Romania	2012	1,249	77%	5.9	0.9	0.2	1.2	2.4	9.1	17.3
Russian Federation	2011	8,965	71%	6.3	1.5	0.5	2.7	5.4	8.2	14.5
Saudi Arabia	2012	189	87%	0.7	0.8	0.3	0.3	0.8	1.2	2.5
Slovakia	2014	731	58%	13.4	0.3	0.2	0.5	2.4	13.2	64.6
South Africa	2013	181	71%	0.3	0.2	0.1	0.2	0.2	0.6	2.1
Spain	2013	2,672	50%	5.7	0.4	0.1	0.5	0.8	2.4	26.7
Sweden	2013	967	55%	10.1	0.2	0.0	0.1	0.4	2.7	48.0
Switzerland	2013	1,766	42%	21.8	0.2	0.3	0.9	1.6	4.1	114.8
Turkey	2013	3,608	52%	4.7	1.3	0.2	0.5	0.6	2.1	51.2
Turkmenistan	2013	27	81%	0.5	0.6	0.4	0.2	0.7	0.7	0.5
Ukraine	2012	2,506	74%	5.5	1.0	0.2	1.7	4.1	7.7	12.4
United Kingdom	2013	5,147	50%	8.1	0.1	0.1	0.4	1.0	3.0	40.5
United States of America	2013	30,208	50%	9.6	0.2	0.0	0.5	1.0	4.4	57.0
Uruguay	2013	49	71%	1.5	0.0	0.0	0.2	0.8	2.4	5.2
Venezuela	2012	675	62%	2.3	0.6	0.3	0.6	1.0	3.0	21.2

Source: National Safety Council tabulations of World Health Organization (WHO) data.
[a]Population estimates based on data from WHO and the U.S. Census Bureau (International Data Base).

INTERNATIONAL
International Drowning Injury-Related Deaths and Death Rates

The International Classification of Diseases (ICD) system identifies drowning by codes W65-W74, which include cases of unintentional drowning and submersion while in or following a fall in a bathtub, swimming pool, or natural body of water. Other specified and unspecified cases of drowning and submersion also are included. Worldwide drowning-related deaths were a projected 362,316 in 2015, resulting in a projected death rate of 5 per 100,000 population.

Unintentional drowning injury-related deaths and death rates by age group, latest year available

Country	Year	Deaths Total	% male	All ages	0 to 4	5 to 14	15 to 24	25 to 44	45 to 64	65 or older
Argentina	2013	450	83%	1.1	2.4	0.6	1.4	0.9	1.0	0.7
Austria	2014	30	73%	0.4	0.0	0.2	0.3	0.1	0.2	1.1
Belarus	2011	733	84%	7.7	3.0	2.1	5.0	9.7	10.3	6.8
Brazil	2013	5,117	87%	2.5	2.9	2.0	3.5	2.5	2.3	2.3
Canada	2011	253	79%	0.7	0.7	0.5	1.0	0.6	0.7	1.0
Chile	2013	325	88%	1.9	1.7	0.6	1.7	1.6	2.9	2.7
Colombia	2012	853	84%	1.9	3.6	1.5	2.4	1.5	1.2	2.9
Costa Rica	2013	102	85%	2.2	2.4	0.9	2.0	1.8	3.0	4.1
Cuba	2013	251	93%	2.2	1.7	2.3	2.2	2.4	2.0	2.5
Czech Republic	2013	177	76%	1.7	0.5	0.5	0.6	1.3	2.6	2.6
Dominican Republic	2012	28	79%	0.3	0.2	0.2	0.6	0.2	0.1	0.4
Ecuador	2013	329	79%	2.1	4.0	1.8	2.4	1.8	1.6	2.4
Egypt	2013	1,965	85%	2.3	3.9	2.7	4.1	1.3	1.0	1.1
Finland	2013	131	77%	2.4	1.0	0.2	0.8	1.1	3.0	6.0
France	2011	918	70%	1.5	1.0	0.3	0.9	0.8	1.7	3.3
Georgia	2014	49	78%	1.3	0.4	0.5	1.6	1.5	0.8	2.7
Germany	2013	465	72%	0.6	0.4	0.3	0.5	0.3	0.5	1.1
Guatemala	2013	342	85%	2.4	1.7	1.6	2.3	2.9	2.3	6.3
Hungary	2013	123	80%	1.2	0.2	0.4	1.5	1.0	1.7	1.5
Israel	2013	55	84%	0.7	0.7	0.3	0.6	0.3	1.1	1.8
Italy	2012	363	82%	0.6	0.2	0.2	0.6	0.6	0.5	1.0
Japan	2013	7,523	53%	6.0	0.6	0.5	0.8	0.7	2.5	19.8
Kazakhstan	2012	872	84%	5.2	3.9	3.7	5.6	6.5	5.6	2.4
Kuwait	2013	26	92%	0.7	1.3	1.2	1.0	0.4	0.0	4.0
Kyrgyzstan	2013	214	69%	3.7	9.3	2.3	1.8	3.8	3.5	3.7
Lithuania	2013	198	82%	6.7	2.0	1.4	4.6	5.0	13.5	4.7
Mexico	2013	1,998	86%	1.7	2.2	1.0	2.0	1.7	1.5	2.7
Netherlands	2013	84	70%	0.5	0.7	0.2	0.5	0.3	0.5	0.9
Nicaragua	2013	138	83%	2.4	0.9	1.0	2.2	3.7	2.7	2.9
Panama	2013	118	83%	3.3	2.1	4.1	3.9	3.1	2.6	4.1
Paraguay	2013	175	84%	2.6	3.4	2.6	3.5	2.6	1.4	2.3
Peru	2013	400	78%	1.3	2.2	0.9	1.3	1.2	1.3	2.2
Poland	2013	884	82%	2.3	0.3	0.5	2.5	1.8	3.5	2.7
Portugal	2013	81	72%	0.8	0.2	0.3	1.0	0.4	0.9	1.3
Puerto Rico	2013	28	82%	0.8	0.5	0.2	0.9	1.1	0.5	1.0
Republic of Korea	2013	622	79%	1.2	0.7	0.5	0.8	0.6	1.5	3.4
Republic of Moldova	2013	159	75%	4.5	3.6	2.1	2.5	3.9	7.0	5.6
Romania	2012	657	82%	3.1	1.6	2.7	3.2	2.1	4.0	4.2
Russian Federation	2011	8,530	84%	6.0	2.6	3.2	4.7	7.6	7.1	4.5
Saudi Arabia	2012	13	77%	0.0	0.2	0.1	0.0	0.0	0.0	0.0
Slovakia	2014	129	80%	2.4	0.7	0.7	1.7	1.6	3.9	3.6
South Africa	2013	1,518	76%	2.9	4.9	3.3	2.4	2.4	2.4	2.4
Spain	2013	422	82%	0.9	0.8	0.5	0.7	0.5	0.9	2.0
Sweden	2013	83	82%	0.9	0.3	0.3	0.7	0.2	1.1	1.9
Switzerland	2013	56	75%	0.7	0.7	0.4	0.9	0.4	0.7	1.2
Turkey	2013	647	81%	0.9	1.3	0.8	1.1	0.6	0.6	1.6
Turkmenistan	2013	66	79%	1.3	3.9	0.2	1.0	1.3	1.5	0.5
Ukraine	2012	2,713	85%	6.0	2.4	2.9	4.8	6.7	7.8	5.3
United Kingdom	2013	262	76%	0.4	0.2	0.1	0.5	0.4	0.5	0.5
United States of America	2013	3,391	77%	1.1	2.1	0.5	1.1	0.9	1.1	1.2
Uruguay	2013	70	79%	2.1	0.9	1.0	2.8	2.3	1.8	3.0
Venezuela	2012	448	82%	1.5	3.1	1.0	2.2	1.3	1.1	1.2

Source: National Safety Council tabulations of World Health Organization (WHO) data.
[a]Population estimates based on data from WHO and the U.S. Census Bureau (International Data Base).

INTERNATIONAL
Occupational Deaths

Counts and rates of fatal work-related injuries are shown on this page and the next. Comparisons between countries should be made with caution and take into account the differences in sources, coverage, and kinds of cases included.

Occupational deaths by country, 2011-2015

Country	2011	2012	2013	2014	2015	Source of data	Worker types[a]	Activities excluded
Injuries only – compensated cases								
Australia	226	229	197	188	—	AR	E	none
Bulgaria	94	77	81	115	—	IR	I	none
Chile	282	322	283	—	—	AR	I	none
Finland	26	—	16	—	—	IR	E	none
France	—	—	542	—	—	IR	I	none
Germany	664	—	606	639	—	IR	I	none
Greece	—	—	—	—	34	IR	I	none
Italy	—	—	—	396	517	IR	I	none
Korea, Republic of	1,271	1,292	1,245	1,123	—	IR	I	none
Lithuania	53	57	60	60	—	LR	E	none
New Zealand	—	48	—	—	—	IR	I	none
Slovenia	18	—	20	25	—	AR	I	none
Zimbabwe	84	91	—	106	—	IR	I	none
Injuries only – reported cases								
Austria	73	98	91	—	67	IR	E	none
Azerbaijan	—	—	66	88	50	LR	E	none
Belarus	169	147	141	107	72	S	E	none
Belgium[c]	82	67	72	—	—	IR	E	none
Cyprus	5	9	9	5	4	LR	E	none
Czech Republic	139	105	—	—	—	LR	—	none
Estonia	19	14	20	16	16	LR	—	none
Hungary	80	62	—	78	84	LR	E	none
Ireland	49	—	40	—	—	LR	—	none
Japan	1,024	1,093	1,030	—	—	S	E	Pub. Admn.
Latvia	34	34	29	—	—	LR	E	none
Moldova, Republic of	—	—	36	34	33	S	E	none
Norway	53	37	48	—	—	LR	E	SF, MT, OOE
Poland	404	348	—	—	263	S	E	Priv. Agr
Russian Federation	1,824	1,820	—	1,699[e]	1,456[e]	S	E	none
Singapore	61	56	59	60	66	AR	E	PDS
Slovakia	38	54	53	—	57	LR	E	none
Spain	335	271	232	246	289	IR	I	none
Sri Lanka	—	—	141	77	—	LR	E	none
Sweden	58	45	33	41	34	AR	—	none
Trinidad and Tobago	—	—	—	6	—	AR	—	—
Turkey	1,710	745	—	—	—	IR	I	none
Ukraine	597	587	474	384	325	AR	I	none
United Kingdom	171	—	148	—	—	LR	E	none
United States[d]	4,693	4,628	4,585	—	—	C	E,SE	none
Injuries and commuting accidents – compensated cases								
Croatia	38	40	27	36	29	IR	E, SE	none
Injuries and commuting accidents – reported cases								
Macau, China[c]	13	19	18	12	—	LR	E	none
Romania	297	240	223	224	199	LR	E,SE	none
Injuries and diseases – compensated cases								
Malta	1	6	—	—	—	AR	—	none
Injuries and diseases – reported cases								
Argentina	558	562	—	427	449	AR	I	none
Hong Kong, China	191	196	188	210	—	LR	E	none
Japan	—	—	—	1,057	972	S	E	Pub. Admn.
Switzerland	192	—	272	222	—	IR	E	none
Injuries, diseases, and commuting accidents – reported cases								
Luxembourg	19	18	22	—	—	IR	I	none
Mexico	1,578	1,534	1,314	1,330	1,444	IR	—	none
Panama[c]	24	24	22	21	—	LR	—	—

Source: International Labour Organization (ILO), ILO Department of Statistics, accessed September 28, 2016, from http://laborsta.ilo.org.
Note: Dash (—) means data not available. See footnotes on page 195.

Source of Data
AR = Administrative reports
C = Census
IR = Insurance records
LR = Labor inspectorate records
S = Survey

Worker Types
E = Employees
I = Insured persons
SE = Self-employed

Economic Activities
MT = Maritime transport
OOE = Offshore oil extraction
PDS = Private domestic service
Priv. Agr = Private farms in agriculture
Pub. Admn. = Public Administration
SF = Sea fishing

INTERNATIONAL
Occupational Death Rates

The International Labour Organization (ILO) estimates that about 2.3 million persons die from work-related incidents and diseases each year. This total equates to about 6,300 worker deaths per day due to an incident or disease from their work, with one worker dying from a work-related incident or disease every 15 seconds. In addition to the human cost of these deaths and injuries, the economic burden of poor safety and health practices is estimated at 4% of global gross domestic product each year.

Source: International Labour Organization. (2016). Accessed September 20, 2016 at http://www.ilo.org/global/topics/safety-and-health-at-work/lang--en/index.htm

Occupational death rates by country, 2011-2015

Country	Coverage[f]	2011	2012	2013	2014	2015
Deaths per 1,000 employees						
Injuries only						
Ireland	RC	0	—	—	—	—
Slovakia	RC	—	3	3	—	—
Injuries and diseases						
Hong Kong, China	RC	0.1	0.1	0.1	0.1	—
Deaths per 100,000 employed persons						
Injuries only						
Australia	CC	2	—	1.7	1.6	—
Austria	RC	2.6	3.4	3.1	—	2.3
Chile	CC	—	—	5.1	—	—
Cyprus	RC	1.5	2.8	2.9	1.7	1.3
Denmark	RC	2	2	—	—	—
Estonia	RC	3.1	2.2	3.2	2.6	2.5
Finland	CC	1.2	—	0.8	—	—
Hungary	RC	2.1	1.6	—	1.9	—
Kyrgyzstan	RC	—	—	6	—	—
Lithuania	RC	5.4	5.6	5.8	5.7	—
Malaysia	RC	9	6	—	—	—
Mexico	RC	—	—	—	7.9	—
Moldova	RC	—	—	6.2	5.9	5.7
Netherlands	RC	0.7	—	—	—	—
Norway[g]	RC	2.1	1.4	1.9	—	—
Romania	RC	—	—	4.7	4.7	4.1
Singapore[h]	RC	2.3	2.1	2.1	1.8	1.9
Slovakia	RC	2	—	—	—	0
Slovenia	CC	2.2	—	—	—	—
Sweden	RC	1	1	1	1	1
Turkey	RC	15.5	6.2	—	—	—
United Kingdom	RC	0.6	—	0.5	—	—
Injuries and commuting accidents						
Brazil	RC	7.4	—	—	—	—
Croatia	CC	2.7	2.9	—	—	2
Israel	CC	2.4	2.1	—	—	—
Macau, China[c]	RC	4	5.5	5	3.1	—
Romania	RC	6.4	5.1	—	—	—
Injuries and diseases						
Malta	CC	0.6	3.5	—	—	—
Switzerland	RC	5	—	7	5.6	—
United States[d, i]	RC	3.5	3.2[b]	3.3[c]	—	—
Injuries, diseases, and commuting accidents						
Israel	CC	—	—	—	2	—
Luxembourg	RC	0	0	0	—	—
Mexico	RC	10.5	9.8	8.1	—	—
Panama[c]	RC	1.6	1.5	1.3	—	—
Deaths per 100,000 persons insured						
Injuries only						
Australia	CC	—	2	—	—	—
Belize	CC	4.5	6.7	—	—	—
Bulgaria	CC	3.6	3	3.1	4.4	—
Chile	CC	5.5	6	—	—	—
France	CC	—	—	0	—	—
Germany	CC	—	—	—	—	1.6
Malaysia	RC	—	—	5	—	5
Mexico	RC	—	—	—	—	8.2
Slovenia	CC	—	—	—	3.1	—
Spain	RC	2.3	1.9	1.7	1.8	2.1
Thailand	CC	—	—	0	—	—
Ukraine	RC	5.8	5.7	5	4.3	4
Injuries and diseases						
Argentina	RC	67.1	—	—	47.4	46.4
Deaths per 100,000 persons insured						
Injuries only						
Japan[j]	RC	0	0	—	1.7	0
Korea, Republic of	CC	0	0	0	0	—

See source and limitations of data on page 194.
Note: Dash (—) indicates data not available
[a] Types of workers included in the data.
[b] Provisional.
[c] Private sector only.
[d] Excludes farms with less than 11 employees.
[e] Official estimates.
[f] Includes reported cases (RC) and compensated cases (CC) of occupational fatalities
[g] Excludes sea fishing, maritime transport, and offshore oil extraction.
[h] Excludes employees in private domestic service.
[i] Excludes federal jurusdictions.
[j] Excludes agriculture.

INTERNATIONAL
Occupational Injuries

Counts and rates of nonfatal work-related injuries are shown on this page and the next. Comparisons between countries should be made with caution and take into account the differences in sources, coverage, and kinds of cases included.

Occupational injuries by country, 2011-2015

Country	2011	2012	2013	2014	2015	Source of data	Worker types[a]	Activities excluded
Injuries only – compensated cases								
Australia	94,714	105,525	107,220	98,980	—	IR	—	none
Bulgaria	2,279	2,314	2,203	2,289	—	IR	I	none
Chile	225,535	214,986	198,551	—	—	AR	I	none
Finland	51,344	—	49,014	—	—	IR	E	none
France	—	—	618,273	—	—	IR	I	none
Germany	1,007,200	—	958,537	955,280	—	IR	I	none
Italy	—	—	—	305,246	290,280	IR	I	none
Lithuania	2,668	2,840	3,082	3,232	—	LR	E	none
New Zealand	—	15,369	—	—	—	IR	—	none
Slovenia	15,200	—	12,904	12,914	—	AR	—	none
Thailand	—	—	5,081	5,270	—	IR	I	none
Injuries only – reported cases								
Azerbaijan	—	—	117	181	111	LR	—	none
Austria	70,374	68,260	59,464	—	57,242	IR	E	none
Belarus	2,180	1,932	1,860	1,726	1,452	S	E	none
Belgium[b]	85,329	77,609	71,008	—	—	IR	E	none
Belize	1,757	1,756	—	—	—	AR	—	none
Cyprus	2,005	1,732	1,529	1,613	1,592	LR	E	none
Czech Republic			42,927	45,058	—	AR	I	none
Denmark	42,491	41,710	—	—	—	AR	—	none
Estonia	3,725	4,133	4,160	4,619	4,758	LR	—	none
Hungary	17,215	16,963	—	19,583	—	LR	E	none
Latvia	1,363	1,476	1,566	—	—	LR	E	none
Netherlands	834,200	908,000	831,800	—	—	S	E	Inst.
Norway	12,051	15,198	—	—	—	LR	—	SF, MT, OOE
Romania	—	—	3,352	3,351	3,815[c]	LR	—	AF
Singapore	10,060	11,057	11,842	—	—	AR	—	PDS
Slovakia	8,789	8,469	8,482	—	9,008	LR	E	none
Spain	511,051	407,073	402,718	423,106	456,496	IR	—	none
Sri Lanka	—	—	—	1,440	—	LR	E	none
Sweden	28,702	29,906	30,480	30,319	31,773	AR	—	none
Turkey	2,216	2,209	—	—	—	IR	E	none
Ukraine	10,317	9,480	—	4,589	4,119	S	I	none
United Kingdom	113,535	—	79,917	—	—	LR	E	—
United States[d]	1,181,290	1,149,270	—	—	—	S	E,SE	Fed., Inst., OT
Injuries and commuting accidents - compensated cases								
Croatia	18,116	15,718	15,432	13,785	15,996	IR	E	none
Israel	63,294	66,264	—	—	—	IR	I	none
Injuries and commuting accidents - reported cases								
Macau, China[b]	4,247	3,352	5,632	7,325	—	LR	E	none
Romania	3,264	3,251	—	—	—	LR	E,SE	AF
Injuries and diseases – compensated cases								
Malta	3,024	3,057	—	—	—	AR	—	none
Injuries and diseases – reported cases								
Argentina	466,086	441,113	—	421,080	422,373	AR	I	none
Hong Kong, China	40,387	39,711	37,839[e]	37,313[e]	—	LR	E	none
Switzerland	93,770	—	95,599	96,056	—	IR	I	none
Injuries, diseases, and commuting accidents – reported cases								
Ecuador	9,338	13,657	—	—	—	AR	—	none
Luxembourg	8,481	8,522	8,473	—	—	IR	I	none
Mexico	536,322	557,782	542,373	527,844	549,542	IR	—	none
Panama[f]	22	30	42	32	—	LR	—	none

Source: International Labour Organization, Department of Statistics, accessed September 1, 2016, from http://www.ilo.org/ilostat/faces/home/statisticaldata
Note: Dash (—) means data not available. See footnotes on page 197.

Source of Data
AR = Administrative reports
IR = Insurance records
LR = Labor inspectorate records
S = Survey

Worker Types
E = Employees
I = Insured persons
SE = Self-employed

Economic Activities
AF = Armed forces
Fed. = Federal jurisdictions
Inst. = Institutional population
MT = Maritime transport

OOE = Offshore oil extraction
OT = Overseas territories
PDS = Private domestic service
SF = Sea fishing

INTERNATIONAL
Occupational Injury Rates

The International Labour Organization (ILO) estimates that about 317 million nonfatal occupational injuries occur annually, many of which result in extended absences from work. This means that every 15 seconds, 153 workers suffer a work-related injury. Provided below are nonfatal injury and illness rates for 40 countries included in the ILO dataset.

Source: International Labour Organization. (2016). Safety and health at work. Accessed September 28, 2016 from www.ilo.org/global/topics/safety-and-health-at-work/lang--en/index.htm.

Occupational injury rates by country, 2011-2015

Country	Coverage[f]	2011	2012	2013	2014	2015
Injuries per 1,000 employees						
Injuries only						
Belarus	RC	0.6	0.5	0.5	0.5	0.4
Ireland	RC	22.5	—	—	—	—
Injuries and diseases						
Hong Kong, China	RC	14.5	14	13.1[e]	12.7[e]	—
Injuries per 1,000 insured employees						
Injuries and diseases						
Argentina	RC	56.1	50.9	—	—	43.7
Injuries per 100,000 employed persons						
Injuries only						
Australia	RC	907.5	1,016.4	1,011.5	—	—
Austria	RC	2,478	2,368	2,051	—	1,947
Bulgaria	CC	—	—	84.7	—	—
Cyprus	RC	613.6	534.4	494.4	541.5	517.8
Denmark	RC	1,588	1,560	—	—	—
Estonia	RC	611.6	661.9	669.6	739.3	742.4
Finland	CC	2,397	—	2,305	—	—
Hungary	RC	451.6	437.4	—	479.4	—
Kyrgyzstan	RC	—	—	38	—	—
Lithuania	RC	269.3	281.1	299.7	308.9	—
Malaysia	RC	747	703	—	—	—
Mexico	RC	—	—	—	3,141.2	3,134.2
Netherlands[g]	RC	11,800	12,800	11,900	—	5,000
New Zealand	CC	—	800	—	—	—
Norway[g]	RC	473.9	586.6	—	—	—
Panama[b]	RC	—	—	2.5	—	—
Qatar[h]	CC	8.9	5.4	3.6[f]	4.9[f]	—
Romania[g]	RC	—	—	70.5	70.6	79
Singapore[g]	RC	—	—	—	403	362
Slovakia	RC	452	430	431.2	—	—
Slovenia	CC	1,858.6	—	—	1,595.2	—
Sweden	RC	636	662	666	656	682
Turkey	RC	20.1	18.5	—	—	—
Ukraine	RC	100.5	91.8	85.4	51.2	51.1
United Kingdom	RC	387.8	—	270.1	—	—
United States[d, g]	RC	1,164	1,118	1,094	1,071	—
Injuries and commuting accidents						
Croatia	CC	1,284.6	1,127.3	1,093.9	986.4	1,131.6
Israel	CC	2,419.5	2,259.6	—	—	—
Macau, China[b]	RC	1,296.4	976.7	1,560.1	1,887.4	1,880.7
Romania[g]	RC	70	69.3	—	—	—
Injuries and diseases						
Malta	CC	1,792.4	1,770.1	—	—	—
Switzerland	RC	2,437.7	—	2,463.8	2,435.1	—
Injuries, diseases, and commuting accidents						
Israel	CC	—	—	—	2,262.9	—
Mexico	RC	3,582.4	3,559.2	3,343	—	—
Panama[b]	RC	1.4	1.9	—	—	—
Injuries per 1,000,000 persons insured						
Injuries only						
Australia	CC	—	—	—	912.8	—
Belize	CC	1,996.9	1,954.4	—	—	—
Bulgaria	CC	88.1	90.2	—	86.5	—
Chile	CC	5,488.3	4,876.2	—	—	—
Germany	CC	—	—	—	—	2,371
Malaysia[b]	RC	—	—	681	—	615
Slovenia	CC	—	—	—	1,595.2	—
Spain	RC	3,504.7	2,838.7	2,997.6	3,100.2	3,241.2
Injuries per 1,000,000 hours worked						
Injuries only						
Belgium[b]	RC	21.4	19.4	17.6	—	—
France	CC	—	—	22.7	—	—
Injuries, diseases, and commuting accidents						
Luxembourg	RC	12.5	12.3	12	—	—

See source and limitations of data on page 196.
Note: Dash (–) indicates data not available
[a] Types of workers included in the data.
[b] Private sector only.
[c] Includes all economic activities.
[d] Excludes federal jurisdictions, occupational diseases, and farms with less than 11 employees.
[e] Government controlled areas.
[f] Includes reported cases (RC) and compensated cases (CC) of occupational fatalities.
[g] See activities excluded in table on page 196.
[h] Excluding injuries not resulting in some degree of disability.

Technical Appendix
Other Sources
Glossary
Index

Highlights

Technical appendix — pgs. 200-204

Other sources — pg. 205

Glossary — pg. 206

Index — pgs. 207-210

INJURY FACTS® 2017

This appendix gives a brief explanation of some of the sources and methods used by the National Safety Council Statistics Department in preparing the estimates of deaths, injuries, and costs presented in this book.

The Council uses four classes to categorize unintentional injuries. The four classes are Motor Vehicle, Work, Home, and Public. Each class represents an environment and an intervention route for injury prevention through a responsible authority such as a police department, an employer, a home owner, or a public health department.

Technical Appendix

This appendix gives a brief explanation of some of the sources and methods used by the National Safety Council Statistics Department in preparing the estimates of deaths, injuries, and costs presented in this book. Because many of the estimates depend on death certificate data provided by the National Center for Health Statistics (NCHS), it begins with a brief introduction to the certification and classification of deaths.

Certification and classification. The medical certification of death involves entering information on the death certificate about the disease or condition directly leading to death, antecedent causes, and other significant conditions. The death certificate is then registered with the appropriate authority and a code is assigned for the underlying cause of death. The underlying cause is defined as "(a) the disease or injury which initiated the train of morbid events leading directly to death, or (b) the circumstances of the accident or violence which produced the fatal injury" (World Health Organization [WHO], 1992). Deaths are classified and coded on the basis of a WHO standard, the *International Statistical Classification of Diseases and Related Health Problems*, commonly known as the International Classification of Diseases or ICD (WHO, 1992). For deaths due to injury and poisoning, the ICD provides a system of "external cause" codes to which the underlying cause of death is assigned. (See pages 24-25 of *Injury Facts* for a condensed list of external cause codes.)

Comparability across ICD revisions. The ICD is revised periodically and these revisions can affect comparability from year to year. The sixth revision (1948) substantially expanded the list of external causes and provided for classifying the place of occurrence. Changes in the classification procedures for the sixth revision as well as the seventh (1958) and eighth (1968) revisions classified as diseases some deaths previously classified as injuries. The eighth revision also expanded and reorganized some external cause sections. The ninth revision (1979), provided more detail on the agency involved, the victims' activity, and the place of occurrence. The tenth revision, which was adopted in the United States effective with 1999 data, completely revised the transportation-related categories. Specific external cause categories affected by the revisions are noted in the historical tables.

The table at the end of this appendix (page 203) shows the ICD-9 codes, the ICD-10 codes, and a comparability ratio for each of the principal causes of unintentional injury death. The comparability ratio represents the net effect of the new revision on statistics for the cause of death. The comparability ratio was obtained by classifying a sample of death certificates under both ICD-9 and ICD-10 and then dividing the number of deaths for a selected cause classified under ICD-10 by the number classified to the most nearly comparable ICD-9 cause. A comparability ratio of 1.00 indicates no net change due to the new classification scheme. A ratio less than 1.00 indicates fewer deaths assigned to a cause under ICD-10 than under ICD-9. A ratio greater than 1.00 indicates an increase in assignment of deaths to a cause under ICD-10 compared to ICD-9.

The broad category of "accidents" or "unintentional injuries" under ICD-9 included complications and misadventures of surgical and medical care (E870-E879) and adverse effects of drugs in therapeutic use (E930-E949). These categories are not included in "accidents" or "unintentional injuries" under ICD-10. In 1998, deaths in these two categories numbered 3,228 and 276, respectively.

Under ICD-9, the code range for falls (E880-E888) included a code for "fracture, cause unspecified" (E887). A similar code does not appear in ICD-10 (W00-W19), which probably accounts for the low comparability ratio (0.8409). In 1998, deaths in code E887 numbered 3,679.

Beginning with 1970 data, tabulations published by NCHS no longer include deaths of nonresident aliens. In 2014, there were 804 such unintentional deaths, of which 290 were motor-vehicle related.

Fatality estimates. The Council uses four classes and three venues to categorize unintentional injuries. The four classes are Motor Vehicle, Work, Home, and Public. Each class represents an environment and an intervention route for injury prevention through a responsible authority such as a police department, an employer, a home owner, or public health department. The three venues are Transportation, Work, and Home and Community.

Motor vehicle. The Motor Vehicle class can be identified by the underlying cause of death (see the table on page 203).

Work. The National Safety Council adopted the Bureau of Labor Statistics' Census of Fatal Occupational Injuries (CFOI) figure, beginning with the 1992 data year, as the authoritative count of unintentional work-related deaths. The CFOI system is described in detail in Toscano and Windau (1994).

The 2-Way Split. After subtracting the Motor Vehicle and Work figures from the unintentional injury total (ICD-10 codes V01-X59, Y85- Y86), the remainder belong to the Home and Public classes. The Home class can be identified by the "place of occurrence" subclassification (code .0) used with most nontransport deaths; the Public class is the remainder. Missing "place of occurrence" information, however, prevents the direct determination of the Home and Public class totals. Because of this, the Council allocates non-motor vehicle, non-work deaths into the Home and Public classes based on the external cause, age group, and cases with specified "place of occurrence." This procedure, known as the 2-Way Split, uses the most recent death certificate data available from the NCHS and the CFOI data for the same calendar year. For each cause-code group and age group combination, the Motor Vehicle and Work deaths are subtracted and the remainder, including those with "place of occurrence" unspecified, are allocated to Home and Public in the same proportion as those with "place of occurrence" specified.

TECHNICAL APPENDIX
OTHER SOURCES | GLOSSARY | INDEX

Technical Appendix (cont.)

The table on page 203 shows the ICD-10 cause-codes and CFOI event codes for the most common causes of unintentional-injury death. The CFOI event codes (BLS, 1992) do not match exactly with ICD cause codes, so there is some error in the allocation of deaths among the classes.

Linking up to current year. Historically the benchmark data published by NCHS can be two years old and the final CFOI data are often one year old. Starting with the 2011 edition of *Injury Facts*, an exponential smoothing technique is used to make current year estimates. Exponential smoothing is a statistical technique to make short term forecasts. In exponential smoothing (as opposed to in moving averages smoothing) older data are given progressively less relative weight (importance) whereas newer data are given progressively greater weight. The results of the exponential smoothing are then compared against the latest reported state data for validation. Recently both NCHS and CFOI has accelerated data reporting, often making exponential smoothing unnecessary. Exponential smoothing was not used in the 2017 edition because 2015 data were available from all sources.

Nonfatal injury estimates. Starting with the 2011 edition of *Injury Facts*, the Council adopted the concept of "medically consulted injury" to define the kinds of injuries included in its estimates. Prior editions of *Injury Facts* used the definition of disabling injury. There is no national injury surveillance system that provides injury estimates on a current basis. The National Health Interview System, a household survey conducted by NCHS (see page 28), produces national estimates using its own definition of medically consulted injury (Adams, Heyman, Vickerie, 2009). A medically consulted injury as defined by NCHS is an injury serious enough that a medical professional was consulted. The Council uses the medically consulted injury estimates from the National Health Interview survey for its motor vehicle, home, and public injury estimates. Starting with the 2016 edition of *Injury Facts* a further refinement of the nonfatal injury estimate was implemented to better account for and remove intentional injuries. Because of this refinement, nonfatal estimates published prior to the 2016 edition are not comparable with current estimates. In addition, the Occupational Safety and Health Administration defines injury or illness using criteria including "Medical treatment beyond first aid." The Council uses the total recordable case estimate defined by OSHA and published by the Bureau of Labor Statistics to estimate the number of workplace injuries. Because BLS's estimate excludes the self-employed, unpaid family workers, and federal government employees, the Council uses total employment estimates, as well as BLS nonfatal estimates, to calculate the total number of nonfatal medically consulted injuries.

Injury-to-death ratios. Because estimates for medically consulted injuries are not available for the current year, the Council uses injury-to-death ratios to estimate nonfatal medically consulted injuries for the current year. Complete documentation of the procedure, effective with the 1993 edition, may be found in Landes, Ginsburg, Hoskin, and Miller (1990). The resulting estimates are not direct measures of nonfatal injuries and should not be compared with prior years.

Population sources. All population figures used in computing rates are estimates taken from various reports published by the Bureau of the Census, U.S. Department of Commerce, on their website (www.census.gov). *Resident* population is used for computing rates.

Costs (pages 8-11). The procedures for estimating the economic losses due to fatal and nonfatal unintentional injuries were extensively revised for the 2016 edition of *Injury Facts*. New components were added, new benchmarks adopted, and a new discount rate assumed. All of these changes resulted in significant cost estimate changes. For this reason, it must be re-emphasized that the cost estimates should not be compared to those in earlier editions of the book. Many of the cost benchmarks relied on by the previous model were originally developed in the late 1980's and early 1990's. The new cost estimate model takes advantage of many new benchmarks, including the CDC WISQARS cost estimates and HCUP (Health Care Utilization Program).

The new cost estimate model results in substantial changes in several of the cost estimates compared to the previous model, with workplace cost estimates particularly impacted. Please note that the changes in cost estimates reflect improvements in estimate procedures, not in actual year to year changes. Provided below is a summary of the extent of the workplace cost estimate changes:
- Total cost estimate is about a quarter lower than previous estimates
- Wage and productivity losses
  - About 40% lower than previous model
  - New model uses the CDC WISQARS cost estimates as a benchmark for work loss and productivity
- Medical expenses
  - About a third lower than previous model
  - New model uses the CDC WISQARS cost estimates and PIRE evaluation of Nationwide Inpatient sample (HCUP) as benchmarks for medical expenses
- Motor-vehicle damage
  - About 50% higher than previous model
  - New model uses Blincoe et al. (2015) as benchmark

The Council's general philosophy underlying its cost estimates is that the figures represent income not received or expenses incurred because of fatal and nonfatal unintentional

Technical Appendix (cont.)

injuries. Stated this way, the Council's cost estimates are a measure of the economic impact of unintentional injuries and may be compared to other economic measures such as gross domestic product, per capita income, or personal consumption expenditures. (See page 109 and "lost quality of life" [page 202] for a discussion of injury costs for cost-benefit analysis.)

The general approach followed was to identify a benchmark unit cost for each component, adjust the benchmark to the current year using an appropriate inflator, estimate the number of cases to which the component applied, and compute the product. Where possible, benchmarks were obtained for each class: Motor Vehicle, Work, Home, and Public.

Wage and productivity losses include the value of wages, fringe benefits, and household production for all classes, and travel delay for the Motor Vehicle class.

Medical and work loss costs of unintentional fatal injuries are based on cost benchmarks from the CDC WISQARS Cost Model and multiplied by the Council's fatal injury estimate. Work loss includes earnings and the value of household production.

Medical and work loss costs for unintentional hospitalized injuries were computed by the Pacific Institute for Research and Evaluation (PIRE) from its costed version of the 2010 Healthcare Cost and Utilization Project (HCUP) Nationwide Inpatient Sample, using readmission rates from HCUP. Work loss includes earnings and the value of household production.

Medical and work loss costs of non-hospitalized injuries are based on costs from the WISQARS Cost Module for ED-treated-and-released injuries and multiplied by the Council's estimate of number of non-hospitalized injuries. Work loss includes earnings and the value of household production.

Cost of motor-vehicle property damage and travel delay costs were computed by PIRE from data used in Blincoe et al. (2015) and then multiplied by the Council's estimates of crash incidence (The Economic and Societal Impact of Motor Vehicle Crashes, 2010 Revised. DOT HS 812-013).

Cost per ambulance transport was benchmarked to National Medical Expenditure Survey (NMES) data and cost per helicopter transport was benchmarked to data in Miller et al. (1993a). The number of cases transported was based on data from Rice and MacKenzie (1989) and the National Electronic Injury Surveillance System.

Administrative expenses include the administrative cost of private and public insurance, which represents the cost of having insurance, and police and legal costs.

The administrative cost of motor-vehicle insurance was the difference between premiums earned (adjusted to remove fire, theft, and casualty premiums) and pure losses incurred, based on data from A. M. Best. Workers' compensation insurance administration was based on A. M. Best data for private carriers and regression estimates using Social Security Administration data for state funds and the self-insured. Administrative costs of public insurance (mainly Medicaid and Medicare) amount to about 4% of the medical expenses paid by public insurance, which were determined from Rice and MacKenzie (1989) and Hensler et al. (1991).

Average police costs for motor-vehicle crashes were computed by PIRE from data used in Blincoe (2015) and multiplied by the Council's estimates of the number of fatal, injury, and property damage crashes.

Travel delay costs were obtained from the Council's estimates of the number of fatal, injury, and property damage crashes and an average delay cost per crash from Miller et al. (1991).

Legal expenses include court costs, and plaintiff's and defendant's time and expenses. Hensler et al. (1991) provided data on the proportion of injured persons who hire a lawyer, file a claim, and get compensation. Kakalik and Pace (1986) provided data on costs per case.

Fire losses were based on data published by the National Fire Protection Association in the *NFPA Journal*. The allocation into the classes was based on the property use for structure fires and other NFPA data for non-structure fires.

Employer uninsured costs for work injuries is an estimate of the productivity costs incurred by employers. It assumes each fatality or permanent injury resulted in four person-months of disruption, serious injuries one person-month, and minor to moderate injuries two person-days. All injuries to nonworkers were assumed to involve two days of worker productivity loss. Average hourly earnings for supervisors and nonsupervisory workers were computed and then multiplied by the incidence and hours lost per case. Property damage and production delays (except motor-vehicle related) are not included in the estimates but can be substantial.

Lost quality of life is the difference between the value of a statistical fatality or statistical injury and the value of after-tax wages, fringe benefits, and household production. Because this does not represent real income not received or expenses incurred, it is not included in the total economic cost figure. If included, the resulting comprehensive costs can be used in cost-benefit analysis because the total costs then represent the maximum amount society should spend to prevent a statistical death or injury. Lost quality of life costs are benchmarked using 2010 NCHS multiple cause of death data and using the Department of Transportation's estimate of $9.1 million (2012 dollars) as the value of a statistical life.

Work deaths and injuries (page 58). The method for estimating total work-related deaths and injuries is discussed above. The breakdown of deaths by industry division for the current year is obtained from CFOI. The estimate of nonfatal medically consulted injuries by industry division is made using the Survey of Occupational Injury and Illness' estimate of total recordable injury and illness after correcting for the exclusion of self-employed, unpaid family workers, and federal government employees.

Technical Appendix (cont.)

Employment. The employment estimates for 1992 to the present were changed for the 1998 edition. Estimates for these years in prior editions are not comparable. The total employment figure used by the Council represents the number of persons in the civilian labor force, aged 16 and older, who were wage or salary workers, self-employed, or unpaid family workers, plus active duty military personnel resident in the United States. The total employment estimate is a combination of three figures – total civilian employment from the Current Population Survey (CPS) as published in *Employment and Earnings*, plus the difference between total resident population and total civilian population, which represents active duty military personnel.

Employment by industry is obtained from an unpublished Bureau of Labor Statistics table titled "Employed and experience unemployed persons by detailed industry and class of worker, Annual Average [year] (based on CPS)."

Time lost (page 62) is the product of the number of cases and the average time lost per case. Deaths average 150 workdays lost in the current year and 5,850 in future years; permanent disabilities involve 75 and 565 days lost in current and future years, respectively; temporary disabilities involve 17 days lost in the current year only. Off-the-job injuries to workers are assumed to result in similar lost time.

Off-the-job (page 63) deaths and injuries are estimated by assuming that employed persons incur injuries at the same rate as the entire population.

Motor vehicle (pages 104-139). Estimates of miles traveled, registered vehicles and licensed drivers are published by the Federal Highway Administration in *Highway Statistics* and *Traffic Volume Trends*.

Selected unintentional-injury code groupings

Manner of injury	ICD-9 codes[a]	ICD-10 codes[b]	Comparability ratio[c]	OICCS v2.01[d] event codes
Unintentional injuries	E800-E869, E880-E929[e]	V01-X59, Y85-Y86	1.0305 (1.0278-1.0333)[f]	12 - 9999
Railway accident	E800-E807	V05, V15, V80.6, V81(.2-.9)	n/a	22
Motor-vehicle accident	E810-E825	V02-V04, V09.0, V09.2, V12-V14, V19.0-V19.2, V19.4-V19.6, V20-V79, V80.3-V80.5, V81.0-V81.1, V82.0-V82.1, V83-V86, V87.0-V87.8, V88.0-V88.8, V89.0, V89.2	0.9754 (0.9742-0.9766)	24, 26, 27
Water transport accident	E830-E838	V90-V94	n/a	25
Air transport accident	E840-E845	V95-V97	n/a	21
Poisoning by solids and liquids	E850-58, E860-66	X40-X49	n/a	55, 59, 1224
Poisoning by gases and vapors	E867-E869			
Falls	E880-E888	W00-W19	0.8409 (0.8313-0.8505)	40, 42-45, 49
Fires and burns	E890-E899	X00-X09	0.9743 (0.9568-0.9918)	31
Drowning[g]	E910	W65-W74	0.9965 (0.9716-1.0213)	561
Choking[h]	E911-E912	W78-W80	n/a	562
Mechanical suffocation	E913	W75-W77, W81-W84	n/a	560, 563, 569
Firearms	E922	W32-W34	1.0579 (1.0331-1.0828)	1211, 1221, 1222

Source: National Safety Council.
Note: n/a means comparability ratio not calculated or does not meet standards of reliability or precision.
[a]WHO (1977).
[b]WHO (1992).
[c]Hoyert, Arias, Smith, et al. (2001). Table III.
[d]BLS (2012), Occupational Injury and Illness Classification Manual, Version 2.01.
[e]The National Safety Council has used E800-E949 for unintentional injuries. The code group in the table omits complications and misadventures of surgical and medical care (E870-E879) and adverse effects of drugs in therapeutic use (E930-E949).
[f]Figures in parentheses are the 95% confidence interval for the comparability ratio.
[g]Excludes transport.
[h]Suffocation by ingestion or inhalation.

TECHNICAL APPENDIX
OTHER SOURCES | GLOSSARY | INDEX

Technical Appendix (cont.)

Berkowitz, M., & Burton, J.F., Jr. (1987). *Permanent Disability Benefits in Workers' Compensation*. Kalamazoo, MI: W.E. Upjohn Institute for Employment Research.

Blincoe, L. J., Miller, T. R., Zaloshnja, E., & Lawrence, B. A. (2015, May). *The economic and societal impact of motor vehicle crashes, 2010.* (Revised) (Report No. DOT HS 812 013). Washington, DC: National Highway Traffic Safety Administration.

Bureau of Labor Statistics [BLS]. (2015, October). *Employer-Reported Workplace Injuries and Illnesses in 2015*. Press release USDL-16-2056.

Bureau of Labor Statistics [BLS]. (2015, December). *National Census of Fatal Occupational Injuries in 2015*. Press release USDL-16-2304.

Hensler, D.R., Marquis, M.S., Abrahamse, A.F., Berry, S.H., Ebener, P.A., Lewis, E.D., Lind, E.A., MacCoun, R.J., Manning, W.G., Rogowski, J.A., & Vaiana, M.E. (1991). *Compensation for Accidental Injuries in the United States*. Santa Monica, CA: The RAND Corporation.

Hoyert, D.L., Arias, E., Smith, B.L., Murphy, S.L., & Kochanek, K.D. (2001). Deaths: final data for 1999. *National Vital Statistics Reports, 49*(8).

Kakalik, J.S., & Pace, N. (1986). *Costs and Compensation Paid in Tort Litigation*. R-3391-ICJ. Santa Monica, CA: The RAND Corporation.

Landes, S.R., Ginsburg, K.M., Hoskin, A.F., & Miller, T.A. (1990). *Estimating Nonfatal Injuries*. Itasca, IL: Statistics Department, National Safety Council.

Miller, T., Viner, J., Rossman, S., Pindus, N., Gellert, W., Douglass, J., Dillingham, A., & Blomquist, G. (1991). *The Costs of Highway Crashes*. Springfield, VA: National Technical Information Service.

Miller, T.R., Brigham, P.A., Cohen, M.A., Douglass, J.B., Galbraith, M.S., Lestina, D.C., Nelkin, V.S., Pindus, N.M., & Smith-Regojo, P. (1993a). Estimating the costs to society of cigarette fire injuries. *Report to Congress in Response to the Fire Safe Cigarette Act of 1990*. Washington, DC: U.S. Consumer Product Safety Commission.

Miller, T.R., Pindus, N.M., Douglass, J.B., & Rossman, S.B. (1993b). *Nonfatal Injury Incidence, Costs, and Consequences: A Data Book*. Washington, DC: The Urban Institute Press.

Occupational Safety and Health Administration. (2005). *OSHA recordkeeping handbook*. OSHA 3245-01R.

Rice, D.P., & MacKenzie, E.J. (1989). *Cost of Injury in the United States: A Report to Congress*. Atlanta, GA: Centers for Disease Control and Prevention.

Adams, P.F., Heyman, K.M., & Vickerie, J.L. (2009). Summary health statistics for the U.S. population: National health interview survey, 2008. *Vital and Health Statistics, Series 10, No. 243*. Hyattsville, MD: National Center of Health Statistics.

Toscano, G., & Windau, J. (1994). The changing character of fatal work injuries. *Monthly Labor Review, 117*(10), 17-28.

World Health Organization. (1977). *Manual of the International Statistical Classification of Diseases, Injuries, and Causes of Death*. Geneva, Switzerland: Author.

World Health Organization. (1992). *International Statistical Classification of Diseases and Related Health Problems – Tenth Revision*. Geneva, Switzerland: Author.

TECHNICAL APPENDIX
OTHER SOURCES | GLOSSARY | INDEX

Other Sources

The following organizations may be useful for obtaining more current data or more detailed information on various subjects in *Injury Facts*.

American Association of Poison Control Centers
(703) 894-1858
www.aapcc.org, info@aapcc.org

Bureau of Labor Statistics
U.S. Department of Labor
(202) 691-5200
www.bls.gov
blsdata_staff@bls.gov

Bureau of the Census
U.S. Department of Commerce
(800) 923-8282
www.census.gov

Centers for Disease Control and Prevention
(800) 232-4636
www.cdc.gov, cdcinfo@cdc.gov

Federal Aviation Administration
U.S. Department of Transportation
(866) 835-5322
www.faa.gov

Federal Highway Administration
U.S. Department of Transportation
(202) 366-4000
www.fhwa.dot.gov
execsecretariat.fhwa@fhwa.dot.gov

Federal Motor Carrier Safety Administration
U.S. Department of Transportation
(800) 832-5660
www.fmcsa.dot.gov

Federal Railroad Administration
U.S. Department of Transportation
(202) 493-6065
www.fra.dot.gov

International Labour Organization
Phone: +41-22-799-6111
Fax: +41-22-798-8685
www.ilo.org
ilo@ilo.org

Mine Safety and Health Administration
(202) 693-9400
www.msha.gov

National Center for Health Statistics
(800) 232-4636
www.cdc.gov/nchs

National Center for Statistics and Analysis
(202) 366-4198 or (800) 934-8517
www.nhtsa.dot.gov
NCSAweb@nhtsa.dot.gov

National Climatic Data Center
(828) 271-4800
www.ncdc.noaa.gov/oa/ncdc.html
ncdc.info@noaa.gov

National Collegiate Athletic Association
(317) 917-6222
www.ncaa.org

National Council on Compensation Insurance
(566) 893-1000
www.ncci.com

National Fire Protection Association
(617) 770-3000 or (800) 344-3555
www.nfpa.org
custserv@nfpa.org

National Highway Traffic Safety Administration
U.S. Department of Transportation
www.nhtsa.gov
(800) 877-8339

National Sporting Goods Association
(800) 815-5422
www.nsga.org
info@nsga.org

Occupational Safety and Health Administration
U.S. Department of Labor
(800) 321-OSHA (6742)
www.osha.gov

Substance Abuse and Mental Health Services Administration
(877) 726-4727
www.samhsa.gov

Transportation Research Board
(202) 334-2934
http://gulliver.trb.org

U.S. Coast Guard
(800) 368-5647
www.uscgboating.org
uscginfoline@gcrm.com

U.S. Consumer Product Safety Commission
(301) 504-7923
www.cpsc.gov
clearinghouse@cpsc.gov

World Health Organization
Phone: +41-22-791-2111
www.who.int
info@who.int

TECHNICAL APPENDIX
OTHER SOURCES | GLOSSARY | INDEX

Glossary

Accident is that occurrence in a sequence of events that produces unintended injury, death, or property damage. Accident refers to the event, not the result of the event (see Unintentional injury). The term "accident" has largely been replaced in the public health community with the term "incident."

Death from incident is a death that occurs within one year of the incident.

Disabling injury is an injury causing death, permanent disability, or any degree of temporary total disability beyond the day of the injury. Starting with the 2012 edition of *Injury Facts*, the definition of disabling injury was replaced by medically consulted injury for all non-fatal injury estimates.

Fatal incident is an incident that results in one or more deaths within one year.

Home is a dwelling and its premises within the property lines including single family dwellings and apartment houses, duplex dwellings, boarding and rooming houses, and seasonal cottages. Excluded from home are barracks, dormitories, and resident institutions.

Incidence rate, as defined by OSHA, is the number of occupational injuries and/or illnesses or lost workdays per 100 full-time employees (see formula on page 76).

Incident is the preferred term for "accident" in the public health community. It refers to the occurrence in a sequence of events that produces unintended injury, death, or property damage. Incident refers to the event, not the result of the event (see Unintentional injury).

Injury is physical harm or damage to the body resulting from an exchange, usually acute, of mechanical, chemical, thermal, or other environmental energy that exceeds the body's tolerance.

Medically consulted injury is an injury serious enough that a medical professional was consulted. For the motor vehicle, home and public venues, the National Safety Council uses the medically consulted injury estimates from the National Health Interview Survey. The Council uses the total recordable case estimate, using OSHA's definition, published by the Bureau of Labor Statistics (BLS) to estimate the number of workplace injuries. Because the BLS estimate excludes self-employed, unpaid family workers, and federal government employees, the Council extrapolates the BLS estimate to reflect the total worker population.

Motor vehicle is any mechanically or electrically powered device not operated on rails, upon which or by which any person or property may be transported upon a land highway. The load on a motor vehicle or trailer attached to it is considered part of the vehicle. Tractors and motorized machinery are included while self-propelled in transit or used for transportation. Non-motor vehicle is any road vehicle other than a motor vehicle, such as a bicycle or animal-drawn vehicle, except a coaster wagon, child's sled, child's tricycle, child's carriage, and similar means of transportation; persons using these latter means of transportation are considered pedestrians.

Motor-vehicle incident is an unstabilized situation that includes at least one harmful event (injury or property damage) involving a motor vehicle in transport (in motion, in readiness for motion, or on a roadway but not parked in a designated parking area) that does not result from discharge of a firearm or explosive device and does not directly result from a cataclysm. [See Committee on Motor Vehicle Traffic Accident Classification (1997), *Manual on Classification of Motor Vehicle Traffic Accidents,* ANSI D16.1-1996, Itasca, IL: National Safety Council.]

Motor-vehicle traffic incident is a motor-vehicle incident that occurs on a trafficway – a way or place, any part of which is open to the use of the public for the purposes of vehicular traffic. A motor-vehicle nontraffic incident is any motor-vehicle incident that occurs entirely in any place other than a trafficway.

Nonfatal injury incident is an incident in which at least one person is injured and no injury results in death.

Occupational illness is any abnormal condition or disorder other than one resulting from an occupational injury caused by exposure to environmental factors associated with employment. It includes acute and chronic illnesses or diseases that may be caused by inhalation, absorption, ingestion, or direct contact (see also pages 73 and 79).

Occupational injury is any injury such as a cut, fracture, sprain, amputation, etc., that results from a work incident or from a single instantaneous exposure in the work environment (see also page 79).

Pedalcycle is a vehicle propelled by human power and operated solely by pedals; excludes mopeds.

Pedestrian is any person involved in a motor-vehicle incident who is not in or upon a motor vehicle or non-motor vehicle. Includes persons injured while using a coaster wagon, child's tricycle, roller skates, etc. Excludes persons boarding, alighting, jumping, or falling from a motor vehicle in transport who are considered occupants of the vehicle.

Permanent disability (or permanent impairment) includes any degree of permanent nonfatal injury. It includes any injury that results in the loss or complete loss of use of any part of the body or in any permanent impairment of functions of the body or a part thereof.

Property damage incident is an incident that results in property damage but in which no person is injured.

Public incident is any incident other than motor vehicle that occurs in the public use of any premises. Includes deaths in recreation (swimming, hunting, etc.), in transportation except motor vehicle, public buildings, etc., and from widespread natural disasters even though some may have happened on home premises. Excludes incidents to people in the course of gainful employment.

Source of injury is the principal object such as tool, machine, or equipment involved in the incident and is usually the object inflicting injury or property damage. Also called agency or agent.

Temporary total disability is an injury that does not result in death or permanent disability but that renders the injured person unable to perform regular duties or activities on one or more full calendar days after the day of the injury.

Total cases include all work-related deaths and illnesses and those work-related injuries that result in loss of consciousness, restriction of work or motion, or transfer to another job, or require medical treatment other than first aid.

Unintentional injury is the preferred term for accidental injury in the public health community. It refers to the result of an incident.

Work hours are the total number of hours worked by all employees. They are usually compiled for various levels, such as an establishment, a company, or an industry. A work hour is the equivalent of one employee working one hour.

Work injuries (including occupational illnesses) are those that arise out of and in the course of gainful employment regardless of where the accident or exposure occurs. Excluded are work injuries to private household workers and injuries occurring in connection with farm chores that are classified as home injuries.

Workers are all persons gainfully employed, including owners, managers, other paid employees, the self-employed, and unpaid family workers but excluding private household workers.

Work/motor vehicle duplication includes work injuries that occur in motor-vehicle incidents (see Work injuries and Motor-vehicle incident).

TECHNICAL APPENDIX
OTHER SOURCES | GLOSSARY | INDEX

Index

A

Accommodation	82, 83
Activity	30
Administrative and support services	82, 83
Adults	19, 39, 163
Advanced safety technologies	119
Age	6, 7, 14-16, 18, 19, 28, 30, 32, 33, 36, 44, 153, 166, 167, 189-193, (see 2016 Ed.; 31)
by class and type	12, 13, 20-23, 26, 28, 38, 39, 48-51, 136-139, 146, 147, 150, 151, 160
by motor vehicle	106, 107, 123, 126, 136-139
work	70, 71, 86-101
Agriculture	58, 61, 70, 71, 73, 79, 80, 83, 87
Air transportation	24, 34, 41, 65, 82, 83, 149-151, 156-158, 169, 179
Airbags	112
Alcohol	25, 42, 108, 114, 115, 129, 160
All-terrain vehicles	125
Ambulatory health care services	82, 83
Amputations	67
Animal or insect, injury by	24, 25, 41, 42
Animal production	80, 83
Apparel manufacturing	80, 83
Arm injury (see Part of body)	
Arts, entertainment, and recreation services	82, 83
Asphyxiation (see Poisoning)	
Assistive safety technology	119
Automobile (see Motor vehicle)	
Aviation	22, 41, 43, 156, 158

B

Back injuries (see also Part of body)	67
Backup collisions	(see 2015 Ed.; 127)
Bathroom	(see 2012 Ed.; 151)
Bathtubs	24, 41, (also 2013 Ed.; 153)
Benchmarking	69-71, 76, 77, 85-101
Beverage and tobacco product manufacturing	80, 83
Bicycle (see Pedalcycle)	
Bites and stings	24, 25, 33, 41-43
Boating injuries	24, 41, 149, 151
Brain injuries, traumatic	(see 2014 Ed.; 153)
Broadcasting (except Internet)	82, 83
Bureau of Labor Statistics	70, 71, 76-101, 182, 183
Burns	13-16, 18, 19, 52-55, 66, 67
Buses	24, 41, 122, 156, 157

C

Cataclysm	25, 34, 42, 43
Cause or source of injury	6, 7, 12-16, 18, 19, 32, 33, 153, 155, 162
home	149-151, 160
motor vehicle	106, 107, 116, 134, 135
work	66, 69-71, 84, 86-101
Cell phones	118
Census of Fatal Occupational Injuries	58, 60, 61, 181
Chemicals manufacturing	80, 83

Child injuries	6, 12-15, 18, 32, 33, 38, 106, 107, 122, 124, 136-139, 146, 147, 150, 151, 154
single year ages	38
Child restraints	111, 113
Choking	6, 7, 12-14, 16-21, 24, 26, 27, 30, 32, 38, 39, 41, 43, 52-55, 143, 145, 146, 147, 149-151, 169, 173, 175-178
Classes, principal, of unintentional injury	2-5, 45-47, 63
Clothing ignition	25, 42
Cold, excessive	25-27, 39, 42, 149, 152, 179
Computer and electronic product mfg.	81, 83
Confined spaces	24, 41
Conflagration (see also Fire, flames, or smoke)	25, 42
Construction	58, 61, 69-75, 79, 80, 83, 89
Construction, work zone	130
Consumer products	153, 155
Contact with objects and equipment	86-101
Contractor	(see 2016 Ed.; 72)
Cost equivalents	11
Costs	5, 8-11, 62-67, 104, 109, 142, 144, 148, 201, 202, (also 2016 Ed.; 65, 153)
Couriers and messengers	82, 83
Crop production	80, 83
Cumulative trauma disorders	66, 67
Cutting or piercing instruments	24, 28, 33, 41, 66, (also 2016 Ed.; 30)

D

Daily death tolls	5
Days lost, work injuries	62, 63
Death calendar	(see 2012 Ed.; 59)
Death rates (see Rates, death)	
Definitions	12, 13, 29, 79, 106, 107, 122, 131, 146, 147, 150, 151, 207
Directional analysis, motor vehicle	116
Disasters	34
Disease	14-16, 43, 73
Distracted driving	108, 110, 118
Distracted walking	(see 2015 Ed.; 153)
Dog bite	24, 33, 41, 43
Drinking (see Alcohol)	
Driver, motor vehicle	104, 126
age	124-126
number of	104, 126, 132, 133
Driveway, motor vehicle	(see 2015 Ed.; 127)
Drowning	6, 7, 12-21, 24, 26, 27, 32, 38, 39, 41, 45, 52-55, 143, 145-147, 149, 150, 166, 169, 175-178, 188, 193
Drugs	25, 42, 160-162, (also 2016 Ed.; 30)

E

Earthquakes	25, 42
Economic loss (see Costs)	
Education	31
Educational and health services	58, 61, 68, 70-75, 79, 82, 98
Educational services	82, 83
Elderly	39
Electric current	25, 42, 43, 179

TECHNICAL APPENDIX
OTHER SOURCES | GLOSSARY | INDEX

Index (cont.)

Electric power	82, 83, *(also 2014 Ed.; 164)*
Electrical equipment manufacturing	81, 83
Emergency department visits	33, 125, 153, *(also 2016 Ed.; 30)*
Emergency vehicles	130
Employer uninsured costs	8, 10, 11, 62
Employment	58, 60, 86-101
Ethnic origin	17, 70, 71, 72, 86-101
Explosions (see also Fires, flames, or smoke)	22, 41
Exposure to harmful substance or environments	86-101
Eye injury (see Part of body)	

F

Fabricated metal manufacturing	81, 83
Face injury (see Part of body)	
Falls	16-21, 18, 24, 26-28, 33, 38, 39, 41, 43, 52-55, 66, 143, 145, 146, 149, 150, 163, 173, 175-178, 181, 192
age	6, 7, 12, 14-16, 18, 20, 21, 26, 28, 32, 150, 163
country	192
home	145, 146
public	149, 150
work	59, 69-72, 84, 86-101
Fatigue	72
Financial activities	58, 61, 73, 79, 82, 83, 96
Finger injury (see Part of body)	
Fire loss	8, 10, 11, 62
Fire or explosion	86-101
Fire, flames, or smoke	6, 7, 12-19, 20, 21, 25-27, 32, 34, 38, 39, 42, 43, 45, 52-55, 143, 145, 149, 150, 164, 166, 167, 169, 175-178, 181, *(also 2016 Ed.; 30)*
Firearms	6, 7, 24, 32, 38, 39, 41, 52-55, 145-147, 149-151, 168, 169, 179
Fireworks	22, 41, *(also 2013 Ed.; 164)*
Fishing	79, 80, 87
recreational	154
Fixed object	106, 116, 134, 135
Flammable fabrics	23, 42
Floods	25, 42, 152
Food manufacturing	80, 83
Food service and drinking places	82, 83
Foot injury (see Part of body)	
Foreign body	24, 33, 41
Forestry	79, 80, 87
Forklift trucks	68
Fractures	67
Furniture and related products mfg.	81, 83

G

Government	58, 59, 61, 101
Grade crossing	159
Graduated licensing	110, 124

H

Hand injury (see Part of body)	
Head injury (see Part of body)	
Health services	72, 82
Hearing loss	73
Heat, excessive	25-27, 39, 42, 149, 152, 179
Helmets	113
Hispanic origin (see Ethnic origin)	
Holidays	129
Home	2-5, 8, 9, 29, 30, 45-47, 63, 144-147
Home and community	142-169
Homicide, assault	3, 14-16, 25, 35-37, 42, 43, 58, 61, 84, 168, *(also 2016 Ed.; 30)*
Hospitals	29, 82, 83, *(also 2016 Ed.; 30)*
Hurricanes	152

I

ICD Ninth Revision	*(see 2001 Ed.; 160)*
ICD Tenth Revision	24, 25, 41, 42, 200, 201
Illness, occupational	73, *(also 2015 Ed.; 72)*
Improper driving	120
Inattention, driver	118
Incidence rates (see Rates, incidence)	
Income	31
Industrial injuries (see Work or specific industry titles)	
Information	58, 61, 73, 79, 82, 95
Ingestion (see Poisoning or Choking)	
Inhalation (see Poisoning or Choking)	
Injury rates (see Rates, incidence; and Rates, work injury)	
Injury totals	2, 3, 5, 28, 58, 63, 104, 116, 142, 144, 148, 154, 155
Insurance administration cost	8, 10, 11, 62
Intentional injuries	3, 23, 35-37, 42, 43
International injury data	188-197

L

Laws, motor vehicle	110, 124
Leading causes of death or injury	6, 7, 14-16, 18, 19, 20, 21, 27, 32, 33, 38, 39, 59, 77, 175-181
Leather and leather products	80, 83
Leg injury (see Part of body)	
Legal intervention	25, 35, 42
Leisure and hospitality	58, 61, 70-74, 79, 82, 99
Lightning	25, 42, 43, 152
Lives saved	2, 112

M

Machinery	24, 41, 179, *(also 2016 Ed.; 30)*
Machinery manufacturing	81, 83
Management of companies and enterprises	82, 83
Manufacturing	58, 61, 70-75, 79-81, 83, 90
Marine (see Water transportation)	
Medical expense	8, 10, 11, 62
Mileage, motor-vehicle	104, 105, 132, 133
Mileage rates (see Rates, death)	
Mining	58, 61, 70-73, 79, 80, 83, 88
Miscellaneous manufacturing	81, 83
Month, motor-vehicle deaths	129
Month, type of event	27, 152
Motorcycles	24, 41, 108, 113, 121

TECHNICAL APPENDIX
OTHER SOURCES | GLOSSARY | INDEX

Index (cont.)

Motor vehicle 2-9, 12, 14-21, 24, 26, 27, 32-34, 38, 39, 41, 43, 45-47, 52-55, 63, 104-139, 156, 157, 173, 175-178, 184, 185, 188
    costs 104, 109
    country 190
    impact of recession 127
    marijuana .... (see 2016 Ed.; 127)
    time of day, day of week 128
    work 65, 66

N

National Health Interview Survey 28-31
National Highway Traffic Safety Administration 131
Natural gas distribution 82, 83
Nature of injury 67, 69-71, 74, 86-101
Noncollision, motor vehicle 107, 116, 134, 135
Nonmetallic mineral product mfg. 81, 83
Nontraffic, motor vehicle 134, 135
Nursing and residential care facilities 82, 83

O

Object, struck by .... 24, 41, (also 2016 Ed.; 30)
Occupant deaths, motor vehicle 112, 121
Occupant protection 108, 111-113
    mandatory use laws 110, 111
Occupant restraints (see Occupant protection)
Occupation of worker 69-71, 86-101
Occupational (see Work)
Occupational health .... 73, (also 2015 Ed.; 72)
Occupational Safety and Health
Administration (OSHA) .... 78-83, 182, 183, (also 2013 Ed.; 73)
Odds of Dying 40-43
Off-the-job injuries 5, 63
Oil and gas extraction 80, 83
Other services 79, 82, 100
Overexertion/overextension 28, 33, 59, 66

P

Paper manufacturing 80, 83
Parking lot, motor vehicle .... (see 2015 Ed.; 127)
Part of body injured .... 67, 69-71, 75, 86-101, (also 2016 Ed.; 31)
Passenger deaths;
    aviation 156-158
    motor vehicle 121, 156, 157
    railroad 156, 157, 159
Passing, improper, motor vehicle 120
Pedalcycle .... 24, 33, 41, 43, 107, 116, 134, 135, 154, 165, (also 2016 Ed.; 30)
Pedestrian 24, 41, 65, 106, 108, 116, 123, 134, 135
Personal and laundry services 82, 83
Petroleum and coal products 80, 83
Pipeline transportation 82, 83
Plastics and rubber products mfg. 81, 83
Playground injuries 153
Poisoning .... 6, 7, 12, 14-21, 25-28, 32, 33, 38, 39, 42, 43, 45, 52-55, 73, 143, 145, 146, 149, 150, 160-162, 166, 167, 169, 173, 175-178, 191, (also 2016 Ed.; 30)
Population 44, 51
Population rates (see Rates, death)
Primary metal mfg. 81, 83
Printing 80, 83
Private industry 70, 71, 79, 80, 83, 86
Products, consumer 155
Professional and business services 58, 61, 70-75, 79, 82, 83, 97
Professional, scientific, and technical services 82, 83
Property damage 8, 10, 11, 62, 104
Public injuries 2-5, 8, 9, 29, 30, 45-47, 63, 148-151
Public utilities 61
Publishing (except Internet) 82, 83

Q

Quarrying (see Mining)

R

Race 17, 70, 71, 86-101
Radiation 25, 42
Railroad 24, 41, 65, 82, 83, 106, 107, 116, 134, 135, 149-151, 156, 157, 159, 169, 179
Rates, death;
    country 189-193, 195
    mileage 104, 105, 129, 132, 133, 156-158, 184, 185
    population;
        age 12-16, 21, 23, 38, 39, 50, 51, 106, 107, 138, 139, 146, 147, 150, 151, 160, 163
        class of unintentional injury 2, 45-47
        country 189, 190-193
        ethnic origin 17-19
        home 144, 146, 147
        home and community 142
        intentional injuries 37
        motor vehicle 2, 12, 14-16, 45-47, 54, 55, 104-107, 132, 133, 138, 139, 184, 185, 190
        public 148, 150, 151
        race 17-19
        regional 174
        sex 14-19, 23, 26
        state 173-177, 180, 184, 185
        trends 44-47, 50, 51, 54, 55, 132, 133, 138, 139, 148
        type of event 12-16, 21, 54, 55, 106, 107, 146, 147, 150, 151, 173, 175-177
        work 2, 45-47, 58
    registration, motor vehicle 104, 132, 133, 185
    work 58, 61, 195
Rates, fatal injury 32
Rates, incidence 73, 78-83, 182, 183
Rates, nonfatal injury .... 33, (also 2016 Ed.; 30, 31)
Rates, work injury 63, 197
Recreation 154
Religious, grantmaking, civic,
and professional organizations 82, 83
Repair and maintenance 82, 83

INJURY FACTS® 2017 EDITION   NATIONAL SAFETY COUNCIL® ■ 209

Index (cont.)

Respiratory conditions 73
Retail trade 58, 61, 70, 71, 73-75, 79, 81-83, 92
Right-of-way violation 120
Risks, age 166, 167

S

Safety belts (see Occupant protection)
School 29, 30
School bus 122
Seasonal trends;
   motor vehicle 129
   type of event 27, 152
Seat belts (see Occupant protection)
Sex 17, 30, 36
   of person injured 27
   of person killed 14-16, 22, 23, 26, 28, 70, 71, 86-101
   of worker 70, 71, 86-101
   type of event 26, 160
Skin diseases and disorders 73
Slip, trip (see Falls, workplace)
Source of injury, work 86-101
Sources, additional 206
Specialty trade contractors 80, 83
Speeding, motor vehicle 108, 117, 120
Sports injuries 30, 154
Sprains, strains 67
State injury records 64, 172-185
Storms 34, 152
Street railways 134, 135
Striking against or struck by .... 24, 27, 28, 33, 41, 66, 179, *(also 2016 Ed.; 30)*
Suffocation by inhalation or ingestion (see Choking)
Suffocation, mechanical .... 13-15, 24, 26, 27, 38, 39, 41, 53, 55, 145-147, 149-151, 169, 178, *(also 2016 Ed.; 30)*
Suicide, self-inflicted injury .... 3, 14-16, 25, 36, 37, 42, 58, 61, 168, *(also 2016 Ed.; 30)*
Surgical and medical complications and misadventures 25, 42
Swimming pools 24, 41

T

Technical appendix 200-205
Textile mills 80, 83
Textile product mills 80, 83
Toe injury (see Part of body)
Tornadoes 34, 152
Transit industry 82, 83
Transportation .... 28, 30, 32-34, 58, 61, 65, 79, 82, 181, *(also 2016 Ed.; 30)*
   public 24, 41, 83, 149-151, 156-159, 169
Transportation and warehousing 70-75, 81, 93
Transportation equipment mfg. 81, 83

Transportation incidents 65
Trends;
   all unintentional-injury deaths .... iv, v, 18, 19, 44, 46-55
   home 45-47, 144, 145, 169
   intentional-injury deaths 37
   motor vehicle 45-47, 52-55, 105, 124, 131-139
   poisoning 45, 52-55, 149, 161, 162
   public 45-47, 148, 149, 153, 169
   work 45-47, 60, 61, 65, 69
   work injury rate 60, 78
Trucking 82, 83
Trucks 24, 41, 120
Type of event .... 6, 7, 12-16, 18, 19, 24-27, 32, 33, 41-43, 52-55, *(also 2016 Ed.; 31)*
   age 6, 7, 12-16, 18, 19, 32, 33, 38, 39
   class;
      home 145-147
      motor vehicle 106, 107, 116, 134, 135
      public 149-151
      work 69-71, 84-101
   sex 14-16, 18, 19, 26

U

Undercount, workplace injuries .... *(see 2015 Ed.; 72)*
Utilities 58, 61, 73, 79, 82, 94

V

Vehicles
   nonmotor 24, 41
   number of 104, 121, 132, 133
   type of 120
Violations, motor vehicle 120
Violence, workplace 86-101, 181

W

Wage loss 8, 10, 11, 62
Warehousing 58, 61, 79, 93
Warehousing and storage 82, 83
Waste management and remediation 82, 83
Water transportation 24, 41, 65, 82, 83, 149-151, 169, 179
Water, sewage, and other systems 82, 83
Weather 34, 152
While you speak! 5
Wholesale trade 58, 61, 70-75, 79, 81, 83, 91
Wood products manufacturing 80, 83
Work injuries .... 2-5, 8, 9, 30, 45-47, 58-101, 181, 194-197, *(also 2016 Ed.; 65, 72)*
   undercount .... *(see 2015 Ed.; 72)*
Work zone 130
Workers' compensation .... 64-67, *(also 2016 Ed.; 65)*